# FACULTY AT WORK

## DATE DUE

| DEC 11 2005 | |
|---|---|
| | |
| | |
| | |
| | |
| | |
| | |
| | |
| | |
| | |
| | |
| | |
| | |
| | |
| | |
| | |
| | |
| | |

GAYLORD                                    PRINTED IN U.S.A.

# FACULTY AT

# WORK

## MOTIVATION, EXPECTATION, SATISFACTION

Robert T. Blackburn & Janet H. Lawrence

The Johns Hopkins University Press

BALTIMORE AND LONDON

© 1995 The Johns Hopkins University Press
All rights reserved. Published 1995
Printed in the United States of America on acid-free paper
04  03  02  01  00  99  98  97  96  95     5  4  3  2  1

The Johns Hopkins University Press
2715 North Charles Street
Baltimore, Maryland 21218-4319
The Johns Hopkins Press Ltd., London

ISBN 0-8018-4942-X

Library of Congress Cataloging-in-Publication Data
will be found at the end of this book.

A catalog record for this book is available
from the British Library.

# CONTENTS

# Contents

# TABLES

## Tables

# Tables

# FIGURES

# *Figures*

# PREFACE

FACULTY FOLKLORE seems almost unbounded, rich with equal measures of dead seriousness and jestful academic argot. The reader may rightfully wonder how we could be so brash as to write a book on faculty and think it could add to what is already well known. We respond by explaining what our aims are, how our effort fits in with those of others who have written on college and university faculty, and what theoretical and methodological stance we take (and why).

Our goals are (1) to draw together empirical evidence on faculty at work, (2) to develop and test a theoretical framework of faculty motivation to engage in different teaching, research, and service activities, and (3) to suggest how administrative practice can be improved so that faculty work lives are enriched and colleges and universities become more productive organizations.

The uniqueness of our contribution is best shown by placing it in the context of earlier books on faculty. While a few volumes predate Logan Wilson's *The Academic Man* (1942)—Claude Bowman's *The College Professor in America* (1938) is one—Wilson's sociological account of faculty in the most highly reputed universities is frequently taken as the benchmark volume. Wilson compensates for his lack of supporting data by the comprehensiveness of his treatment. Paul Lazarsfeld and Wagner Thielens's *The Academic Mind: Social Scientists in a Time of Crisis* (1958) reports the results of the first interview survey of faculty, carried out in 1954 to trace the effects of the Joseph McCarthy era on professorial behavior. Talcott Parsons and Gerald Platt's *The American Academic Professions: A Pilot Study* (1968) is based on a mail survey of a small sample of faculty conducted in 1964 to test a hypothesis concerning the stratification of U.S. colleges and universities.

In 1969 the American Council on Education and the Carnegie Foundation for the Advancement of Teaching launched the first of what became a series of national surveys of faculty (1969, 1972, 1975, 1984, 1988). These surveys resulted in a number of books on selected topics. The authors were sociologists and political scientists, and their books reflect those conceptual

*Preface*

backgrounds—for example, looking for correlates of liberal versus conservative faculty dispositions with place of work, scholarly publications, attitudes toward students, or religious background. Examples of such works include Seymour Lipset and Everett Ladd, *Jewish Academics in the United States: Their Achievements, Culture, and Politics* (1971); Ladd and Lipset, *Professors, Unions, and American Higher Education* (1973); Ladd and Lipset, *The Divided Academy* (1975); Peter Blau, *The Organization of Academic Work* (1973); Saul Feldman, *Escape from the Doll's House* (1973); Stephen Steinberg, *The Academic Melting Pot* (1974); and Martin Trow, *Teachers and Students* (1975). The surveys that provided the databases for these books were essentially a single questionnaire that varied from administration to administration only on what happened to be the current issue in higher education at the moment—student power, Vietnam, collective bargaining in the professoriate, faculty morale.

This spate of early publications was capped off by Burton Clark's *The Academic Life: Small Worlds, Different Worlds* (1987). In between, Martin Finkelstein's *The American Academic Profession: A Synthesis of Social Scientific Inquiry since World War II* (1984a) examined the journal literature on faculty that had been published prior to 1980 and took a broader view of what might be safely concluded about faculty in their different roles and in their personal lives. Howard Bowen and Jack Schuster's *American Professors: A National Resource Imperiled* (1986) describes faculty life and the structure of higher education in the United States, but the interviews on which the book is based deal almost exclusively with faculty morale at that point in time (1984).

In part, then, our book addresses a significant hiatus—10 years of mostly unreported research growing at an exponential rate. More than a need for updating, however, we see in the existing literature a need for theoretical frameworks grounded in contemporary psychological and sociological theory—a perspective that assumes that faculty consciously and cognitively assess their work environment and respond to their perceptions, an ongoing process that leads to reevaluations of one's self, reinterpretations of one's environment, and shifts in behavior and productivity. Our theoretical framework, and our empirical tests of it in a variety of disciplines and institutions, we take to be our principal contribution to the present and future understanding of faculty at work.

As for where we stand, philosophically and methodologically, our studies are clearly in the quantitative domain. At the same time, we would strenuously object to anyone who labeled us "logical empiricists" or "reductionists" and thereby dismissed our work out of hand. We fully acknowledge the limitations of survey data, which the majority of our data are. We do not

xiv

forget that the indicators of our constructs are always lacking in complete-
ness, that their correspondence with reality is always limited, and that our
measures are seldom as precise as we would wish them to be; we remind the
reader of these limitations throughout the book. We do not assert universal
truths, and we know that what we have learned is restricted by context and
time, both of which we deal with when we can. (Appendix G discusses these
concerns at greater length.)

Our basic survey data set speaks in faculty voices, not sociological jar-
gon. (Our writing also sets aside the dispassionate scholarly-journal subjective voice. When we say *we,* we mean ourselves, RTB and JHL.) We began
by taping exploratory interviews with faculty in our neighborhood at the
University of Michigan, a mix of individuals from a variety of disciplines,
institutional types, ages, genders, and races/ethnicities. From our analysis of
these tapes we developed a structured interview schedule and preliminary
paper-and-pencil questionnaires. We used them with 120 faculty from four
college and university types. Their open-ended responses provided us with
the language for the questionnaire items in our 1987–88 NCRIPTAL (National Center for Research to Improve Postsecondary Teaching and Learning) national survey, reproduced in appendix H. We also relied on our
longitudinal interview study of University of Michigan faculty. (See Bieber,
Lawrence, & Blackburn, 1993.)

In short, while the tests of our theoretical framework used quantitative
data, the items for the constructs were qualitatively generated. All in all,
then, despite the avalanche of ideological critics of data analyses that rely
heavily on contemporary statistical procedures, we believe that our research
position and methods contribute significantly and appropriately to answer-
ing our primary research question, "What motivates faculty?"

Turning now to those to whom we are especially indebted, the abundance
of people creates a problem for us. Our less-than-satisfactory solution has
been to create some categories, place persons in one or another of them, and
list them alphabetically. Citations in the bibliography provide additional
recognition to those who were joint authors with us on research conference
paper presentations or published articles, some two dozen and more.

The following graduate students were joint authors with us on either
research conference papers or articles in scholarly journals (or both): Richard
Bentley, Jeffery Bieber, Raymond Brown, Ellyn Dickman, Kenneth Frank,
Kathy Hart, Georgina Herzberg, Rita Knuesel, Vincent Linder, Christopher
Mackie, Rosemary Meiland, Virginia Polk Okoloko, Judith Pitney, Kay
Saulsberry, Terrence Street, Lois Trautvetter, and Kwang-suk Yoon.

The following supported our efforts in a number of ways—composing tables, typing manuscripts, and keeping our records both during NCRIP-TAL and afterwards: Chris Eldred, Jane Elliot, Rose Garcia, Mary Joscelyn, Cindy LaSovage, and Wei Zhou.

Secretaries Betty Piccione, Peggy Plawchan, Priscilla Rice, and Linda Stiles helped in all of the above ways, and more.

Faculty everywhere aided us in critiquing our studies and our documents, responding to our ideas—the off-the-wall as well as the reasonably sound ones—and providing what only colleagues invaluably can provide. With us almost weekly for five years of NCRIPTAL projects were Kim Cameron, Robert Kozma, Malcolm Lowther, Wilbert McKeachie, Marvin Peterson, and Joan Stark. (Stephen Ross from Memphis State joined us on one project, as did a number of visiting postdoctoral scholars from time to time.)

A number of graduate students graciously proofed and critiqued our studies and this manuscript. We are thankful to Carol Hughes, Lisa Mets, Clifford Wilcox, and students in the College and University Faculty seminar.

At the Johns Hopkins University Press, we are now thankful that Jackie Wehmueller found potential in our early manuscript and encouraged us to go on. She also found two superb faculty readers for whose suggestions and critique we are deeply indebted. And Mary Yates has turned a pretty rough manuscript into a most readable book.

Last, we thank the following for granting permission to reproduce materials under their jurisdiction:

Ernest Boyer, President, the Carnegie Foundation for the Advancement of Teaching, for permission to use tables 1 and 2 (pp. 3 and 4) and the definitions of the Carnegie types (pp. 7 and 8) as they appear in the 1987 edition of *A Classification of Institutions of Higher Education* (Princeton, N.J.: Carnegie Foundation for the Advancement of Teaching).

*Change Magazine*, vol. 24, no. 4 (July/August 1992), pp. 31–32, for permission to quote, in chapter 4, from Bieber, Lawrence, and Blackburn, "Through the Years: Faculty and Their Changing Institutions." Reprinted with permission of the Helen Dwight Reid Educational Foundation. Published by Heldref Publications, 1319 Eighteenth Street, N.W., Washington, D.C., 20036-1802. Copyright 1992.

Carol Hollenshead, Director, Center for the Education of Women, University of Michigan, for permission to use the two figures from her *Women at the University of Michigan* (Ann Arbor: University of Michigan, Office of the President, February 1992).

Lewis Lapham, Editor, *Harper's Magazine,* December 1991, p. 54, for permission to quote from Louis Menand's article, "What Are Universities For? The Real Crisis on Campus Is One of Identity," as the paragraphs appear at the close of the epilogue.

John Smart, Editor, *Higher Education: Handbook of Theory and Research,* vol. 1 (New York: Agathon, 1985), pp. 260–261, for the selections from Mary Frank Fox's chapter, "Publication, Performance, and Reward in Science and Scholarship," quoted in chapter 3.

Joan Stark, Director, NCRIPTAL, University of Michigan, for permission to reproduce our faculty and administrator *Faculty at Work* surveys.

Joan Stark, Editor, *Review of Higher Education,* vol. 17, no. 3 (1994), for permission to reprint table 2 from p. 278 of Blackburn, Wenzel, and Bieber, "Minority vs. Majority Faculty Publication Performance: A Research Note."

C. Whitehead, Editor, *Education Research and Perspectives* (formerly *The Australian Journal of Higher Education*), vol. 4, no. 1 (1970), for permission to adopt parts of Robert T. Blackburn's "Legends of Academe U.S.A., 1970: Filters, Philtres, and Potions," as they appear in the epilogue.

# INTRODUCTION

Universities are among the world's most dominant and enduring social organizations. Since their creation universities have withstood untold social and political upheavals. Their original roles, of preparing men for the ministry and transmitting a culture to future generations, have been supplemented by new ones. Universities now prepare students to join the many professions; they critique society; and they produce knowledge.

While the evolution of higher education in the United States has been irregular, it has nonetheless been spectacular, and it has not been equaled elsewhere. The growth in the number of institutions alone is staggering: since the 1636 founding of Harvard College, some 3,500 postsecondary institutions have come into existence in this country. Ezra Cornell's "any body, any study" dream has become a reality. Having achieved, in the last half of the nineteenth century, the amalgamation of the English college and the German graduate research institution, the American university has emerged as the acknowledged world leader. Our scholars no longer go abroad to become distinguished researchers. Rather, people from all over the globe come to our shores for the best in advanced studies.

Unlike governments in most other countries, the U.S. government has invested in these institutions for its research needs rather than build research establishments of its own. The universities have also provided experts to address the nation's economic and foreign affairs problems. The arts—music, drama, and dance as well as the visual arts—have settled in the university and been welcomed. So have the intelligentsia, the literary and social critics who formerly operated as private individuals. Greenwich Village is no longer an art colony (Jacoby, 1987).

Universities have also become, in many ways, the equivalent of the country's giant industrial corporations, with all the bureaucratic accouterments—vice presidents for everything, for example, where once a dean or two handled it all. Major growth has been dependent on external monies, especially from the federal government. Federal regulations accompany those dollars, and the paperwork and monitoring nearly choke administrative offices. Still, our colleges and universities have been, and remain, remarkably humane organizations.

The universities have permitted a wide spectrum of behavior and now accept persons from all backgrounds. But they have records of behavior they wish had never taken place—exclusion of students and faculty on grounds of religion, gender, and ethnicity, for example. They are truly conservative organizations with changes much more often having come from without than from within. (Deconstructionism and the demise of the literary canon are exceptions.) They typically resist the periodic attacks on their procedures and actions, though attacks occur with almost predictable regularity. Institutional autonomy has always been more rhetoric than reality. Even the private hilltop liberal arts college cannot avoid alienating some alumni when it implements a change in policy or practice.

While the focus of concern changes from time to time, there are recurring themes and targets. Not all critics aim their charges at faculty, but faculty are the target of many poisoned arrows. Today one hears that faculty have abandoned students for their laboratories and carrels, that the time they should be spending teaching now goes into the writing of trivial articles no one reads, that they are cheating students by depriving them of a liberal education, and that they are only interested in teaching courses in their specialty. While relatively few critics advance these overstated charges, it is probably true that the gap between specialization and a liberal education has widened.

Faculty have always been accused of corrupting the values of their charges, turning them into atheists and revolutionaries. Today they are said to demand that their colleagues be "politically correct" or be excommunicated. The muckrakers are having a field day (Anderson, 1992; Cheney, 1990; Douglas, 1992; D'Souza, 1991; Huber, 1992; Kimball, 1990; Smith, 1991; Sykes, 1988, 1990).

At the same time, faculty experience pressures from within. Experts predict an intensification of already tight fiscal restraints—also a perpetual state of affairs within higher education. Administrators reduce support staffs; they lay off colleagues; they do not replace the departed and retired. More faculty compete for fewer grants, those resources administrators exhort them to acquire. It is not only every tub (school or department) on its own bottom; it is every faculty member in her or his own Jacuzzi. Faculty salaries have increased at roughly the same rate as inflation over the past two decades, but to many the dollar amount sounds high. Faculty salaries are the largest single component of a college or university's budget.

When faculty look upward, they see a burgeoning administration, one that is becoming increasingly distant from them. Involvement in decision making, the collegial norm, has more than waned; it appears to have ended. Power is fully in the hands of the bureaucrats. They reward the rich (business, medicine, engineering, law) and starve the poor (art, education, philosophy). They impose multiculturalism on their institution and expect faculty to know how to cope with the results. While new ideas about the implications of gender, ethnicity, and social class present exciting challenges, they simultaneously appear to bring more underprepared students into faculty members' classrooms and thereby compound their purported teaching "problem." Faculty are to recruit students and professors of color, preferably female, if they want favors from above. Quite understandably, they find themselves confronting a conflicting set of expectations.

In addition, faculty report that they have witnessed a marked change over the past decade or so in the institutional climate in which they work. Some feel guilty because of the power they have as the gatekeepers to almost all the professions. While their students make clear that careerism is more important to them than learning for its own sake—not a novel phenomenon in the history of higher education—many faculty members are genuinely disturbed by what seems to be a permanent loss in the traditional canons of scholarship. Especially in the humanities, but also in some social sciences, what constitutes truth and genuine knowledge seems to have become a matter of completely personal and relative judgment. Deconstruction and postmodernism have carried the day in literature in several leading departments. Anyone's idea is as good as anyone else's. How can one judge an assistant professor's work when there is no consensus on what constitutes high-quality scholarship? However, in economics and the natural sciences, the traditional views of sound scholarship generally prevail. Even those faculty sympathetic to the ongoing debates subscribe to "cognitive rationality" as the unquestioned premise of the university—search for truth and verify it with "empirical reality testing," in Berger's (1991, p. 328) words.

Competition has replaced collegiality. The pressures to publish—the requirement for a successful university career for some time now—and to secure grants have intensified. The university has been hiring superspecialists who seem to have no time for cross-disciplinary intellectual conversations. Their training immerses them in a language all their own, one others cannot understand. They are "foreigners in their own land."[1] Their immediate colleagues who joined the university with them are now competitors courting the same funding agencies. Organizational anxiety has replaced the formerly supportive, cooperative environment (Bieber, Lawrence, & Blackburn, 1992).

Faculty are at the heart of this perceived turmoil. They are a large workforce—about 550,000 full-time professors and nearly an equal number of part-timers. They are often not understood—at times, indeed, even misunderstood. Simultaneously, many outside the academy envy their autonomy, especially their control of their time. It is therefore important to study faculty, to learn about not only how they actually behave but also why they behave as they do. These are the aims of this book.

## The Context

Our focus is on the individual faculty member. However, one needs to understand the context in which academics work. Before we turn to how we will achieve our aims, we present a broad picture of the academic context in which our inquiry takes place. We display some information about the institutions in which faculty work, the numbers of people we are talking about, where they are located in this maze of colleges and universities, and how the picture has been changing in the last 25 years.[2]

We use the institutional classification system of the Carnegie Foundation for the Advancement of Teaching (1987), as does nearly all research on faculty. We exclude faculty in private two-year colleges and specialized institutions because the data on them are inadequate.[3] Sometimes we display demographics on all faculty. For example, we present data on the numbers of hours faculty spend in the classroom, and on the great variation that exists among those in different institutional types and in different disciplines. We also show the total number of hours faculty give to their job. For instance, those in community colleges can spend three times as many hours teaching as do those in research universities, yet the latter devote more hours per week to their academic work than do the former, 57 versus 44 hours. At other times we have selected only faculty in the disciplines commonly found in every institutional type. Then our subjects are full-time appointees in the largest departments within three broad fields of knowledge: English and history (humanities), biology, chemistry, and mathematics (natural sciences), and political science, psychology, and sociology (social sciences).[4]

Table I.1 displays data on U.S. colleges and universities grouped by their Carnegie classification. It contains the number of institutions within each category, the percentage of the total number of colleges and universities (3,389) that each category represents, the percentage of all students (12.3 million) enrolled in institutions of each type, and the average student body size for each institutional type. For example, there are 45 public research university I (Res-I) institutions; another 25 are under private control. These 70 universities represent only 2.1 percent of all U.S. colleges and universities. Still, they educate 12.8 percent of the students. They average 22,557 students per university, the largest average student body of all institutional types.[5]

Table I.1  Carnegie Classification of Colleges and Universities

| | Number of Institutions | | | % of All Institutions | Enrollments (Thousands) | | | Average | % of All Enrollments |
|---|---|---|---|---|---|---|---|---|---|
| | Public | Private | Total | | Public | Private | Total | | |
| Research I | 45 | 25 | 70 | 2.1 | 1,258 | 321 | 1,579 | 22.6 | 12.8 |
| Research II | 26 | 7 | 33 | 1.0 | 541 | 78 | 619 | 18.8 | 5.0 |
| Doctoral I | 29 | 22 | 51 | 1.5 | 467 | 195 | 662 | 13.0 | 5.4 |
| Doctoral II | 34 | 25 | 59 | 1.7 | 389 | 179 | 568 | 9.6 | 4.6 |
| Subtotal | 134 | 79 | 213 | 6.3 | 2,655 | 773 | 3,428 | 16.1 | 27.9 |
| Comprehensive I | 285 | 142 | 427 | 12.6 | 2,272 | 697 | 2,969 | 7.0 | 24.1 |
| Comprehensive II | 47 | 127 | 174 | 5.1 | 97 | 240 | 337 | 1.9 | 2.7 |
| Subtotal | 332 | 269 | 601 | 17.7 | 2,369 | 937 | 3,306 | 5.5 | 26.9 |
| Liberal arts I | 1 | 124 | 125 | 3.7 | 4 | 187 | 191 | 1.5 | 1.6 |
| Liberal arts II | 30 | 409 | 439 | 13.0 | 49 | 342 | 391 | 0.9 | 3.2 |
| Subtotal | 31 | 533 | 564 | 16.6 | 53 | 529 | 582 | 1.0 | 4.7 |
| Two-year institutions | 985 | 383 | 1,368 | 40.4 | 4,250 | 268 | 4,518 | 3.3 | 36.7 |
| Specialized institutions | 66 | 577 | 643 | 19.0 | 131 | 338 | 469 | 0.7 | 3.8 |
| Total | 1,548 | 1,841 | 3,389 | 100.0 | 9,458 | 2,845 | 12,303 | 3.6 | 100.0 |

*Source:* Carnegie Foundation for the Advancement of Teaching (1987), pp. 3 and 4.

5

*Research and doctoral universities* offer a wide range of baccalaureate programs, commit themselves to graduate education, and give a high priority to research. (See appendix A for the defining characteristics of each institutional type.) They differ from one another in the amount of federal support received for research and development: $33.5 million or more annually for Res-I's, a smaller amount but one above $12.5 million for Res-II's. They also differ in the number of Ph.D.'s awarded per year: 50 or more in many fields for Res-I's and -II's, 40 or more in at least five different fields for doctoral universities (Doc-I's and -II's). Res-I professors have a pervasive influence on faculty norms everywhere. Still, they compose less than 13 percent of the workforce.

*Comprehensive universities and colleges* (Comp-I's and -II's) offer graduate work through the master's degree and in professional fields (e.g., engineering). Comp-I's are larger than Comp-II's. Many of these colleges and universities began as two-year normal schools, later expanded to become four-year state colleges, added master's degree programs, and subsequently were renamed universities. Some also offer doctoral degrees in selected fields.

The principal difference between the two types of *liberal arts colleges* (LAC-I's and -II's) resides in the selectivity of their admissions and in their financial health (e.g., endowment size). LAC-I's have students with higher SAT scores, enjoy larger endowments, and cost more. Faculty in LAC-I's work almost exclusively in private institutions. (There is only one public LAC-I.) While there are 125 LAC-I's, they enroll less than 2 percent of the students.

*Two-year colleges* are predominantly the junior and community colleges (CCs) and technical institutes some states have. They typically do not offer work beyond the first two years of the bachelor's degree.[6] They provide liberal arts course equivalents to the first two years of four-year institutions, but their largest sections are vocational and technical programs of varying length, ranging from a single course to a full two years (e.g., a certificate in nursing).

*Specialized institutions* offer anywhere from a bachelor's to a doctor's degree. They are not attached to colleges or universities. Theological seminaries, medical centers, and independent schools of art and music fall into this category.

The Carnegie classification subdivides each category according to type of control, private or public. Institutional control affects formal organization (e.g., appointment and composition of the governing board), public responsibilities (e.g., open vs. closed meetings), compliance with federal laws (e.g., affirmative action), and other matters. Most of these differences, however, influence faculty lives only minimally.[7] Consequently, we almost always collapse the public/private distinction when reporting faculty behaviors across institutional types.

As for where faculty work in this maze of large and small, public and private, undergraduate and graduate, general and specialized curricula, a few rules of thumb prevail. A student-to-faculty ratio generally holds within an institutional category, but there is 100 percent or more variation between categories. Res-I's and LAC-I's experience the lowest student-to-faculty ratios—from 8 or 12 to 1.[8] CCs, Comp-I's, and Doc-II's typically have ratios of more than 20 to 1. One could accurately estimate the number of faculty in the United States were these ratios known with precision. Unfortunately, ignorance prevails and precludes our knowing the actual numbers of faculty in the workplace. Nonetheless, we move from this overview of institutional types to estimates of how many faculty work in the profession.

In estimating the magnitude of the workforce, we rely heavily on different people's assessments of what it is and how large it will become. Table I.2 contains the current data.

One is at first overwhelmed by the discrepancies in the data, actual counts as well as projections.[9] For example, for 1981 the National Center for Educational Statistics (NCES, 1989 [NCES-2000]) said there were 461,000 full-time faculty; the American Council on Education (1987) reported 470,000; and Bowen and Schuster (1986) claimed 537,000, more than a 25 percent difference. For 1987 the U.S. Department of Education's Office of Educational Research and Improvement (OERI) reported the number as 466,000 in one publication (NCES, 1989) and as 491,000 in another (NCES, 1990a [NSOPF88]). Projections for 1995 range from a low of 421,000 full-time (NCES, 1989) to a high of 537,000 (Bowen & Schuster, 1986), a 28 percent difference. One reason for the discrepancies is that there is no commonly accepted definition of *full-time*.[10] Another difficulty is that there are no licensing or certification requirements for faculty as there are, say, for medical doctors. We are simply unable to count the number of faculty accurately.

Even though there are disagreements as to what the actual numbers are, we continue to deal with a large workforce, a population that doubled during the 1960s. From the mid-1970s to the mid-1980s the total numbers changed little. Some areas grew and prospered (computer science, business) while others declined and struggled to obtain needed resources (education, philosophy).

In order to describe this workforce accurately, we have circumscribed our general ignorance by calculating quite precise estimates of the numbers of faculty in the eight selected disciplines identified earlier. We accomplished

Table I.2   Actual and Projected Numbers of Full- and Part-Time Faculty, 1980–2012

| | NCES-2000 (NCES 1989) | | 1986–87 Fact Book (ACE 1987) | | NSOPF88 (NCES 1990a) | | Bowen & Sosa (1989) | Bowen & Schuster (1986) | |
|---|---|---|---|---|---|---|---|---|---|
| | FT | PT | FT | PT | FT | PT | A&S FT | FT | PT |
| 1980 | 450 | 236 | 458 | 238 | | | | | |
| 1981 | 461 | 244 | 470 | 246 | | | | 537 | 466 |
| 1982 | 462 | 248 | 472 | 249 | | | | | |
| 1983 | 471 | 254 | 465 | 246 | | | | | |
| 1984 | 462 | 255 | 460 | 243 | | | | | |
| 1985 | 459 | 246 | 454 | 240 | | | | | |
| 1986 | 459 | 263 | | | 487 | | | 426–455 | 194–207 |
| 1987 | 466 | 269 | | | 491 | 180 | 139–334 | | |
| 1988 | 467 | 275 | | | | | | | |
| 1989 | 458–501 | 271–297 | | | | | | | |
| 1990 | 453–509 | 273–303 | 437 | 233 | | | | 399–458 | 182–212 |
| 1992 | 435–503 | 273–305 | | | | | 131–141 | | |
| 1995 | 421–491 | 271–303 | | | | | | 410–537 | 111–212 |
| 1997 | 425–500 | 269–303 | | | | | 129–152 | | |
| 2000 | 444–527 | 267–302 | | | | | | 398–470 | 113–222 |
| 2002 | | | | | | | 138–158 | | |
| 2005 | | | | | | | | 434–501 | 122–228 |
| 2007 | | | | | | | 143–164 | | |
| 2010 | | | | | | | | 450–521 | 127–237 |
| 2012 | | | | | | | 144–165 | | |

*Notes:* All numbers are in thousands. Where ranges are shown, the figures represent the range between the authors' lowest and highest projections. If no value was reported, the cell was left blank. Numbers are for full-time regular and part-time regular faculty, except in the entries for Bowen and Sosa (all years); theirs are full-time arts and science faculty only. Bowen and Sosa report numbers only for the initial year of their projection period (1987); the other values shown were calculated (see their appendix D).

our somewhat complicated procedure for Res-I through Comp-I Carnegie types (Bentley, Blackburn, & Bieber, 1990; Blackburn & Lawrence, 1989). We could extend our method to incorporate Comp-II's and LACs.[11] It is doubtful, however, whether one could determine the actual number of full-time faculty in CCs even if one had large quantities of money and time. Basic reference works such as the American Council on Education's *Fact Book* (1987) do not exist for these institutions. In addition, the mix of part-time and full-time faculty is so great today, and so different from what it was 20 years ago, that there is no realistic hope of acquiring the proper correction factor to use on early survey data sets.

The descriptive data we present, then, are limited and cannot be generalized to all disciplines and all institutions. As a rule of thumb, we know that liberal arts colleges and public two-year colleges have a higher-than-average proportion of female professors. On average, LAC-I's have a smaller percentage of minority faculty and community colleges a higher percentage.[12]

Figure I.1 displays the numbers of faculty in eight disciplines in all institutional types at four points in time beginning with 1969 (the year of the first in a series of national surveys).[13] Public Comp-I's house the largest number of faculty and exhibit the greatest growth over the past two decades. Today, fewest faculty work in the private Res-II universities. These institutions also show the most stable numbers. Other institutional types grew during the late 1960s and the 1980s, although public Res-II faculty numbers fell during the last time period.

The faculty work context involves more than how many of them there are and where they work, as important as both questions are. U.S. higher education operates within a highly stratified system, and the Carnegie classification depicts the hierarchical structure almost perfectly. Setting aside private two-year and special institutions, the pecking order from Res-I's to CCs is exactly as depicted on the Carnegie scale, except for LAC-I's. Faculty status goes down the scale, with LAC-I's set off to the side of Res-II's. Both have high-pedigree faculty and scholarly concerns. Neither, however, has as much publishing activity among their faculty as Res-I's do. They also differ in size and in their dedication to undergraduate liberal arts education.

Faculty work context also varies with academic discipline. Faculty in philosophy departments lead different lives from their colleagues across campus in physics departments. Disciplines have gender concentrations, with more women occupying positions in psychology than in economics. In addition, disciplines have ethnic saturations, with Asian Americans especially prevalent in the physical and health sciences and African Americans found primarily in the social sciences. We develop these differences in chapters 2 and 3.

Figure I.1   Changes in Faculty Numbers, by Carnegie Type and Control

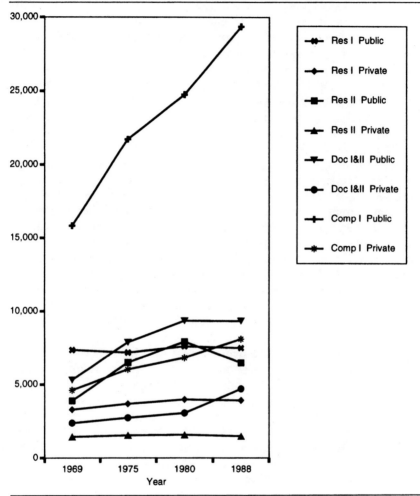

*Source:* Data from Bentley, Blackburn, and Bieber (1990), tables 3–6.

## Overview

Returning to the book's aims, it is no easy task to answer the questions of how faculty behave and why. We are dealing with all the complexities of human behavior. As we became more involved in conducting research on faculty and in examining the studies that others have done, it struck us that the existing research suffered from an absence of sound theory guiding the investigations. When theory was present, the conceptual framework was most often too restrictive. It depended almost exclusively on demographic attributes of age and sex and on career experiences of where the professor had gone to graduate school and was currently working. The research literature was too often overwhelmingly descriptive, a kind of Gallup poll of faculty demographics and opinions. At best it contained simple correlations. The need was not for more surveys and larger numbers of respondents, but rather for data that would explain and predict faculty behavior and outcomes—for example, publications (Long, 1992).

We have created a theoretical framework that addresses these complexities, and more important, we have tapped faculty members' cognitions— their self-evaluations of their interests and efficacy (competence and ability to influence outcomes) and their perceptions of the environment (what it expects and what it rewards).

We have divided this book into three major sections. Part 1 we call "Setting the Stage and Developing the Framework." Chapter 1 establishes the theoretical bases for the framework and takes the reader through the choices we made and the reasons for them. It ends with a display of the major components of the framework and their relationships with one another.

Chapters 2 and 3 explain the conceptual meaning of each of the variables used to measure the constructs in our theoretical framework. Here we turn to the research literature and discuss the studies that utilize our variables, if and when the study relates the variable to a faculty behavior (teaching, conducting research, contributing service) or product (a published article, a new curriculum).[14] Chapter 3 closes with a presentation of the primary research conclusions, the ways in which the findings make faculty behavior understandable, and how the results can be used to inform administrative actions with regard to increasing faculty vitality and institutional productivity. (We warn the reader, however, that in chapter 7 we show that administrators and faculty frequently do not see the same work environment in the same way.)

Part 2 we call "Testing and Using the Framework." Here we describe the studies we have conducted to evaluate our framework. Chapter 4 considers investigations in which faculty publication is the outcome variable. Chapter 5 takes teaching as the behavior to be predicted. Chapter 6 deals with the third faculty role, service and scholarship, about which little research exists. Each of these chapters closes with the principal findings, the light they shed on faculty behavior, and their implications for arranging the work environment. Chapter 7, as indicated above, compares administrator and faculty views of the same workplace.

Part 3, a discussion of what we learned, summarizes our findings and speculates about the future.


We turn now to the theoretical framework.

# PART ONE

Setting the Stage
and Developing
the Framework

# 1

# THE THEORETICAL
# FRAMEWORK

In this chapter we advance a conceptualization of faculty role performance and achievement. The theoretical perspective we take is that characteristics of individuals and their employing institution combine and lead to variations in faculty motivation, behavior, and productivity. We begin the explanation of our framework by defining its key structural components. We then review select motivation theories and propose alternative explanations for how different individual and environmental factors affect faculty role performance.

## Properties of Individuals and Their Work Environments

Empirical studies of faculty work performance tend to focus exclusively on properties of either the individual or the environment that lead to variations in behavior and productivity. Individual properties are characteristics of faculty members—for example, sociodemographic characteristics, aptitudes, and values that can affect their access to opportunities, their capacity to meet performance expectations, and their commitment to different facets of faculty roles. Environmental properties are features of a situation—such as intellectual resources, institutional norms, or physical plant—that can constrain or enhance role performance. In this chapter we identify the individual and environmental constructs in our framework. In chapters 2 and 3 we review the empirical evidence regarding the influence of these factors on faculty behavior.

### Properties of Individuals

We identify four individual constructs within our framework as antecedents to faculty behavior: sociodemographic characteristics, career, self-knowledge, and social knowledge. Among the most widely studied *socio-demographic* characteristics are chronological age, race/ethnicity, and gender. The literature suggests that these variables influence behavior indirectly by limiting or enhancing one's access to resources and opportunities. Empirical data suggest that men and women and older and younger people have different psychological needs that influence their behavior. Furthermore, writers argue that men and women, as well as members of different ethnic groups, receive qualitatively different responses to their behavior. This feedback affects individuals' perceptions of themselves and of their environments and, ultimately, their role performance.

We conceive of the *career* construct as having several key properties. Career includes the graduate socialization experiences of individuals, in particular the type of preparation they received in research and teaching as well as the conceptions of the faculty role they learned. We also include as career variables one's academic discipline and the type of institution in which one works, since the normative structures of the disciplines as well as those of the employing institution influence individual beliefs and priorities. The career construct also includes an individual's pattern or sequence of academic or administrative positions and her or his present position within a college or university. Career age—the number of years one has had a full-time faculty appointment—indicates the extent of faculty experience and adjusts for chronological age differences that can falsely identify maturity and wisdom. At the same time, career age serves as a surrogate for the skills and knowledge an individual has acquired. Finally, we incorporate prior accomplishments such as publication record, awards for outstanding teaching, and grants and fellowships obtained as properties of career. Although there are clearly other aspects of career we might include, prior studies suggest that these are the most salient. In addition, they affect one's ability to influence decisions within academic units and to acquire resources to support one's work, both within and outside the employing institution. Moreover, these indicators of past success often predict an individual's assessments of her or his capacity to engage in future professional activities.

*Self-knowledge* delineates a third construct antecedent to faculty behavior. Self-knowledge serves as an indicator of one's understanding of self, or self-referent thought. It is a measure of self-image and self-assessed competence in selected professional activities, as well as one's sense of efficacy in situations. Self-knowledge encompasses an individual's personal attitudes and values with respect to the importance of certain aspects of the faculty role (e.g., teaching, research, service). One's dispositions, such as ambition, persistence, and supportiveness, are also part of this theoretical construct. They affect levels of engagement in different activities, the proportion of the effort given to the different faculty roles of teaching, research, service, and scholarship. Studies in higher education and other settings indicate that these individual characteristics are key correlates of behavior and often mediate the influence of other factors on behavior. For example, faculty members' self-efficacy judgments may mediate the influence of their professional status on their participation in organizational decision making.

Broadly defined, *social knowledge* represents how individuals perceive their environment. It includes faculty members' understanding of how others expect them to behave (subjective norms) and their beliefs about others in the environment, individuals with whom they interact and on whom they may depend. Research conducted by House (1981), Pelz and Andrews (1976), and others (e.g., Austin & Gamson, 1983; Neumann & Finaly-Neumann, 1990) underscores the importance of social knowledge through their findings that productive scholars perceive that their work environments offered collegial support and autonomy. The dimensions of social knowledge we distinguish are similar to those that Moos (1976, 1979) believes characterize an organization's social climate. We do, however, depart from conventional definitions of this construct in that we include as part of social knowledge the prototypes or cognitive representations of valued faculty members that individuals carry in their heads and may use to guide their decisions about how to behave (Abelson & Levi, 1984; Cohen, 1981; Nisbet & Ross, 1980; Staw, 1983).

### Properties of the Environment

We define properties of the environment as the objective characteristics of the work setting that exist, separate and apart from individual faculty perceptions of it. We also include in the framework situations that arise in individuals' personal lives that can affect role performance. The three environmental constructs are environmental conditions, environmental responses, and social contingencies.

The *environmental conditions* construct represents the structural and normative features of the university or college. One set of factors is the fiscal well-being of an institution, its geographical location, the composition of a department's faculty, and the system of faculty governance. These structural features can affect faculty access to resources they need in order to carry out their research. A second set—the composition of the student body and the quality of library, laboratory, and other instructional resources—can influence faculty teaching. A third set consists of normative features such as the understanding of the mission of a college or university shared by faculty and administrators. Normative features can also exert pervasive effects on behavior. We define environmental conditions in terms of these properties.

17

The *environmental response* construct includes the different types of formal feedback that faculty receive about their role performance. Perhaps today the most significant of these responses for the faculty member is the awarding of tenure. However, there are myriad sources of information, both within and outside the employing institution, that indicate to faculty members that they are achieving important goals. Faculty receive evaluations from students in their classes, from discipline peers who review their publications and grant applications, from colleagues and administrators who consider their proposals for curricular revisions, requests for graduate research assistants, instructional materials, and the like. These responses operationalize the normative climate of the institution. The shared understanding of the institution's mission and of what is central to a particular academic unit in part shapes decisions about awarding tenure or committing institutional resources to faculty projects.

The third environmental construct, *social contingencies,* includes events that happen in faculty members' personal lives and affect their work. The birth of a child or the health problems of a parent or spouse, for example, put demands on one's emotional state and time and can restrict the level of effort given to work. Some events are under the control of individuals (e.g., coaching a child's soccer team), whereas others are not (e.g., health problems). Hence, the social contingencies construct includes conditions that exist for short or long periods of time and factors that vary in terms of an individual's control over them.

## Motivation Processes

We turn now from the question of what affects faculty behavior and productivity (the structural dimension of our framework) to the question of how these factors influence behavior and productivity (the process dimension). Explaining individual and group differences in motivated behavior— that is, their tendencies to initiate and sustain a given activity—is a central concern for researchers in many fields, including higher education. Hence, we examine different theoretical perspectives on motivation for some answers to the process question.

For the purpose of discussion, we group motivation theories into two categories, noncognitive and cognitive. We also focus on motivation in achievement contexts, situations in which there are performance outcomes that define levels of success. This emphasis reflects the reality of the academic context in which faculty and students are constantly being evaluated or evaluating themselves against standards of performance.

## Noncognitive Theories of Motivation

A key assumption of noncognitive theories is that internal needs, personality dispositions, and external incentives and rewards will cause an individual to behave in predictable ways. Little or no human cognition is required, as any learning about how to behave involves noncognitive conditioning of the bond between these stimuli and responses. Among the theories that fall within this category are stage theories of personality and career development as well as reinforcement and dispositional theories of motivation.

### Personality and Career Development Theories

Interest in adult development has heightened with the aging of the American population. During the last 20 years the number of theories of personality development and life-course patterns has grown rapidly. (See Baltes & Brim [1983] for a review of these theories.) The majority of these theoretical perspectives are characterized by a focus on the ontogenetic needs that guide behavior at different periods in the life span. The central proposition is that at different development stages, individuals are compelled by particular needs or psychobiological states to act in characteristic ways. Various researchers offer biographical, empirical, and clinical evidence to support the argument that there are predictable crises experienced by all people during a particular period in their lives, and that there are predictable goals that individuals set for themselves as they resolve these dilemmas (e.g., Gould, 1978; Levinson, Darrow, Klein, Levinson, & McKee, 1978; Taylor & Ellison, 1967). However, some scholars criticize this literature for its inattention to the social contexts in which individuals age (see, e.g., Dannefer, 1984).

An alternative perspective, life-course theory, assumes that development is shaped by interactions between age-determined psychological and biological changes in the individual and environmental factors (Featherman, 1983). From this perspective, cohort membership must be taken into account, along with chronological age, because the knowledge and societal conditions that predominate during critical periods of socialization can vary and affect the pattern of development that characterizes a generation. For example, this view takes it to be critical to know when one attended school or entered the workforce in order to interpret longitudinal data on intelligence or educational and work values (cf. Schaie, 1983).

Some researchers (e.g., Levinson et al., 1978) have examined the impact of personality development changes on work life. Others (e.g., Hall & Mansfield, 1975) have proposed sequences of career stages, each with a set

19

of distinctive pressures or needs that lead individuals to behave in particular ways and to find certain activities most satisfying. Super, Crites, Hummerl, Moser, Overstreet, and Warnath (1957) and Super (1980), for example, divide careers into four stages that progress from an exploratory phase to establishment, then to maintenance, and finally to a stage of decline. Each stage has a set of goals that individuals feel they must accomplish, and hence these goals motivate behavior.

## Reinforcement Theories

Reinforcement theory holds that behavior (response) is caused by the environment (stimuli), that different factors in the environment motivate different responses from an individual (Atkinson, 1977). According to behaviorist theory, individuals create stimulus-response bonds through a form of noncognitive learning (conditioning), and the response that occurs in a situation is the one most strongly associated with the stimulus.

Experimental studies led behaviorist researchers to conclude that people behave in ways that maximize rewards and minimize punishment. This principle is central to socialization theory as well as to organizational psychology models and management practices that assume that the selective reinforcement of desired behavior (contingent reinforcement) will motivate people to behave in ways that are socially and organizationally desired (Staw, 1983). Critics of this contingency reinforcement approach to behavior modification note that certain activities are intrinsically motivating; for example, people engage in research because they find the process innately rewarding (Deci, Nezlek, & Sheinman, 1981; Lepper, Greene, & Nisbet, 1973). Thus, the introduction of extrinsic rewards for research, such as salary incentives, can diminish the strength of incentives that are intrinsic to the activity itself and so can lead faculty to conduct research solely for the financial gains. The concern is that once the extrinsic rewards are removed, or not increased, individuals may no longer engage in the desired activity. In other words, the selective reinforcement of behavior results in long-term conformity only if the conditions that originally led to the behavior are maintained.

## Dispositional Theories

Clark Hull modified the basic stimulus-response formulation of motivation to take into account individual differences in needs that could heighten or diminish the strength of a stimulus, a change that was critical to the subsequent development of motivation theory. The highly influential works of Atkinson (1957), Atkinson and Feather (1966), Atkinson and Raynor (1974), McClelland (1961), and McClelland, Atkinson, Clark, and Lowell

(1953) conceptualized the achievement motive as a relatively stable desire, or need—namely, to excel in reference to a standard of excellence. They assumed that this predisposition was an enduring personality trait learned during childhood through the process of socialization. Atkinson predicted that achievement motives would cause individuals to seek out and persist in activities that differed in their degree of challenge. Individuals high in the need for achievement would exhibit motivated behavior under more challenging environmental conditions, whereas those low in the need for achievement would be more motivated under less challenging conditions.

While there are many dispositions that could motivate behavior, achievement and affiliation have received the most attention in the education literature in part because achievement and affiliative behaviors are important to success in academic settings. However, the behaviors associated with these two motives are contradictory. The achievement motive leads to competitive behavior, whereas the affiliation motive results in cooperative and supportive behavior. Achievement and affiliation are also a focus of attention because some researchers have found differences in the needs of men and women (e.g., Astin, 1969; Belenky, Clinchy, Goldberger, & Tarule, 1986; Fausto-Sterling, 1992, p. 123). These researchers would attribute variations in performance on a given task to sex differences. For example, female faculty's greater interest in teaching is motivated by their stronger need for affiliation, a need more likely to be satisfied with students in the classroom than with colleagues in research settings.

### Cognitive Theories of Motivation

Psychologists who synthesized research on decision making with need and reinforcement conceptualizations of motivation share a common premise. Motivation is a function of individuals' subjective estimates of the probability of task success (expectancy) and of the consequences of their actions (value). In other words, cognitive theories of motivation assume that people make decisions about how to behave by evaluating their capacity to respond to situations and estimating their possible losses and gains. Many theories are refinements of this general view of motivation. We review four that are most relevant to research on college and university faculty. Specifically, we focus attention on expectancy, attribution, efficacy, and information-processing theories.

### Expectancy Theories

Weiner (1985, p. 555) states that "every major cognitive motivational theorist includes the expectancy of goal attainment among the determinants of action." While Atkinson's perspective emphasizes the dispositional features of achievement motivation, Weiner grounds his view in expectancy theory. Contrary to initial predictions that achievement-oriented people would seek high challenge, empirical evidence indicated that individuals who were high in achievement motivation were more likely to exhibit motivated behavior under conditions where the chances of failure and success were equal. Hence, Atkinson modified his initial theoretical model to include situational determinants as well as internalized needs. He took achievement behavior to be a function of the motive to avoid failure and approach success (achievement disposition), the expectancy for success (expectancy), and the incentive value of the task (value).

Vroom's (1964) model of work motivation applies the expectancy perspective to the workplace. He posited that individuals are motivated to work when they expect that job performance will lead to desired outcomes and when they value work activities. In contrast to Atkinson, Vroom tended to emphasize the motivational value of the work situation itself, such as wages and opportunities for promotion, more than the characteristics of individuals, such as their abilities and interests.

Maehr and Braskamp's (1986) personal investment theory attends to both the individual and the contextual aspects of motivation in the workplace. Their expectancy theory posits that people are constantly making decisions about how to invest their time and effort. Motivation to perform a task varies in relation to the meaning it has for an individual. Meaning is determined by a person's sense of self and by personal incentives that evolve and change over time as a result of social learning. The sense of self includes one's estimates of personal control over the situation, self-competence, and goal-directedness. Personal incentives are the outcomes that the individual wants to achieve in different situations. For example, someone may seek collegial approval of a course proposal during informal conversations with other faculty members or seek more formal recognition of her or his accomplishments through merit salary increases. Personal investment theory assumes, then, that an individual's choices of activities, as well as decisions about the level of effort to expend and persistence toward goals, are motivated behaviors and are contingent on her or his personal sense of self and the subjective value of the activity. Compared with the other expectancy theories described above, this perspective tends to emphasize the value component of the expectancy value formulation. (The expectancy value formulation refers to expectancy theories' key premise that these theoretical constructs interact.)

## Attribution Theories

Another elaboration of the expectancy value formulation of motivation focuses on individuals' causal attributions that influence their expectancy of success and their responses to performance outcomes (Weiner, 1985). This view holds that in achievement situations individuals tend to believe that success is caused by factors within the individual and in the environment. These factors vary in terms of their locus, stability, and controllability. Specifically, causal attributions differ depending on an individual's perceptions as to (1) whether the conditions that determine success are primarily under one's own control or under the control of others (locus of control); (2) whether the causal factors are stable or variable (e.g., individual aptitude may be constant across situations, whereas environmental resources may vary); and (3) whether the internal factors can or cannot be controlled by the individual (e.g., one can regulate the amount of effort allocated to an activity but may have less control over causes such as artistic aptitude). Weiner argues that causal attributions are important antecedents of expectancies because they can raise or lower a person's estimations of her or his probable success.

Weiner's attributional perspective extends theory in one other important way. He proposes that affective reactions to performance outcomes influence the subjective value of goal achievement (e.g., task value). For example, successful performance attributed to personal effort and skill may result in feelings of satisfaction, whereas success attributed to chance may result in surprise. Weiner reasons that the causal attribution of success to skill and effort along with the positive feelings it brings will lead individuals to ascribe greater value to the task. Hence, this attributional approach predicts that the value component of the expectancy formulation of motivation will be greater in subsequent situations. Individuals will be more motivated to engage in an activity in which they expect to be successful and when previous engagement in that activity brought them personal satisfaction.

## Efficacy Theories

The self-efficacy theories of Bandura (1977a, 1982) and Bandura and Wood (1989) incorporate features of Weiner's attribution model of motivation. However, Bandura focuses attention on individuals' assessments of the personal resources they bring to a situation in addition to their causal attributions and affective responses to previous performance outcomes. Bandura argues that self-referent thought, in which people judge their abilities to complete a task successfully (self-efficacy), influences their levels of goal-directed behavior (motivation).

In keeping with other cognitive motivation theories, self-efficacy theory predicts that level of effort and persistence on task will vary in relation to an individual's level of goal commitment; the greater the subjective value of the goal, the higher the level of goal-directed behavior. Further, efficacy theory posits that the level of engagement in a task will increase as confidence in one's capacity to meet situational demands and one's beliefs that effort will lead to desired outcomes (self-efficacy) increase in strength.

Self-efficacy is not a fixed trait or disposition. Rather, it is a "dynamic construct" that takes into account features of a task and the environment in which it is embedded as well as an individual's competence, past experience, and success with the task. Unlike self-esteem and self-concept, which tend to be more global assessments of the self across several situations, self-efficacy is task-specific and varies in relation to experience, learning, and performance feedback (Bandura, 1982).

According to Bandura, the causal attributions people make regarding their past performance become focal points of subsequent efficacy judgments. The distinctions people draw between factors that are under their control and those that are under the control of others are particularly influential when they are assessing their self-efficacy. Furthermore, their affective response to past experience influences these judgments (Gist & Mitchell, 1992; Weiner, 1985).

The features of a task as well as its social context are also focal points as individuals estimate their self-efficacy. People evaluate the difficulty of a task by comparing those features that come easily to them with those that are more difficult. In addition, they take into consideration what kinds of resources they will need to complete the task and whether or not they have access to them. In instances where the task requires coordinated effort, individuals estimate the probability that others will fulfill their obligations (Bandura & Wood, 1989).

Gist and Mitchell (1992) offer the following insights:

> The assessment of task requirements and attributional analysis of experience provide some sense of what it will take to do well on the task in terms of ability and motivational components and in terms of the relative contributions of these to performance. However, these two antecedent processes appear to yield necessary but insufficient data in the formation of self-efficacy. There remains an examination of self and setting by which the individual assesses the availability of specific resources and constraints for performing the task at various levels. This assessment requires consideration of personal factors (e.g., skill level, anxiety, desire, available effort) as well as situational factors (e.g., competing demands, distractions) that impinge on future performance. (p. 190)

### Information-Processing Theories

As noted earlier, the cognitive theories of motivation conceptualize the motivation process as a form of decision making in which individuals conduct detailed analyses of their potential losses and gains and the resources that can be brought to bear on a situation. One weakness of this perspective is that it does not necessarily differentiate decisions that require a great deal of cognitive energy from those that are less complicated (Staw, 1983).

Researchers have begun to distinguish between more in-depth and superficial analyses of situations that guide decisions about how to behave (Bargh & Pietrononaco, 1976; Kihlstrom, 1983). Abelson and Levi (1984), Buss and Craik (1983), Cantor, Mischel, and Schwartz (1982), Gersick and Hackman (1990), Langer (1989), Mitchell and Beach (1990), and Nuttin (1984) are among the researchers working to identify the schemas, prototypes, and scripts people use. These writers assert that we process information in different ways, depending on the situation. In situations that are unfamiliar, complex, or potentially costly, the process of interpretation and decisions about a course of action require the kinds of judgments suggested by the cognitive motivation theorists. They maintain, however, that in familiar situations we apply heuristic strategies that we carry in our heads. Showers and Cantor (1985, p. 278) state, "In actuality, the active cognitive processes of selection, combination, and reinterpretation are often neither necessary nor efficient; individuals seem to do just fine using the most available and ready-made interpretations."

Research on the interconnections between social cognition and motivation offers some insights into distinctions that might be drawn between in-depth processing and rudimentary forms of situational analysis. This literature suggests that the motivational elements that affect efficacy and value judgments can also influence the cognitive strategies people use to interpret and decide on plans of action. It appears that individuals' expertise, goals, and mood affect their strategies for responding to situations (Showers & Cantor, 1985).

People's expertise affects how they interpret situations. Individuals with a larger repertoire of information to draw upon may develop several alternative interpretations and courses of action, whereas those with less relevant expertise may see only one. Expertise also allows people to develop more efficient and automatic strategies that require less intellectual effort to be devoted to planning courses of action (Petty, Cacioppo, & Goldman, 1981). Personal goals are another factor that affects the strategies people develop. Studies show that individuals whose subjective goal is to maintain their self-image may increase their effort if they expect to succeed and diminish their effort if they expect to fail, regardless of the incentives offered by others (Carver & Scheier, 1983). Mood can also influence one's interpretation of a situation and one's strategy for responding to it. Individuals in positive moods are more likely to identify multiple interpretations and action plans, whereas those who are despondent may be more rigid in their interpretations and actions (Showers & Cantor, 1985).

## Faculty Role Performance and Achievement: A Theoretical Framework

The theoretical framework that we propose integrates the research on faculty role performance and productivity with motivation theories. As noted earlier, we derived the theoretical constructs representing properties of the individual and environment from the higher-education literature. From the motivation research we extrapolated the hypothetical paths through which different individual and situational factors may influence behavior and productivity.

The framework models both immediate and future productivity as affected by ongoing interactions between individual faculty members and their work environments. The key premises underlying the framework are as follows. First, academic institutions are achievement-laden environments in which the evaluation of faculty, student, and administrator performance is ongoing. Second, faculty use assessments of themselves and their social contexts to make meaningful decisions about their actions. However, not all decisions require the same level of detailed situation analysis. Third, experience over time leads individuals to modify their understanding of their work environments as well as their self-images. These changes can affect the subjective incentive value of different facets of work, and consequently a faculty member's level of engagement in different activities can shift. Fourth, some types of self-referent thought and perceptions of the work environment are fairly enduring, whereas others change frequently on the basis of personal feedback and vicarious experience.

We base the placement of the individual and environmental constructs within the framework on the results of empirical studies of faculty careers and cognitive motivation research. Specifically, we propose that sociodemographic characteristics exert direct effects on individuals' career and self-knowledge. We also propose that the career construct in our theoretical framework can mediate the impact of some sociodemographic characteristics on self-knowledge. (See figure 1.1.)

The first hypothesized paths are supported by sociological studies of social stratification and mobility demonstrating that individuals' access to career opportunities can vary depending on their ethnicity and sex. These paths are also supported by psychological developmental theories suggesting that personal goals and commitments vary with age, and by life-course theories asserting that cohorts are socialized to different values and vary in

Figure 1.1   Theoretical Framework

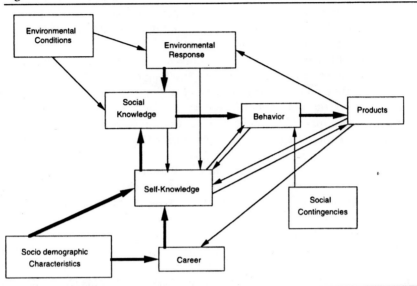

*Note:* The thick, heavier arrows signify strong, direct effects of the variables in one category on the variables in the category the arrow points to. The thin arrows acknowledge that there are weaker effects between several of the principal constructs.

expertise depending on when they received their graduate preparation (Chubin, Porter, & Boeckman, 1981; Long, 1978; Reskin, 1978). The possibility that career may mediate the effects of sociodemographic characteristics is suggested by the work of Allison and Stewart (1974) on the Matthew effect. Specifically, they have demonstrated that individuals who are high achievers early on tend to continue to be high producers throughout their careers because they enjoy greater access to funds for their research. Allison and Stewart conclude that the effects of age on role performance are mediated by this process of "accumulative advantage."

We base the placement of self-knowledge ahead of social knowledge primarily on the results of cognitive motivation research. In most of the empirical studies, the data suggest that individuals' understanding of themselves (e.g., their self-assessed competence, personality dispositions, efficacy) predict how they perceive their environments (e.g., norms, resources) more frequently than environmental perceptions predict this self-understanding (Kanfer & Ackerman, 1974; Wigfield & Braskamp, 1985).

We conceptualize social knowledge as the key link between self-referent thought, the other individual variables, and behavior. This construct owes its placement to the fact that social knowledge is influenced by both self-knowledge and environmental response. While performance feedback clearly affects perceptions of organizational priorities and individual competence, cognitive theories assume that motivation is a function of both individual characteristics and perceptions of the environment. We decided, therefore, to take this into account by showing that behavior is a result of the cumulative effects of self-knowledge and social knowledge. However, we leave open the possibility that the personal incentive value of an activity or some developmental issue that needs to be resolved may directly affect behavior even despite the faculty member's knowledge of her or his work environment.

The environmental constructs in the theoretical framework have both direct and indirect effects on behavior. We assume that social contingencies exert direct effects on behavior in that they typically place constraints on the time and energy one has to engage in activities. We also assume that environmental conditions exert influence over behavior indirectly through social knowledge. As noted earlier, the normative context of an institution has pervasive effects on the individuals within it. Environmental conditions affect faculty members' understanding of the standards of performance that predominate and the resources the institution can make available (social knowledge). We believe that certain resources affect role performance to the extent that faculty know they exist, and therefore that differences in this knowledge have the potential to affect behavior.

Environmental conditions also indirectly influence social knowledge through environmental responses. Standards of performance that are embedded in the institution's normative context in part shape direct feedback on performance. These standards also help determine decisions about requests for assistance with individuals' work. In effect, then, these environmental responses translate the more abstract shared understanding of an institution's goals into specific messages about organizational priorities and role expectations. This proposition reflects the reinforcement principles of behaviorist psychology and socialization theory as well as the social learning precepts that are central to cognitive motivation theories. We show that the effects of feedback on behavior are mediated by social knowledge because research indicates that individuals will not necessarily interpret the same feedback in a similar fashion. Feedback is filtered through previous experiences, personal priorities, and competencies, and one's interpretation of it is colored by the credibility one attributes to its source (Bandura, 1982).

We define *behavior* as the specific activities a faculty member engages in as well as the levels of effort expended. We take *productivity,* on the other hand, to be the specific outcomes achieved by individuals—that is, articles published, teaching awards received, grants and fellowships obtained, and the like. Because the framework is longitudinal, we indicate that productivity has effects on self-knowledge and career. The assumption is that levels of achievement in different activity areas can influence faculty members' self-knowledge and career. For example, acquisition of a grant to support one's research after a long period without funding may result in specific changes in one's sense of competence and efficacy. These changes in self-knowledge can in turn affect one's views of colleagues (social knowledge) and the level of effort one devotes to research (behavior). Furthermore, performance at high levels of achievement over time can affect one's career, such as status within one's institution and discipline.

Different theoretical perspectives on motivation suggest specific paths through which the various theoretical constructs in the framework influence faculty behavior. In the following chapters we explain these perspectives in more detail and discuss the supporting empirical evidence. In particular, chapters 2 and 3 present the research literature for the variables we use in our studies for each of the theoretical framework's constructs.

# 2

# THE VARIABLES: SOCIO-
# DEMOGRAPHICS AND CAREER

This CHAPTER AND THE NEXT ONE present empirical evidence about each of the theoretical framework's constructs. We indicate the measures used to assess the variables as we display and describe the constructs advanced to assay the variables. In each instance we report the variable's relationship to either a behavior or a product—the principal outcomes of the framework.

Behavior and product, then, are critical constructs. We pause to define them and to tell their typical indicators and measures. We also point out an indicator's limitations and discuss its reliability and accuracy.

## Behaviors and Products

*Behaviors* are faculty activities, such as leading a class discussion, reading new materials that will be used in teaching or in research, conducting an experiment, reviewing a manuscript, participating in meetings—a wide assortment of teaching, scholarly, research, and service activities. Time spent represents a measure of a behavior (e.g., hours given to teaching). However, we do not consider a student's rating of Professor A as a good lecturer or a colleague's judgment that Professor B is a good researcher to be indicators of behaviors. These are opinions and beliefs, not activities.[1]

*Products* are concrete objects, such as a new syllabus, a published article, a painting, a monograph, a chapter in a book, a software program, a musical score, a video for explaining a difficult concept in a course—again, a wide assortment of faculty creations.

As straightforward as this distinction sounds, it contains complications and complexities. Teaching requires more than preparing new materials and keeping abreast of new knowledge. It involves grading papers, preparing examinations, helping students who are having difficulty, spending time in the laboratory—a long list of activities. Moreover, effective teaching is more than a list of specific activities; it is an art, a performance. We can identify some pedagogical components. However, teaching qua teaching remains something more than the sum of its parts.

A research product, say a published article, also serves as a limited indicator of what constitutes research: having a novel idea, creating a way to demonstrate a hypothesis, inventing a means to explore it, preparing a way to communicate it—a long list of activities that again does not fully capture the construct we call research. In sum, every construct has limitations, some more serious than others.

So do the measures of constructs. Most often the information we collect on a construct is the *quantity* of the measure, not its *quality*. Of course, quality matters more. A new syllabus of little assistance to the student may be a product, but hardly something of value. An article deemed wanting or in error by colleagues who read it makes at best a minimal contribution— namely, by showing what not to do. Time spent on an activity does not guarantee the quality of the effort.

At the same time, there are partial quality controls for some behaviors and products. Those that do exist fall almost exclusively within the research role, not in the teaching, scholarship, or service ones. For research, faculty experts in the field in which the professor is conducting research serve as judges on the quality of a manuscript or a proposal. This peer-review process sorts out most of the wheat from the chaff. Still, as with every human enterprise, it is not a perfect system. A flawed kernel may be discovered in the highest-rated journal, and an original, important mutant may initially be rejected as unimportant, unworthy.

Some faculty productivity studies have utilized frequency of citations of an article as a measure of the quality of a professor's work; we cite some such studies below. The more frequently other scholars use an author's work, the higher its value (quality). Citation counts correlate highly (around .7) with the quantity of articles a faculty member publishes. Without going into detail, citation counts as a research construct also have some shortcomings. (See, e.g., Lindsey, 1989; Wallmark & Sedig, 1986.)

Another limitation of our behavior and product variables lies in the ways in which data are collected. Faculty report the activities they engage in, but there is usually no documentation to corroborate their replies. On questionnaires or during interviews they tell how much effort they give to different activities, how frequently they redesign courses, publish articles, write reports, counsel students. They provide time estimates for the extent of their activities. But rarely do researchers collect records to verify what the respon-

31

dents report. Consequently errors exist—not because faculty distort the truth, but simply because inaccuracies and uncertainties are inevitable. Nonetheless, reliability studies provide a high degree of confidence in the collected data. Research designed to corroborate faculty work activities and products strongly supports the accuracy of the information faculty provide. These investigations include getting faculty to keep diaries, interviewing spouses for how many hours faculty work, and comparing vitae with reported publications (Allison & Stewart, 1974; Blackburn, Boberg, O'Connell, & Pellino, 1980; Clark & Centra, 1985).

With these limitations and understandings in mind, we turn now to what the research literature contains on each of our theoretical framework's constructs—sociodemographics and career in this chapter, self-knowledge and social knowledge in the next one. We do not report all studies. Rather, we select the stronger ones. When the findings differ from one another, we suggest why and draw the soundest inferences.

## Sociodemographics

As our theoretical framework shows, we place age, sex, and race in the category of sociodemographics, an individual's fixed characteristics.

### Age

We begin with the professorial age distribution and how it has been changing over the past two decades. Figure 2.1 displays the data.[2] The figure reveals the dramatic shift in younger faculty from 1969 to 1980. The proportion of those aged 35 or younger fell from 32.1 percent of the workforce to 6.8 percent. The slight increase to 8.5 percent in 1988 indicates the beginning of a new cohort of junior faculty and a widening gap between junior and senior faculty. Also in 1988, nearly a quarter were older than 55; more than 60 percent were older than 45.[3]

Bowen and Schuster (1986), Lawrence, Blackburn, and Yoon (1987), and the National Science Foundation (1988), among others, have addressed various dimensions of faculty aging. As fewer graduate students seek academic careers, the faculty shortage projected to occur before the end of the 1990s has become an age-related issue. A second problem is that accelerating retirements are increasing educational costs.[4] A third concern centers on the continuity of faculty leadership, since there is a hiatus in the age distribution in many units resulting from the fact that the number of new appointments was close to zero over the decade of the 1970s. Faculty fall at either end of the age spectrum. There are relatively few in the middle to ascend to positions of leadership. A belief that declining faculty productivity accompanies aging constitutes a fourth issue.

Figure 2.1   Distribution of Faculty by Age

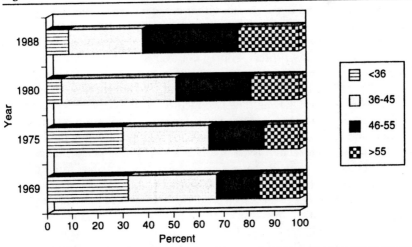

*Source:* National surveys.
*Note:* Data are for faculty in the eight disciplines who work in Res-I's through Comp-I's, not all U.S. academics. In addition, we have adjusted the numbers from the four surveys to their proper proportions to take into account survey sampling errors related to nonrespondents.

Pundits have predicted faculty shortages more than once in the past—most recently in the 1960s, when the country's higher-education system exploded. New community colleges opened at the rate of one per week. Other institutional types operated at full student capacity. An inadequate supply of faculty was inevitable.[5] Experts predicted disaster. Yet someone taught classes, and students passed through the system. Today's faculty-shortage prognoses rest on better databases. Still, forecasters disagree sharply on the magnitude and timing of the shortage.[6] Embedded within the shortage issue is the question of the nation's future supply of scientists. As the United States competes for world leadership, knowledge constitutes a primary product. Here the data (National Science Foundation, 1988) confirm the steady decline of U.S. doctorates over the past 15 years.[7]

The third age-related issue mentioned above—the hiatus in future faculty institutional leadership because of the gap that occurred with the economic downturn and reduced hiring of the mid-1970s to mid-1980s—has affected other aspects of the workplace. Many departments now have "two cultures," a young and an old, with but a handful of middle-aged faculty in between. Communication between them is strained. Some of the gap is social—differing stages of family development, two-career young couples

33

versus single-income seniors. Another gap is ideological—differing beliefs about what matters in the world. Other breaches are intellectual. The new hires' interests lie more with theory and less with practice. The new economists build theoretical models and consult less with business and industry. Recently minted law professors may not even sit for the state's bar exams and pay but casual attention to courtroom tactics. The novice assistant professor of English relishes deconstruction, not another traditionally approached piece on Dickens. The two faculty cultures can converse on little but trivia anymore. As a consequence, department cohesion fractures, curricular and requirement debates intensify, and students may be the losers.

The fourth age-related issue involves the declining performance that is asserted to accompany increasing years. A veritable petrified forest of faculty deadwood is already in hand, and unless our higher-educational institutions prune the older professorial crop, the nation's key knowledge production industry will tumble—or so some university presidents believe. Not long ago a small set of academic administrators and higher-education spokespersons persuaded senators that the federal law uncapping mandatory retirement at age 70 should exempt university professors (and firefighters and police officers).[8]

The relationship between age and creative work engrosses people. Fascination with child prodigies at one end of the life course and prolific octogenarians such as a Pablo Casals or Rexford Tugwell at the other have piqued the interest of artists as well as academicians. Shakespeare's seven stages (*As You Like It*) reappear as the anthropologist's rites of passage, Erickson's (1963) developmental stages, Perry's (1968) steps of cognitive development, Levinson, Darrow, Klein, Levinson, and McKee's (1978) periods of turmoil and calm, and a host of other delineations of the sequence of events humans pass through on their course from birth to death.

Moreover, age has more than practical consequences. Many link it to, and frequently advance it as, the cause of motivated interests. Theories contend that different levels and kinds of creative motivation occur at different ages. We examine four contesting theoretical predictions of age as a motivator of faculty productivity. We present the expectations of four basic conceptual frameworks and cite illustrative research pieces conducted within each theoretical framework.

Before going on, however, we need to note that faculty productivity studies have employed different creativity indicators. The variations cause problems for comparing research findings that utilize different measures. For example, some investigators have focused on the age at which an individual produced her or his most creative work, an estimation that can itself spark debate among those who judge a discovery's significance. Others take overall scholarly output or scholarly articles per unit of time as the creative measure. Despite the limitations different productivity measures impose and the dimensions of the creative construct they fail to capture, the submitted article includes the peer-review process and retains a quality component when the place of publication ("leading" journal) is taken into account. Academicians generally agree that an article published in the "right" place serves as a fair indicator of creative work (J. R. Cole, 1979).

Most of the studies we examine use as their measure of productivity the scholarly article, despite its inappropriateness for humanists and people in the arts.[9] This decision imposes the restriction that in most studies the subjects are overwhelmingly Caucasian males in the natural and social sciences.

In order to reduce the composite data and provide meaningful structure to the discussion, we group faculty productivity and age studies into four theoretical categories—biological, psychological, sociological, and social-psychological (life-course).[10] We next display representative data from selected studies within each category.

## The Biological Perspective

The principal position of the biological perspective is that intellectual powers peak at an early age and deteriorate thereafter. Declining mental capacity and function accompany aging in the same way that other parts of the body become less flexible and agile as the years go by. One wins the Nobel Prize for work done at an early age, even though the honor may not be bestowed until later in life. Most often the laureate continues to be "productive" after that principal discovery. However, the quality and impact of later work rarely match what was accomplished at an earlier age (Zuckerman, 1967). Adams's (1946), Lehman's (1953, 1958, 1966), and Dennis's (1956, 1966) studies fall into this category.[11] Figure 2.2 exhibits the general pattern that subscribers to this view predict.

## The Psychological (Stages) Perspective

The psychological perspective attributes motivation to be the cause of productivity and probes agents that produce changes in motivation at different stages in the career. Critical events in life (e.g., marriage, children) and career (e.g., tenure, retirement) are said to cause changes in one's motivation level. By way of illustration, to explain the saddle-shaped hump productivity curve Pelz and Andrews (1976) uncovered, one hypothesizes the following: The newly appointed assistant professor in a research university knows that tenure and promotion to associate professor require appreciable publications. A recently completed dissertation serves as a source of articles and the foundation for ongoing research. Hence productivity rises in the early years. Once these goals are met—that is, success and security have been

35

Figure 2.2   Biological Framework

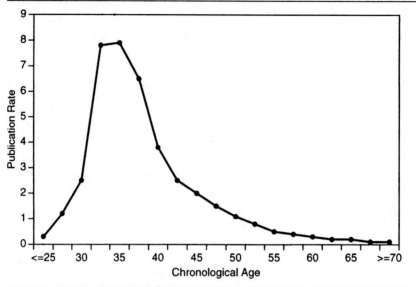

*Source:* Data constructed by authors from various studies.
*Note:* Vertical scale is not arithmetical but rather extends from less (bottom) to more (top).

achieved—the motivation to publish recedes and output drops. It rises again later in order for the faculty member to secure promotion to full professor. Then it declines, for no rewards remain. Figure 2.3 shows "typical" findings from these studies.

Baldwin and Blackburn (1981), Bayer and Dutton (1977), Blackburn (1985), Blackburn, Behymer, and Hall (1978), Entrekin and Everett (1981), and Horner, Rushton, and Vernon (1986) have presented data on changing productivity over the course of a career. Their data most often come from national surveys of faculty conducted between 1969 and 1989 and tend to select arts and science faculty.[12] Schuttenberg, Patterson, and Sutton (1986) obtained for faculty at a professional school (education) results similar to those obtained by Davis (1990) in a survey of 788 faculty from a variety of disciplines and institutional types. The general finding is no correlation between age and career stage and publications.[13]

### The Sociological Perspective

Socialization theory predicts that people acquire patterns of behavior—including doing and publishing research—during their preparation for their

Figure 2.3   Psychological Framework

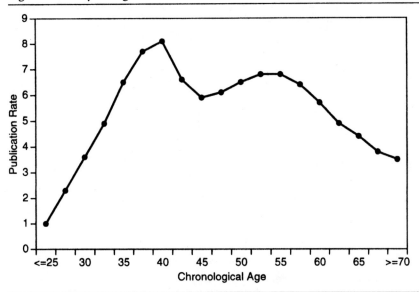

*Source:* Data constructed by authors from various studies.
*Note:* Vertical scale is not arithmetical but rather extends from less (bottom) to more (top).

career. This perspective assumes that values and patterns are long-lasting and not easily altered. Graduate school training inculcates the motivation to publish. While this motivation is established at an early age and varies according to the expectations of faculty at different universities, once the novitiate faculty member is socialized, the learned values and behaviors persist. Socialization theory predicts that faculty educated and trained in graduate departments where research is the dominant value will be more prolific scholars than will those who attended institutions less committed to the research role.

Studies by Clark (1986), Clemente and Hendricks (1973), S. Cole (1979), Crane (1972), Long, Allison, and McGinnis (1979), Pfeffer (1981), and Reskin (1979, 1985) demonstrate that high producers remain high producers over the course of their career, while initially low producers remain below average. The employing department's productivity pattern, however, can alter the pattern somewhat. High-output departments raise the level of lower producers, and vice versa. In addition, a department's faculty age distribution can introduce some minor changes into the publication pattern. Different age cohorts can produce at different rates (S. Cole,

Figure 2.4    Sociological Framework

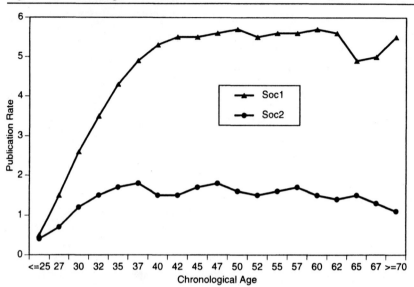

*Source:* Data constructed by authors from various studies.
*Notes:* Vertical scale is not arithmetical but rather extends from less (bottom) to more (top).
Soc1 = high producers; Soc2 = low producers.

1979; Pfeffer, Leong, & Strehl, 1976). For the most part, though, socialization theory predicts a relatively flat curve. Figure 2.4 depicts the socialization theory expectation.

Data are not as plentiful for socialization predictions as they are for the other theories. Still, some studies indicate close approximations to a rather stable pattern after an early rise, the initial upsurge being attributed to "getting started on the job."

### The Social-Psychological (Life-Course) Perspective

The social-psychological perspective combines personal motivators (interests, competencies) with the individual's perceptions of the work environment (beliefs about what the institution rewards, the kind and degree of support perceived for engaging in research). This theory expects that received rewards will lead to increased scholarly output that will accumulate over the course of the career. Those who succeed receive the resources to undertake new research—the more, the more. Merton (1968) called it the Matthew effect. Allison and Stewart (1974) documented the prediction.

Social-psychological theory thus has distinct predicted curves for different individuals. For example, age at first publication will affect productivity over time. The younger one is at first publication, the more one will publish at future points in time. Allison and Stewart (1974), Bentley (1990), Clemente (1973), Horner, Rushton, and Vernon (1986), and Raymond (1967) have data on accumulative advantage and publication at an early age.

Lawrence and Blackburn (1986) discover more complex patterns that are a consequence of our theoretical framework. Figure 2.5 displays these age productivity patterns. The three curves represent different individual productivity levels, ones that do not necessarily rise and fall together, because individuals will differentially be motivated or perceive what the environment rewards at different career points.

### Discussion

Obviously not all four theoretical accounts can be "correct." Even recognizing each one's limitations and errors, many still believe that there is *a*

Figure 2.5   Social-Psychological Framework

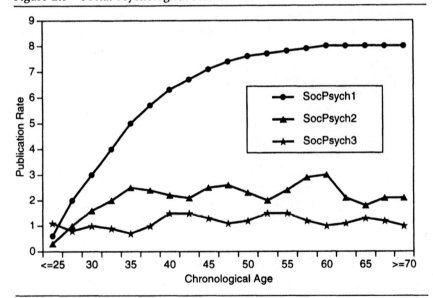

*Source:* Data constructed by authors from various studies.
*Notes:* Vertical scale is not arithmetical but rather extends from less (bottom) to more (top). SocPsych1, SocPsych2, and SocPsych3 represent the productivity curves of three individuals.

cycle of faculty productivity that is age-determined. Beginning faculty will follow a predictable curve, if only we could find it. Figures 2.6 and 2.7 shatter that seductive assumption.

In figure 2.6 productivity data sets have been taken from five different sources and graphed on top of one another. Each has a different but "legitimate" indicator of output and runs over a slightly different age span. Where the plots do overlap, however, one readily notes that at each point in time where one or another curve is going up, another is going down, and vice versa. There is some relationship with Levinson et al.'s (1978) period of tranquillity after promotion to associate professor and before attaining full professorship. Most of the curves are dipping during this period. The overall message, though, is that age and productivity have no predictable, direct relationship to one another.

Figure 2.7 has "curves" constructed from four national surveys, from 1969 through 1988. These data raise another set of unanswerable questions. The earliest curve, 1969, is somewhat like figure 2.3. Indeed, that database is the foundation for many of the explanations advanced for age and publication patterns.[14] Since 1969, however, different patterns have emerged. While the relationship between age and productivity was curvilinear and the age correlations near zero in the years prior to 1988, the slope has now become appreciably negative ($r = -.20, p \leq .001$).[15] That is, the youngest group now produces the most.

To predict where the 1988 cohort will be on this chart when they enter the next age category would seem to be pure speculation, a roll of the dice. Will they continue at their current rate, one higher than any other group at any age has ever achieved? Will they now increase their output in order to achieve tenure, as the earliest data show? Just how many articles per year can faculty produce? And maintain over 40 years? Should we expect an upper limit? Will these 1988 assistant professors automatically be promoted, since they have already produced more than the cohort in front of them, all of whom have tenure? Will they burn out because of the high pace at which they have been operating? Will their publication curve decline to zero over the next 30 years, maybe with even a total collapse in a few years? With no recovery?

Why is it so difficult to ascertain the relationship between age and scholarly productivity? Is motivation to publish really not directly related to age? That is, are the theories fallacious? Is age so interconnected with other variables that it cannot be sorted out for its effect? Perhaps what people do at different ages is done in response not to developmental needs but rather to cognitive assessments and to the unexpected events that confront indi-

Figure 2.6    Transitional Periods and Productivity

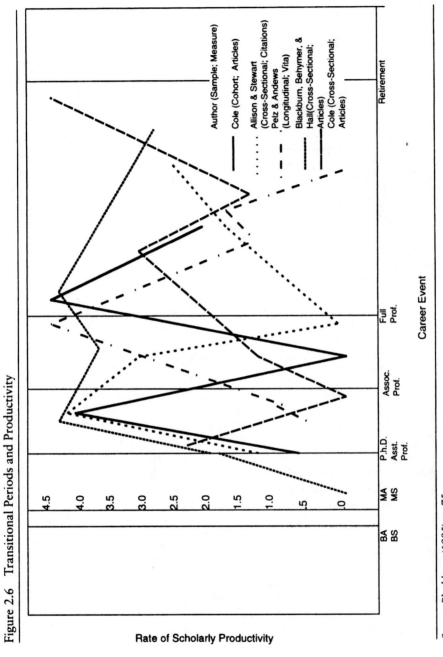

*Source:* Blackburn (1985), p. 75.

*Note:* Transitional periods from Levinson et al. (1978). Productivity data from Allison and Stewart (1974), S. Cole (1979), Pelz and Andrews (1976), and Blackburn, Behymer, and Hall (1978).

Figure 2.7    Productivity Data from Four National Surveys

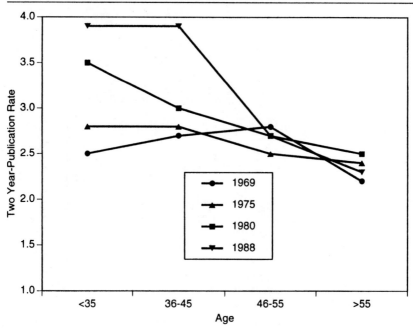

*Source:* National surveys.

viduals almost daily—successes and failures, new opportunities and lost chances, joys and sorrows.

One major deficiency in every study has been its failure—perhaps *inability* is the better word—to take into account historical changes in the environment and the consequences for workers. This shortcoming exists for both longitudinal and cross-sectional databases. Cross-sectional data have successive cohorts working under a different set of conditions when they move into the next age range, conditions that may favor output in one instance and dampen it in another. In the case of longitudinal data, if one begins with a sample that extends over an appreciable age range (say, 28 to 68), different historical effects have already occurred. If one begins with a cohort of nearly identical-age faculty and follows them for 40 years, one could begin to sort out historical effects. However, at the end one would have no grounds for generalizing as to what a future cohort will go through and how their productivity will change over time.[16]

## Sex/Gender

For some, describing the faculty population by selected subgroups (e.g., sex/gender[17] and race/ethnicity) and not by others (e.g., religious or political beliefs) smacks of some indefensible bias (e.g., political correctness), since no a priori reason exists that these background characteristics should be significantly related to an academic career. One can support the questioner's case by showing that women's and minorities' contributions to knowledge have for the most part been not abundant, perhaps even less than their small percentages of the profession. For both reasons, then, some argue that subgroups are not important to include.

For other people, however, a number of matters related to sex/gender and to race/ethnicity deserve special attention because of past, present, and future conditions of the professoriate. One deals with discrimination—that of the blatant past being well documented and that of the present, while less explicit and more often subtle, still not eliminated. (See, e.g., Barbezat, 1989; Smart, 1991.) Women and minorities have been denied admission to an occupation that prides itself on judging creations on the basis of their merit, certainly not on the nonuniversalistic attributes of sex/gender and race/ethnicity. Still, women and minorities have been, and still are, disallowed full access. Generally, colleges and universities have responded positively to affirmative action, not only to comply with federal regulations and to retain federal dollar support but also because they now acknowledge their past sins. For the first time in decades women enjoy an advantage in securing a faculty position, "other things being equal." Their numbers are increasing because of equity concerns. The social and structural hurdles they encounter after being hired, however, are another story.

Accompanying the feeling of personal guilt that members of the academy may harbor, social pressures affecting academic life have descended on colleges and universities—from foundations and the federal government, among other sources—to increase the numbers of underrepresented groups among both students and faculty. Some evidence supports the belief that if the disadvantaged in this country are to have a fair chance to succeed in higher education, faculty role models are crucial. Their absence today hinders the retribution owed to disadvantaged groups.

Proponents of faculty positions for women and minorities also point to the changing pattern of U.S. demographics—the rapidly growing proportion of this country's non-Caucasian population, irreversible trends of such a magnitude that in an infinitesimal historical interval, the Caucasian majority will cease to be one (and, of course, at least half of the emerging dominant group will be women). Leadership depends upon an educated population. The forthcoming disadvantaged majority must be superbly educated if the country is to function. We must eradicate the present imbalances.

Others defending the position for more women and minority faculty— and some share some of the positions already put forth—make their case on the basis of national needs. Despite the reduced threats of international war, the United States competes intensely in world markets, ones that strongly depend upon being on the cutting technological edge. Caucasian males have been abandoning graduate studies in the sciences and engineering at a steady rate for over a decade now. The future supply of needed national talent in these fields depends upon increasing the number of women and minorities studying them—fields in which these groups are now most underrepresented. Policymakers now see women and minorities as the major untapped resource in the country. Setting aside past discriminations, the nation says it now wants their potential to be realized.

In addition, a small faculty coterie favors special attention to women and minorities because they believe the introduction of women's studies and African American studies, curricular innovations that accompanied the civil rights and affirmative action movements of the late 1960s and early 1970s, have enriched scholarship. Women's first new inroads into higher education's heterosexual Caucasian male establishment took place through women's studies, a "field" that possessed no legitimacy in the academy.[18] In response to social pressures, universities allowed women to launch "programs" within the standard curriculum but most often did not award these programs degree-granting status. Still, feminist scholarship emerged, especially in history and in literature. Sometimes it found a home in the semilegitimate units of "American studies." Starting as an outlet for female research, but not being accepted by promotion committees as genuine scholarship, feminist research has (almost completely) become a legitimate knowledge source. Early journals such as the *Psychology of Women Quarterly* have acquired recognition and status. Some traditional academics acknowledge the new and enriched insights feminist scholars provide. Even some white male professors who basically detest a "feminist perspective" now confess that, having read an insightful piece of feminist scholarship, they must take into consideration what has been argued. The skeptics have to reconsider what they had believed was immutable. Some men rejoice in the enriched intellectual environment that women have created.

Sex correlates with a number of faculty behaviors (e.g., publications) and other characteristics (e.g., discipline), although researchers debate its predictive power. The relationships, though, are hardly causal. Being a woman does not ipso facto cause one not to be a mathematician. For example, survey opinion data indicate that women prefer the teaching role more than men do. But it remains unclear whether the preference stems from real or perceived exclusion from the research role, from the formal demands traditional (male) research imposes, or from female needs for nurturing. Whatever the explanation, sex retains high importance for the reasons noted above and beyond its predictive power.

## The Data

Since the onset of affirmative action, gender statistics have poured out of Washington and other repositories. Sorting noncorroborating documents continues to be a problem. We stay with the national surveys we have been reporting and supplement them with data from the National Center for Educational Statistics (NCES) and the National Research Council (NRC), two dependable sources.

Table 2.1 discloses the distribution of women faculty by institutional type (top set) and by discipline (bottom set). With respect to where female

Table 2.1  Distribution of Female Faculty by Carnegie Type and Discipline

|  | 1969 | | 1975 | | 1980 | | 1988 | |
|---|---|---|---|---|---|---|---|---|
|  | % | N | % | N | % | N | % | N |
| *Carnegie type* | | | | | | | | |
| Res-I | 6.2 | 88 | 8.7 | 86 | 12.0 | 49 | 17.9 | 103 |
| Res-II | 7.6 | 36 | 9.0 | 54 | 10.6 | 28 | 22.5 | 54 |
| Doc-I | 7.0 | 44 | 10.5 | 30 | 9.1 | 29 | 20.5 | 60 |
| Doc-II | 10.3 | 18 | 13.3 | 51 | 12.7 | 19 | 18.4 | 57 |
| Comp-I | 11.3 | 48 | 15.8 | 195 | 17.8 | 62 | 19.3 | 183 |
| All | 7.5 | 234 | 11.9 | 416 | 12.6 | 187 | 19.3 | 457 |
| Chi-square | 14.4 | | 33.1 | | 13.3 | | 2.8 | |
| Significance | .00 | | .00 | | .01 | | .60 | |
| *Discipline* | | | | | | | | |
| Chemistry | 2.7 | 12 | 4.5 | 20 | 3.2 | 6 | 9.4 | 25 |
| Math/stat. | 5.2 | 28 | 5.4 | 30 | 6.2 | 15 | 13.4 | 40 |
| Biology | 12.8 | 31 | 9.8 | 33 | 13.9 | 21 | 15.7 | 49 |
| Psychology | 11.7 | 50 | 17.1 | 66 | 20.4 | 41 | 21.8 | 72 |
| Sociology | 5.6 | 13 | 17.6 | 49 | 17.1 | 25 | 23.6 | 51 |
| Political science | 4.3 | 12 | 6.4 | 21 | 7.5 | 10 | 10.9 | 24 |
| English | 12.9 | 73 | 22.7 | 156 | 23.1 | 53 | 33.6 | 146 |
| History | 3.7 | 15 | 8.6 | 41 | 8.0 | 16 | 17.2 | 50 |
| All | 7.5 | 234 | 11.9 | 416 | 12.6 | 187 | 19.3 | 457 |
| Chi-square | 76.1 | | 155.9 | | 68.3 | | 97.9 | |
| Significance | .00 | | .00 | | .00 | | .00 | |

*Source:* National surveys.

academics are located within the system, with but one exception their percentage is the smallest in the research universities (the most desired locations in terms of resources) and greatest in the comprehensive colleges and universities (where resources are the least).[19]

Simultaneously, the percentage of women in each institutional type generally increases at each successive point in time.[20] The greatest percentage gain has been in the research universities. Moreover, the differences between the female percentages for the various institutional types have changed from being significant in 1969, 1975, and 1980 (see the chi-square probabilities) to being not significant in 1988 ($p = .60$).

Table 2.1 also shows, however, that the natural sciences and mathematics, while increasingly feminized, have a long way to go to reach parity. Very large chi-squares demonstrate that significant differences persist between the disciplines. History and sociology exhibit the greatest percentage gains over the two decades. When starting from far back, one witnesses dramatic percentage increases. For example, in 1969 none of the top-rated sociology departments in the country had a woman faculty member at any rank (Rossi, 1970).[21] The reader also needs to observe the actual numbers, not just the percentages. By way of illustration, in 1969 there were only 12 female chemistry faculty in the sample of 132 universities, for an average of about 1 woman chemist per 10 institutions; 9 out of 10 institutions had none.[22]

We now look more closely at the relationship between gender and motivation and examine what prior research on women and productivity has learned.

A cruel but understandable irony pervades the historical record. When data collection began in the 1960s, research was displacing teaching as the valued faculty role. Consequently, when sociologists and psychologists got around to collecting data, they did so to explain why some faculty produced more than others—that is, published more articles and books. Their subjects were the then current faculty, an overwhelmingly male and Caucasian population. In addition, the researchers taught at Res-I universities, institutions employing the smallest proportion of women. Their view from the top shaped the flood of surveys on faculty behaviors and opinions: Parsons and Platt (1968); the Carnegie Commission and the American Council on Education (ACE) in 1969 (Bayer, 1970); ACE in 1972 (Trow, 1975); the Carnegie Commission in 1975 (Roizen, Fulton, & Trow, 1978); and the Carnegie Foundation for the Advancement of Teaching in 1984 and 1989 (Carnegie, 1984, 1989b).

In more than one way, then, the possibility for understanding female academics ended the day it began. The researchers looked in the mirror and found variables that accounted for their own superior position: Ph.D. as their highest degree, national ranking of their graduate school, quality rating of their place of work, religion in which raised (not Catholic or Southern Baptist), parents' education and social class, politically liberal orientation— in short, the features of male WASPs and Jews. They apparently did not entertain hypotheses that there could be different factors related to female success. From their vantage point, academe was a pure meritocracy and could not possibly discriminate against women. (In science, e.g., see J. R. Cole, 1979.) Quite simply, motivation for research occurred during socialization into the academic career.

In the doubling of the total faculty workforce during the 1960s, from some 250,000 to 500,000, the number of women also increased by a factor of two. Their proportion and status, however, changed not at all. (See figure 2.8.) Still, enough women now work in the system that they too can be studied— but by the same men, and a few women, on the same independent and dependent variables. Women have lost on nearly every indicator— fewer publications, lower degrees, inferior graduate schools and place of work, lower rank, fewer with tenure.

The stacked situation had one fruitful outcome. Scholars had to address the natural question as to why female academics performed poorly vis-à-vis male professors. Researchers launched new investigations. Speculations abound: women publish less because they are more highly motivated to teach (a nurturing, motherly activity), because they lack the drive and commitment needed to succeed in research, because they have children, because they are tokens—a long list of explanations. The studies are alike in one regard. The standard of success continues to be the male model and its rules. The studies also explain only small amounts of the variance. In addition, female academic behavior remains inadequately accounted for.

Still, if women's motivations differ from men's, researchers have taken erroneous avenues toward understanding their behaviors. The low predictive power of the male variables attests to that fact. So as we turn to the gender literature, we are prepared to find disappointing information. When we report studies with our framework and introduce some motivation variables, we uncover increased explanatory power and richer insights into female academic behaviors (chapters 4–7, especially chapter 4). However, a great deal remains to be done.

## The Literature

As was the case with age as a predictor of productivity, sex too most often links with other characteristics and attributes as well as with cultural and structural conditions. Difficulties arise when trying to estimate the effect sex

Figure 2.8   Women in Regular Instructional Ranks, 1978–1979 to 1989–1990

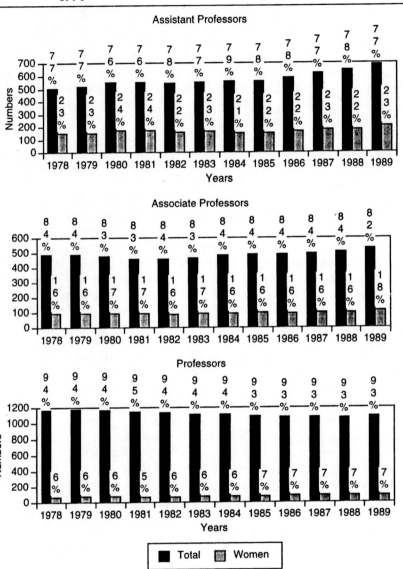

itself has on work performance. Researchers typically try to control for those variables they believe correlate most closely with sex. No one has taken everything into account. Keeping the complexities in mind, we turn to the research literature.[23]

More than 50 studies demonstrate that women publish less than men, even when age and other important social attributes are taken into account (Zuckerman, 1991). Examples are Astin (1978, 1984), Bayer and Astin (1975), Bouillon (1987), J. R. Cole (1979), Cole and Cole (1973), Cole and Zuckerman (1987), Finkelstein (1984b), Fox (1985a), Kyvik (1990), and Zuckerman and Cole (1975). More recent studies report near or exact equivalence between the sexes. Rubin and Powell (1987) found no sex difference in publication output for social work faculty, nor did MacKie (1985) and McNamee, Willis, and Rotchford (1990) for sociology faculty (although the latter found more co-authorships among the women), Garkland (1990) for library and information science faculty, and Rieger (1990) for professors in teacher education. Even in other countries, Allen (1990) in Australian universities and Noordenbos (1992) in Belgian institutions found no difference between men's and women's publication rates.

Turning to how women's publication record has changed over time, figure 2.9 displays the gains that women have made in two-year publication rate since 1969.[24] The data show that the publication gap between men and women has narrowed considerably since 1969. As a result, by 1988 no statistically significant difference in two-year publication rate existed between men and women, although men still published at a slightly higher two-year rate: 3.1 compared with 2.8 publications. Women advance in rank more slowly (Hollenshead, 1992; Long, Allison, & McGinnis, 1993; Tien, 1994) and are paid less even when their productivity is the same (Milem & Dey, 1993; Regan & Volkwein, 1993; Tuckman, Gapinski, & Hagemann, 1977).

Figures 2.10–2.12 plot the relationship between sex and two-year publication rate for three selected disciplines—biology, psychology, and English. The narrowing trend in publication output appears in all three disciplines. The largest gap persists in biology, where women averaged 2.6 publications in the past two years as compared with 3.1 for men, not a statistically significant difference.

Still, the restricted information obtained from typical statistical procedures (e.g., anovas) or from the use of gender as a dummy variable in regression analyses limits many of these gender-difference studies. That is, the studies are straight female/male comparisons. We do not learn what predicts for women. Neither statistical approach allows a determination of the relative power of the predictive variables, the critical information

49

Figure 2.9    Two-Year Publication Rate, by Sex

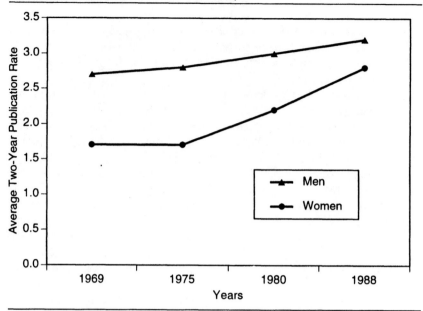

*Source:* National surveys.

Figure 2.10    Two-Year Publication Rate in Biology, by Sex

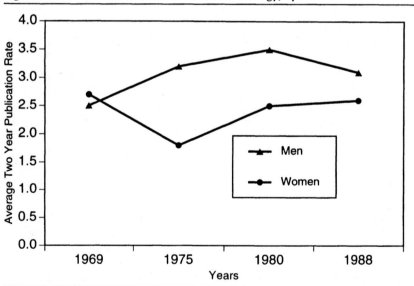

*Source:* National surveys.

Figure 2.11   Two-Year Publication Rate in Psychology, by Sex

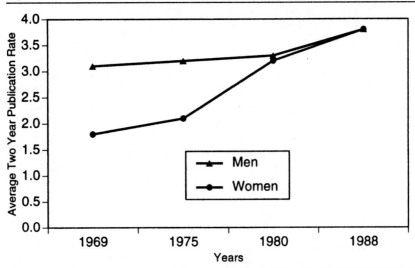

*Source:* National surveys.

Figure 2.12   Two-Year Publication Rate in English, by Sex

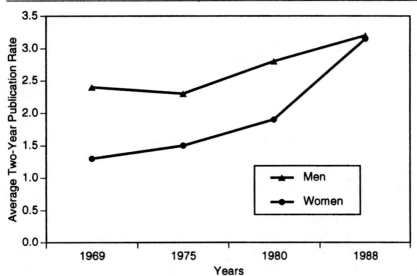

*Source:* National surveys.

needed for setting policy in recruiting women and having them succeed.

Only in the past two decades have studies begun to focus on differences between female and male faculty with respect to their research role (Blackburn & Holbert, 1986; Creswell, 1985; Lawrence & Blackburn, 1988). Rosenfeld (1981, 1984) compares the sexes, but her concern is with the career mobility of academic psychologists, not productivity. Reskin's (1976) study had a sample of male and female chemists who received their Ph.D. between 1955 and 1961. The principal focus was on the consequences of a postdoctoral fellowship. Reskin has a mix of academic chemists and persons in industry or not employed (more frequently women). Her independent variables account for less than 10 percent of the explained variance on publication. Reskin's (1978) later study introduces more variables, separates out noncontinuously employed women, and achieves slightly higher accounted-for variance.

Long's (1990) recent inquiry adds to Reskin's by including female Ph.D.'s from 1950 to 1967. The one productivity comparison uses the number of articles in a three-year period ending the 11th year after the Ph.D. Long regressed publications against variables that account for 13 percent of the variance for the women and 12 percent of the variance for the men. Perhaps as a result of the small percentages of achieved variances, Long advances an attractive hypothesis for why fewer women than men succeed. It relates to having children, an area several scholars have investigated. Ahern and Scott (1981), Astin (1984), Ferber and Loeb (1973), Hamovitch and Morgenstern (1977), and Toren (1991) found no evidence that child rearing is related to the number of publications of academic women. Thomas and McKenzie (1986) in the United States found that married women with children published more, and Kyvik (1990) in Norway found that childless women—married and unmarried—published less. At the same time, Hargens, McCann, and Reskin (1978) found an inverse relationship between fertility and productivity, one that was true for both sexes. Clearly, the final record is not in as yet. Long (1990) speculates that having children is not what matters directly. What does make a difference is that women are less likely to be regularly in contact with ongoing research projects and their dissertation chairs. Hence they frequently do not become authors and joint authors at the outset of their career (pre- and immediate post-Ph.D.). As other studies indicate (Clemente, 1973; Horner, Rushton, & Vernon, 1986; Lightfield, 1971; Reskin, 1977), early publication strongly predicts rate of publication at all successive career points. Women miss a critical career event. At the same time, when Long (1992) followed up on the sample of men and women scientists he had reported on earlier (Long, 1978; Long, Allison, & McGinnis, 1979), he found that although the women were still publishing less, their work was more frequently cited by other scholars.

In a study examining women in selected "female" and "male" disciplines at three points in time (1969, 1975, and 1988), Lawrence, Blackburn, Trautvetter, Hart, and Herzberg (1990) found that a number of career variables predicted productivity.[25] The best publication predictors differed at the three points in time. In 1969 all career variables contributed to differences between the disciplines in the number of published articles over the career, with academic rank predicting approximately 14 percent of the explained variance. Highest degree and academic rank were strong predictors of the number of books published over the career, Ph.D. holders publishing significantly more than non-Ph.D.'s. In 1975 Ph.D. full professors in Res-I's were the most active publishers, with chemists and psychologists publishing more articles and English faculty more books. The 1988 results were similar, although there were no differences between disciplines when it came to publishing books. Women are but a couple of years younger than men (less experience: figure 2.13), are less likely to be tenured and hence are at lower ranks (figure 2.14), and are less likely to have grants (figures 2.15 and 2.16), especially federal ones that have the larger dollar support. All factors predict lower output.[26]

In accounting for reported sex differences in research productivity, studies usually point to the disparate institutional locations of female and male faculty. Men are more likely to work in the major universities, with lower teaching loads and greater research resources (Astin, 1978; Blackburn, Behymer, & Hall, 1978; Persell, 1983). Past research has been mixed on whether or not sex differences in publication rates persist when controlling for their relevant correlates. Blackburn, Behymer, and Hall (1978) reported that sex differences disappear when multivariate analysis controls for such factors as institutional affiliation, preference for research, rank, and age. Bentley and Blackburn (1991) and Clemente (1973) also discovered that when environmental variables (e.g., place of work) are controlled for, sex differences either disappear completely or are reduced to a minor factor. However, other studies have found significant sex differences even after controlling for other productivity correlates (J. R. Cole, 1979; Helmrich, Spence, Beane, Lucker, & Matthews, 1980).

Explanations for sex differences in publication output tend to fall into one of two categories: (1) various kinds of social factors (e.g., sex discrimination) or (2) psychological factors (e.g., interest in research, cognitive abilities, commitment to marriage and family). However, little empirical research distinguishing female and male faculty has investigated how personal attributes, perceptions of the environment, socialization, and environmental conditions function to influence the perceptions and judgments asso-

Figure 2.13   Average Age, by Sex

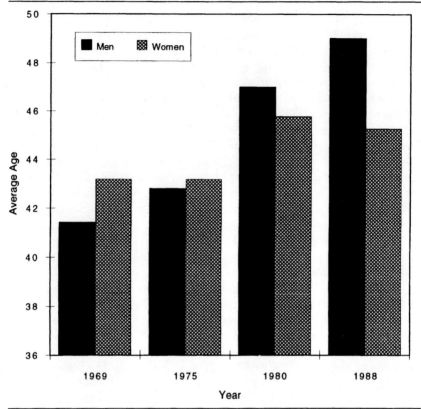

*Source:* National surveys.

ciated with publication output. Moreover, researchers rarely identify the sources of motivation. Rather, they infer motivation from changes in behavior, intentions, or outcomes (e.g., publication rate). Employing either a sociological or a psychological model by itself loses valuable information about sex differences.

In addition, prevailing theories assume that an individual's response is compliance to environmental rewards. They do not address the extent to which cognitive processes affect behavior. Individual motivation, the tendency to initiate and sustain a certain activity, needs to be explored within the context of the work environment. Some researchers have suggested that academic men and women respond to different motivators regarding role performance, and that these different motivators could play a role in sex differences in publication output (Astin, 1984; Astin & Bayer, 1979; Hornig, 1984; Humphreys, 1984; Long, 1987; Zuckerman & Cole, 1975). By way of illustration, Pavel's (1991) study of 2,438 liberal arts college faculty found that the principal motivator for men was freedom in their work, whereas for women it was being of service to others.

Sex having proved to be at best a weak predictor and one needing to be understood in conjunction with other factors, numerous hypotheses surfaced, some of which have been explored with research. Fear of success (Horner, 1972), tokenism (Kanter, 1977),[27] women's ways of seeing the world (Gilligan, 1982), and biological differences (Rossi, 1980) are four. Dwyer, Flynn, and Inman (1991, p. 195) develop four broad theoretical constructs:

1. From Aisenberg and Harrington (1988), Boice and Jones (1984), and Helmrich et al. (1980) they compose a personality and situation correlate category.

2. From Clark and Corcoran (1986) and Youn (1988) they develop an accumulative disadvantage and human capital theory.

Figure 2.14    Appointment Status (Tenure), by Sex

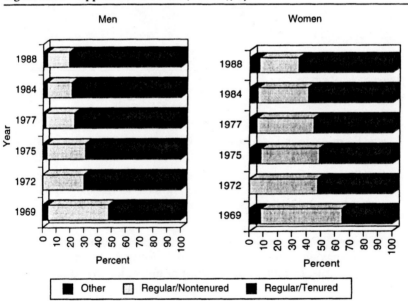

*Source:* National surveys.

Figure 2.15  Faculty with Institutional Grants, by Sex

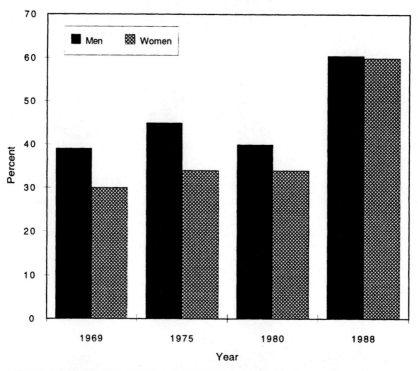

*Source:* National surveys.

3. From Armour, Furhmann, and Wergin (1990), Chamberlain (1989), and Fox (1985) they compose a structural model.

4. From Fox and Faver (1984), Rodgers and Maranto (1989), and Trautvetter and Blackburn (1990) they combine sociodemographic, career, self-knowledge, social knowledge, and behavior (our book's theoretical framework and terms).

To this more conceptual list one could add specific explanations such as women not having mentors, being noncompetitive and nonaggressive, being perfectionists, lacking social support at home, having to follow a husband's moves, experiencing discrimination, and more.[28] We report female and male sex differences under psychological characteristics in chapter 3.

## Race/Ethnicity

Many kinds of subgroups exist within both the majority and minority populations.[29] Treating them collectively, as they are almost always treated, seriously distorts the actual state of affairs. For example, Asian Americans include diverse populations—Koreans, Japanese, Chinese, as well as others. Moreover, within any nationality numerous subsets differ appreciably from one another in what they value and how they behave. So do Native Americans, African Americans, Hispanics, and Caucasians. At a minimum, Caucasians have religious, political, and social class differences (as do others). Within all of these subpopulations there exist still other groups whose academic lives differ from those of the dominant culture. See, for example, Bensimon (1992) on being a lesbian, gay, or bisexual faculty member, Ryan and Sackrey (1984) and Tokarczyk and Fay (1993) on coming into academe from a low social class, and James and Farmer (1993) on being a black

Figure 2.16   Faculty with Federal Grants, by Sex

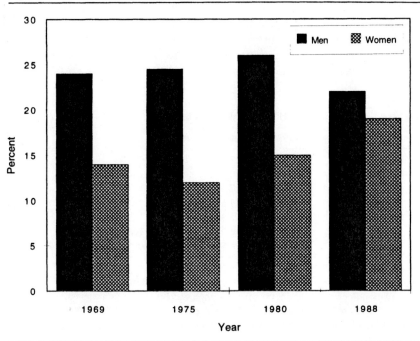

*Source:* National surveys.

woman in white academe. With this caveat, we turn to the "standard" ethnic groups of this country.

Since the numbers here are smaller than those in the female population, the shortage-of-scientists argument carries less weight. (See table 2.2 for population estimates.) However, social justice considerations and the accompanying need for role models persist and warrant the inclusion of data on these groups to round out the larger setting.

Only sparse data exist for Native American, African American, Asian American, and Hispanic faculty. Those that do exist are open to question, over time as well as in the actual population. Native Americans are less than 1 percent. In round numbers, African American faculty are 3 to 4 percent. Counts of Hispanics range from 0.5 percent to 3 percent. Table 2.3 displays the data from the National Center for Educational Statistics (1990a) 1988 survey of faculty.[30]

The institutional affiliation of the different groups varies. For example, African Americans make up 8 percent of the faculty in liberal arts colleges—their largest proportion in any institutional type. The number, however, can distort reality inasmuch as about one-half of the 100 historically black colleges and universities (HBCUs) in this country are private liberal arts colleges and have a high proportion of African American faculty.

Even greater variation from a random race/ethnicity distribution occurs when one examines work location by discipline or program area. Table 2.3

Table 2.2    Distribution of U.S. Population by Minority Group, 1980–2000 (Percent)

|  | 1980 | 1982 | 1985 | 1990 | 1995 | 2000 |
|---|---|---|---|---|---|---|
| Black | 11.7 | 11.9 | 12.1 | 12.5 | 12.9 | 13.3 |
| Hispanic | 6.4 | 6.8 | 7.2 | 7.9 | 8.6 | 9.4 |
| Asian[a] | 2.3 | 2.5 | 2.7 | 3.0 | 3.3 | 3.5 |
| Total minority | 20.4 | 21.5 | 22.0 | 23.4 | 24.8 | 26.2 |
| White | 79.6 | 78.8 | 78.0 | 76.6 | 75.2 | 73.8 |
| Total % | 100.0 | 100.0 | 100.0 | 100.0 | 100.0 | 100.0 |
| Total N (000s) | 226,546 | 232,925 | 239,959 | 250,795 | 260,868 | 269,444 |

*Source:* Deskins (1990), p. 6.

*Note:* The table is based on the following sources: U.S. Bureau of the Census, Current Population Reports, ser. p-25, no. 1022, *United States Population Estimates by Age, Sex, and Race: 1980 to 1987* (Washington, DC: U.S. Government Printing Office, 1988), and no. 995, *Projections of Hispanic Population: 1983 to 2080* (Washington, DC: U.S. Government Printing Office, 1986).

a. In 1980 Asian and Native American populations were reported in the U.S. Census of Population as separate groups. Here both groups are combined and referred to as Asian.

Table 2.3    Distribution of Full-Time Regular Faculty by Race/Ethnicity, Type and
Control of Institution, and Program Area, Fall 1987

|  | *Total N* *Responding* *(unweighted)* | *Amer.* *Indian* | *Asian* | *Black* | *Hispanic* | *White* |
|---|---|---|---|---|---|---|
|  |  | *Race/Ethnicity (%)* | | | | |
| All institutions[a] | 6,265 | 0.84 | 4.36 | 3.26 | 2.05 | 89.49 |
| By type and control |  |  |  |  |  |  |
| Public research | 1,283 | 0.72 | 4.98 | 1.69 | 2.18 | 90.42 |
| Private research | 429 | 0.00 | 3.74 | 6.14 | 4.70 | 85.42 |
| Public doctoral[b] | 770 | 1.06 | 5.25 | 1.86 | 0.71 | 91.12 |
| Private doctoral[c] | 216 | 0.36 | 10.40 | 1.81 | 1.45 | 85.98 |
| Public comp. | 1,276 | 0.77 | 5.82 | 3.51 | 1.88 | 88.03 |
| Private comp. | 653 | 1.19 | 4.40 | 1.79 | 1.40 | 91.22 |
| Liberal arts | 555 | 1.19 | 2.68 | 8.30 | 0.95 | 86.88 |
| Public two-year[d] | 849 | 1.27 | 1.94 | 3.06 | 2.75 | 90.97 |
| Other[e] | 162 | 0.00 | 0.98 | 2.94 | 0.99 | 95.10 |
| Four-year institutions | 5,182 | 0.78 | 5.12 | 3.32 | 1.92 | 88.86 |
| By program area |  |  |  |  |  |  |
| Agr./home econ. | 230 | 1.56 | 1.42 | 0.32 | 3.02 | 93.68 |
| Business | 228 | 1.44 | 9.03 | 2.84 | 0.70 | 86.00 |
| Education | 485 | 1.08 | 1.28 | 6.57 | 2.84 | 88.23 |
| Engineering | 184 | 0.00 | 14.58 | 0.54 | 1.45 | 83.43 |
| Fine arts | 363 | 0.61 | 1.76 | 3.41 | 2.93 | 91.29 |
| Health sciences | 450 | 0.77 | 6.97 | 2.86 | 1.00 | 88.40 |
| Humanities | 1,870 | 0.80 | 1.85 | 2.54 | 3.95 | 90.85 |
| Natural sciences | 625 | 0.52 | 7.17 | 1.43 | 1.86 | 89.03 |
| Social sciences | 348 | 0.97 | 2.48 | 5.01 | 2.09 | 89.45 |
| Other fields | 399 | 0.64 | 3.87 | 6.07 | 0.92 | 88.50 |

*Source:* National Center for Educational Statistics (1990a).

a. All accredited, nonproprietary U.S. postsecondary institutions that grant a two-year (A.A.) or higher degree and whose accreditation at the higher education level is recognized by the U.S. Department of Education.

b. Include publicly controlled institutions classified by the Carnegie Foundation as specialized medical schools.

c. Include privately controlled institutions classified by the Carnegie Foundation as specialized medical schools.

d. Respondents from private two-year colleges are included only in "all institutions" because there are too few cases for a reliable estimate.

e. Religious and other specialized institutions, except medical, that offer degrees ranging from the bachelor's to the doctorate.

reveals that African American faculty are more frequently in education and the social sciences, whereas Asian Americans are less frequently in these fields but are prevalent in engineering, business, and the health and natural sciences.[31]

Table 2.4 shows the differential promotion rates for ethnic faculty who were assistant professors in 1977 in four-year colleges and universities. The right-most column adds whites to the three minority groups reported. Fewer blacks were promoted to the top two ranks than Hispanics or Asian Americans. The last two groups did better than the national averages. By 1985 Asian Americans exceeded the national average of promotions to full professor by more than a factor of two (56 percent vs. 26 percent), whereas the black figure (15 percent) is more than 10 percentage points below the national average. During the nine-year interval from 1977 (base year as assistant professors), blacks lagged behind all others in promotion rate and time lapse to promotion (Brown, 1988, p. 21).

Stanford University's internal study of faculty perceptions of the institution's work environment (University Committee, 1989) is illuminating inas-

Table 2.4   Promotion Decisions of Full-Time Minority S/E and Humanities Faculty Who Were Assistant Professors in 1977 in Four-Year Colleges and Universities, U.S Citizens, 1981 and 1985 (Percent)

|  | Black | Hispanic | Asian American | U.S. Total |
|---|---|---|---|---|
| **1981** | | | | |
| Number | 277 | 479 | 276 | 23,726 |
| Full professor | 2.2 | 7.5 | 30.8 | 2.7 |
| Associate professor | 59.6 | 66.8 | 50.7 | 62.7 |
| Assistant professor | 35.7 | 25.3 | 17.8 | 32.3 |
| Institution administration | 0.7 | 0.0 | 1.1 | 1.2 |
| Other[a] | 1.8 | 0.4 | 0.7 | 1.1 |
| **1985** | | | | |
| Number | 217 | 363 | 273 | 18,423 |
| Full professor | 15.2 | 30.9 | 56.4 | 25.9 |
| Associate professor | 68.7 | 57.9 | 40.3 | 64.9 |
| Assistant professor | 12.0 | 8.0 | 1.7 | 6.7 |
| Institution administration | 4.1 | 2.7 | 1.4 | 1.6 |
| Other[a] | 0.0 | 0.3 | 1.2 | 0.9 |

*Source:* National Research Council (1990).

*Note:* Includes native-born and naturalized citizens.

a. Includes adjunct faculty.

60

much as it displays beliefs and opinions held by each of four groups—Asian American, African American, Hispanic, and Caucasian. Stanford learned that Asian American and Caucasian faculty view the institution in much the same way, but frequently quite differently from African American and Hispanic faculty. By way of illustration, African American and Hispanic faculty feel that they have less time available for research than do other faculty at their level in their department. Asian American and Caucasian faculty most likely strongly disagree with that feeling. Combined group differences also exist as to how active deans should be in recruiting and retaining minority faculty, what the obstacles are to increasing the number of minority faculty, and how sincere the university has been in achieving affirmative action goals. Asian Americans and Caucasians see active leadership, more obstacles, and more sincerity than do Hispanics and African Americans, the African Americans always being the most removed from the Caucasians. On many other perception items in the survey, however, Hispanics are closer to Asian Americans and Caucasians than they are to the African American faculty.[32] Welch's (1992) authors writing on beginning female African American faculty describe their struggles as they try to launch a successful career in traditionally white institutions (TWIs).

As for the track record to date, before the civil rights movement African Americans were almost exclusively in HBCUs and accounted for about 3 percent of the total faculty population (Exum, 1983). Numbers increased to over 19,000 by 1976–1977 but have declined steadily since then (Carter & Wilson, 1987). Moreover, the number of African American students receiving the Ph.D. has been declining steadily over the past decade, even though the total number of Ph.D.'s awarded each year has remained nearly constant. In the case of mathematics, African American women and men both constitute but a very small percentage of those receiving the Ph.D. during the decade 1977–1987. There are no signs of an increasing trend. The situation in law looks more impressive for African American women than for men, but these are percentages. The actual numbers are small. Furthermore, the spurt in the late 1970s seems to have tapered off appreciably. These data paint a pessimistic picture of the future health of colleges and universities.

Using National Research Council data, Deskins (1990) shows that between 1977 and 1988 the number of Ph.D.'s (in all fields) earned by African American students fell 20 percent; the number increased 47 percent for Hispanics and 36 percent for Asian Americans, and decreased 57 percent for Native Americans. Over this same interval Caucasian Ph.D. acquisition dropped 9 percent, while that for nonresident aliens increased 79 percent.[33]

Without a pool of graduates to draw from, the immediate prospect for increasing minority representation appears gloomy. Moreover, a new minority of Ph.D.'s are selecting other than academic careers (Patitu & Tack, 1991). In part because numbers are smaller, black studies has not become as solidly established as a field of scholarship as women's studies. Its place in the university remains marginal and hence endangered. At the same time, the pattern of declining enrollments in HBCUs has reversed itself during the past two years. Students who receive their undergraduate education at these institutions go on to graduate school in a higher proportion than do black students in TWIs. Perhaps the decline in graduate education is about to reverse itself.

Having laid out some of the demographics on race and ethnicity, we now turn to the literature for their relationship to research output. It is not immediately clear why race/ethnicity would relate to productivity or to motivation. No evidence supports intelligence differences between racial or ethnic groups. One might speculate that certain values with respect to conducting and publishing research differ between non-Caucasian female and male groups and between ethnic groups. However, no data exist that would sustain such hypotheses. Social reasons lead one to expect that portions of some groups would publish less—namely, those who have been economically and socially disadvantaged and have had inferior schooling and training. Still, some Caucasian subsets suffer similar disadvantages (Ryan & Sackery, 1984), as do African American women from lower social classes (Tokarczyk & Fay, 1993).

Only a handful of studies correlate race with productivity, but not because investigators do not want to find such correlations.[34] Quite the contrary. Ever since the 1954 Supreme Court decision and the presidential executive orders of the 1960s (and after), African American faculty and black higher education have received extensive attention. One focus has been on the HBCUs—about 100 of them—with some pundits saying that they should be shut down because of their poor resources and the less-than-adequate training of their faculty (Jencks & Riesman, 1968). Others point out not only the historic role of these institutions but also the fact that a disproportionate number of this country's African American leaders graduated from HBCUs (Elmore & Blackburn, 1983).

Beginning with the 1969 survey conducted by the Carnegie Commission and the American Council on Education (Bayer, 1970) and continuing through the 1990 national survey of the Higher Education Research Institute (n.d.), African American faculty have received questionnaires that, among other things, asked for information about how much they have published.[35] Only one productivity study of African American faculty based on these data banks has been published (Freeman, 1978).

We do not know why other researchers have not analyzed these data, but we know why we have not. The numbers are small, too low in many instances. For example, of the 60,028 faculty who responded to the 1969 survey, 188 were employed at HBCUs. Of these 188, 92 were African Americans (6 did not respond to the race question).[36] One knows that institutional type and discipline need to be taken into account, but doing so reduces the numbers in any one category to sizes that prohibit analysis. The numbers of minority respondents are small not only because of the small actual population but also because their response rate falls below an acceptable level, so low that one cannot have confidence that the findings are reliable and can be generalized.[37]

Another focus has been on integration and diversity. TWIs compete with one another, and with HBCUs, to recruit the "best" African American faculty from an inadequate and shrinking pool. Affirmative action fans these flames but fails to produce more African American Ph.D.'s.

We now turn to the few existing studies. Comparing African American and Caucasian faculty at TWIs, both Rafky (1972) and Freeman (1978) found that African Americans published significantly less.[38] Scott (1981) studied African American faculty in New England TWIs. He discovered that their productivity increased as their amount of contact with Caucasian faculty increased.[39] Blackburn and Young (1985) discovered differences in most disciplines when Caucasian faculty in TWIs were compared with African American faculty in HBCUs in two southern states, Caucasians publishing more. In a national study focusing on African American faculty in social work, Schiele (1991) found them to be publishing slightly less than the overall social work faculty. Women of color clearly are being promoted at a lower rate, or are leaving their institution at a higher rate, or both, than Caucasian men (Banks, 1984; Exum, Menges, Watkins, & Berglund, 1984; Johnsrud & Saddao, 1993; Wyche & Graves, 1992). (See figure 2.17.)

On the other hand, Elmore and Blackburn (1983) found no difference in publication output between black and white faculty in Big 10 universities, nor did Vroom (1991) for faculty in graduate schools of social work. In his study of African American faculty alienation, Jackson (1991) discovered that this fairly widespread condition, especially among untenured assistant professors, was not associated with faculty productivity. Blackburn, Wenzel, and Bieber (1994) examined the NCES 1988 data tape for differences between minority and majority publication rates as reported at that time. Small Ns made most discipline comparisons impossible. Those that could be tested are shown in table 2.5. As can be seen, publication output differed significantly in only three instances.

The outcomes can be explained and bear no relationship to racial differ-

Figure 2.17   Women of Color in Regular Instructional Ranks, 1978–1979 to 1989–1990, Ann Arbor Campus

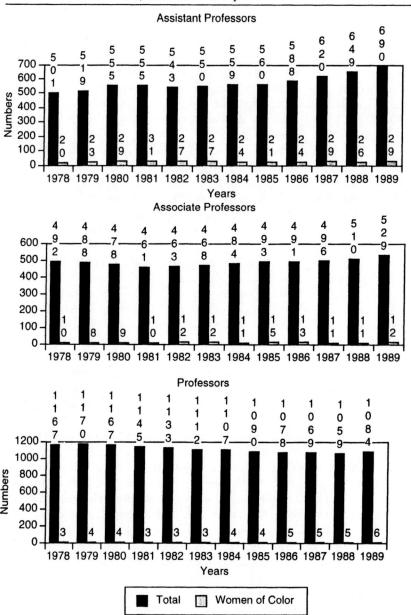

*Source:* Hollenshead (1992).

*Note:* Includes women who are African American, Asian American, Native American, and Hispanic.

Table 2.5    T-Tests for Minority/Majority Faculty Two-Year Publication Rates, by
Institutional Type and Discipline

| | | Minority | | | Majority | | | p Values Mean Diff. | p Values % Untenured Diff. |
|---|---|---|---|---|---|---|---|---|---|
| Type | Discipline | Mean | SD | N | Mean | SD | N | | |
| | | Hispanic | | | Caucasian | | | | |
| Res | Foreign lang. | 10.3 | 6.5 | 22 | 9.9 | 11.4 | 118 | .82 | .28 |
| Doc | Foreign lang. | 9.2 | 7.6 | 10 | 8.3 | 9.4 | 63 | .75 | .33 |
| Comp | Foreign lang. | 6.8 | 10.0 | 21 | 5.7 | 8.1 | 113 | .64 | .67 |
| | | Asian American | | | Caucasian | | | | |
| Res | Health sci. | 13.2 | 9.0 | 12 | 18.1 | 20.5 | 212 | .11 | .18 |
| Res | Engineering | 15.1 | 8.3 | 9 | 12.1 | 8.4 | 66 | .34 | .13 |
| Res | Natural sci.* | 9.6 | 9.1 | 19 | 16.6 | 33.8 | 203 | .03 | .11 |
| Res | Foreign lang. | 7.4 | 6.4 | 13 | 9.9 | 11.4 | 118 | .24 | .23 |
| Comp | Natural sci. | 5.0 | 4.7 | 12 | 7.1 | 19.2 | 201 | .28 | .64 |
| Comp | Business | 4.1 | 2.9 | 10 | 6.4 | 10.0 | 81 | .11 | .18 |
| Comp | Engineering | 6.6 | 6.2 | 11 | 5.3 | 8.8 | 60 | .57 | .05 |
| Doc | Natural sci. | 7.7 | 7.1 | 6 | 10.2 | 11.3 | 92 | .44 | .86 |
| | | African American | | | Caucasian | | | | |
| Res | Health sci.* | 4.0 | 5.0 | 8 | 18.1 | 20.5 | 212 | .00 | .40 |
| Comp | Educ. | 7.9 | 6.4 | 6 | 10.8 | 20.7 | 204 | .25 | .92 |
| Comp | English | 4.6 | 6.1 | 8 | 9.8 | 23.5 | 173 | .08 | .69 |
| Doc | Educ.* | 8.8 | 5.5 | 6 | 15.8 | 19.3 | 83 | .04 | .00 |

*Source:* Blackburn, Wenzel, and Bieber (1994), p. 278.

* $p < .05$.

ences. Over half of the African American faculty in TWIs are in education and a few social science fields, disciplines that publish at an appreciably lower rate than do the sciences (where the faculty circa 1970 were almost exclusively Caucasian—as they still are, though with an increasing number of Asian Americans). Res-I's reward faculty on the single standard of scholarly publications. The African American and Caucasian faculty in the Elmore and Blackburn study (all Res-I's) had identical pedigrees—Ph.D.'s from the leading universities.[40] The same explanation holds for Vroom's sample. While Blackburn and Young compared African American and Caucasian faculty at the same institutional type, one cannot equate the HBCU and TWI work environments. The resources for conducting research—

libraries, laboratories, support staff, money for equipment and travel to professional meetings, graduate research assistants—are vastly inferior at the HBCUs. Both the teaching and the student advising and counseling loads are heavier.

## Career

We now consider career variables—characteristics, attributes, and behaviors that accrue to individuals because of the life they have led. In contrast to age, sex/gender, and race/ethnicity, career variables such as specialization (discipline), graduate school attended, highest degree earned, place of work, rank and tenure status, career age, publication record, satisfaction with career—all these are things that one has done or experienced, things not set by birth.[41] These variables affect one's values, beliefs, and self-image (self-knowledge) as well as one's publication output. We detail the ones we use in our theoretical framework.

The situation now becomes more complex. Career variables almost always correlate with age and with one another. Career age relates directly to chronological age, because passage of time is one of the two elements employed to measure it. Older faculty hold higher ranks.[42] Highest degree correlates with place of work, because four-year institutions, but not two-year ones, require the doctorate. Graduate school attended correlates with place of work, the Res-I universities being almost completely staffed by graduates of that set of institutions. Rank and tenure status correlate, because one is typically awarded tenure when promoted to associate professor. The research literature reported below quite often does not statistically control for some of these correlations.

### Academic Discipline

We do not know why and when faculty selected the discipline they did. When we ask faculty how they happened to become an anthropologist, geologist, historian, or whatever, there are as many different answers as there are persons interviewed. Some seem to have backed into their specialty by accident, not even knowing that it existed. Others were strongly influenced by a teacher, often an undergraduate professor. One astronomer knew what he was going to become at age four, when his father had him look through a telescope. From then on, stargazing was all he ever wanted to do. And today as he approaches retirement, he counts the days to his scheduled time on the big telescope across the country.

Whatever created the marriage between the person and the discipline, her or his life develops in predictable ways that are unique to each specialty. We find vast differences among academic disciplines with regard to how faculty life is lived and the career one experiences. Disciplines differ from one another in the time required to earn the Ph.D. (over 10 years in the humanities and about 5 in the natural sciences), the custom of working alone or in teams, the definition of an honored product (a book in the humanities, a research article in the sciences), the value accorded teaching and the time given to it (higher in the humanities), and salaries (higher in the sciences).[43] Becher (1981) first advanced research styles as the differentiating principle but later (1989) called the disciplines academic tribes having distinct languages. They have a lifestyle and language of their own. When a mathematician calls the proof of a theorem "beautiful," it carries a different meaning from that of an artist complimenting a colleague on a painting (Geertz, 1983, pp. 158–159). Whitley (1978) shows how both the organization of academic work and research strategies differ across scientific fields.[44]

So many differences exist across fields of study when it comes to productivity that we always "control" for discipline. That is, we do not directly compare psychology professors' publication numbers with those of historians. When we compare men and women, or other groups, we do so within a discipline, not across.[45]

Bayer and Dutton (1977) plotted best-fit faculty productivity curves (with age) for seven selected science, engineering, and social science fields. The patterns differ appreciably from one another. Kyvik (1990) believes that the discrepancies between disciplines arise from differences in their development, particularly the speed of knowledge production and technological advance. Others suggest paradigm agreement as an explanation. Beyer and Stevens (1974) compared faculty in chemistry, physics, political science, and sociology and discovered differences in types of publications (and in forms of communication, support, and other variables). Using the same data bank as Beyer and Stevens, Neumann (1978) found different predictors for publication and grant securing across the four fields. Pfeffer, Leong, and Strehl (1976) detected significant differences in faculty publication rates in chemistry, sociology, and political science. They believe that the higher rate in chemistry results from that field's better-developed paradigm—that is, the agreement among its scholars as to what constitutes good and proper research. When Baird (1991) examined publication levels in 228 doctoral research departments in 23 disciplines, he found the most productive discipline averaging more than 10 times the mean of the least productive discipline (although there was great variation within disciplines as well). Wanner, Lewis, and Gregorio (1981) discovered that natural scientists publish nearly half again as many articles as social scientists and two and one-half times more than humanists. For books, social scientists lead; natural scientists are last.

### Graduate School

A Ph.D. is a Ph.D. is a Ph.D., so many say. However, the university awarding that degree affects one's career, in day-to-day experiences as well as in predicting outcomes, including productivity.

As demonstrated in the introduction, the United States has a stratified higher-education system. Everyone judges some colleges and universities superior to others. Those in the highest stratum are acclaimed as the country's elite. Their degrees carry a kennel club pedigree and confer special privileges on their recipients. Our status-conscious society finds no difficulty in acknowledging differential recognitions.

Res-I universities possess the greatest physical and fiscal resources— libraries, laboratories, endowment, grants. In addition, their faculty publish more than do faculty at other colleges and universities. More of their faculty enjoy national and international reputations. They have Nobel laureates on staff, enroll students with the highest test scores, and support the highest proportion of graduate research assistants. Postdoctoral fellows add to the intellectual climate. These institutions are blessed with many riches. In addition, they appear to be getting wealthier while others suffer and struggle. This is the Matthew effect at the institutional level—an advantage that accrues to those colleges and universities that already have (Bentley & Blackburn, 1991).[46] (See table 2.6.)

Colleges and universities that seek promising scholars turn to graduates

Table 2.6    Federal Grants, by Carnegie Type

|  | 1969 | | 1975 | | 1980 | | 1988 | |
|---|---|---|---|---|---|---|---|---|
|  | % | N | % | N | % | N | % | N |
| Res-I | 38.5 | 758 | 44.5 | 637 | 45.2 | 266 | 39.3 | 368 |
| Res-II | 35.2 | 374 | 34.7 | 452 | 28.9 | 215 | 33.3 | 261 |
| Doc-I | 28.2 | 411 | 31.1 | 266 | 35.9 | 181 | 30.2 | 217 |
| Doc-II | 16.1 | 120 | 18.5 | 348 | 16.5 | 104 | 21.6 | 236 |
| Comp-I | 10.2 | 1,400 | 11.2 | 1,633 | 14.6 | 727 | 12.4 | 1,218 |
| Average | 22.9 | 3,063 | 23.1 | 3,336 | 24.8 | 1,493 | 21.9 | 2,300 |
| Chi-square | 273.2 | | 342.8 | | 117.6 | | 152.5 | |
| Significance | .00 | | .00 | | .00 | | .00 | |

*Source:* National surveys.

of Res-I universities. They believe they are brighter, better educated, and better trained to conduct research.[47] Dissertation chairs serve as mentors and sponsor their graduates. The hiring institution knows that a relationship with the graduating university will continue, at least long enough for the new hire to launch a successful career. Research data support the argument made and the beliefs held. A wide assortment of studies over time and in a variety of settings and disciplines demonstrate that graduates of Res-I's produce more scholarship than faculty graduating from any other institutional category (Bayer & Folger, 1966; Clark & Centra, 1985; Clemente, 1973; Clemente & Sturgis, 1974; Crane, 1965; Lightfield, 1971; Long, 1978; Oromaner, 1981; Reskin, 1977). Using longitudinal data on psychology faculty, Deitsch (1989) found that the prestige of the baccalaureate school affected the prestige of the doctoral university, which in turn acted throughout the faculty member's career. Reskin (1976) also found that the caliber of the graduate school led to prestigious postdoctoral fellowships, which in turn led to high-status positions and scientific productivity—for men. Women gained no advantage from postdoctoral appointments.

The one finding that tempers the relationship comes from Long's (1978) study. He found that the effect of graduate school prestige wanes with the passage of time and that place of work matters more. We turn to that variable shortly.

### Highest Degree

Being a professor requires no licensing—no examinations to take at the institutional, state, national, or international level, and no boards to pass in order to practice (as lawyers and physicians do). One can even be hired as a professor without a college degree.[48]

The educational attainment level required for an introductory faculty position varies among the Carnegie types. In the main, U.S. two-year colleges say that knowledge acquired in earning a master's degree meets the minimum level needed for instruction in the arts and sciences. Faculty who teach in vocational and technical programs frequently offer their experience, not their formal schooling, as their credential. One need not earn the doctorate to secure tenure in a community college, although now nearly 30 percent of the community college faculty hold the highest degree, an appreciable increase from the less than 5 percent but 20 years ago (Lawrence, Blackburn, Hart, & Saulsberry, 1989).[49]

The Ph.D. is the expected entry degree for faculty in most four-year colleges and universities who teach in arts and science disciplines. For some professional fields the master's degree remains the terminal (highest expected) degree—in architecture, for example.[50] One reason why advanced education and training are required relates to instruction; the other involves the research role.

Advanced courses at the undergraduate level call on faculty knowledge that extends beyond what was learned at the master's level. Conducting research requires not only advanced knowledge but also the intellectual and technical skills to carry it out. The dissertation experience not only certifies research skills but also demonstrates the kind of perseverance scholarly inquiry requires. Ph.D. programs provide these prerequisites.[51] We turn first to the pool of qualified faculty and then to the question of how the supply of Ph.D.'s has been changing over time, especially with respect to underrepresented faculty groups—women and minorities.

The pattern of Ph.D. production over the past two decades can be seen in figure 2.18. These percentages are for women in science (mathematics, physics, biology, etc.) and engineering (mechanical, electrical, environmental, etc.) fields. The National Science Foundation (NSF) includes psychology as a separate science and places all of the other social sciences in another category within its larger designation of "social science." Women are much more likely to earn their doctorate in the humanities and psychology than in engineering or physics.[52] The 1960s unveiled a phenomenal growth rate. The

Figure 2.18   Ph.D.'s Earned by U.S. Citizens, by Sex

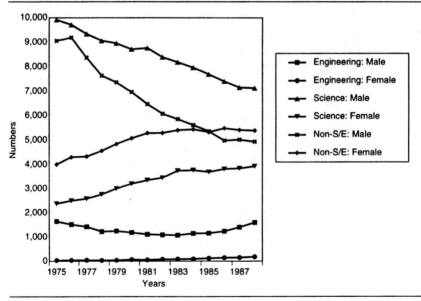

*Source:* National Science Foundation (1989).

number of Ph.D.'s granted per year increased from 9,733 to 25,743, a 164 percent gain. Ph.D. degrees in science and engineering increased at nearly the same rate. Doctorates earned by women increased more than threefold. Still, the percentage of Ph.D.'s in science and engineering earned by women during the same decade only increased from 7.1 percent to 9.2 percent.

Annual Ph.D. production has been remarkably stable since 1970. The composition of those earning the degree, however, has changed dramatically. Women more than doubled their proportion during the 1970s. The percentage rise during the 1980s has been slower.[53]

As can be seen in figure 2.18 above, an even more extraordinary gender change has occurred since 1975. In 13 years the percentage of men earning Ph.D.'s has declined in every category—by approximately 10 percent in engineering, 15 percent in science, and 20 percent in nonscience. After 1985 women exceed men in the non-S/E fields. Since the actual numbers of degrees have remained essentially constant over this period, the increases are in real numbers as well. Table 2.7 provides a more detailed set of data, by discipline and by sex, and documents changes in Ph.D. acquisition.

The third revolutionary phenomenon that took place during this period is the increase in the percentage of Ph.D.'s earned by foreign students,

Table 2.7    The Movement toward Gender Parity among Doctorate Recipients, by Field

| | Number of Doctorates in 1979 | | Number of Doctorates in 1985 | | % of Women in Field | | | % Growth, 1979–85 | |
|---|---|---|---|---|---|---|---|---|---|
| | Women | Men | Women | Men | 1979 | 1985 | Diff. 79–85 | Women | Men |
| Mathematics | 194 | 1,265 | 194 | 942 | 13.3 | 17.1 | 3.8 | 0.0 | -25.5 |
| Computer sci. | 40 | 277 | 68 | 518 | 12.6 | 11.6 | -1.0 | 70.0 | 87.0 |
| Physics/astron. | 97 | 1,906 | 146 | 1,763 | 4.8 | 7.6 | 2.8 | 50.5 | -7.5 |
| Chemistry | 375 | 2,799 | 582 | 2,597 | 11.8 | 18.3 | 6.5 | 55.2 | -7.2 |
| Earth/environ. | 116 | 1,146 | 181 | 905 | 9.2 | 16.7 | 7.5 | 56.0 | -21.0 |
| Engineering | 99 | 4,160 | 242 | 4,347 | 2.3 | 5.3 | 2.9 | 144.4 | 4.5 |
| Agriculture | 98 | 1,234 | 248 | 1,476 | 7.4 | 14.4 | 7.0 | 153.1 | 19.6 |
| Medical sci. | 313 | 917 | 880 | 984 | 25.4 | 47.2 | 21.8 | 181.2 | 7.3 |
| Biological sci. | 1,377 | 4,238 | 2,149 | 4,371 | 24.5 | 33.0 | 8.4 | 56.1 | 3.1 |
| Psychology | 2,157 | 3,729 | 3,136 | 3,273 | 36.6 | 48.9 | 12.3 | 45.4 | -12.2 |
| Social sci. | 1,385 | 4,639 | 1,757 | 3,626 | 23.0 | 32.6 | 9.6 | 26.9 | -21.8 |
| Humanities | 3,066 | 4,789 | 2,813 | 3,539 | 39.0 | 44.3 | 5.3 | -8.3 | -26.1 |
| Total | 9,317 | 31,099 | 12,396 | 28,341 | 23.1 | 30.4 | 7.4 | 33.0 | -8.9 |

*Source:* Heath and Tuckman (1989), p. 706.

especially in engineering and mathematics. Figure 2.19 shows that in 1978 foreign students were already earning over 30 percent of the engineering doctorates. By 1988 they had increased their share to over 40 percent. Earned mathematics Ph.D.'s more than doubled, from less than 20 percent to over 40 percent.

Since the foreign students in these fields are overwhelmingly men, removing them from the figures considerably alters the share of degrees earned by U.S. female citizens. In all non-S/E fields U.S. women earned 52 percent of the Ph.D.'s awarded in 1988. (See figure 2.18 above.) They earned 32 percent of the science doctorates awarded to U.S. citizens in 1988, up from 17 percent in 1975. Women's shares of Ph.D.'s in both psychology and the life sciences—where they have always been more strongly represented—have increased since 1975, from 32 percent to 55 percent and from 21 percent to 35 percent, respectively. (See table 2.8.)

Turning to the literature, one finds to no great surprise that those with Ph.D.'s publish more than those who do not have that degree (Dickson, 1983). The relationship, however, while not spurious, can mislead. When institutional type is controlled, the correlation essentially disappears. Fewer community college faculty have the Ph.D. Almost all research university faculty do. (See figure 2.20.) The former are teaching institutions, and the latter are places where publication is the norm. Degree predicts almost nothing within most institutional types.

Figure 2.19    Science and Engineering Ph.D.'s Earned by Non–U.S. Citizens

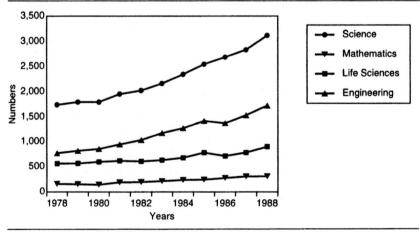

*Source:* National Science Foundation (1989).
*Note:* Includes only foreigners on temporary visas.

Table 2.8    Psychology and Life Sciences Ph.D.'s of U.S. Citizens, by Field and Sex

| | Psychology | | | | Life Sciences | | | |
|---|---|---|---|---|---|---|---|---|
| | M | F | Total | F% | M | F | Total | F% |
| 1975 | 1,746 | 806 | 2,552 | 32 | 2,760 | 713 | 3,473 | 21 |
| 1976 | 1,832 | 895 | 2,727 | 33 | 2,804 | 693 | 3,497 | 20 |
| 1977 | 1,767 | 1,007 | 2,774 | 36 | 2,702 | 694 | 3,396 | 20 |
| 1978 | 1,770 | 1,034 | 2,804 | 37 | 2,744 | 778 | 3,522 | 22 |
| 1979 | 1,700 | 1,150 | 2,850 | 40 | 2,814 | 860 | 3,674 | 23 |
| 1980 | 1,637 | 1,222 | 2,859 | 43 | 2,871 | 978 | 3,849 | 25 |
| 1981 | 1,746 | 1,365 | 3,111 | 44 | 2,859 | 1,032 | 3,891 | 27 |
| 1982 | 1,556 | 1,320 | 2,876 | 46 | 2,851 | 1,113 | 3,964 | 28 |
| 1983 | 1,576 | 1,468 | 3,044 | 48 | 2,688 | 1,171 | 3,859 | 30 |
| 1984 | 1,440 | 1,495 | 2,935 | 51 | 2,773 | 1,137 | 3,910 | 29 |
| 1985 | 1,396 | 1,409 | 2,805 | 50 | 2,678 | 1,151 | 3,829 | 30 |
| 1986 | 1,330 | 1,436 | 2,766 | 52 | 2,513 | 1,191 | 3,704 | 32 |
| 1987 | 1,262 | 1,490 | 2,752 | 54 | 2,375 | 1,193 | 3,568 | 33 |
| 1988 | 1,179 | 1,462 | 2,641 | 55 | 2,373 | 1,285 | 3,658 | 35 |

*Source:* National Science Foundation (1989).

## Place of Work

Faculty members' place of work correlates with their scholarly productivity. Those who secured positions at research universities did so on the basis of their research interest and their successful record. That is, the motivation to engage in research had already been demonstrated. Those seeking positions where teaching receives the major emphasis go to institutions where research expectations and requirements are lower. Motivation for teaching is expressed in the institutional selection process. (It is also the case today that people with scholarly interests have difficulty finding positions in research universities.)

The relationship between productivity and place of work has other consequences. Long (1978) has demonstrated that faculty who move from a highly productive institution to a less productive one publish at a reduced rate, while those who move in the opposite direction increase their output.[54] A large number of studies confirm this relationship in a variety of settings and academic disciplines (Anderson, 1978; Blackburn, Behymer, & Hall, 1978; Blau, 1973; Bouillon, 1987; Cole & Cole, 1973; Crane, 1965; Deitsch, 1989; Fulton & Trow, 1974; Long, 1978; Long & McGinnis, 1981; Oromaner, 1981; Over, 1982; Reskin, 1977, 1979; Wispe, 1969).

Long (1978) finds that the effect of place of employment on productivity

Figure 2.20   Faculty with Ph.D.'s, by Institutional Type

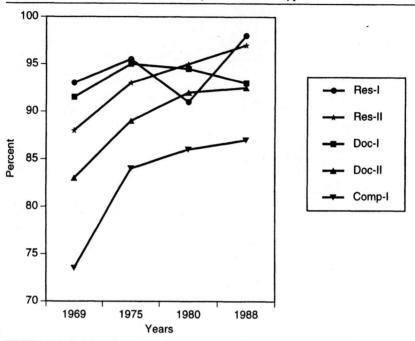

*Source:* National surveys.

is not only strong but also increases in importance over time. Figures 2.21 (on grants) and 2.22 (on lifetime books published) show the unchanging relationship to Carnegie type from Res-I to Comp-I institutions. Endler (1977) discovered a similar phenomenon in Canadian university psychology departments. The high producers and most cited authors taught in the leading departments and universities. The same phenomenon occurs in professional schools, such as library science schools (Budd & Seavey, 1990) and schools of business administration (Moore et al., 1992). Academic life in the lower-rated institutions, the ones Caesar (1992) calls "invisible colleges," differs dramatically from that in Res-I's. Place of work remains an important variable in our theoretical framework.

## Professorial Rank and Tenure

As career variables, academic rank and tenure represent a status individuals acquire as a consequence of their performance. One generally begins as an assistant professor and has seven years in which to demonstrate competencies that merit promotion to the associate rank and the awarding of

Figure 2.21    Standardized Sponsored Grants, by Institutional Type

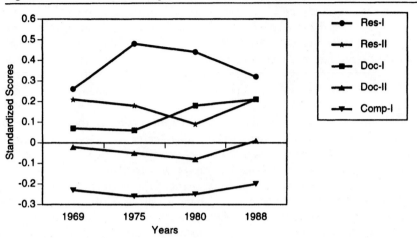

*Source:* National surveys.
*Note:* Adjusted by differences by discipline.

Figure 2.22    Lifetime Books Published, by Institutional Type

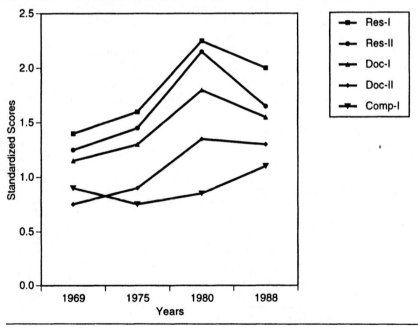

*Source:* National surveys.

tenure, a continuing life appointment. Table 2.9 shows the data on rank. As would be expected, age, career age, and rank (and tenure) are highly interrelated. One sees the same pattern as witnessed for age: decreasing numbers of assistant professors (new hires) from 1969 to 1980, followed by an increase in 1988. (See figure 2.1 above.) Similarly, the percentage of full professors increases from 31.4 percent in 1969 to 52.6 percent in 1980. The fall-off in 1988 indicates the onset of increased numbers of retirements over the past few years.[55]

Figure 2.23 exhibits the percentage differences between men and women in the various academic ranks.[56] The "other" category includes instructors, lecturers, and other titles such as visiting or adjunct professor, all of which are not tenure-track positions but rather year-to-year contracts with no credit being accumulated toward a permanent appointment and an authentic career.[57] Persons in this category have no promise of a continuing appointment. (These low-status positions were common two decades ago.) Note that nearly 40 percent of the women did not have ranked positions in 1969. Today these appointment types constitute a much smaller percentage of full-time faculty. Still, women more frequently occupy these lower-status and insecure positions.

While the percentage of women who are full professors has increased from about 13 percent in 1969 to 25 percent in 1988, the male percentages rose from about 30 percent to approximately 50 percent. That is, men continue to hold the highest-status titles.

Figure 2.14, above, contains similar data. The percentage of women who have acquired tenure is appreciably greater in 1988 than in 1969. However, their numbers still lag behind those of men.[58] In addition, data from a highly competitive environment, a Res-I university, indicate no gain for women over the 10-year interval 1978–1988. During this period, as was seen in figures 2.8 and 2.17, above, the percentage of female associate and full professors remained essentially constant for the University of Michigan, an

Table 2.9   Distribution of Faculty by Rank

|                 | 1969 | | 1975 | | 1980 | | 1988 | |
|-----------------|------|-------|------|-------|------|-------|------|-------|
|                 | N    | %     | N    | %     | N    | %     | N    | %     |
| Assistant prof. | 1,228 | 38.8 | 1,149 | 32.6 | 161 | 10.8 | 471 | 19.8 |
| Associate prof. | 943  | 29.8  | 1,097 | 31.1 | 547 | 36.6 | 731 | 30.7 |
| Full prof.      | 996  | 31.4  | 1,278 | 36.3 | 785 | 52.6 | 1,181 | 49.6 |
| All             | 3,167 | 100.0 | 3,524 | 100.0 | 1,493 | 100.0 | 2,383 | 100.0 |

*Source:* National surveys.

Figure 2.23   Academic Rank, by Sex

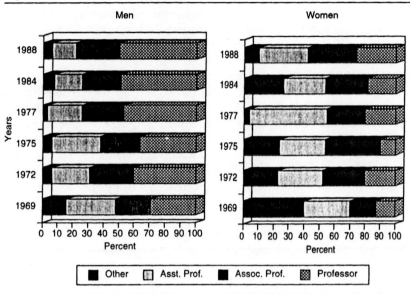

*Source:* National surveys.

institution with a strong affirmative action program and a commitment to increasing the numbers of women and minority faculty. Yet women either were not promoted or left as soon as they were (Hollenshead, 1992).

Having laid out some of the demographics on rank and tenure, we now turn to the literature for their relationships to research output. Until 1988, the studies showed small, positive correlations between rank—and hence tenure and age—and publication rate as well as total career publications (Blackburn, Behymer, & Hall, 1978; Bonzi, 1992; Cornette, 1987; Hickson, 1991). Explanations for the direction of the relationship are of two kinds. One is artificial; the other calls upon experience. Neither directly involves motivation.

The statistical relationship comes about in part because of institutional practices. As noted, one has to publish in order to be awarded tenure and be promoted in universities. "Publish or perish" is the popular phrase. To the degree to which this norm is practiced, the survivors—namely, those in the higher ranks—are the ones who have published, while the assistant professors are still learning how to turn research into publications. They have published less. Hence the positive relationship between rank and productivity follows.

The experience explanation for publication output is just that—experience. One learns how to be a publishing researcher, and the skill increases with time, age and rank being the accompanying attributes. Cumulative advantage enters once again. Those who have been successful researchers acquire increased resources over time.

The oversupply of potential faculty for a limited number of openings has changed in the past few years so as to turn this positive relationship into a negative one (Bentley & Blackburn, 1991). Colleges and universities capitalized on the buyer's market. They hired active publishers rather than select new Ph.D.'s on the basis of future promise, the typical hiring practice of the 1960s and 1970s. Now the assistant professors are publishing at a higher rate than the full professors. In addition, the new hires, already successful in the art, know that gaining tenure is contingent upon a successful research performance. They are motivated to publish at rates not heretofore witnessed in higher education. Tien and Blackburn (1993) used the 1984 Carnegie survey data to examine faculty publication rates just prior to and immediately after expected (average) promotion time, to test the degree to which promotion (an external reward) acts as a motivator. The findings were mixed. For some, publication rates rose just prior to the promotion date and dropped afterward. For others, especially full professors having no prospects of further promotion as a reward, publishing continued at the former level. Such continuous performance suggests that they find research intrinsically motivating.

Despite the essential lack of relationship between rank and publications and the strong relationship between tenure and rank, many believe that once tenure is awarded, faculty publication rates will drop. Slothfulness sets in. They quit working and go fishing. Along with Tein and Blackburn, two studies that tested this belief (Bridgwater, Walsh, & Walkenbach, 1982; Holley, 1977) expose its untruth.

## Career Age

More experience in a business means more savvy on what it takes to succeed. Most often we do not know exactly how long a person has been a faculty member, but we do know the date at which the highest degree was awarded. We take the difference between that date and the survey date as the person's career age. This procedure underestimates a true career age for those faculty who had taken a position before completing their highest degree, and it overestimates the career age if the person did not launch a faculty career for some time after completing the final degree.[59]

Table 2.10 contains career age data. The data support the hypothesis of the graying of the professoriate. Career age increases at each successive data

Table 2.10   Distribution of Faculty by Career Age

| | 1969 | | 1975 | | 1980 | | 1988 | |
|---|---|---|---|---|---|---|---|---|
| | N | % | N | % | N | % | N | % |
| < 6 years | 1,149 | 36.5 | 966 | 27.9 | 95 | 6.4 | 232 | 9.8 |
| 6 to 10 years | 698 | 22.2 | 910 | 26.3 | 358 | 24.2 | 301 | 12.7 |
| 11 to 15 years | 407 | 12.9 | 594 | 17.1 | 398 | 26.9 | 433 | 18.2 |
| 16 to 20 years | 407 | 12.9 | 365 | 10.5 | 257 | 17.4 | 612 | 25.8 |
| 21 to 25 years | 143 | 4.5 | 327 | 9.4 | 171 | 11.6 | 406 | 17.1 |
| > 25 years | 344 | 10.9 | 304 | 8.8 | 199 | 13.5 | 391 | 16.5 |
| All | 3,148 | 100.0 | 3,466 | 100.0 | 1,478 | 100.0 | 2,375 | 100.0 |

*Source:* National surveys.

collection point. The average rose from 11.5 years in 1969 to 17.3 in 1988. Fewer faculty have been entering the profession, and fewer have been leaving. The age distribution has simply shifted to the older end. This trend is expected to end shortly, however, because the departures are accelerating and replacements at the young end are also slowly increasing. Both average chronological age and career age will soon decline.[60] The share of those having less than six years of experience dropped from 36.5 percent in 1969 to 6.4 percent in 1980 but increased to 9.8 percent in 1988.

Career age is an important variable, because people earn their degrees at quite different ages, and so actual age as an indicator of productivity can be misleading. People in the natural sciences and mathematics earn their degrees, on average, some six years younger than those in the humanities—under 30 to over 30. When one examines career publication data, dividing it by career age is important so that a rate can be established and individuals compared on a fair basis.

Career age correlates slightly, and positively, with productivity (Bentley & Blackburn, 1991; Bonzi, 1992; Bouillon, 1987; Dickson, 1983; Oromaner, 1973a), a finding consistent with the small correlation found with rank (for rank correlates with career age). Recall, however, that the recent findings of Bentley and Blackburn (1991) demonstrate that younger faculty—those of lower rank and lower career age—are publishing at a higher rate than senior faculty. The often reported career age/publications relationship may disappear, or may already have done so.

### Publication Record

Not surprisingly, how prolific one has been predicts how prolific one will be. Those who have published frequently in the past are more likely to publish more in the future. Studies using the national surveys of faculty collect information on both their total career publications and how much they have published in the last two years. While the last two years is not the future, it is the most current measure we have. Past publication—career total minus the last two years—correlates with most recent publication. Like tenure and higher rank, it is a characteristic of established faculty members. Trautvetter and Blackburn (1990) found this variable to be an exceptionally strong predictor for men and women in science and mathematics, as did the test of our theoretical framework. (See chapter 4.)

Early publication, including publication before the doctorate, predicts future production rate and total production (Gaston, 1978; Long, Allison, & McGinnis, 1979; Raymond, 1967; Reskin, 1977). Early publishers become prolific publishers. As they publish, they get grants. As they get grants, they publish. We noted this phenomenon above in the social-psychological explanation for age and publication data. It accounts in part for the fact that a very small percentage of faculty produce the majority of the research literature.

In all, then, with the exception of publication record, career variables by themselves are informative, individually and collectively, but questionable and not especially strong predictors of faculty behaviors—producing research, in this instance.

# 3

## THE VARIABLES: SELF-KNOWLEDGE, SOCIAL KNOWLEDGE, BEHAVIORS, AND ENVIRONMENTAL CONSTRUCTS

W$_E$ NOW MOVE TO what the research literature offers concerning the remaining constructs in our theoretical framework. (Return to figure 1.1 and the major arrows that sequentially connect the constructs and order the presentation of this and the preceding chapter.) We begin with self-knowledge and social knowledge. We then turn to behaviors, a construct first developed at the outset of chapter 2. At the end of the chapter we briefly discuss our framework's environmental constructs—environmental conditions, environmental responses, and social contingencies.

### Self-Knowledge

The self-knowledge category contains a number of variables—interest in and preference for a role, commitment, efficacy (competence and influence), psychological attributes. It includes self-perceptions that relate directly to behaviors and products in the various academic roles—teaching, scholarship, research, and service—and to the perceptions of the environment that we call social knowledge.

These cognitive variables differ from sociodemographic and career variables not only in their conceptual status but also in their immediacy. The connection between such factors as interest and motivation are obviously direct. Unlike gender and race, they have a potential for change—in the course of a day as well as over a career.[1]

Self-knowledge variables, while salient, fluctuate. Historical events over which I have minimal control (e.g., a financial crisis, a change in institutional priorities set by a new president, war—what we call environmental conditions) can influence them. Still, as we will see when we test our theory for the behaviors faculty exhibit and their creations, the self-knowledge variables are important predictors.[2]

We include in this category two indicators of interest, one of commitment, and two of efficacy.

*Interest*

How people allocate their work effort reflects their interest in different activities—assuming that the job provides options. Faculty do not differ from others in this regard. What distinguishes academics from most other professional groups is the latitude they enjoy in how they spend their time. Even as salaried employees of an organization, they have fewer hours of committed task time than do most lawyers in a corporation, doctors in a hospital, engineers in a firm—almost any group one can name. Only some self-employed individuals have more latitude. Artists and writers do, but dentists do not. Patient clientele pretty much dictates the dentist's weekly schedule.

While teaching work loads, as higher education calls specified assignments, vary from institution to institution—one or two courses per term in graduate departments in research universities, five or even more courses in community colleges—the committed number of hours is relatively small. A five-course load, a schedule four-year college and university faculty consider extraordinarily heavy, means 15 class hours, perhaps 4 office hours, and 2 committee hours per week—just about half of the American 40-hour workweek.

At the same time, faculty report working many more than 50 hours a week, a number that has been corroborated more than once since the 1960s (French, Tupper, & Mueller, 1965; Yuker, 1984). Even faculty with the maximum contracted classroom and office hour time can spend more than 30 hours each week engaged in activities that interest them most. These numbers, of course, exaggerate reality. One has to spend time preparing for class, grading papers and examinations, and attending to other matters that accompany the different roles—keeping up to date by reading, for example. In fact, one could spend all of one's time in teaching-related activities if desired. Some faculty do. Others give a bare minimum outside of class, calling on past notes, reusing old examinations, requiring few written assignments.

In short, faculty have a privileged opportunity to satisfy their interests.[3] Some faculty in the same organization with equivalent assignments and known institutional expectations can diverge appreciably in how they allocate their efforts. Furthermore, no supervisor—department chair, dean—

monitors that unassigned time. As for what is required or accomplished outside the formal assignments, instructors are really not accountable to anyone except themselves.[4]

Our measures of faculty interest fail to capture this rich diversity, if ever any data could. Still, one question appears on nearly all of the surveys and allows a comparison across time as well as insights on how faculty differ across institutional types and disciplines. The common item asks faculty to indicate whether their interests reside heavily in research or in teaching, or, when both, toward which they lean. Figure 3.1 and table 3.1 display how faculty interest in research has been changing over time. Here we see a consistent pattern by institutional category, from highest research interest in universities to lowest in comprehensive institutions.[5] As shown in the table, a discernable pattern of increasing interest in research occurs at each successive time of testing in all three categories, the exception being a slight dip among faculty in Doc-II's and Comp-I's in 1975. Larger numbers of faculty express a principal interest in research today.

Figure 3.1   Faculty Primarily Interested in Research, by Institutional Type

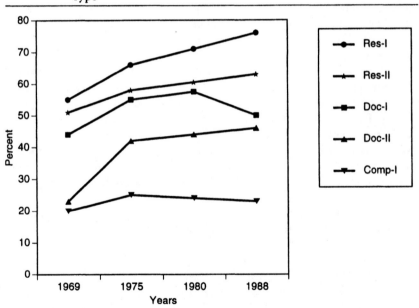

*Source:* National surveys.
*Note:* Data unavailable in 1980. Graph has extrapolations.

Table 3.1    Faculty Primarily Interested in Research (Percent)

|      | *Category 1* | *Category 2* | *Category 3* |
|------|------|------|------|
| 1969 | 54 | 28 | 22 |
| 1975 | 60 | 29 | 20 |
| 1988 | 74 | 48 | 29 |

*Source:* National surveys.

*Note:* Category 1 = Res-I and -II; category 2 = Doc-I and LAC-I; category 3 = Doc-II and Comp-I and -II.

A principal interest in research varies across institutional types, as shown in table 3.2. The percentage of faculty primarily interested in research ranges from 79 at Res-I universities to 7 at community colleges. With the exception of LAC-I's, interest declines linearly across the Carnegie types.

Table 3.3 displays differences in faculty interest in teaching across selected disciplines and institutional types. Community college faculty have the highest interest—their average score is 0.93 on a scale that runs from 0 (low interest) to 1 (high interest)—and the least variation across or within the disciplines. Res-I university faculty, on the other hand, express the least interest in teaching. Their 0.21 average complements their research interest.[6] Differences occur across disciplines in Res-I's. English faculty indicate more than twice the interest in teaching as do the faculty in both of the sciences.

We have a second interest indicator for the different faculty roles. Here faculty reported what percentage of their work effort they would prefer to give to teaching, scholarship, research, and service in a typical week of the term. The questionnaire indicates the kinds of activities included within each role.[7] This interest indicator differs from the first one. Time allocations may vary appreciably between two individuals who both have a high interest in a certain role. A faculty member at a liberal arts college may prefer to give her or his major effort to teaching but still maintain a very high interest in scholarship.

Tables 3.4 and 3.5 show how this measure varies by institutional type and academic discipline.[8] As was the case for interest in research (table 3.2),

Table 3.2    Faculty Interest in Research, by Institutional Type (Percent)

|  | Res-I | Res-II | Doc-I | Doc-II | Comp-I | Comp-II | LAC-I | LAC-II | CC |
|--|--|--|--|--|--|--|--|--|--|
| Interest | 79 | 68 | 51 | 49 | 25 | 13 | 26 | 14 | 7 |

*Source:* NCRIPTAL survey.

84

Table 3.3    Faculty Interest in Teaching in Selected Disciplines and Institutional Types

|          | English | | Chemistry | | Psychology | |
|----------|------|------|------|------|------|------|
|          | Mean | SD   | Mean | SD   | Mean | SD   |
| CCs      | 0.91 | 0.28 | 0.95 | 0.22 | 0.92 | 0.27 |
| Comp-I's | 0.75 | 0.43 | 0.81 | 0.40 | 0.67 | 0.47 |
| Res-I's  | 0.34 | 0.48 | 0.13 | 0.33 | 0.15 | 0.30 |

*Source:* NCRIPTAL survey.
*Note:* Numbers are standardized scores that can range from 0 (low) to 1 (high).

table 3.4 shows an almost linear decline from Res-I faculty wanting to give 42 percent of their effort to research to CC faculty saying 4 percent. That interest and personal preference co-vary is what one would expect two similar indicators to do. That there is a high degree of agreement between preferred percentage of effort allocated to the role and interest in the role supports the argument made above that faculty allocate time to their different roles in proportion to their interests, not specifically in proportion to their institution's assignments.

Table 3.5, like table 3.3, shows community college faculty's higher preference for teaching and the lack of differences across disciplines when the mission is teaching, not research. It also elucidates the differences across disciplines within Res-I universities, although they are not as large as they were on the interest indicator.

While not a particularly strong predictor, interest does correlate with research productivity. (See Fulton & Trow, 1974; Rowe, 1976). Aisenberg and Harrington's (1988) interviews with female academics illustrate the strong interest they have in teaching and service and their weaker interest in research, a relationship that can in part account for women's lower publication rates. In her study of role conflict and teaching effectiveness as measured by student ratings, Miller (1988) learned that as the discrepancy between preferred and actual time spent on the tasks that comprise the teaching role and the research role increases, teaching effectiveness tends to decrease.

Table 3.4    Faculty Preference for Time Given to Research, by Institutional Type (Percent)

|            | Res-I | Res-II | Doc-I | Doc-II | Comp-I | Comp-II | LAC-I | LAC-II | CC |
|------------|-------|--------|-------|--------|--------|---------|-------|--------|----|
| Preference | 42    | 36     | 34    | 31     | 19     | 8       | 14    | 9      | 4  |

*Source:* NCRIPTAL survey.

Table 3.5   Faculty Preference for Time Given to Teaching in Selected Disciplines and Institutional Types (Percent)

|  | English | | Chemistry | | Psychology | |
|---|---|---|---|---|---|---|
|  | *Mean* | *SD* | *Mean* | *SD* | *Mean* | *SD* |
| CCs | 60.5 | 15.6 | 68.2 | 16.7 | 59.5 | 17.3 |
| Comp-I's | 53.0 | 16.0 | 55.0 | 15.5 | 46.5 | 16.4 |
| Res-I's | 37.3 | 12.9 | 28.0 | 9.5 | 26.0 | 12.9 |

*Source:* NCRIPTAL survey.

## Commitment

Along with interest, theory expects a commitment to an activity to correlate with the expectation of such commitment. Commitment does not imply exclusive devotion to a role, but it does express a vow or promise to succeed in the activity to the best of one's ability. Our interviewed faculty characterized the valued faculty member as one who committed herself or himself to either teaching or research, or both. Our survey asked the respondents to tell us how committed they were to the two roles. We will see that the variable has a relationship to publications. We have been unable, however, to find studies that use this variable.

## Efficacy

People need to have a sense of ownership and to feel in control of choices, options, and opportunities—that is, a sense of self-efficacy (Maehr & Braskamp, 1986). Deci (1975) believes that one's intrinsic motivation varies directly with feelings of personal control. According to Bandura (1977a), individuals employ different sources of information to judge their efficacy level—for example, performance accomplishments or successfully persuading others to their point of view.

A distinction exists between the information contained in environmental events and information as processed and transferred by the individual. Consequently, the impact of information on one's efficacy will depend upon "how it is cognitively appraised" (Bandura, 1977a, p. 200). For example, success with minimal effort may foster ability and reinforce efficacy, while success achieved through a high expenditure of effort may produce a lower sense of efficacy. Bandura proposes that individuals "can give up trying because they lack a sense of self-efficacy in achieving the required behavior, or they may be assured of their capabilities, but give up trying because they expect their behavior to have no effect on an unresponsive environment or to be consistently punished" (p. 204).

One dimension of self-efficacy is one's competence; another is one's ability to influence outcomes. We treat both next.

*Competence*

People can specify their ability to perform different roles. Most likely they estimate their competence to carry out specific functions and to accomplish certain kinds of tasks on the basis of various kinds of evidence. Here we present findings regarding faculty members' perceptions of their competence for teaching and for conducting research.

Faculty receive feedback on their teaching competence from a variety of sources—directly in the classroom from student responses to what transpires, from comments in conversations with colleagues and advisees, and from systematic student evaluations at the end of a course. In some institutions—for example, in unionized two-year colleges—the contract may specify supervisor classroom visitations and evaluations, another response mechanism. Overall, faculty give highest credence to evaluations from students and from themselves when it comes to judging how skilled they are in the teaching role (Blackburn, Boberg, O'Connell, & Pellino, 1980).

Tables 3.6–3.9 display faculty responses as to how they rate themselves as teachers and lecturers. On a four-point scale ranging from "highly" to "not at all" effective, one sees that faculty rate their teaching highly, even those who work in research universities, where the popular belief is that professors do not care about pedagogy. Self-assessments of teaching effectiveness are not as high among research and doctoral-institution faculty as among liberal arts and community college faculty. Still, well over 95 percent in all types rate themselves in one of the top two categories. Fewer differences exist across institutional types when it comes to skill as a lecturer.

When placing these data up against the frequent and well-publicized complaints about poor teaching in our colleges and universities, one might conclude that faculty possess inflated egos with respect to their pedagogical competence. The evidence, however, rests on the faculty side. Faculty generally receive high ratings from students on standardized evaluation forms. By way of illustration, at the University of Michigan the average overall student rating of faculty teaching is above 4 on a five-point scale (McKeachie, 1979a).

Turning to research competence, we have two indicators—publishing and obtaining grants. Faculty reported the degree to which skills in these areas were characteristic of themselves. Tables 3.10–3.13 display the findings.

Generally, faculty reported that they were publishers and that they obtained grants. The institutional type pattern is what one would expect, given

Table 3.6    Faculty Self-Report on Teaching Effectiveness, by Institutional Type (Percent)

| How Effective? | Res-I | Res-II | Doc-I | Doc-II | Comp-I | Comp-II | LAC-I | LAC-II | CC |
|---|---|---|---|---|---|---|---|---|---|
| Not at all | 0.3 | 0.4 | 0.0 | 0.4 | 0.0 | 0.0 | 0.0 | 0.8 | 0.0 |
| Slightly | 3.5 | 5.2 | 3.4 | 3.3 | 1.7 | 0.8 | 1.6 | 1.6 | 0.2 |
| Somewhat | 47.4 | 45.5 | 41.1 | 35.0 | 34.8 | 40.5 | 35.6 | 31.4 | 26.6 |
| Highly | 48.8 | 48.9 | 55.4 | 61.4 | 63.4 | 58.8 | 62.8 | 66.3 | 73.2 |

Table 3.7    Faculty Self-Report on Teaching Effectiveness, by Discipline (Percent)

| How Effective? | Bio. | Chem. | Math/ Stat. | Engl. | Hist. | Poli. Sci. | Psych. | Soc. |
|---|---|---|---|---|---|---|---|---|
| Not at all | 0.2 | 0.0 | 0.2 | 0.1 | 0.0 | 0.3 | 0.0 | 0.6 |
| Slightly | 2.1 | 3.0 | 2.6 | 0.6 | 1.1 | 2.3 | 2.3 | 3.3 |
| Somewhat | 37.7 | 37.7 | 33.2 | 31.3 | 34.7 | 38.7 | 39.6 | 39.2 |
| Highly | 60.0 | 59.3 | 64.0 | 68.0 | 64.2 | 58.7 | 58.1 | 56.9 |

Table 3.8    Faculty Self-Report on Being a Good Lecturer, by Institutional Type (Percent)

| How Characteristic? | Res-I | Res-II | Doc-I | Doc-II | Comp-I | Comp-II | LAC-I | LAC-II | CC |
|---|---|---|---|---|---|---|---|---|---|
| Not at all | 0.9 | 3.5 | 0.3 | 1.6 | 0.9 | 2.3 | 0.0 | 2.0 | 1.1 |
| Slightly | 15.5 | 22.9 | 14.0 | 14.8 | 10.5 | 17.2 | 10.9 | 16.1 | 9.9 |
| Somewhat | 50.0 | 47.1 | 50.9 | 44.0 | 50.3 | 53.1 | 55.2 | 50.6 | 46.5 |
| Highly | 33.7 | 26.4 | 34.9 | 39.5 | 38.3 | 27.3 | 33.9 | 31.4 | 42.5 |

Table 3.9    Faculty Self-Report on Being a Good Lecturer, by Discipline (Percent)

| How Characteristic? | Bio. | Chem. | Math/ Stat. | Engl. | Hist. | Poli. Sci. | Psych. | Soc. |
|---|---|---|---|---|---|---|---|---|
| Not at all | 0.4 | 0.0 | 0.7 | 2.8 | 0.2 | 1.6 | 1.3 | 1.2 |
| Slightly | 11.5 | 13.2 | 11.6 | 16.3 | 8.9 | 10.7 | 11.6 | 14.6 |
| Somewhat | 51.3 | 47.1 | 54.1 | 46.2 | 45.4 | 47.2 | 51.1 | 50.3 |
| Highly | 36.9 | 39.7 | 33.7 | 34.7 | 45.4 | 40.4 | 36.1 | 33.8 |

*Source:* NCRIPTAL survey.

the different college and university aims. Disciplines differ less when it comes to publishing. However, biology and chemistry faculty judge their competence in securing outside funding higher than do faculty in the other disciplines—simply, one supposes, because there is more money to be obtained in these fields, and consequently faculty have enjoyed more success in acquiring grants.

Table 3.10   Faculty Self-Report on Publishing, by Institutional Type (Percent)

| *How Characteristic?* | Res-I | Res-II | Doc-I | Doc-II | Comp-I | Comp-II | LAC-I | LAC-II | CC |
|---|---|---|---|---|---|---|---|---|---|
| Not at all | 3.5 | 7.0 | 5.4 | 11.8 | 24.1 | 34.6 | 33.3 | 43.6 | 58.9 |
| Slightly | 10.4 | 12.7 | 21.7 | 18.0 | 30.7 | 33.1 | 19.8 | 26.6 | 22.1 |
| Somewhat | 39.6 | 41.0 | 38.2 | 40.8 | 27.6 | 22.3 | 25.0 | 20.1 | 11.7 |
| Highly | 46.5 | 39.3 | 34.8 | 29.4 | 17.5 | 10.0 | 21.9 | 9.7 | 7.2 |

Table 3.11   Faculty Self-Report on Publishing, by Discipline (Percent)

| *How Characteristic?* | Bio. | Chem. | Math/ Stat. | Engl. | Hist. | Poli. Sci. | Psych. | Soc. |
|---|---|---|---|---|---|---|---|---|
| Not at all | 30.4 | 24.2 | 44.2 | 28.3 | 18.8 | 16.5 | 20.3 | 25.7 |
| Slightly | 24.4 | 21.4 | 23.7 | 23.5 | 18.6 | 25.2 | 24.4 | 21.0 |
| Somewhat | 25.1 | .31.1 | 18.3 | 25.8 | 34.4 | 32.0 | 28.8 | 31.4 |
| Highly | 20.1 | 23.3 | 13.8 | 22.3 | 28.2 | 26.2 | 26.5 | 21.9 |

Table 3.12   Faculty Self-Report on Obtaining Grants, by Institutional Type (Percent)

| *How Characteristic?* | Res-I | Res-II | Doc-I | Doc-II | Comp-I | Comp-II | LAC-I | LAC-II | CC |
|---|---|---|---|---|---|---|---|---|---|
| Not at all | 24.9 | 27.1 | 27.6 | 39.8 | 45.9 | 45.8 | 47.1 | 54.7 | 73.2 |
| Slightly | 22.3 | 28.4 | 33.0 | 33.7 | 32.1 | 30.5 | 28.8 | 27.9 | 18.6 |
| Somewhat | 25.3 | 25.8 | 20.5 | 19.1 | 15.3 | 15.3 | 13.1 | 12.8 | 5.6 |
| Highly | 27.5 | 18.8 | 19.0 | 7.3 | 6.6 | 8.4 | 11.0 | 4.7 | 2.7 |

Table 3.13   Faculty Self-Report on Obtaining Grants, by Discipline (Percent)

| *How Characteristic?* | Bio. | Chem. | Math/ Stat. | Engl. | Hist. | Poli. Sci. | Psych. | Soc. |
|---|---|---|---|---|---|---|---|---|
| Not at all | 40.3 | 28.5 | 63.3 | 52.3 | 39.5 | 42.3 | 45.5 | 39.8 |
| Slightly | 24.0 | 27.1 | 22.6 | 27.0 | 29.2 | 28.5 | 30.1 | 31.9 |
| Somewhat | 19.9 | 24.4 | 7.9 | 14.2 | 19.1 | 19.6 | 15.4 | 17.0 |
| Highly | 17.7 | 20.0 | 6.2 | 6.5 | 12.3 | 9.6 | 9.0 | 11.2 |

*Source:* NCRIPTAL survey.

## Influence

More complex than assessing one's competence is assessing one's ability to influence teaching and research outcomes—to take two examples from the survey, student learning and having a manuscript accepted for publication. According to theory, the more specific the outcome, the more accurate should be the estimate of one's influence. Moreover, I expect my success in influencing outcomes to vary more from day to day than my teaching skills. One month I might be able to secure some extra funds from the dean's office for travel to a conference. My efficacy receives a boost. On a later occasion I will be turned down. My efficacy drops.

Tables 3.14–3.17 provide information on teaching and research efficacy. As can be seen, all faculty believe they have an appreciable influence on student learning. However, faculty in doctoral and research universities do not believe it as strongly as do liberal arts and two-year college faculty. Their belief may be weaker because their institutions tend to be larger, and they don't have as much contact with students as do faculty in the institutions more heavily devoted to teaching. Or it may be because they really believe that other sources—student peers, readings, and libraries—primarily influence student learning, and that they as faculty members are not as critical to the educational process. As for faculty believing they can influence decisions about publishing their work, the pattern across institutional types reverses. Res-I faculty express the highest efficacy and CC faculty the lowest. Again, there are few differences across disciplines.

Landino and Owen (1988) and Schoen and Winocur (1988) published the first studies utilizing efficacy as a key variable. Each study has limitations of sample size and response rate. Still, they are important contributions. For example, Schoen and Winocur connect lower self-efficacy scores among female faculty to their concentration in the lower academic ranks. While not a direct measure of productivity, low output correlates with assistant-professor rank. Rieger (1990) found that high-producing faculty were individuals who believed they were well respected as researchers and scholars— that is, their efficacy was strong. In a study of 284 faculty in a variety of schools and colleges within one university, Vasil (1991) obtained a significant relationship between research self-efficacy and research productivity.

## Psychological Characteristics

We postulate that certain personal dispositions relate to the amount of effort given to the different faculty roles. For example, research almost always requires resources above and beyond what the institution can directly provide. It is often necessary to secure outside funding. Moreover, grant seekers outnumber available grants. One infers, then, that the more ambitious and competitive faculty are going to be more successful—better at "grantsmanship," as the saying goes. When we factor-analyzed the data, a third item—perseverance—combined with these two variables; we labeled this factor "personal disposition for research." Publishers tend to attribute

Table 3.14   Faculty Self-Report on Influence on Student Learning, by Institutional Type (Percent)

| How Much Influence? | Res-I | Res-II | Doc-I | Doc-II | Comp-I | Comp-II | LAC-I | LAC-II | CC |
|---|---|---|---|---|---|---|---|---|---|
| Really none | 0.2 | 0.0 | 0.3 | 0.0 | 0.3 | 0.0 | 0.0 | 0.0 | 0.2 |
| Minor | 3.5 | 7.5 | 3.6 | 2.0 | 2.6 | 2.3 | 2.1 | 3.0 | 1.5 |
| Some | 46.4 | 45.2 | 53.1 | 41.8 | 45.2 | 42.0 | 29.2 | 39.2 | 35.7 |
| Substantial | 49.9 | 47.3 | 43.1 | 56.2 | 51.9 | 55.7 | 68.8 | 57.8 | 62.5 |

Table 3.15   Faculty Self-Report on Influence on Student Learning, by Discipline (Percent)

| How Much Influence? | Bio. | Chem. | Math/ Stat. | Engl. | Hist. | Poli. Sci. | Psych. | Soc. |
|---|---|---|---|---|---|---|---|---|
| Really none | 0.4 | 24.2 | 0.3 | 0.1 | 0.2 | 16.5 | 0.2 | 0.3 |
| Minor | 3.1 | 3.9 | 3.1 | 2.7 | 3.4 | 2.5 | 2.9 | 2.4 |
| Some | 35.9 | 40.6 | 38.3 | 37.7 | 50.4 | 46.8 | 43.4 | 53.1 |
| Substantial | 60.6 | 55.6 | 58.3 | 59.5 | 45.9 | 50.8 | 53.5 | 44.2 |

Table 3.16   Faculty Self-Report on Influence on Publication, by Institutional Type (Percent)

| How Much Influence? | Res-I | Res-II | Doc-I | Doc-II | Comp-I | Comp-II | LAC-I | LAC-II | CC |
|---|---|---|---|---|---|---|---|---|---|
| Really none | 5.1 | 9.4 | 6.1 | 7.3 | 14.3 | 21.4 | 16.4 | 17.6 | 20.9 |
| Minor | 8.8 | 12.3 | 19.6 | 17.3 | 22.9 | 23.7 | 19.0 | 25.4 | 24.8 |
| Some | 27.4 | 30.7 | 32.6 | 33.9 | 32.6 | 37.4 | 29.6 | 34.0 | 35.8 |
| Substantial | 58.7 | 47.5 | 41.7 | 41.5 | 30.2 | 17.6 | 34.9 | 23.0 | 18.5 |

Table 3.17   Faculty Self-Report on Influence on Publication, by Discipline (Percent)

| How Much Influence? | Bio. | Chem. | Math/ Stat. | Engl. | Hist. | Poli. Sci. | Psych. | Soc. |
|---|---|---|---|---|---|---|---|---|
| Really none | 10.3 | 11.3 | 20.2 | 15.6 | 15.5 | 10.2 | 7.7 | 13.5 |
| Minor | 18.1 | 19.3 | 24.2 | 25.6 | 15.3 | 21.0 | 14.2 | 18.8 |
| Some | 32.4 | 28.5 | 30.4 | 3.4 | 35.6 | 35.9 | 31.4 | 34.7 |
| Substantial | 39.2 | 40.9 | 25.2 | 24.9 | 33.6 | 33.0 | 46.7 | 32.9 |

*Source:* NCRIPTAL survey.

their successes to their personal characteristics and their failures to external circumstances (Crittenden & Wiley, 1985). We also know that faculty who collaborate with co-authors have a higher acceptance rate of their articles (Smart & Bayer, 1986).

Tables 3.18–3.21 display the differences in self-assessed ambition and competitiveness by institutional type and discipline. While the differences are not exceptionally large, the university faculty believe they are more ambitious and competitive, especially when one combines the two highest categories ("highly" plus "somewhat characteristic"). Res-I faculty are 77 percent (46.1 + 30.9) in the "somewhat" and "highly characteristic" categories for ambition, versus 58 percent for the community college faculty, and 64 percent versus 50 percent for competitiveness. Again, the differences across disciplines are not as strong.

Turning to the personality characteristics of those inclined toward teaching, tables 3.22–3.25 display the data on how personable and supportive faculty feel they are. Faculty in the teaching institutions score higher on these personality dimensions than do faculty working in the research settings. It also appears that the science and mathematics faculty are the lowest on these dimensions, fitting the stereotype of the distant, objective white-coated transmitter of knowledge. Taylor, Locke, Lee, and Gist (1984), in their study of professional faculty in a large public eastern university, found Type A behavior to be directly related to both quantity and quality indices of faculty research productivity. Plomp (1990) used citation data for 338 professors in Dutch medical schools and found, among other things, that individual talent is the most decisive factor in accounting for the most prolific researchers. In a study of highly successful researchers in mass communication, Boice (1989) found that personal motivation was the strongest productivity factor. At the same time, he learned that untenured faculty had their problems with getting published. Procrastination correlated with failure. Christensen and Jansen (1992) had an identical finding in their study of industrial education faculty.

There are, of course, many psychological variables that may be relevant beyond the ones included in our research. For example, there is a growing literature on psychological differences between men and women advanced to explain why Caucasian men are more career-successful than women, especially in the sciences.[9] While most studies do not have measures relating to productivity, we recognize and report them, for future research will likely incorporate them.

Basically, the sexes are intellectually equal (Zuckerman, 1991, p. 34; Fox, 1991, p. 188). However, there appear to be sex differences in some dimensions of intelligence.[10] Women score higher verbally (Tavris & Wade,

Table 3.18   Faculty Self-Report on Ambition, by Institutional Type (Percent)

| How Characteristic? | Res-I | Res-II | Doc-I | Doc-II | Comp-I | Comp-II | LAC-I | LAC-II | CC |
|---|---|---|---|---|---|---|---|---|---|
| Not at all | 3.8 | 8.3 | 3.9 | 5.4 | 8.5 | 10.9 | 7.4 | 7.1 | 9.3 |
| Slightly | 19.2 | 25.2 | 26.5 | 25.2 | 30.9 | 23.4 | 30.3 | 28.1 | 32.4 |
| Somewhat | 46.1 | 42.7 | 43.5 | 46.7 | 40.0 | 39.8 | 40.4 | 45.5 | 35.4 |
| Highly | 30.9 | 23.9 | 2.6 | 22.7 | 20.6 | 25.8 | 21.8 | 19.4 | 23.0 |

Table 3.19   Faculty Self-Report on Ambition, by Discipline (Percent)

| How Characteristic? | Bio. | Chem. | Math/ Stat. | Engl. | Hist. | Poli. Sci. | Psych. | Soc. |
|---|---|---|---|---|---|---|---|---|
| Not at all | 4.9 | 4.5 | 7.2 | 10.8 | 9.7 | 5.0 | 6.0 | 8.4 |
| Slightly | 21.3 | 26.8 | 29.9 | 31.0 | 28.2 | 26.3 | 27.0 | 23.0 |
| Somewhat | 44.7 | 43.6 | 38.5 | 38.4 | 40.8 | 42.7 | 43.2 | 43.5 |
| Highly | 29.1 | 25.1 | 24.3 | 19.8 | 21.4 | 26.0 | 23.8 | 25.2 |

Table 3.20   Faculty Self-Report on Competitiveness, by Institutional Type

| How Characteristic? | Res-I | Res-II | Doc-I | Doc-II | Comp-I | Comp-II | LAC-I | LAC-II | CC |
|---|---|---|---|---|---|---|---|---|---|
| Not at all | 8.2 | 12.8 | 9.6 | 9.5 | 14.2 | 11.7 | 16.6 | 11.9 | 16.5 |
| Slightly | 27.8 | 32.4 | 27.5 | 35.0 | 31.7 | 29.7 | 37.4 | 36.8 | 33.6 |
| Somewhat | 41.0 | 36.5 | 44.5 | 22.2 | 37.4 | 38.3 | 33.7 | 36.4 | 31.5 |
| Highly | 23.0 | 18.3 | 18.5 | 22.2 | 16.7 | 20.3 | 12.3 | 15.0 | 18.4 |

Table 3.21   Faculty Self-Report on Competitiveness, by Discipline (Percent)

| How Characteristic? | Bio. | Chem. | Math/ Stat. | Engl. | Hist. | Poli. Sci. | Psych. | Soc. |
|---|---|---|---|---|---|---|---|---|
| Not at all | 11.0 | 5.7 | 10.1 | 17.9 | 14.6 | 11.0 | 13.8 | 14.6 |
| Slightly | 27.3 | 29.7 | 32.6 | 32.0 | 31.3 | 29.3 | 36.8 | 32.0 |
| Somewhat | 39.6 | 39.2 | 36.5 | 35.3 | 36.3 | 38.0 | 35.1 | 36.0 |
| Highly | 22.1 | 25.4 | 20.8 | 14.8 | 17.8 | 21.7 | 14.3 | 17.4 |

*Source:* NCRIPTAL survey.

1984, p. 42) and lower mathematically (Zuckerman, 1991, p. 49) on the SATs. Men possess better spatial visualization (Fausto-Sterling, 1992, p. 25; Newcombe, Bandura, & Taylor, 1983; Tavris & Wade, 1984, p. 42), an attribute many chemistry faculty believe to be critical for success in their

Table 3.22   Faculty Self-Report on Being Personable, by Institutional Type (Percent)

| How Characteristic? | Res-I | Res-II | Doc-I | Doc-II | Comp-I | Comp-II | LAC-I | LAC-II | CC |
|---|---|---|---|---|---|---|---|---|---|
| Not at all | 2.2 | 1.4 | 0.6 | 0.8 | 0.9 | 0.0 | 0.0 | 1.6 | 0.6 |
| Slightly | 15.2 | 14.7 | 9.6 | 10.7 | 12.2 | 11.7 | 11.8 | 9.5 | 8.3 |
| Somewhat | 49.0 | 48.4 | 48.7 | 54.3 | 50.4 | 50.0 | 38.0 | 49.4 | 41.1 |
| Highly | 33.6 | 35.5 | 41.2 | 34.2 | 36.5 | 38.3 | 50.3 | 39.5 | 50.0 |

Table 3.23   Faculty Self-Report on Being Personable, by Discipline (Percent)

| How Characteristic? | Bio. | Chem. | Math/ Stat. | Engl. | Hist. | Poli. Sci. | Psych. | Soc. |
|---|---|---|---|---|---|---|---|---|
| Not at all | 0.9 | 0.5 | 1.7 | 0.6 | 0.9 | 0.7 | 1.5 | 0.6 |
| Slightly | 11.6 | 12.2 | 11.9 | 10.2 | 10.6 | 12.1 | 11.3 | 11.1 |
| Somewhat | 48.0 | 53.7 | 50.5 | 44.0 | 46.0 | 43.6 | 44.0 | 40.9 |
| Highly | 39.5 | 33.7 | 35.8 | 45.2 | 42.4 | 43.6 | 43.2 | 47.4 |

Table 3.24   Faculty Self-Report on Being Supportive, by Institutional Type (Percent)

| How Characteristic? | Res-I | Res-II | Doc-I | Doc-II | Comp-I | Comp-II | LAC-I | LAC-II | CC |
|---|---|---|---|---|---|---|---|---|---|
| Not at all | 0.4 | 0.0 | 1.2 | 0.4 | 0.6 | 0.0 | 0.0 | 0.0 | 0.0 |
| Slightly | 11.5 | 8.6 | 9.3 | 6.6 | 5.4 | 3.1 | 3.7 | 6.3 | 6.0 |
| Somewhat | 45.4 | 46.4 | 44.3 | 49.0 | 44.1 | 43.0 | 38.3 | 38.7 | 35.2 |
| Highly | 42.7 | 45.0 | 45.2 | 44.0 | 49.9 | 53.9 | 58.0 | 54.9 | 58.8 |

Table 3.25   Faculty Self-Report on Being Supportive, by Discipline (Percent)

| How Characteristic? | Bio. | Chem. | Math/ Stat. | Engl. | Hist. | Poli. Sci. | Psych. | Soc. |
|---|---|---|---|---|---|---|---|---|
| Not at all | 0.2 | 0.0 | 0.5 | 0.2 | 0.9 | 0.7 | 0.2 | 0.0 |
| Slightly | 6.0 | 6.0 | 7.7 | 5.3 | 6.8 | 8.0 | 7.9 | 6.3 |
| Somewhat | 41.8 | 45.2 | 41.1 | 39.8 | 39.9 | 46.2 | 39.8 | 40.6 |
| Highly | 52.1 | 48.8 | 50.7 | 54.7 | 52.4 | 45.2 | 52.1 | 53.1 |

*Source:* NCRIPTAL survey.

discipline (consider the three-dimensional model of atoms and molecules). Data have been interpreted to support hypotheses that men are more logical (Namenwirth, 1986, p. 19) and are better reasoners (Schiebinger, 1987, p. 33). Namenwirth (1986, p. 19) also claims that men are more intelligent and inventive. When trying to make sense of unsorted data, women tend to look for similarities, whereas men note and emphasize differences (Longino & Doell, 1983, p. 185). Women make use of metaphors in coming to know something; men know by "seeing" (Belenky, Clinchy, Goldberger, & Tarule, 1986, pp. 17–18).

Women are more subjective and irrational (Schiebinger, 1987, p. 33; Keller, 1985, p. 7), whereas men are more objective (Keller, 1985, p. 7; Namenwirth, 1986, p. 19). Women are more sensitive, timid, and emotional; men are more courageous and are more frequently risk-takers (Namenwirth, 1986, p. 19). Women have lower expectations for success; men are more certain of their authority (Belenky et al., 1986, p. 221) and more forceful (Namenwirth, 1986, p. 19). Men can be more driven and competitive than women (Fox & Faver, 1981, pp. 131–132; Hamovich & Morgenstern, 1977; Keller & Moglen, 1987). Male faculty enjoy the institutional research image more than their female colleagues do (Fulton & Trow, 1974).

Female scientists think they are not taken seriously and believe they are less competent than their male colleagues (e.g., Etaugh & Kasley, 1981; Frieze & Hanusa, 1984; Ramaley, 1978; Tidball, 1976; Widom & Burke, 1978; Zuckerman & Cole, 1975). Astin's (1969) early report speculated that women with more publications had a stronger sense of self-competence, thus leading to more publications. More recently, Linn and Hyde (1989) stated that sex differences in confidence may contribute to differential career success.

Fear of female success has conflicting support—Horner (1972) claims yes and Paludi (1987) says no. Women fear a loss of femininity, whereas men are more aggressive (Tavris & Wade, 1984, p. 43; Fausto-Sterling, 1992, p. 123), hasty, and fickle (Fausto-Sterling, 1992, p. 156). Women are more likely to attribute success to luck, whereas men attribute their successes to skill (Belenky et al., 1986, p. 196; Zuckerman, 1991, p. 79). Keller (1985, pp. 9, 70) sees men as more impersonal and disinterested, more alienated and autonomous. Namenwirth (1986, pp. 20–21) views men as potent, powerful, fearless, authoritative, and dominating. Belenky et al. (1986, p. 115) see men as fearing intimacy. Women are also seen as more easily depressed (Fausto-Sterling, 1992, p. 155), self-sacrificing, self-effacing, and modest (Namenwirth, 1986, p. 19). While seen as more passive, women respond to positive reinforcement (Astin, 1991, p. 59; Cole & Zuckerman, 1984).

The psychological-need literature is sparse for sex differences. Women have a need for encouragement, whereas men's needs are for prestige, personal power, authority, and dominance (Hood, 1985, pp. 114–116;

Namenwirth, 1986, pp. 19–21). Fausto-Sterling (1992, p. 123) says women possess a need for attachment, whereas men need to dominate.

Women value home (love and family) and nature, whereas men value work and the mind. Women value feeling; men accord reason a higher value (Blackman, 1986; Keller, 1985, pp. 9, 63; Trigg & Perlman, 1976).[11] Astin (1978) finds that women's goals are to facilitate, help, and provide direction; men's are to contribute to theory.[12] Belenky et al. (1986, p. 208) say women's goals are to please; men's are to grow intellectually. Fausto-Sterling (1992, p. 6; 1989, p. 319) says men have a desire to provide.

When it comes to interpersonal relationships, women favor warmth and attachment; men prefer power over another (Keller, 1985, p. 7). Women value kindness and dependence in a relationship; men seek independence (Namenwirth, 1986, p. 19). Women prefer connectedness versus detachment, closeness and empathy versus distance (Belenky et al., 1986, pp. 226–229). Women listen; men speak (p. 45). Women start with affirmation; men wait for it (p. 194). Women value community and collaboration and want network patterns to evolve; men expect a hierarchy, arbitrary requirements, and adversarial relationships (pp. 221, 229). Women have difficulty asserting authority, considering themselves as authorities, expressing themselves in public, gaining the respect of others, and utilizing their abilities at work (p. 45).

As stated at the outset, correlations with research productivity are not known. If evidence supports the hypothetical relationships advanced above, we will still need to explore the effects on faculty outside the natural and physical sciences, for women are having better career success in the social sciences and the humanities, at least in some disciplines.[13] One expects other differences to arise when researchers incorporate female racial and ethnic minorities.

Fox (1985b, pp. 260–261) has reviewed the literature that extends beyond motivation and attitude. While most of these studies involve small and unrepresentative samples, and the inferences are more frequently suggestive rather than demonstrative, we reproduce Fox's important contribution:

> A second variant of this perspective focuses not so much on motivation and attitude as on "stamina" or the capacity to work hard, tolerate frustration, and persist in the pursuit of long-range goals (Merton, 1973; Zuckerman, 1970). A third variety of the psychological perspective is represented by clinical investigations of (1) the emotional styles (Cattell and Drevdahl, 1955; Knapp, 1963; Roe, 1953, 1964); (2) the biographical backgrounds—early childhood experiences, sources of satisfaction and dissatisfaction, attitudes, values, and interests (Chambers, 1964; Roe, 1952; Stein, 1962; Taylor and Banon, 1975; Taylor and Ellison, 1967); and (3) the cognitive

structure of productive scientists (Cropley and Field, 1969; Eiduson, 1962; Gordon and Morse, 1970; Selye, 1964; Wilkes, 1980).

From the above studies, we find that certain psychological and attitudinal factors do correlate with publication. The biographical studies, especially, make clear that autonomy or self-direction is characteristic of the most productive. This is apparent in their early preferences for teachers who let them alone, in attitudes toward religion, and in personal relations. Productive scientists and scholars tend to be detached from their immediate families and wider social relations and attached, instead, to the inanimate objects and abstract ideas of their work (Chambers, 1964; Stein, 1962; Taylor and Ellison, 1967).

Further, data suggest the superior stamina of the high producers, revealing them as absorbed, involved, and indefatigable workers (Bernard, 1964; Eiduson, 1962; Pelz and Andrews, 1976; Zuckerman, 1970). Driven by curiosity, ambition, or need for achievement, high producers tend to organize their lives around their work.

In cognitive and perceptual styles, productive scholars and scientists also exhibit certain modes of perceiving and thinking, including a capacity to play with ideas, stave off intellectual closure, and tolerate ambiguity and abstraction (Eiduson, 1962; Gordon and Morse, 1970; Selye, 1964). The emphasis here is upon style rather than level of ability. Measured ability level, in fact, correlates very weakly with productivity and achievement in science (Cole and Cole, 1973). Although high IQ may be a prerequisite for doctoral training, once the degree is obtained, differences in measured ability do not predict subsequent levels of performance (Cole and Cole, 1973). Rather, persons with equal ability differ markedly in the way they deploy intellectual resources (see Cropley and Field, 1969).

The fundamental problem of the psychological perspective is that personality traits and attributes do not exist in a vacuum (Andrews, 1975). These individual traits and dispositions are strongly affected by the social and organizational context in which they exist. Andrews discovered that measured creativity, for example, does not result in productivity unless scientists have strong motivation, diverse activities, and the capacity to exercise power and influence over decisions. Likewise, other studies fail to support a direct relationship between measured creativity and measured performance (Connor, 1974; Gordon and Morse, 1970), and suggest the "interface of psychological capability and organizational requisite" (Gordon and Morse, 1970) as the nexus of research performance. However, unlike Andrews' investigation, these others do not actually test the extent to which organizational context mediates psychological characteristics and productivity. Thus, the link between individual attributes and environments remains a critical area for investigation.

Compared to the large number of psychological studies, those on work habits are few, and the commentary on the subject tends to be speculative (see, for example, Stinchcombe, 1966). Exceptions include Hargens' (1978) study, which focuses upon disciplinary context, and Simon's (1974) study of the work practices of eminent scholars. Hargens' work reports that habits relate to productivity according to the level of "routine" or "predictability" in the work. Thus in chemistry, a more routinized discipline, time spent in research and engagement in multiple projects are associated with productivity, while in less routinized fields such as mathematics these work practices have a weak to non-existent impact upon output. Simon's study reports that, as a group, eminent scholars have certain work patterns: they devote enormous time to research (some working 365 days of the year); they work on several projects at once; they tend to devote mornings to writing.

### Satisfaction/Morale

Many postulate that satisfaction with work and career relates to productivity. Low-morale workers contest the organization's expectations. Satisfied workers turn out more and better products. This rationale's attractiveness, however, exceeds the evidence supporting it. McNeece (1981) learned that job satisfaction had little effect on the publication rates of graduate social work faculty.

Most surveys employ indirect and questionable measures of satisfaction and morale. Instead of being asked directly how satisfied they are with their career, faculty have had to express a degree of agreement/disagreement with such statements as "This (the college I am at) is a good place for me" and "If I were to start my career over, I would become a professor." While many of the national surveys contain these or parallel items, they unfortunately do not ask them in an identical way. Inquiring as to whether one would become a professor again given an opportunity to start afresh will not produce the same percentage of positive responses as negative responses when the question is asked in the opposite manner, that is, "Given a chance to start over, would you *not* become a professor?"

Other difficulties reside with the construct's questionable reliability, its openness to fluctuations, and the changes in the ways the environment responds to faculty. Today I may have had a proposal turned down; tomorrow I may receive public recognition for my work. My "typical" morale is not likely to be the same on both days.

Despite the shortcomings of the measures, the studies show a consistent outcome. Studies consistently tell us that older, tenured, full professors are the most satisfied faculty. (See, e.g., Clark, 1986.)

Ascertaining the direction of the relationship between satisfaction and productivity also presents a problem. Is it that faculty who are satisfied produce more? Or is it that successful faculty producing more experience greater satisfaction? With these issues and limitations in mind, we report the few studies relating satisfaction and morale with productivity.

Bowen and Schuster's (1986) interviews with faculty present a gloomy picture of life in academe in the mid-1980s. Unfortunately, their data are not linked with faculty publication records, so we do not know if low morale and high dissatisfaction are related. Terpstra, Olson, and Lockerman (1982) uncovered for business and economics professors a negative relationship between their publication output and their satisfaction with a new management system in their organization. The more they disliked the system, the more they produced. On the other hand, there are conditions that lead to reduced faculty output. Kerlin and Dunlap's (1993) recent case study of the prolonged austerity and retrenchment in Oregon's higher-education system shows the very low morale of faculty and their perceptions that the necessary support for research has eroded precipitously. One predicts that faculty publications will drop should this state persist for long.

## Social Knowledge

By a faculty member's social knowledge we mean her or his perceptions of various aspects of the work environment. Faculty form beliefs from experiences with colleagues, administrators, committee decisions, faculty meetings, institutional rules and norms, and professional association practices. These beliefs constitute their social knowledge.

Faculty need not be accurate and correct in their judgments of what behaviors the different constituencies reward. Still, these perceptions motivate their behaviors. In addition, faculty regularly test their social knowledge. They receive feedback on their behaviors (e.g., a merit salary increase after obtaining a grant; no merit increase for advising additional students). Some environmental responses confirm the currently held social knowledge. Other responses motivate faculty to revise their environmental perceptions and to modify their behaviors. In part, social knowledge follows from self-knowledge and from environmental responses to faculty behaviors. (See figure 1.1.) We expect social knowledge, then, to motivate and account for faculty behaviors.

We select those indicators that most frequently have been assessed at different points in time. Unfortunately, as was the case with self-knowledge variables, the items are not always identical from survey to survey. Inferences about changes have to be made with caution. Moreover, the earlier surveys have few social knowledge indicators, so some that we employ in our theoretical framework exist only for the 1988 NCRIPTAL data collection.

Faculty perceptions of the support they receive influence their motivations for engaging in some activities and not in others. The devotion of energy to creating new courses and learning new pedagogical techniques dampens when one sees that necessary resources are hard to come by and senior faculty believe such effort has no value. Professors have knowledge of support (both social and material), institutional preferences for how they should allocate their effort, and the reward structure of the organization.

## Social Support

A professor's decision to act in some ways and not in others is influenced by comments—especially feedback received from colleagues, but also that from students and administrators. These we call social responses. (Money and specialized technological assistance are also critical. These we call material variables. See below.)

## Colleague Commitment

Faculty estimate colleagues' commitment to the various roles by their expressions and actions—across the campus and, particularly, within the department. Our colleague commitment measure is a factor that expresses the perceived strength of faculty commitment in the institution as a whole and within the member's department. By way of illustration, table 3.26 selectively displays the comparisons across three institutional types and three disciplines for colleague commitment to the teaching role. The scores can range from a low of 0 to a high of 4.

The pattern resembles that seen when faculty expressed their interest in teaching. (See table 3.3 above.) Faculty in CCs perceive a higher departmental and institutional commitment to teaching than do faculty in Comp-I's and Res-I's, the latter perceiving the lowest commitment level. Res-I English faculty perceive higher commitment than do their colleagues across campus. (They also expressed a higher personal interest in and preference for teach-

Table 3.26  Colleague Commitment to Teaching

|  | English | | Chemistry | | Psychology | |
|---|---|---|---|---|---|---|
|  | Mean | SD | Mean | SD | Mean | SD |
| CCs | 3.55 | 0.63 | 3.79 | 0.54 | 3.73 | 0.54 |
| Comp-I's | 3.19 | 0.63 | 3.30 | 0.69 | 3.22 | 0.71 |
| Res-I's | 2.89 | 0.68 | 2.64 | 0.69 | 2.40 | 0.60 |

*Source:* NCRIPTAL survey.

*Note:* Numbers are standardized scores that can range from 0 (low) to 4 (high).

ing.) That difference, however, does not hold for English faculty in the two other institutional types.

Colleague commitment also accompanies the norms of behavior, including publication output. In their study of 84 professors at a large midwestern university, Jauch, Glueck, and Osborn (1978) found no relationship between a faculty member's institutional loyalty and her or his productivity. However, researchers with the strongest professional commitment, that is, commitment to their discipline, had higher research productivity. In a study of 179 chemists, biologists, physicists, and mathematicians who changed institutions between 1961 and 1965, Allison and Long (1990) found that scientists who moved to universities whose departmental national rating was appreciably higher than that of the institution they had left increased their productivity 25 percent. For scientists who moved to lower-rated departments, there was a substantial decrease in both their average number of publications and the average number of citations to their publications. Braxton (1983) has supporting data.

*Intellectual Climate*

A related construct is intellectual climate—the atmosphere in which faculty work, the stimulation they receive from immediate colleagues on their campus, scholars who visit to present colloquia and lectures, researchers they know professionally, graduate students, professional association meetings and committees, and the like. When the atmosphere is a lively, stimulating one, faculty can float an idea, even a half-baked one, and receive a considered response. A professor can obtain the reinforcement needed to plunge on. For many, good colleagues are sources of ideas, criticism, and even pressure to do good work—encouragement and very strong motivation.

Several studies over the years and across disciplines support the relationship between this construct and publication output. Babchuk and Bates (1962), Blau (1973), Braxton (1983), de Meuse (1987), Fox and Faver (1982, 1984), Louis, Blumenthal, Gluck, and Stoto (1988), Oromaner (1975), Over (1982), Parsons and Platt (1968), Pelz and Andrews (1976), and Reskin (1978) find positive relationships between the intellectual climate colleagues provide and publication rate. Blau's (1974) study of a physics group concluded that the most effective environment for production was a few direct associates in the ongoing research project and a wider set of colleagues who knew the relevant theory.

Paisley (1972) and Perrucci, O'Flaherty, and Marshall (1983) have studies involving communications with peers around the world. This is a phenomenon Price and Beaver (1966) and Crane (1965, 1972) called the "invisible college," a no-formal-structure organization.[14] High-producing individuals actively interact with colleagues quite irrespective of geographical constraints, with communications made easier daily by electronic mail networks.

## Consensus and Support

Enjoying colleague consensus about matters that affect teaching—for example, what the content of the curriculum should be—allows one to engage in pedagogical endeavors knowing that those who matter support one's effort. Motivation to devote effort to teaching should be low when there is a lack of agreement, or even conflict, as to what is to be taught and how. When faculty also judge that adequate support facilities exist, physical (laboratories, libraries) as well as human (clerical and student assistance)— that is, when they feel that the institution seems to care about good teaching—motivation to devote effort to instructional matters should be high.

These two items, consensus and support, combined in our analysis to form a single factor. Table 3.27 reveals that there were no strong differences among institutional types. Overall, chemistry faculty perceived the strongest consensus and support for teaching. How important this difference is with respect to outcome variables such as grants obtained or research published has not been tested. The difference favoring consensus within chemistry over English and psychology may be nothing more than a fairly long established agreement within the discipline, an agreement reinforced by the American Chemical Society, as to what constitutes a basic curriculum (one a department must have in order to receive accreditation).

## Leadership

Leadership—the activities of the department chair—has a weak relationship with productivity, even when the chair is lending moral as well as

Table 3.27 Faculty Consensus Regarding Teaching

|  | English | | Chemistry | | Psychology | |
|---|---|---|---|---|---|---|
|  | *Mean* | *SD* | *Mean* | *SD* | *Mean* | *SD* |
| CCs | 3.10 | 1.00 | 3.37 | 0.92 | 3.07 | 0.96 |
| Comp-I's | 2.74 | 1.10 | 3.19 | 1.00 | 2.94 | 0.88 |
| Res-I's | 2.79 | 1.10 | 3.18 | 0.89 | 2.93 | 0.85 |

*Source:* NCRIPTAL survey.

*Note:* Numbers are standardized scores that can range from 0 (low) to 4 (high).

monetary support (Coltrin & Glueck, 1977; Glueck & Thorp, 1974). Hill and French (1967) actually found a negative relationship: faculty who were more negative about departmental leadership published more.

Our NCRIPTAL studies had little success with this variable. In general, faculty gave little credence to feedback they received from their chairs. Whether it concerned their teaching, their research, or their scholarship, faculty valued more highly the assessment of their colleagues and their students. Moreover, when we asked them to evaluate their immediate superior (chair, in most all cases) in terms of skills, values, professionalism, experience/background, and personality (see question 12 of the survey reproduced in appendix H), faculty seldom differentiated their responses. They tended to rate the person either consistently high or consistently low on all dimensions. The place of leadership for faculty as it relates to enhancing creative work needs extended investigation.

### Material Support

Conducting research costs money. One expense is that fraction of a professor's salary allocated to research, a proportion that can range from essentially zero to nearly 100 percent. Even a small research activity requires funding in the form of equipment (books, chemicals, computers), professional interaction (phone calls, conference attendance), and professional assistance (students, clericals). As one moves into big science one adds to this list expensive machines plus extensive building space, with their overhead costs. The need for dollars quickly exceeds institutional resources.

The funding agency's grant normally includes salary money for the professor, dollars available to hire another professor to teach what the faculty member with the grant normally teaches. Faculty with grants, then, not only have motivations to do more research—they competed for the money to aid their research efforts—but they also have time and support. One expects faculty with grants to be more productive than those without. Several studies confirm the expectation. (See, e.g., Bentley, 1990; Liebert, 1976, 1977; Meador et al., 1992; Neumann, 1978; Pfeffer & Konrad, 1991; Williams & Blackburn, 1988.) However, Rong, Grant, and Ward (1989) do not find this to be true for women.

One also expects faculty at institutions with richer resources to publish more. This expectation is confirmed by Van House's (1990) study of the relationship between library resources—more serials, larger collections, more professional librarians—and number of publications by science and engineering faculty, a link Cartter (1966) established some time ago. This finding is also supported by Rushton and Meltzer (1981).

### Perceived Institutional Preference

#### Preference for Teaching

As free as faculty are to allocate their effort to different activities, they hold beliefs about how their college or university wants them to spend their time and what their institution expects them to accomplish. Faculty behaviors are motivated by perceived institutional preferences on time allocation to the principal roles of teaching and research.[15]

Table 3.28 displays data on percentage of time allotted to teaching: (1) the actual time allocation reported by faculty, (2) the allocation they believe their institution prefers, and (3) the allocation they themselves prefer. The first and third categories (interest and personal preference) are self-knowledge variables, while the second (institutional preference) is a social knowledge variable.

Conspicuous differences in time allocated to teaching appear across institutional types. Differences across disciplines are smaller within institutional types. On average, CC faculty reported twice as much time given to teaching as did Res-I faculty (70 percent vs. 35 percent). All faculty said they believe their institutions would prefer them to give less effort to teaching than they

Table 3.28  Preference for Teaching (Percent)

|  | English | | Chemistry | | Psychology | |
|---|---|---|---|---|---|---|
|  | *Mean* | *SD* | *Mean* | *SD* | *Mean* | *SD* |
| *Time allocation reported* | | | | | | |
| CCs | 70 | 16 | 75 | 16 | 66 | 19 |
| Comp-I's | 62 | 18 | 63 | 18 | 54 | 18 |
| Res-I's | 44 | 21 | 29 | 17 | 32 | 14 |
| *Time allocation preferred by institution* | | | | | | |
| CCs | 66 | 17 | 75 | 12 | 67 | 18 |
| Comp-I's | 52 | 20 | 56 | 16 | 52 | 19 |
| Res-I's | 46 | 16 | 31 | 12 | 28 | 12 |
| *Time allocation preferred by faculty* | | | | | | |
| CCs | 60 | 16 | 68 | 17 | 60 | 17 |
| Comp-I's | 53 | 16 | 55 | 16 | 46 | 16 |
| Res-I's | 37 | 13 | 28 | 10 | 26 | 13 |

*Source:* NCRIPTAL survey.

do (68 percent at CCs, 53 percent at Comp-I's, and 31 percent at Res-I's). At the same time, most faculty would prefer to do even less teaching than they believe the institution expects (62 percent at CCs, 51 percent at Comp-I's, and 31 percent at Res-I's). CC and Comp-I faculty would prefer to do some 8–9 percent less teaching than they currently do; Res-I faculty would prefer about 4 percent less.

Somewhat more variation in time given to teaching prevails across disciplines in the research universities. Faculty with access to grants (e.g., in chemistry and psychology) earn teaching-released time. English faculty have less external funding. They give appreciably above the institutional average in teaching time. Furthermore, humanities faculty have traditionally taken teaching as a fundamental component of their profession, a basic value that differentiates them from natural and social science faculty.

On average, the actual allocated effort and the perceived percentage the institution prefers closely agree, the largest differences (about 10 percent) occurring with English faculty in Comp-I's. They spend more time teaching than they think their institution wants them to and more than they would prefer to give.

At the same time, the standard deviations are around 15 percent, a number sufficiently large to indicate that even when agreement exists on average, appreciable variation persists within each of the disciplines and within each of the institutional types. Many faculty have not surrendered to the institution's perceived desire.

*Preference for Research, Scholarship, and Service*

Remember that in our framework, "research" deals with published products, whereas "scholarship" involves keeping up-to-date with the literature and other intellectual activity. (See the definitions in question 13 of appendix H.) With respect to interest in research, we found (as expected) very high percentages in research universities and low percentages in Comp-II's, LAC-I's and -II's, and CCs. Personal preferences for time given to research follow the same pattern. In the universities, perceived institutional preference and personal preference are similar. However, in the Comp-II's, LAC-I's and -II's, and CCs, personal preference for time given to research is less than what faculty believe the administration wants.

As for scholarship, personal preference and actual effort are in accord, and both are less than what faculty perceive their institutions to prefer. This is true across all institutional types. Similarly, personal preference and perceived institutional preference for time given to service are essentially the same across all institutional types, with faculty unexpectedly preferring to give a little more effort than they believe the administration wants.

### Who and What the Institution Values

As will be seen in chapter 7 on administrator and faculty views of the workplace, appreciable differences sometimes exist between the two constituencies as to who and what is valued. (The differences vary by institutional type.) Irrespective of which group, if either, has the correct perception, faculty will continue to be motivated by their perception of the environment—what it honors, values, and rewards. There may be talk about good teaching or making contributions to the community or state, but if faculty do not see these activities rewarded, such talk may even be a negative motivator. That is, the credence accorded to administrators may weaken, and their ability to lead may diminish.

Empirical evidence to support these assertions is slim. What does exist are a few studies that correlate salary, an external reward, with faculty publications (Hansen, Weisbrod, & Strauss, 1978; Lewis, Wanner, & Gregorio, 1979; Tuckman, 1976). The correlations are positive, and the salary benefit, when accrued over time, is appreciable for high publishers. What clouds the correlation, however, is the causal direction of the relationship. The economists (e.g., Tuckman) conclude that faculty publish in order to earn more money. Those who believe the principal motivation to be intrinsic (e.g., McKeachie, 1979b) say that faculty publish because they like to. It just so happens that their institution rewards them more than it does those who publish less.

## Behaviors

We now turn to the penultimate category of variables that lead to products, namely behaviors, a construct we developed at the outset of chapter 2. As seen in figure 1.1, it is the faculty members' social knowledge that leads to behaviors, which in turn lead to the products they produce.[16] (Note the heavy arrows.)

Our theoretical framework postulates that motivations lead to behaviors, to activities in the domains of teaching, research, scholarship, and service. To the extent that they have options, faculty members will allocate their efforts to those activities toward which they are most motivated—by interest, by self-knowledge concerning their competence and their chances of success, and by the social knowledge they trust with regard to what students, peers, and administrators value and reward. Presumably, then, that effort will lead to products.

While all of the above runs consistent with our theoretical framework, only a few studies link behaviors to outcomes—time spent teaching linked to a new syllabus, a computerized course package, a new set of lectures; time spent conducting research linked to a scientific invention, an article in a scholarly journal; time spent chairing dissertations linked to joint publications; time spent in the scholarship role linked to giving collegewide lectures, presentations at scholarly conferences; time spent performing service linked to a revised curriculum, a new major and minor sequence, an improved governance structure. The absence most likely stems from the difficulty of establishing agreed-upon measures of outcomes (products) and adequate indicators beyond time spent with regard to the activities. For example, does the activity of reading a large number of works to prepare a lecture lead to better student learning?[17]

The exception to this vast void involves faculty grant activity. Grant activity does not include the effort given to preparing grant proposals—no small amount of time and energy; rather, it entails the consequences of a successful proposal. Working with grant support correlates with publications. Table 3.29 exhibits the number and percentage of faculty in Res-I through Comp-I institutions who received different types of grants at four different points in time. While the percentage of faculty who have received federal grants has remained nearly constant, appreciable increases have taken place in both institutional and "other" funding sources (e.g., state,

Table 3.29   Distribution of Faculty Receiving Grants in Past Year, by Grant Type

|  | 1969 | | 1975 | | 1980 | | 1988 | |
|---|---|---|---|---|---|---|---|---|
|  | N | % | N | % | N | % | N | % |
| *Institutional* | | | | | | | | |
| Yes | 1,187 | 38 | 1,455 | 43 | 581 | 39 | 1,345 | 59 |
| No | 1,870 | 61 | 1,916 | 56 | 892 | 60 | 899 | 40 |
| *Federal* | | | | | | | | |
| Yes | 694 | 23 | 769 | 23 | 364 | 24 | 477 | 22 |
| No | 2,332 | 77 | 2,558 | 76 | 1,111 | 75 | 1,680 | 77 |
| *Industrial* | | | | | | | | |
| Yes | 71 | 2 | 127 | 4 | 60 | 4 | 132 | 6 |
| No | 2,956 | 97 | 3,012 | 96 | 1,413 | 95 | 1,933 | 93 |
| *Other*[a] | | | | | | | | |
| Yes | 454 | 14 | 611 | 17 | 229 | 15 | 583 | 27 |
| No | 2,633 | 85 | 2,899 | 82 | 1,244 | 84 | 1,575 | 73 |

*Source:* National surveys.

a. Includes state and local governments, foundations, and unspecified.

local government, and foundation grants). When it comes to actual dollars, table 3.30 shows that federal monies, while having dropped from over 70 percent of the dollars awarded to 60 percent, remain by far faculty's principal grant source.

Table 3.31 shows the variations among the eight disciplines we have been examining. The sciences, including psychology, receive the giant share of the federal and industrial dollars, whereas the humanities depend almost exclusively on institutional and "other" sources, both appreciably smaller in real dollar amounts.

The National Science Board (1981) data demonstrate a striking decline in the output of articles by U.S. mathematicians after the severe drop in federal grants that occurred during the 1970s. Bentley and Blackburn (1991) have demonstrated how institutional grant acquisition can accumulate over time so that those universities that had more get more, the same

Table 3.30  Support for U.S. Academic R&D, by Grant Type

|  | Institutional | | Federal | | Industrial | | Other | |
|---|---|---|---|---|---|---|---|---|
|  | $ | % | $ | % | $ | % | $ | % |
| 1969 (est.) | 223 | 10.0 | 1,600 | 71.9 | 60 | 2.7 | 342 | 15.4 |
| 1970 | 243 | 10.4 | 1,647 | 70.5 | 61 | 2.6 | 384 | 16.5 |
| 1971 | 274 | 11.0 | 1,724 | 69.0 | 70 | 2.8 | 432 | 17.2 |
| 1972 | 305 | 11.6 | 1,795 | 68.3 | 74 | 2.8 | 456 | 17.3 |
| 1973 | 318 | 11.0 | 1,985 | 68.8 | 84 | 2.9 | 497 | 17.3 |
| 1974 | 368 | 12.2 | 2,032 | 67.2 | 95 | 3.1 | 527 | 17.5 |
| 1975 | 417 | 12.3 | 2,288 | 67.3 | 113 | 3.3 | 581 | 17.1 |
| 1976 | 446 | 12.0 | 2,512 | 67.3 | 123 | 3.3 | 649 | 17.4 |
| 1977 | 514 | 12.6 | 2,726 | 67.0 | 139 | 3.4 | 688 | 17.0 |
| 1978 | 625 | 13.5 | 3,059 | 66.1 | 170 | 3.7 | 771 | 16.7 |
| 1979 | 726 | 13.6 | 3,593 | 67.1 | 194 | 3.6 | 844 | 15.7 |
| 1980 | 835 | 13.8 | 4,096 | 67.6 | 238 | 3.9 | 892 | 14.7 |
| 1981 | 1,009 | 14.7 | 4,561 | 66.6 | 293 | 4.3 | 982 | 14.4 |
| 1982 | 1,122 | 15.3 | 4,759 | 65.0 | 339 | 4.6 | 1,104 | 15.1 |
| 1983 | 1,315 | 16.7 | 4,980 | 63.2 | 388 | 4.9 | 1,201 | 15.2 |
| 1984 | 1,424 | 16.5 | 5,425 | 62.9 | 474 | 5.5 | 1,301 | 15.1 |
| 1985 | 1,632 | 16.8 | 6,064 | 62.6 | 556 | 5.8 | 1,439 | 14.8 |
| 1986 | 1,877 | 17.2 | 6,713 | 61.4 | 692 | 6.3 | 1,643 | 15.1 |
| 1987 | 2,126 | 17.6 | 7,326 | 60.6 | 777 | 6.4 | 1,853 | 15.4 |
| 1988 (est.) | 2,346 | 18.0 | 7,800 | 60.0 | 850 | 6.5 | 2,004 | 15.5 |

*Source:* National Science Board (1989), pp. 296–297.
*Note:* Dollars in millions.

Table 3.31 Distribution of Faculty Receiving Grants in Past Year, by Discipline and Grant Type

|  | 1969 | | 1975 | | 1980 | | 1988 | |
|---|---|---|---|---|---|---|---|---|
|  | N | % | N | % | N | % | N | % |
| *Institutional* | | | | | | | | |
| Chemistry | 234 | 20.2 | 268 | 18.4 | 104 | 17.9 | 165 | 12.3 |
| Mathematics | 82 | 7.1 | 125 | 8.6 | 44 | 7.6 | 168 | 12.5 |
| Biology | 191 | 16.5 | 254 | 17.5 | 97 | 16.7 | 197 | 14.6 |
| Psychology | 192 | 14 | 231 | 15.9 | 66 | 11.4 | 186 | 13.8 |
| Sociology | 82 | 7.1 | 120 | 8.2 | 55 | 9.5 | 110 | 8.2 |
| Political science | 94 | 8.1 | 108 | 7.4 | 51 | 8.8 | 124 | 9.2 |
| English | 161 | 13.9 | 202 | 13.9 | 93 | 16.0 | 235 | 17.5 |
| History | 151 | 13.1 | 147 | 10.1 | 71 | 12.2 | 160 | 11.9 |
| Total | 1,187 | 100.0 | 1,455 | 100.0 | 581 | 100.0 | 1,345 | 100.0 |
| *Federal* | | | | | | | | |
| Chemistry | 160 | 23.1 | 159 | 20.7 | 72 | 19.8 | 96 | 20.1 |
| Mathematics | 144 | 20.7 | 132 | 17.2 | 63 | 17.3 | 65 | 13.6 |
| Biology | 139 | 20.0 | 166 | 21.6 | 67 | 18.4 | 96 | 20.1 |
| Psychology | 123 | 17.7 | 120 | 15.6 | 56 | 15.4 | 62 | 13.0 |
| Sociology | 56 | 8.1 | 63 | 8.2 | 25 | 6.9 | 44 | 9.2 |
| Political science | 29 | 4.2 | 50 | 6.5 | 22 | 6.0 | 30 | 6.3 |
| English | 14 | 2.0 | 32 | 4.2 | 28 | 7.7 | 42 | 8.8 |
| History | 29 | 4.2 | 47 | 6.1 | 31 | 8.5 | 42 | 8.8 |
| Total | 694 | 100.0 | 769 | 100.0 | 364 | 100.0 | 477 | 100.0 |
| *Industry* | | | | | | | | |
| Chemistry | 31 | 43.7 | 38 | 29.9 | 22 | 36.7 | 35 | 26.5 |
| Mathematics | 13 | 18.3 | 13 | 10.2 | 9 | 15 | 19 | 14.4 |
| Biology | 9 | 12.7 | 40 | 31.5 | 4 | 16.7 | 27 | 20.5 |
| Psychology | 3 | 4.2 | 14 | 11 | 11 | 18.3 | 13 | 9.8 |
| Sociology | 4 | 5.6 | 1 | 0.8 | 4 | 6.7 | 16 | 12.1 |
| Political science | 3 | 4.2 | 11 | 8.7 | 5 | 8.3 | 9 | 6.8 |
| English | 6 | 8.5 | 5 | 3.9 | 0 | 0 | 9 | 6.8 |
| History | 2 | 2.8 | 5 | 3.9 | 5 | 8.3 | 4 | 3 |
| Total | 71 | 100.0 | 127 | 100.0 | 60 | 100.0 | 132 | 100.0 |
| *Other*[a] | | | | | | | | |
| Chemistry | 86 | 18.9 | 106 | 17.3 | 47 | 20.5 | 84 | 14.4 |
| Mathematics | 19 | 4.2 | 31 | 5.1 | 15 | 6.6 | 58 | 9.9 |
| Biology | 69 | 15.2 | 126 | 20.6 | 46 | 20.1 | 103 | 17.7 |
| Psychology | 58 | 12.8 | 77 | 12.6 | 19 | 8.3 | 60 | 10.3 |
| Sociology | 37 | 8.1 | 62 | 10.1 | 29 | 12.7 | 62 | 10.6 |
| Political science | 52 | 11.5 | 68 | 11.1 | 21 | 9.2 | 63 | 10.8 |
| English | 69 | 15.2 | 54 | 8.8 | 23 | 10 | 75 | 12.9 |
| History | 64 | 14.1 | 87 | 12.2 | 29 | 12.7 | 78 | 13.4 |
| Total | 454 | 100.0 | 611 | 100 | 229 | 100.0 | 583 | 100.0 |

*Source:* National surveys.
a. Includes state and local governments, foundations, and unspecified.

phenomenon seen before with respect to individual faculty. These are the universities with the high-producing faculty.

## Environmental Constructs

### *Environmental Conditions*

As indicated in chapter 1, our theoretical framework recognizes that factors outside the workplace can affect publication output (and other kinds of behaviors and products as well). As obvious as many effects are—for example, foundation or federal funding in new areas spawning research, or conversely the stopping of external dollars reducing output—they have not been documented in the literature. In addition, money is not the only environmental stimulant. National commissions on curricula and teaching have sent some institutions into overhauling their academic programs. However, scholars rarely trace cause and effect and report it in the literature.

### *Environmental Response*

As the theoretical framework makes clear, publications can lead to an environmental response. They can result in a promotion, tenure, a merit raise, increased clerical support, more money for attending national conferences, a graduate research assistant. Such outcomes, singularly or collectively, will act on both one's self-knowledge and one's social knowledge. One's assessment of one's competence as a researcher is likely to rise, and one's view of what the organization values will probably be altered. If what happened was what was expected, the confirmation will strengthen an already held assessment of the environment; if faculty had not expected such rich returns, now they will for the future. The cyclical and longitudinal nature of the framework suggests that these reassessments of self-knowledge and social knowledge will provide motivation to alter behavior. Assuming that these outcomes were desirable ones, the framework predicts more grant activity, and consequently more publications.

Allison and Stewart (1974) provide corroborating evidence. Those who are successful in publishing receive the resources to publish even more. Their output increases at a more rapid rate than that of their colleagues who have done less—and who presumably have been rewarded less. As Fairweather (1993) showed, a research-oriented reward structure dominates in every institutional type, from Res-I's to CCs. For sociologists, Lightfield (1971) discovered that the early years in a career were critical. About three-quarters of those whose research was cited by other scholars in the first five years continued to publish and be cited again, whereas those whose research was not cited in the initial period stopped publishing. Cole and Cole (1973) and Cole and Zuckerman (1984) obtained similar results studying faculty in the natural sciences. McKeachie, Salthouse, and Linn (1978) and Kasten (1984), in their studies of factors affecting promotion, imply that faculty learn vicariously by observing one another's experiences in the environment. These observations—who succeeds and who does not—affect self-knowledge and social knowledge.

### Social Contingencies

There can be a variety of events that will appreciably affect individuals' productivity—family responsibilities, an extended illness. Unfortunately, there are no studies that recount the consequences of these conditions for faculty behavior and output.[18]

The studies mentioned here illuminate much about faculty at work, more with regard to research than teaching. At the same time, we note that too few investigations rest on a strong, or any, theoretical foundation. Consequently, one would expect the generally low correlations and little explained variance that the literature discloses. We founded our framework on sound theory and the best existing knowledge about faculty. Chapters 4 and 5 test and utilize the theoretical framework.

# PART TWO

Testing and
Using the
Framework

# 4

# FACULTY RESEARCH

P<small>UBLISH OR PERISH</small>" became a hackneyed phrase many years ago. Faculty spoke it more in jest than in seriousness, for they knew that most of their colleagues wrote little or nothing and still survived to live out their academic career. Today, however, publishing has replaced teaching as the principal faculty role in universities and has become an increasingly important criterion for promotion, tenure, and career success in four-year colleges. More faculty are publishing more articles and books in a mushrooming mass of journals and presses.

Several now attack this flood of literature, claiming that most of it is trivia. The critics allege that most of what appears in print never should have been written or published, that faculty simply grind out verbiage to fatten their vitae so as to qualify for the next step up the academic ladder. Faculty carve a single piece of research into bits so that one possibly decent publication instead becomes three or four fragmented articles. High-quality work has all but disappeared. So the critics say.

On the other side, even those who complain the loudest acknowledge the importance of research and our need for new knowledge. They know we have health and social problems needing solutions. They recognize the technological competition this country faces from other nations of the world. They grant the fact that our universities generate more research than all other agencies combined. They see too that this research is not designed to destroy nature or life, although other very different groups of concerned individuals believe that this is precisely what faculty research does to animals in the name of health and the weapons of war, in the name of biology, physics, and engineering.

Today's more competitive academic environment endangers a faculty member's chances for success. A career depends upon becoming known for one's work. Teaching, as important as it is, remains a local phenomenon. One can earn a reputation at home as a distinguished pedagogue. Very rarely, however, does that reputation extend beyond the immediate campus. Moreover, teaching excellence seldom brings national recognition to the institution, a goal high on the administration's list.

Besides wanting to pass their knowledge on to the next generation and to get young people excited about ideas and learning, those who choose the professorial career do so because research attracts them. Research is solving puzzles, doing it all day, every day. It's fun. If successful, one derives a modest income from it, enough to buy books and to pay for the children's music lessons.

Successful research differs from excellence in teaching. Research affects one's career. Recognized scholars, individuals whose reputations transcend the local college or university, judge a researcher's creations. Disciplinary leaders around the world award the prizes, confer on a faculty member a reputation that cannot be gained from colleagues at home. Published research leads to promotions and tenure. Higher salaries come with publications. Administrators like you. Neighbors see your picture in the local paper. Seeing your name in print supplies a momentary high. Many good things happen to those who publish.

In order to appreciate the magnitude of the academic publishing business, we briefly step back to sketch a partial picture of what has happened in the world of scholarship since World War II—a true watershed period—before looking at the evidence and passing judgment on the critics' claims. As noted above, teaching, not research, used to be the central faculty role. When Jencks and Riesman (1968) wrote *Academic Revolution,* university faculty were shifting their priorities. Jencks and Riesman called this change the "professionalization of faculty." Commitment to their professional associations and to their colleagues around the world challenged faculty members' institutional allegiance.[1] They found excitement both in new discoveries and in the dissemination of what they had learned. Nisbet (1992) has written of his graduate school days at Berkeley, describing how he joined the faculty upon completion of his Ph.D. during the Great Depression and how life changed at his university after World War II. There was no doubt in his and his most distinguished peers' minds in the 1930s that they would do research as one of their duties. However, being an excellent teacher, preparing outstanding lectures—these came first for even the most famous of the faculty at Berkeley. War research fell heavily on the universities, from covert operations such as radar to the atomic bomb. Washington money continued after 1945 to win the technological races with friendly as well as hostile nations. The pendulum has not swung back. As administrators and faculty acknowledge, research is the name of the game.

A few figures illustrate the magnitude of the knowledge production in-

116

dustry and the role universities have played in it, how it has changed, and to what degree.[2] To begin, the number of university presses doubled between 1948 and 1958. The 727 titles these presses published in 1948 increased to about 2,300 in 1966 (Douglas, 1992, p. 97). Between 1978 and 1988 more than 29,000 new scientific journals were launched (*Chronicle of Higher Education,* March 28, 1990, p. A13). Mooney (1991, p. A17) reports that during 1989–1990 there were a million refereed articles and 300,000 books, chapters, and monographs published.[3] A faculty member, on average, contributed one article and the equivalent of half a book (chapter or monograph) each year. (Research university professors averaged twice that output.) At the same time, the amount of available space for faculty publications has not been uniform across the disciplines. Between 1972 and 1988, journal pages for psychologists grew at a half-again faster rate than the number of psychology faculty. That is, there was about 50 percent more journal space in which psychology faculty could publish in 1988 than there was in 1972 (Bieber & Blackburn, 1993). Over this same period, publication space for English faculty decreased and competition for it increased. For example, *Publications of the Modern Language Association* (*PMLA*) now prints only half as many articles per issue as it did 20 years ago.

Besides publication differences among the disciplines, two fascinating studies show that the places where knowledge is produced are anything but randomly distributed around the world, including within the United States. When Deutsch, Platt, and Senghaas (1971) were examining the conditions that led to the 62 most significant scholarly contributions in the social sciences around the world between 1900 and 1965, they noted that the majority came from very few locations. Of the 101 different scholars involved in these 62 landmark contributions, the majority were Europeans until 1929; after 1930 the majority were Americans. For the entire 65 years the total number of scholars included 53 Americans, 44 Europeans, and 4 from other locations. Three centers—Chicago, Cambridge (Mass.), and New York—were the residences of more than half of the American professoriate contributors. Washington (D.C.), Ann Arbor, and New Haven provided another quarter (p. 458). That is, three-fourths of these landmark discoveries took place in but a handful of universities.

As we saw in chapter 2, place of work strongly predicts scholarly output. More recently, *Science Watch* counted all scientific papers indexed by the Institute for Scientific Information's *Science Citation Index* during 1991, about 600,000 of them. Approximately 25 percent came from people in but 25 cities, 14 of them in the United States. The *Scientist* (1993, p. 15) reproduced that article. Table 4.1 from it provides the details.

Between 1981 and 1991 the average growth in the number of scientific

Table 4.1    The World's Research-Rich Cities

| Rank | City | 1991 Papers | Rank | City | 1991 Papers |
|------|------|-------------|------|------|-------------|
| 1 | Moscow | 14,541 | 14 | Houston | 4,911 |
| 2 | London | 14,051 | 15 | San Diego–La Jolla, CA | 4,740 |
| 3 | Boston-Cambridge, MA | 12,480 | 16 | Stanford–Palo Alto, CA | 4,201 |
| 4 | Tokyo | 11,582 | 17 | Seattle | 4,055 |
| 5 | New York | 8,551 | 18 | Berlin | 4,040 |
| 6 | Paris | 7,964 | 19 | Ann Arbor, MI | 3,907 |
| 7 | Los Angeles | 6,601 | 20 | Montreal | 3,895 |
| 8 | Bethesda | 6,233 | 21 | Toronto | 3,887 |
| 9 | Philadelphia | 6,183 | 22 | Cambridge, England | 3,850 |
| 10 | Osaka, Japan | 5,408 | 23 | San Francisco | 3,773 |
| 11 | Washington, DC | 5,388 | 24 | Kyoto, Japan | 3,679 |
| 12 | Chicago | 5,174 | 25 | Oxford, England | 3,597 |
| 13 | Baltimore | 4,933 | | | |

*Source: Scientist* (1993), p. 15, reproducing data from *Science Watch/ISI's Science Citation Index* (1991).

papers produced at these locations was about 25 percent. One might expect research activity to be high in cities such as Boston-Cambridge (with Harvard, the Massachusetts Institute of Technology, Boston College, Boston University, and the University of Massachusetts–Boston, as well as 50 other higher-education institutions), New York (with Columbia, New York University, Cornell Medical Center, and several other universities), and Chicago (with the University of Chicago, Northwestern, the University of Illinois–Chicago, Loyola, DePaul, and Roosevelt). But Baltimore is essentially Johns Hopkins (although the University of Maryland–Baltimore is also there); Stanford–Palo Alto *is* Stanford; and Ann Arbor *is* the University of Michigan. Single institutions can be highly productive organizations when staffed with talented faculty, when resources are adequate, and when colleague interaction is valued.

What has created this worldwide explosion of knowledge? Most likely a number of factors—societal needs and requests; competition among universities to be recognized as the best (with faculty publication rates determining the standings); attempts to satisfy faculty members' intrinsic desires while incidentally providing extrinsic rewards. The multiplication of journals is the most understandable phenomenon. As knowledge grows and more people participate in its production, interesting subbranches of inquiry emerge. They grow, and mitosis sets in. Journals spring up to handle the new specialties that arise. The newly founded fields grow. Then they split, an inevitable process. New questions spawn other journals for communicating with colleagues on the current state of the enterprise.

Do faculty play the game the critics accuse them of? Sure, some do. Others try to solve what they and others believe are the important problems. We see the vast majority of faculty in the latter category.

What about the quality of this tremendous outpouring of new knowledge? Here the answer is not easy. From Deutsch, Platt, and Senghaas (1971) and the data from the *Scientist* (1993) we see that quality and quantity go together, a fact researchers have established by correlating numbers of articles with citations received. (See chapter 2.) Bieber, Blackburn, and De Vries's (1991) effort to establish the criteria for high-quality publications basically failed, especially in English literature (one of the three disciplines studied). Faculty agreed that rhetorical style is an essential criterion for an English essay, but they did not agree on what constitutes good style. Quality is a social construct and no doubt will always have a debatable element. One knows it when one sees it, even if its criteria cannot be specified. (See Pirsig, 1974, p. 179.)[4]

On the other hand, one need only scan the leading social science journals of the past 15 years and contrast them with today's to see a significant upgrade in quality.[5] Faculty today would not submit most of the articles published then, or even write them in the first place. Theory has become richer; databases are larger and more reliable; new methodologies have become available; computing power and techniques have advanced; and faculty training is more sophisticated. Everything supports higher-quality output.

The consequences are many. The knowledge explosion has affected the entire higher-education enterprise on nearly every front: expenses (the costs for library subscriptions to the old standard journals have risen, and there is pressure to subscribe to the new ones as well); the length of faculty education and training; the need for continuing education to keep abreast; the machinery the university now must have and regularly repair and update. Most important of all, publishing has affected faculty lives and careers. We designed our theoretical framework to increase the understanding of faculty in the research role. The studies we now report are ones that test and use our framework with research behavior and, most frequently, with products as the outcomes.

Here we present the results of five studies in which faculty research is the outcome. Each is taken directly from research papers we presented at national conferences (Lawrence, Frank, Bieber, Bentley, Blackburn, & Trautvetter, 1989; Lawrence, Blackburn, & Trautvetter, 1989; Blackburn, Bieber, Lawrence, & Trautvetter, 1991;[6] Trautvetter & Blackburn, 1990; Lawrence, Bieber, Blackburn, Saulsberry, Trautvetter, Hart, & Frank, 1989). The first details an analysis of faculty in eight Res-I universities, our first and most exhaustive test of the theoretical framework. The second extends the test of the theoretical framework to two additional institutional types. The third includes all institutional types and adds two more kinds of research output. The fourth uses the framework to explore sex differences in research output in the sciences. Before presenting the fifth study, which introduces a longitudinal component to the research, we briefly report the outcomes of three other studies using the framework with other databases. We close the chapter with a summary of the personal and contextual variables that correlate with faculty research output and present strategies institutions might adapt should they wish to increase individual and unit research accomplishments.

## Faculty in Research I Universities

As noted in chapter 2, the existing research on scholarly productivity has focused primarily on the direct effects of sociodemographic, career, and sometimes organizational factors. A handful of scholars have investigated the relationships between productivity and selected faculty perceptions of their employing institutions or of higher education in general—that is, their social knowledge. Even fewer have explored the relationships between productivity and a faculty member's personal educational values and beliefs. Although useful in a predictive sense, these studies do not adequately explain the process by which a faculty member's sociodemographic characteristics, career (educational background, status), perceptions (self-knowledge and social knowledge), and behaviors affect publication rates. Our explanatory causal framework identifies both direct and indirect effects of the variables that best portray such a process and provide key insights into the motivation of productive researchers. (See chapter 1.)

Current research also lacks longitudinal data on faculty perceptions, behavior, and productivity. Although a few researchers have described productivity changes through time-ordered analyses using citation indexes and vitae (Allison & Stewart, 1974; Long, 1978; Reskin, 1985), these studies fall short of explaining how individuals relate to their environments and how these interactions may change and influence scholarly output over time. For example, Allison and Stewart's notion that some professors achieve early recognition for their work, and that this reputation gives them an edge over their peers in competition for funds and publication (the accumulative advantage process), was based on cross-sequential analysis of citation indexes and not longitudinal data.

The data assess the influence of key environmental and individual variables on the rate of publication (last two years). We trace the effect of each variable within the constructs of our framework. We now describe our database.

### Data and Sample

The data for the first study described here come from "Faculty at Work," a national survey of faculty conducted by the National Center for Research to Improve Postsecondary Teaching and Learning (NCRIPTAL) from November 1987 through January 1988.[7] (See appendix H.) We drew the faculty sample (N = 4,240) from the nine Carnegie classification categories (Carnegie, 1976) and across eight disciplines selected to represent a cross-section of the liberal arts (English and history for the humanities; biology, chemistry, and mathematics for the natural sciences; and psychology, political science, and sociology for the social sciences). We carried out our survey sample selection in two stages. First, we stratified institutions by Carnegie category. Then we estimated both the number of faculty members in each category and the percentage of all faculty in the United States who fell into each category. Second, we selected institutions at random until the final sample corresponded to the national distribution of faculty across Carnegie classification categories.[8]

We used only respondents from Res-I institutions in this test of the theoretical framework, because the major portion of publications are from these faculty. The resulting sample is of sufficient size (N = 637) to examine many of the individual/environment relationships specified in the framework. The faculty distribution across the disciplines is biology, 13.5 percent; chemistry, 12.1 percent; mathematics/statistics, 10.1 percent; English, 13.8 percent; history, 12.1 percent; political science, 10.7 percent; psychology, 13.2 percent; and sociology, 9.6 percent. The sample is predominantly male (78.5 percent), white (90 percent), and tenured (71.6 percent). The majority earned their highest degree in a Res-I institution (73.8 percent) and achieved the highest degree offered in their fields, namely, Ph.D., J.D., or M.D. (95.5 percent).

Individuals vary in both chronological age (mean = 47.2, standard deviation = 9.6) and career age (defined as the number of years elapsed since earning the highest degree: M = 18.5, SD = 9.6). Their ranks are assistant professor (19.5 percent), associate professor (24.8 percent), and professor (55.7 percent). Further, sufficient numbers of respondents had been reviewed for tenure or had been promoted between 1985 and 1987 (N = 85) to permit meaningful analysis of the effect this environmental response had on social knowledge, behavior, and productivity.

121

In addition to standard sociodemographic and career indices, the survey instrument contains measures of faculty perceptions of their universities and of their own efficacy (sense of organizational influence/personal control, competence), values and beliefs, and psychological dispositions. The instrument includes a variety of items that assess current distribution of effort, current rate of publication, and prior rate of publication (up to 1985). These publication output measures allowed us to distinguish between the individual's past publication performance (a career variable in the framework) and current rate of publication (an outcome variable), and therefore to test the effect of prior accomplishments on current performance. Unlike most previous surveys, our rate of publication is a continuous variable. It provides a refined discrimination among respondents.[9]

### Variables

The theoretical framework evaluated in this study includes six of the nine theoretical constructs specified in figure 4.1: sociodemographic characteristics, career, self-knowledge, social knowledge, environmental response, and productivity.

We used discrete measures (e.g., sex, race, age, discipline, university where employed) and factors to test the framework. We derived the factors by submitting all survey items that assessed each of the six constructs to varimax factor rotation analyses. The factor analyses isolated the following measures and factors:

Three measures of career: (1) status, (2) past productivity record, and (3) graduate education background

Twelve factors defining four theoretically distinct types of self-knowledge: (1) self-competence, (2) self-efficacy, (3) values and beliefs, and (4) dispositions

Thirteen social knowledge factors that fell into three categories: (1) inferences about the organization as a whole (e.g., what the university values), (2) perceptions of administrators, and (3) perceptions of faculty

Under environmental responses, four factors defining both local and off-campus feedback the last two years: (1) awarded promotion/tenure, (2) hours of clerical assistance, (3) hours of graduate student assistance, and (4) requests to review manuscripts for publication

Nine behavior factors: (1) service on dissertation committees, (2) attendance at local research lectures/seminars, (3) involvement in off-campus activities, (4) publication/proposal effort (number submitted during the last two years), (5) time given to research in the current term, (6) work effort, (7) collaboration with colleagues, and (8 and 9) two factors representing different configurations of classroom teaching activities

122

Figure 4.1    Variables Used in Testing the Theoretical Framework

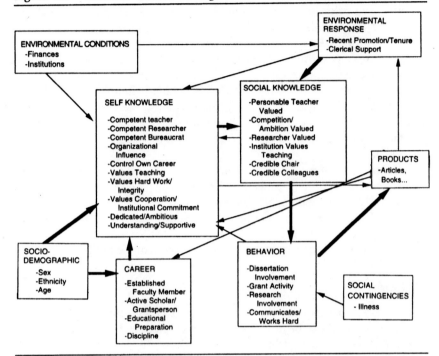

*Note:* See note to figure 1.1 for interpreting thicker and thinner arrows.

We used all 41 factors and the discrete measures of sociodemographic characteristics in the testing of the framework. Appendix B describes the measures from each of the six variable sets that entered the regression analyses. (The teaching variables are the focus of chapter 5.)

### Data Analysis

The causal theoretical framework posits that each set of variables will directly affect the one it precedes. For example, sociodemographic characteristics will influence career, career will influence self-knowledge, and so on. It also assumes that the influence of career, self-knowledge, and social knowledge variables on current publication rate will be indirect. These variables are being mediated by the variables that follow them in the causal sequence. For example, the effect of social knowledge on publication would be mediated by behavior.

We estimated the direct and indirect effects of each construct in the framework by means of a stepwise multiple regression analysis. To estimate the direct effects, we regressed publication rate for the past two years—total number of professional writings published or accepted for publication during this time period—against all causally antecedent variables in the theoretical framework. In this analysis we entered each set of endogenous variables—for example, sociodemographic, career, self-knowledge, social knowledge, environmental response, and behavior—one at a time.[10]

We employed standard path analysis to estimate indirect effects. Each of the endogenous variables was regressed against the causally antecedent variables in the framework. This regression analysis was repeated for each of the variables subsumed under career, self-knowledge, social knowledge, and behavior.

The theoretical framework is longitudinal. However, the data set represents only one point in time, with some retrospective information. As a result, only certain temporal relationships can be tested. These are indicated by the thicker arrows in figure 4.1. In addition, two of the exogenous variables, determined primarily from forces that are outside of the framework, are not included in this analysis: environmental conditions and social contingencies.[11]

### Results

Table 4.2 summarizes the results of the stepwise multiple regressions. The beta weights can be interpreted as direct effects.[12] The relative size and sign of the standardized beta weights indicate the amount of positive or negative change in publication output—the dependent measure—that is attributable to each predictor variable with the influence of every other variable in the equation held constant.

### Direct Effects

The data in table 4.2 show the amount of variance in each of the variables that is predicted by all of its antecedents as well as the betas for each of the predictors. By way of illustration, column 6 indicates how much variation in the measure "established faculty member" is attributable to the sociodemographic variables by displaying the betas for each of the sociodemographic variables that entered the equation. Following standard practice, we discuss only those betas with a magnitude of .05 or greater that are statistically significant at $p \leq .05$.

The theoretical framework assumes that sociodemographic characteristics may directly affect career and self-knowledge, or that the effects on self-knowledge may be mediated by career. (The indirect effects are discussed in the next section.) The findings suggest that being female may have directly influenced discipline affiliation (columns 9–15). Women are in English (column 11) and psychology (14), but not in chemistry (9). Being a woman also had a strong negative effect on being an established faculty member (beta = −.904, $p \leq .001$), a factor including career age, rank, tenure status, and administrative experience.

The data also show that chronological age had significant direct effects on three self-knowledge variables: self-competence, values/beliefs, and disposition. Older faculty members rated themselves lower on research competence and ambition (columns 17 and 24) and reported strong teaching values (21). Race had a direct positive effect on research competence (17). Asian Americans expressed high research competence. Disposition measures (24, 25) had a negative effect on sense of control over one's career (20).

The percentage of explained variance for the career variables predicting self-knowledge ranged from 25.6 percent for research competence (column 17) to 3.7 percent for teaching competence (16). The established faculty member (6) and active scholar/grantsperson (7) variables were the strongest publication predictors. Both had positive direct effects on professors' self-ascribed research ability (research competence, 17) and tendency to be ambitious, competitive, perseverant, and dedicated (dedicated/ambitious, 24). Standing within the university (established faculty member) also led professors to believe they exerted organizational influence (19). In contrast with earlier studies, which conclude that such power is awarded primarily on the basis of scholarly reputation (Fulton & Trow, 1974), professors' cumulative research record (active scholar/grantsperson, 7) did not affect their perceptions of organizational influence (19). However, in keeping with extant research (Lawrence & Blackburn, 1985), the active scholars/grantspersons appear to have less regard for teaching (21).

Among the self-knowledge variables, the self-efficacy, value, and personal disposition variables had the strongest influence on social knowledge. In particular, the impression is that competitiveness and ambition are valued traits (explained variance is 26.2 percent). Professors' sense of control over their careers predicted their perceptions of the credibility of university administrators and faculty colleagues (columns 32 and 33). The faculty members' own valuation of teaching (21) influenced these perceptions of department/unit chairs and colleagues.[13] The largest direct effect on social knowledge was exerted by a disposition variable. Faculty who described themselves as ambitious, competitive, dedicated, and perseverant thought their universities valued these characteristics (29).

The environmental response variables did not have strong direct effects on social knowledge.

The social knowledge variables were not strong predictors of behavior. However, the data indicate that career and self-knowledge variables have

Table 4.2  Path Analysis Data

| | 6 | 7 | 8 | 9 | 10 | 11 | 12 | 13 | 14 | 15 | 16 | 17 | 18 | 19 | 20 | 21 |
|---|---|---|---|---|---|---|---|---|---|---|---|---|---|---|---|---|
| 1 Female | -.904c | -.047 | -.046 | -.105a | -.056 | .160c | -.017 | -.061 | .092a | .041 | .034 | -.081a | .021 | -.109a | -.001 | .025 |
| 2 DAsian | .015 | .017 | .031 | -.015 | .022 | .004 | .014 | .020 | -.044 | -.034 | .035 | .125b | -.016 | -.005 | -.087a | -.044 |
| 3 DOther | .007 | -.048 | .014 | .067 | .120b | -.016 | .015 | -.048 | -.059 | .019 | .033 | .071 | .011 | -.041 | -.139b | .000 |
| 4 DBlack | -.017 | -.086a | -.005 | -.023 | .012 | .043 | .042 | .030 | .068 | .033 | .056 | .021 | .032 | -.003 | -.078 | -.002 |
| 5 Age | .767c | -.021 | .075 | -.007 | .001 | .042 | .056 | .055 | .007 | -.024 | -.077 | -.184b | -.013 | -.172a | -.134a | .252c |
| 6 Estab. faculty | | | | | | | | | | | .133 | .167b | .018 | .284c | .016 | .006 |
| 7 Active scholar/ grantsperson | | | | | | | | | | | | | | | | |
| 8 Edu. background | | | | | | | | | | | .000 | .401c | -.127b | .044 | .179c | -.306c |
| 9 DChemistry | | | | | | | | | | | -.002 | -.036 | -.126b | .056 | .037 | -.061 |
| 10 DMath | | | | | | | | | | | -.009 | -.030 | -.076 | .031 | .080 | -.053 |
| 11 DEnglish | | | | | | | | | | | .002 | -.212c | .158b | -.151b | -.044 | .023 |
| 12 DHistory | | | | | | | | | | | .116 | -.034 | -.035 | -.009 | -.130a | .141a |
| 13 DPolitical science | | | | | | | | | | | .124a | .055 | -.057 | .017 | -.044 | .081 |
| 14 DPsychology | | | | | | | | | | | .090 | .050 | -.007 | .025 | .018 | -.012 |
| 15 DSociology | | | | | | | | | | | .068 | -.045 | -.048 | -.066 | .110a | -.041 |
| 16 Competent teacher | | | | | | | | | | | -.004 | .021 | -.038 | -.042 | -.017 | .008 |
| 17 Comp. researcher | | | | | | | | | | | | | | | | |
| 18 Comp. bureaucrat | | | | | | | | | | | | | | | | |
| 19 Org. influence | | | | | | | | | | | | | | | | |
| 20 Control over career | | | | | | | | | | | | | | | | |
| 21 Values teaching | | | | | | | | | | | | | | | | |
| 22 Values hard work/ integrity | | | | | | | | | | | | | | | | |

| | | |
|---|---|---|
| 23 | Values cooperation/ inst. commitment | |
| 24 | Dedic./ambitious | |
| 25 | Understanding/ supportive | |
| 26 | Recent promotion/ tenure | |
| 27 | Clerical support | |
| 28 | Personable teacher valued | |
| 29 | Competition/ ambition valued | |
| 30 | Researcher valued | |
| 31 | Inst. values teaching | |
| 32 | Credible chair | |
| 33 | Credible colleagues | |
| 34 | Diss. involvement | |
| 35 | Grant involvement | |
| 36 | Research involve. | |
| 37 | Communicates/ works hard | |
| 38 | Two-year pub. rate | |
| $R^2$ | .626 .012 .010 .017 .019 .028 .005 .012 .018 .005 .037 .256 .049 .089 .146 .226 | |

*Continued next page*

Table 4.2—*Continued*

| | 22 | 23 | 24 | 25 | 26 | 27 | 28 | 29 | 30 | 31 | 32 | 33 | 34 | 35 | 36 | 37 | 38 |
|---|---|---|---|---|---|---|---|---|---|---|---|---|---|---|---|---|---|
| 1 Female | .039 | -.118a | .069 | .014 | .076 | -.021 | .003 | .001 | -.031 | .073 | .090 | .064 | -.039 | -.230 | -.076 | .010 | -.008 |
| 2 DAsian | .013 | .067 | .075 | .025 | .016 | .042 | .002 | -.043 | .046 | -.019 | .036 | .057 | .034 | -.064 | -.011 | -.041 | .013 |
| 3 DOther | -.048 | .077 | .045 | .025 | .003 | .005 | .004 | -.046 | .015 | .006 | .032 | .089 | .073 | -.103 | -.022 | .047 | .022 |
| 4 DBlack | .058 | .086 | .133b | .136b | .006 | -.009 | .076 | -.018 | .033 | -.040 | .032 | .029 | -.024 | -.007 | -.076 | -.040 | .032 |
| 5 Age | -.046 | -.022 | -.335c | -.062 | -.089 | -.228b | .079 | -.072 | .095 | -.087 | .041 | .110 | .176 | -.315a | .001 | -.109 | .100 |
| 6 Estab. faculty | -.011 | .153a | .261c | .082 | -.337c | .380c | .075 | .047 | -.115 | .113 | .071 | -.141 | -.071 | .106 | .042 | -.006 | -.049 |
| 7 Active scholar/grantsperson | .058 | .043 | .218c | -.128b | -.011 | .083 | -.084 | -.074 | -.086 | .046 | -.059 | -.084 | .180b | .243c | .010 | .138 | .172a |
| 8 Edu. background | .067 | -.010 | .068 | -.024 | .062 | .008 | -.067 | .026 | -.009 | -.047 | -.055 | .048 | .015 | .038 | -.098 | -.039 | -.112 |
| 9 DChemistry | .057 | .121a | .078 | .070 | .031 | .084 | -.144 | -.006 | -.065 | -.031 | -.011 | -.106 | .222b | .016 | .045 | .035 | .029 |
| 10 DMath | -.100 | -.135a | -.150b | -.084 | -.013 | -.143a | -.139 | -.165a | -.104 | .077 | .010 | -.123 | -.081 | -.182 | -.068 | .191a | .094 |
| 11 DEnglish | .091 | -.020 | -.022 | .092 | -.008 | -.028 | -.032 | -.103 | -.166a | .056 | .065 | -.090 | .004 | -.161a | -.111 | .117 | .174a |
| 12 DHistory | .077 | .025 | -.039 | .014 | .036 | -.043 | -.089 | -.159a | -.163a | -.015 | -.039 | -.084 | .020 | -.204a | -.114 | .284b | .032 |
| 13 DPolitical science | .152a | .019 | .104 | .010 | -.103 | -.091 | -.087 | -.160a | -.245b | .009 | -.034 | -.163a | .129 | -.235b | .000 | .214a | .036 |
| 14 DPsychology | .057 | .061 | -.076 | .101 | -.014 | -.029 | -.105 | -.044 | -.063 | -.055 | .018 | -.099 | .151 | -.243b | .000 | .102 | .027 |
| 15 DSociology | .061 | .067 | -.055 | .039 | -.070 | -.128a | -.153a | -.099 | -.115 | .060 | .096 | -.038 | .113 | -.163a | -.020 | .139 | -.005 |
| 16 Competent teacher | | | | | | | .024 | -.033 | .161a | -.027 | .068 | -.027 | .030 | .084 | .004 | -.067 | -.038 |
| 17 Comp. researcher | | | | | | | .103 | -.131 | -.017 | .077 | .034 | .054 | -.050 | .186b | .099 | .091 | .047 |
| 18 Comp. bureaucrat | | | | | | | .026 | -.157a | .028 | -.043 | .027 | -.003 | -.045 | -.046 | .031 | .000 | -.062 |
| 19 Org. influence | | | | | | | .046 | .002 | .150a | -.082 | .209c | .181b | .042 | .075 | .051 | .036 | -.014 |
| 20 Control over career | | | | | | | .000 | .073 | .093 | -.103 | .100 | .011 | .139 | .034 | .014 | -.031 | .044 |
| 21 Values teaching | | | | | | | -.127 | .017 | -.014 | .003 | .085 | .027 | -.009 | -.090 | -.451c | -.019 | .134 |
| 22 Values hard work/integrity | | | | | | | .058 | -.094 | .095 | .044 | -.044 | .640 | -.098 | .052 | .072 | .000 | -.073 |

| Variable | 1 | 2 | 3 | 4 | 5 | 6 | 7 | 8 | 9 | 10 | 11 | 12 | 13 | 14 | 15 | 16 | 17 |
|---|---|---|---|---|---|---|---|---|---|---|---|---|---|---|---|---|---|
| 23 Values cooperation/ inst. commitment | | | | | | | .111 | .032 | .117 | .009 | .149b | .150b | .036 | .004 | -.031 | .041 | -.123 |
| 24 Dedic./ambitious | | | | | | | .033 | .419c | -.062 | .071 | .035 | .066 | -.066 | -.041 | -.117 | .235b | .016 |
| 25 Understanding/ supportive | | | | | | | .079 | .140a | .047 | .020 | .074 | .033 | .187a | -.014 | .011 | -.012 | .020 |
| 26 Recent promotion/ tenure | | | | | | | .143a | .070 | -.001 | .011 | .035 | .017 | | | | | |
| 27 Clerical support | | | | | | | .011 | -.113 | .040 | .095 | .123a | .127a | | | | | |
| 28 Personable teacher valued | | | | | | | | | | | | | -.130a | .039 | .025 | -.002 | .054 |
| 29 Competition/ ambition valued | | | | | | | | | | | | | -.039 | .057 | .141a | -.045 | -.046 |
| 30 Researcher valued | | | | | | | | | | | | | .092 | -.113 | .047 | -.004 | -.032 |
| 31 Inst. values teaching | | | | | | | | | | | | | -.041 | .050 | -.127a | .005 | .050 |
| 32 Credible chair | | | | | | | | | | | | | .134 | -.087 | .106 | .042 | -.086 |
| 33 Credible colleagues | | | | | | | | | | | | | -.146 | .018 | -.088 | .022 | .083 |
| 34 Diss. involvement | | | | | | | | | | | | | | | | | .315c |
| 35 Grant involvement | | | | | | | | | | | | | | | | | .328c |
| 36 Research involve. | | | | | | | | | | | | | | | | | .382c |
| 37 Communicates/ works hard | | | | | | | | | | | | | | | | | .283c |
| 38 Two-year pub. rate | | | | | | | | | | | | | | | | | |
| $R^2$ | .062 | .103 | .177 | .064 | .222 | .103 | .130 | .262 | .237 | .159 | .217 | .185 | .298 | .377 | .453 | .247 | .502 |

*Note:* The letter D before a variable's name (e.g., DAsian, DChemistry) indicates that it was a dummy variable in the data analysis.

a: $p \leq .05$.   b: $p \leq .01$.   c: $p \leq .001$.

significant betas for one or more of the behaviors that do directly affect productivity (columns 34–37).

As predicted, professors' current research behavior had the strongest direct effects on their publication rates during this time period. The betas for the behavior variables ranged from .283 for communicates/works hard (37) to .382 for research involvement (36). All betas were significant at $p \leq .001$.

## Indirect Effects

The causal theoretical framework postulates that the effects of socio-demographic, career, self-knowledge, and social knowledge variables on publication rate would be mediated by behavior. In other words, these variables would have direct effects on behavior variables that in turn enhance publication rate. The framework assumes that faculty members will develop strategies to increase their publication rates based on their understanding of themselves and their environment. The strategies manifest themselves as different behaviors, all of which lead directly to publication. Therefore, to understand the motivation process, one must trace the antecedents of the different behaviors.

The data presented in table 4.2 support the general proposition that behavior mediates the influence of the antecedent variables on current publication rate. All predictor variables (column 38) account for 50.2 percent of the explained variance in publication rate.[14]

The data displayed in table 4.3 show that in the initial stages of the hierarchical regression, the increase in percentage of the explained variance was significant as we added each successive set of variables. (See the bottom row of the table.) When behavior variables were added, the effect of cumulative research record (active scholar/grantsperson) diminished substantially, from a beta of .338 to .172. However, the increase in percentage of explained variance remained significant. Constructs placed earlier in the framework have little predictive value once we take into account constructs that are temporally closer to the outcome. This finding supports the ordering of the theoretical framework.

Table 4.4 shows which of the predictors exert their influence through the four different behaviors, namely, dissertation involvement, grant involvement, research involvement, and communicates/works hard. We report the data in this manner to show both changes in the amount of predicted variance in each behavior and changes in the direct effects of variables as they enter into the regression in the causal sequence.

Beginning with dissertation involvement, the findings indicate that three career variables and one self-knowledge variable have stable effects on this behavior. Active scholars/grantspersons, faculty members with appoint-

Table 4.3  Variations in Publication Rate Predicted by Variable Sets

| | 1 | 2 | 3 | 4 | 5 |
|---|---|---|---|---|---|
| *Sociodemographic* | | | | | |
| Female | -.073 | -.050 | -.034 | -.040 | -.008 |
| Asian | -.005 | -.011 | -.024 | -.022 | .013 |
| Other | -.002 | .004 | .012 | -.012 | .022 |
| Black | -.052 | -.010 | -.008 | -.015 | .032 |
| Age | -.062 | -.078 | .009 | .017 | .100 |
| *Career* | | | | | |
| Established faculty member | | .047 | -.014 | -.024 | -.049 |
| Active scholar/grantsperson | | *.452* | *.333* | *.338* | *.172* |
| Educational preparation | | *-.136* | *-.143* | *-.151* | -.112 |
| Chemistry | | .094 | .083 | .101 | .029 |
| Mathematics | | -.066 | -.032 | -.014 | .094 |
| English | | .031 | .049 | .062 | *.174* |
| History | | -.039 | -.048 | -.024 | .032 |
| Political science | | .000 | -.009 | .005 | .036 |
| Psychology | | -.019 | -.026 | -.012 | .027 |
| Sociology | | -.053 | -.041 | -.026 | -.005 |
| *Self-knowledge* | | | | | |
| Competent teacher | | | -.002 | .005 | -.038 |
| Competent researcher | | | *.149* | .129 | .047 |
| Competent bureaucrat | | | -.078 | -.071 | -.062 |
| Organizational influence | | | .061 | .073 | -.014 |
| Control over career | | | .097 | .094 | .044 |
| Values teaching | | | -.066 | .079 | .134 |
| Values hard work/integrity | | | -.061 | -.061 | -.073 |
| Values cooperation/commit. | | | -.080 | -.090 | -.123 |
| Dedicated/ambitious | | | .048 | .039 | .016 |
| Understanding/supportive | | | .079 | .084 | .020 |
| *Social knowledge* | | | | | |
| Personable teacher valued | | | | .053 | .054 |
| Competition/ambition valued | | | | .026 | -.046 |
| Researcher valued | | | | -.053 | -.032 |
| Institution values teaching | | | | .037 | .050 |
| Credible chair | | | | -.005 | -.086 |
| Credible colleagues | | | | .017 | .083 |
| *Behavior* | | | | | |
| Dissertation involvement | | | | | *.315* |
| Grant involvement | | | | | *.328* |
| Research involvement | | | | | *.382* |
| Communicates/works hard | | | | | *.283* |
| *Percentage of explained variance* | 1.0 | *28.7* | *34.7* | 35.6 | *50.2* |

*Source:* NCRIPTAL survey.

*Notes:* Numbers are standardized betas. Bold, italicized entries are at $p \leq .05$.

Table 4.4   Variations in Behavior Predicted by Antecedent Variables

| | Dissertation Involvement | | | | Grant Involvement | | | | Research Involvement | | | | Communicates/Works Hard | | | |
|---|---|---|---|---|---|---|---|---|---|---|---|---|---|---|---|---|
| | 1 | 2 | 3 | 4 | 1 | 2 | 3 | 4 | 1 | 2 | 3 | 4 | 1 | 2 | 3 | 4 |
| **Sociodemographic** | | | | | | | | | | | | | | | | |
| Female | -.075 | -.062 | -.050 | -.039 | -.079 | -.024 | -.030 | -.230 | -.123 | -.091 | -.069 | -.076 | -.021 | -.003 | .011 | .010 |
| Asian | .009 | .013 | .034 | .034 | -.038 | -.051 | -.076 | -.064 | .017 | .022 | .006 | -.011 | .002 | -.008 | -.040 | -.041 |
| Other | .024 | .034 | .055 | .073 | -.089 | -.074 | -.086 | -.103 | -.086 | -.059 | -.043 | -.022 | .064 | .070 | .054 | .047 |
| Black | -.051 | -.027 | -.027 | -.024 | -.011 | .028 | .012 | -.007 | -.105 | -.066 | -.054 | -.076 | .001 | -.001 | -.027 | -.040 |
| Age | .115 | .145 | .161 | .176 | -.289 | -.363 | -.309 | -.315 | -.104 | -.105 | .018 | .001 | -.111 | -.226 | -.130 | -.109 |
| **Career** | | | | | | | | | | | | | | | | |
| Estab. faculty member | | -.046 | -.083 | -.071 | | .129 | .117 | .106 | | .037 | .016 | .042 | | .117 | .011 | -.006 |
| Active scholar/grantsperson | | .187 | .201 | .180 | | .293 | .246 | .243 | | .169 | -.019 | .010 | | .283 | .155 | .138 |
| Educational prep. | | .035 | .039 | .015 | | .034 | .009 | .038 | | -.069 | -.078 | -.098 | | -.052 | -.047 | -.039 |
| Chemistry | | .272 | .247 | .222 | | .048 | .041 | .016 | | .039 | .025 | .045 | | .041 | .027 | .035 |
| Mathematics | | -.037 | -.035 | -.081 | | -.204 | -.193 | -.182 | | -.160 | -.133 | -.068 | | .134 | .198 | .191 |
| English | | .023 | .023 | .004 | | -.132 | -.134 | -.161 | | -.214 | -.165 | -.111 | | .145 | .147 | .117 |
| History | | .056 | .054 | .020 | | -.155 | -.166 | -.204 | | -.179 | -.172 | -.114 | | .322 | .314 | .284 |
| Political science | | .142 | .152 | .129 | | -.178 | -.203 | -.235 | | -.017 | -.030 | .000 | | .257 | .233 | .214 |
| Psychology | | .210 | .171 | .151 | | -.224 | -.232 | -.243 | | .039 | .005 | .000 | | .075 | .095 | .102 |
| Sociology | | .154 | .152 | .133 | | -.156 | -.154 | -.163 | | -.048 | -.046 | -.020 | | .151 | .160 | .139 |
| **Self-knowledge** | | | | | | | | | | | | | | | | |
| Competent teacher | | | .057 | .030 | | | .158 | .084 | | | .021 | .004 | | | -.071 | -.067 |
| Competent researcher | | | -.065 | -.050 | | | .089 | .186 | | | .085 | .009 | | | .108 | .091 |
| Comp. bureaucrat | | | -.040 | -.045 | | | -.065 | -.046 | | | .012 | .031 | | | .004 | .000 |
| Org. influence | | | .063 | .042 | | | .007 | .075 | | | .015 | .051 | | | .015 | .036 |

| | (1) | (2) | (3) | (4) | (5) | (6) | (7) | (8) | (9) | (10) | (11) | (12) | (13) | (14) | (15) | (16) |
|---|---|---|---|---|---|---|---|---|---|---|---|---|---|---|---|---|
| Control over career | | | .174 | .139 | | | -.006 | .034 | | | .047 | .014 | | | -.047 | -.031 |
| Values teaching | | | .018 | -.009 | | | -.096 | -.090 | | | *-.428* | *-.451* | | | -.004 | -.019 |
| Values hard work/integrity | | | -.125 | -.098 | | | .058 | .052 | | | .033 | .072 | | | -.010 | .000 |
| Values coop./commit. | | | .023 | .036 | | | -.015 | .004 | | | -.070 | -.031 | | | .027 | .041 |
| Dedicated/ambitious | | | .021 | -.006 | | | -.002 | -.041 | | | -.059 | -.117 | | | .222 | .235 |
| Understanding/supportive | | | .162 | .187 | | | .011 | -.014 | | | .028 | .011 | | | -.013 | -.012 |
| *Social knowledge* | | | | | | | | | | | | | | | | |
| Personable teacher valued | | | | -.130 | | | | .039 | | | | .025 | | | | -.002 |
| Competition/ambition valued | | | | -.039 | | | | .057 | | | | .141 | | | | -.045 |
| Researcher valued | | | | .092 | | | | -.113 | | | | .047 | | | | -.004 |
| Inst. values teaching | | | | -.041 | | | | .050 | | | | -.127 | | | | .055 |
| Credible chair | | | | .134 | | | | -.087 | | | | .106 | | | | .042 |
| Credible colleagues | | | | -.146 | | | | .018 | | | | -.088 | | | | .022 |
| *Percentage of explained variance* | 2.6 | 17.8 | 23.9 | 29.8 | 7.9 | 29.1 | 33.1 | 33.7 | 3.6 | 18.0 | 36.8 | 45.3 | 8.1 | 14.1 | 22.4 | 24.7 |

*Source:* NCRIPTAL survey.

*Notes:* Numbers are standardized betas. Bold, italicized numbers are at $p \leq .05$ for betas and change in variance explained.

ments in the sciences, and individuals who describe themselves as understanding and supportive were more likely to supervise dissertation research. The combination of variables fits with the process of accumulative advantage described by Allison and Stewart (1974). The findings from the present study show that professors with strong cumulative records as researchers (active scholars/grantspersons) were more likely to be supervising dissertations. Chairing dissertations can be a strategy used by these faculty to increase their publication rates. Dissertation activity frequently leads to articles co-authored with students whose dissertations are part of faculty members' ongoing research programs. It can also be the case that students seek faculty with strong records to chair their dissertations.

The findings vis-à-vis grant involvement underscore this interpretation. The data show that active scholars/grantspersons are more likely to spend time on the preparation of proposals than on other research activities. However, the findings also suggest that people engage in activities they believe they do well in. In the final regression of the path analysis, faculty members who thought they were competent researchers were more involved with grants than were those who rated their research competency low. Furthermore, the betas for the sciences were positive, and the betas for the humanities were negative.[15] One could infer from these discipline findings that people engage in grant activities when they think the probabilities for success are greater—for example, more funding is available for the sciences—or when the funds are needed for support people and equipment to conduct research.

Although chronological age exerted a substantial negative impact on current grant involvement, its direct effect was reduced as the self-knowledge and social knowledge variables entered the regression. Perhaps older professors in research universities who are not engaged with grant proposals do not feel as competent as researchers when compared with younger professors.

Research involvement, the amount of time given to research in the present term, exerted the strongest direct effect on current publication rate (beta $= .382, p \leq .001$; column 36 in table 4.2). It appears that those who allocate time to research use it in ways that result in publication. It is, however, such a general measure that few antecedents predict it. The variable with the most significant direct effect, "values teaching" (column 21 in table 4.2), had a negative influence (beta $= -.451, p \leq .001$). This instance may be the clearest example of personal values resulting in a decision to devote effort to activities other than research (probably teaching, but perhaps committee and service work). Apparently faculty make this decision irrespective of their inferences about the organizational climate, because the respondents' personal values did not directly affect their perceptions of their institution's emphasis on teaching. (See column 31 in table 4.2.)

Last, the behavior "communicates/works hard" (working long hours, talking about research at conferences and over the phone) has a link to a personality trait. Although writers have speculated about how a professor's personality might influence productivity, there has been little direct empirical research on the question (Baldwin & Blackburn, 1981; Chambers, 1964; Knapp, 1963; Roe, 1964; Zacharias & Mathis, 1982). Our data indicate that the self-ascribed tendencies to be dedicated, perseverant, ambitious, and competitive (dedicated/ambitious) had a significant direct effect on time spent communicating with colleagues about research and pursuing professional activities (communicates/works hard). Communication may involve collaboration on research that leads directly to publications—or arguably, those who are ambitious may also be inclined to communicate with persons who might provide funding or technical assistance that would enable them to carry out their research.

### Discussion

The causal theoretical framework evaluated explained 50 percent of the variance in publication rate during a two-year time period. By far the strongest predictors of publication rate were the actual activities (behaviors) professors engaged in during this time. The data suggest, however, that individual differences in career patterns as well as competence, values and beliefs, disposition, and perceptions of the organization lead professors to distribute their effort in different ways. The data also show that self-knowledge exerts an indirect effect on productivity as mediated by behavior.

Because our framework is temporal, the retrospective data did allow us to assess the impact of an individual's previous research accomplishments on current rate of publication. The findings corroborated earlier studies, concluding that professors with strong cumulative research records tend to be more prolific publishers. The data also fit with other research on expectancy theory and work motivation in that the self-knowledge and social knowledge variables together accounted for as little as 4.6 percent and as much as 27.3 percent of the explained variance in grant involvement and research involvement, respectively (Wahba & House, 1981). Even though the overall impact was not great, the type of influence exerted by these two sets of variables is important in understanding why certain individuals engage in different behaviors.

One provocative inference follows from an examination of the impact of self-knowledge and social knowledge on current publication rate. Self-knowledge variables (primarily research competence) explained 6 percent of the variance in rate, whereas social knowledge accounted for less than 1 percent of the predicted variance and actually suppressed the direct effect of respondents' sense of research competence. Staw (1983) argues that an organization's reward system can become detrimental when an activity is overemphasized. The incentive that is inherent in the activity itself may be diminished and be replaced by the extrinsic reward that is given for performance. In brief, professors may begin to engage in research not because they enjoy the process itself but because it is the basis for merit salary increases and promotion.

With over 50 percent of the variance accounted for—an appreciable increase from the typical 15 percent reported in earlier studies—we claim an initial success. Our theoretical framework has incorporated a number of important variables.

## Research in Three Institutional Types

In this second study we determine if our theoretical framework of publication productivity applies to professors in two additional institutional types—doctoral and comprehensive colleges and universities. The analyses enable us to address several important questions about the extent to which organizational factors, individual differences in preparation, prior activities, and perceptions influence faculty publication, and to take preliminary steps toward developing generalizations about what motivates professors to publish.

Several factors have hampered attempts to develop a theoretical framework of faculty motivation that is relevant to different types of institutions. Key limitations include the lack of identical measures from individuals in the same disciplines but different postsecondary institutions, and the scarcity of longitudinal data. Although a few researchers have described productivity changes through time-ordered analyses using citation indexes or curriculum vitae (Allison & Stewart, 1974; Hammel, 1980; Long, 1978; Reskin, 1985), these studies fall short of explaining how individuals relate to their environments and how these interactions may change and influence scholarly output over time. For example, the notion that some professors achieve early recognition for their work, and that this reputation gives them an edge over their peers in competition for funds and publication—the accumulative advantage process—was, as we noted above, based on cross-sequential analysis of citation indexes and little additional longitudinal data (Allison & Stewart, 1974).

The faculty in our NCRIPTAL sample from research universities (N = 601), doctoral universities (N = 366), and comprehensive colleges and

universities (N = 1,004) were similar in terms of sociodemographic characteristics and disciplinary affiliations. (See table 4.5.) However, the average
two-year publication rates varied across settings. The research university
faculty had the highest rate (M = 6.1, SD = 6.6), followed by doctoral
faculty (M = 4.0, SD = 5.3) and comprehensive faculty (M = 2.1, SD =
3.7).[16]

Each factor analysis resulted in a different number of factors as well as
different factor structures for each institutional type. However, the intercorrelations among factors were small for all institutions (coefficients ranged

Table 4.5    Distribution of Institutional Samples across Sociodemographic Variables

|  | *Res-I* | *Doc-I* | *Comp-I* |
|---|---|---|---|
| Number of institutions | 7 | 6 | 26 |
| Number of faculty respondents | 601 | 366 | 1,004 |
| Percent female | 17.9 | 19.4 | 19.2 |
| Percent Ph.D. | 97.7 | 93.7 | 86.7 |
| Discipline (%) | | | |
|   Biology | 14.2 | 10.5 | 13.9 |
|   Chemistry | 12.2 | 10.5 | 10.8 |
|   Math/statistics | 10.7 | 11.9 | 14.6 |
|   English | 14.9 | 20.2 | 20.4 |
|   History | 12.9 | 13.9 | 10.8 |
|   Political science | 10.8 | 10.0 | 8.4 |
|   Psychology | 13.6 | 15.0 | 13.4 |
|   Sociology | 10.7 | 8.0 | 7.7 |
| Rank (%) | | | |
|   Assistant professor | 15.4 | 15.7 | 18.6 |
|   Associate professor | 24.8 | 31.4 | 31.2 |
|   Full professor | 58.5 | 52.9 | 49.9 |
|   Other | 1.4 | 0.0 | 0.3 |
| Appointment (%) | | | |
|   Regular appt. w/ tenure | 82.7 | 81.6 | 82.3 |
|   Regular appt. w/o tenure | 14.6 | 15.9 | 15.4 |
|   Other | 2.7 | 2.5 | 2.3 |
| Race (%) | | | |
|   Caucasian/white | 94.8 | 95.8 | 93.5 |
|   Black, Asian, and other | 5.2 | 4.2 | 6.5 |
| Number of pubs. in last two years | | | |
|   Mean | 6.1 | 4.0 | 2.1 |
|   SD | 6.6 | 5.3 | 3.7 |

*Source:* NCRIPTAL survey.

from $r = -.20$ to $r = .20$). Consequently, it seems reasonable to assume that the factors were measuring different aspects of each of the framework's constructs; that is, they were not related. We entered a total of 61, 67, and 68 variables into the regressions for Res-I, Doc-I, and Comp-I institutions, respectively. In all instances social knowledge subsumed the largest number of variables (24 for Res-I's, 22 for Doc-I's, and 21 for Comp-I's). The fewest variables were under career (3). We define each in appendix B.[17]

We accounted for environmental conditions by running separate regressions for each of the Carnegie institutional types. Our procedure assumes that the colleges and universities within each category are sufficiently similar in terms of mission, the quality of students and faculty, and institutional resources for research. While variations within a group undoubtedly exist, they are likely to be less than the differences between institutional types. The publication output (table 4.5) demonstrates appreciable differences on the key outcome variable. (See the next to last row for the average number of publications in the last two years per faculty member.)

### Effects of Theoretical Constructs on Productivity

#### Res-I Institutions

The results of the regression analysis with publication rate (total publications in the last two years) as the outcome variable are shown in table 4.6.[18] The variables entered into the regression accounted for 58.5 percent of the explained variance in publication rate at Res-I universities.

Table 4.6 and other similarly structured tables in this chapter are to be read as follows. There are two numerical entries for each institutional type. The one in the first column shows the percentage of the variance in the outcome variable (percent effort given to research) that is attributable to the other (predicting) variables as each is entered into the regression analysis. The second column shows the significance level for each variable that was found to be significant at $p \le .05$ after all of the variables had been entered into the regression analysis. A value of $p \le .05$ means that a value of the magnitude shown would occur by chance less often than 5 times out of 100.

The variables were entered in the order of the framework, that is, as they are displayed in the tables when read from top to bottom. Sometimes we entered the entire set of our construct measures as a single step. (That is the case for table 4.6.) Other times we entered the variables one at a time. (That is the case for table 4.8.) The tables show the total explained variance at each successive step. Once the percentage of explained variance is above 2 percent, it is significant at $p \le .05$, the exact value depending upon the size of the sample for that institutional type: the larger the number of faculty, the smaller the percentage can be and still be significant. When the entry of a

Table 4.6    Predicting Percent Effort Given to Research

| | Res-I | | Doc-I | | Comp-I | |
|---|---|---|---|---|---|---|
| | % Var. | p | % Var. | p | % Var. | p |
| *Sociodemographic* | 0 | | 1 | | 1 | |
| Female | | | | | | |
| Race | | | | -.05 | | |
| Age | | | | .001 | | |
| *Career* | **29** | | **41** | | **13** | |
| Academic discipline | | .01 | | .05 | | |
| Active scholar/grantsperson | | | | .001 | | |
| Educational preparation | | | | | | |
| Established faculty member | | | | -.01 | | |
| *Self-knowledge* | 36 | | **51** | | **28** | |
| Committed to teaching | | .01 | | -.01 | | |
| Values cooperation/ inst. commitment | | -.01 | | | | |
| Values disciplined-focused teaching | | -0.5 | | | | |
| Values scholarship | | -.01 | | | | |
| Competent researcher | | | | .01 | | |
| Responsible faculty member | | | | | | |
| *Environmental response* | **36** | | 53 | | **30** | |
| Journal editorial work | | | | | | .05 |
| *Social knowledge* | 38 | | 62 | | 31 | |
| Credible colleagues | | .05 | 47 | | | |
| Faculty committed to teaching | | | 47 | .001 | | |
| Students are motivated | | | **50** | -.01 | | |
| Teacher control needed | | | 50 | .05 | | |
| Course relevance important | | | 51 | .05 | | |
| Credibility of alumni | | | | -.05 | | |
| Students are competitive | | | | .05 | | |
| Well-rounded teacher valued | | | | -.01 | | |
| Ambition/dedication valued | | | | .001 | | |
| Salary equity | | | | -.01 | | |
| Institution values scholarship | | | | .001 | | |
| *Behavior* | **58** | | **78** | | **39** | |
| Grant preparation | | .001 | | | | .001 |
| High research effort | | .001 | | .001 | | .001 |
| Communicates/works hard | | .001 | | | | |
| Applying for fellowship | | .001 | | .01 | | |
| Attends local res. seminars | | .001 | | | | |
| Dissertation work | | | | .001 | | |
| Org. decision making | | | | -0.5 | | |

*Source:* Lawrence, Blackburn, Trautvetter (1989).

*Note:* Bold, italicized entries are at $p \leq .05$.

variable into the regression produces a significant increase in the percentage of variance accounted for, the value appears in bold italics.

By way of illustration, note the first entry for Res-I institutions in table 4.6. When all three sociodemographic variables—sex, race, and age—were entered, the percentage of variance accounted for was less than 1 percent, and hence zero is entered. That is, these variables had no effect on the outcome variable. In addition, none proved to be a significant predictor after all of the variables had been entered, so no entry is recorded in the *p* (probability) column for female, race, or age.

The second entry was the set of career variables—academic discipline, active scholar/grantsperson, educational preparation, and established faculty member. They significantly increased the percentage of variance accounted for to 29 percent. After all of the variables had been entered into the analysis, discipline was statistically significant at $p \leq .01$. When a minus sign precedes a *p* value (as it does, e.g., on three of the self-knowledge variables), it means the opposite (here, e.g., that more prolific publishers do *not* highly value cooperation and institutional commitment). The entry of the self-knowledge variables increased the percentage of the variance accounted for to 36 percent, but this was not a statistically significant increase. (The number therefore appears in the table in regular type.) At the end one sees that 58 percent of the variance in the publication rate of research universities was attributed to the entire set of variables.

Behavior variables most strongly predicted publication rate. All of the behavior variables were strong predictors ($p \leq .001$). Specifically, faculty members who published more during the two years prior to the survey had been actively involved in the preparation of grant proposals and had given more time to research and less to teaching. The prolific publishers had also spent more time working and communicating with colleagues about scholarly and research issues or had been actively engaged in applying for fellowships. Faculty members who attended seminars or made presentations about their research on their own campuses also published at a higher rate.

The results further suggest that the behavior variables mediated the direct effects of the career, self-knowledge, and social knowledge variables. The direct effects of faculty members' educational preparation and cumulative publication or grant record—all publications and proposals submitted before 1985—weakened and dropped out completely when behaviors were entered. On the other hand, the effects of selected measures of self-knowledge and social knowledge became significant only after the behaviors were entered. A personal commitment to teaching had a positive effect on publication, suggesting that productive publishers may also have a concern about their teaching. The negative sign for "values scholarship" indicates, however, that persons who prefer to spend time on activities that enhance their teaching knowledge or skills are not necessarily publishing. The emergence of the social knowledge factor "credible colleagues"—a perception that one's colleagues give valuable feedback on both one's teaching and one's scholarship—suggests that the behavior "communicates/works hard" enhances its effect. Professors who find their colleagues' critiques useful apparently communicate with them more often about research activities.

*Doc-I Institutions*

The variables entered into the regressions appear to be particularly potent within the doctoral universities, accounting for 77.5 percent of the explained variation in current publication rate. The results indicate that at least one measure of each of the theoretical framework's constructs influenced publication. The strongest predictor was a behavior variable, high research involvement. This factor means that a professor was giving more time to research and less to teaching in the current term, and had been actively submitting grant proposals and articles for publication over the last two years. Next came a second behavior, dissertation work, a factor that shows a faculty member's high level of involvement in students' doctoral research and comprehensive examinations. Self-knowledge in the form of greater commitment to research than teaching, signified by the negative sign for "committed to teaching," continued to influence publication rate from initial entry through the final step in the regression. Likewise, a career factor, active scholar/grantsperson, representing one's cumulative research record as of 1985, exerted a continuous influence on publication rate, although its effect diminished. On the other hand, chronological age (a sociodemographic variable) became an important predictor only when behavior entered the framework and indicated that older professors were publishing at a higher rate. Last, "institution values scholarship," the perception that one's university encourages scholarship (social knowledge), also had a positive impact on publication rate.

Generally speaking, the systematic controls on behavior enhanced the impact of the other variables in the framework. The only variable that entered the regression and did not remain through the last step was journal editorial work, a factor indicating involvement in reviews and editing submitted articles. The fact that seven of the social knowledge variables came to exert significant effects on publication rate after we controlled for behavior indicates, however, that these important views of students and organizational climate are not transmitted through the behavior variables specified in this regression.

*Comp-I Institutions*

The framework's theoretical constructs account for 39 percent of the variance for Comp-I institutions, a highly significant amount even though less than for the other two types. Two behavior variables—grant preparation, signifying active involvement in grant preparation, and high research effort, signifying high involvement in research over the past two years—provide the strongest publication predictors. While their strengths were not especially large, both were significant at $p \leq .001$. The only other variable that remained in the final regression was an environmental response factor, journal editorial work. It identifies faculty members actively involved in reviewing articles for journals and serving on the editorial board of a journal. This factor was significant at $p \leq .05$ but is not a strong predictor.

As for the other components of the framework, only one sociodemographic variable, age, appeared in step one but did not account for a significant amount of the explained variance. (The negative value indicates that younger faculty in Comp-I's published more.) No sociodemographic variable remained after all variables had been entered into the regression.

Active scholar/grantsperson, a career variable representing people who were actively publishing books and articles and submitting grant proposals, was initially statistically significant, but its direct effects were mediated when the behavior variables were entered. Further, the strength of the career measures diminished at each succeeding step. Their strength weakens with the addition of the variables in the subsequent theoretical categories.

Three self-knowledge variables—values discipline-focused teaching, competent researcher, and committed to teaching—initially entered the regression. The two teaching factors have negative signs. To the extent that teaching and research are in competition with one another—that is, are opposite ends of a continuum—one interprets the negative teaching signs as positive research ones. No variables subsumed under the social knowledge construct were significant. The direct effects of social knowledge also disappear when behavior variables are entered at the end. The increase in explained variance at each successive step was significant at $p \leq .01$, except for when social knowledge was introduced. This finding further suggests that faculty perceptions of their environment relate to their personal values, competence, and psychological dispositions.

*Discussion*

The results of this study support the proposed theoretical framework for understanding faculty publication differences. The variables taken into account predicted 77.5 percent, 58.5 percent, and 39.0 percent of the variance

142

in two-year publication rates in the doctoral, research, and comprehensive institutions, respectively. As each group of variables entered into the regression, the amount of explained variance increased in a linear fashion. However, except for the career and behavior variables, which always produced significant changes in the explained variance, the size of the increase was not always significant.

In Res-I's the self-knowledge, environmental response, and social knowledge variables together accounted for very little variance in publication rate. None of these variable groups produced a significant change in the productivity measure. In the Doc-I's the self-knowledge measures produced a significant change in the amount of predicted variance, but environmental response and social knowledge measures did not. Both the self-knowledge and environmental response variables increased the explained variance in publication rate within the Comp-I's.

Although the items in this factor are not identical for all three institutional types, the career variable active scholar/grantsperson stays as an important predictor. This finding suggests that past role performance does indeed influence current productivity. A self-knowledge variable, commitment to teaching, is the same factor for all institutions, but among research university faculty it has positive direct effects on publication, and among the doctoral faculty it has a negative effect. One behavior, the high research involvement factor, was important in the comprehensive and doctoral institutions. However, only three of the behavior items in this factor were the same. These items indicate that faculty who devoted more time to research than to other activities, and who conversed with others about research, also submitted larger numbers of manuscripts for publication. Overall, the theoretical framework taps important constructs for different institutional settings and shows that one needs to take into account where faculty members work when making inferences regarding their motivations toward research and publishing.

We defer further generalizations and implications for practice until the conclusion of the next study. It extends the framework to all institutional types.

## All Institutional Types and Other Indicators of Research

We now turn to expanding the framework's applicability to include all institutional types and to two additional indicators of research. We retain typical scholarly publications—articles, book chapters, research proposals and reports, submitted and accepted professional writings—as the product indicator. We add one other behavior as a dependent variable: making

143

conference presentations. A conference presentation may or may not have a formal paper. Even if it does, it may not result in a published article or monograph. In our theoretical framework, then, conference presentations are behaviors, not products. Conversations with colleagues about research processes and progress are important behaviors. A research product can result.

The productions of scholarly publications were once the almost exclusive domain of research and doctoral universities. Today, however, faculty nearly everywhere perceive pressure to obtain external funding, conduct research, and publish their findings. Liberal arts college faculty with their strong teaching mission also find that good teaching evaluations may not suffice to obtain tenure.

The increasing emphasis on the faculty research role may be the result of administrators' desires for enhanced institutional reputation and economic stability. It could also be the outgrowth of an increased interest on the part of faculty in conducting research as a consequence of their graduate school training. Regardless of the reason, more faculty at all institutional types indicate that they would prefer to give more of their work effort to research than they currently give. The needed extra time, they say, would take away from the effort they now give to service. They would prefer the effort they give to teaching to stay about as it is (Carnegie Foundation for the Advancement of Teaching, 1989a).

Consequently, empirical studies that have the research role as their focus are important. We need to know the relative effect of different kinds of motivators on faculty behavior, specifically on their propensity to engage in research.[19]

We used responses from faculty in our same nine Carnegie institutional types. Our institutions span the spectrum of faculty role expectations, from very little research and medium-sized classes with no graduate student assistance in community colleges to a significant research effort and graduate seminars mixed with large classes and supervising teaching assistants in research universities. Before analyzing three specific outcome components of the study, we first used the percentage of effort the faculty member gave to the role as the dependent variable. This procedure allowed us to ascertain the degree to which the sociodemographic, career, self-knowledge, and social knowledge variables explained the faculty behavior of conducting research. We then employed this behavior variable as a predictor for the product (scholarly publications) and the two role-specific behaviors (conference presentations and conversations regarding research).

We begin by giving a broad picture of what the faculty in this study are like. Table 4.7 displays selected sociodemographic, career, self-knowledge, and social knowledge variables by institutional type.

Table 4.7 Selected Demographic, Career, Self-Knowledge, and Social Knowledge Variables (Percent)

|  | Res-I | Res-II | Doc-I | Doc-II | Comp-I | Comp-II | LAC-I | LAC-II | CC |
|---|---|---|---|---|---|---|---|---|---|
| Number | 597 | 244 | 360 | 251 | 996 | 135 | 194 | 263 | 845 |
| Female | 18 | 23 | 19 | 19 | 19 | 23 | 30 | 35 | 30 |
| Graduate school | 78 | 60 | 59 | 56 | 51 | 38 | 52 | 32 | 33 |
| Lecturer | 1 | 0 | 0 | 0 | 0 | 0 | 0 | 1 | 1 |
| Instructor | 0 | 0 | 0 | 0 | 0 | 1 | 0 | 3 | 18 |
| Assistant prof. | 15 | 30 | 16 | 26 | 18 | 26 | 29 | 24 | 10 |
| Associate prof. | 25 | 35 | 31 | 32 | 31 | 26 | 29 | 31 | 26 |
| Professor | 58 | 35 | 52 | 42 | 50 | 47 | 42 | 41 | 43 |
| Career age (actual) | 19 | 17 | 18 | 17 | 18 | 19 | 17 | 16 | 18 |
| Interest in research | 79 | 68 | 51 | 49 | 25 | 13 | 26 | 14 | 7 |
| Personal pref. for research | 42 | 36 | 34 | 31 | 19 | 8 | 14 | 9 | 4 |
| Institutional pref. for research | 39 | 36 | 32 | 31 | 20 | 15 | 20 | 15 | 10 |

*Source:* NCRIPTAL survey.

The sociodemographic and career variables reveal what other studies have demonstrated: that women are underrepresented, more so in universities than in liberal arts and community colleges (see chapter 2); and that Ph.D.-producing universities, especially Res-I's, have more faculty who graduated from Res-I universities (Breneman & Youn, 1988). The top select their faculty from the top. Most who earn their Ph.D.'s from Res-I's want to be on the faculty in a Res-I. The combined factors lead to a highly inbred faculty in Res-I's.

Career age is similar across institutional types. Since the average age of earning the highest degree is about 29 years, the average actual age of these faculty is approximately 47 years. Res-I's and -II's have a markedly higher percentage of full professors, an indication that research matters most in these universities. Rapid promotion and a competitive environment favor those who are successful in this role.

"Interest in research" means that these faculty have said they have a higher interest in research than in teaching, but not that they have no interest in teaching, and vice versa. By way of illustration, 75 percent of Comp-I faculty (100 percent minus 25 percent) have a higher interest in teaching than in research. Most, however, still have some interest in doing research, just as the 25 percent whose greater interest is research maintain an interest in teaching. The very high percentages for interest in research in research universities and the low percentages in Comp-II's, LAC-II's, and CCs conform to expectations.

Personal preferences for time given to research follow the same pattern. University faculty agree on perceived institutional preference for research effort and personal preference for research effort. However, in the two- and four-year colleges, personal preference for research effort is less than what faculty believe the administration wants. The discrepancies can be a source of stress.

In summary, colleges and universities differ appreciably on the variables the framework uses to predict research behavior and output. (Appreciable variation also exists among institutions within a Carnegie category.) The study, then, tests the framework's ability to enlighten us about faculty with differing characteristics in a variety of work environments.

Table 4.8    Predicting Percent Effort Given to Research

|  | *Res-I* | | *Res-II* | | *Doc-I* | | *Doc-II* | |
|---|---|---|---|---|---|---|---|---|
|  | *% Var.* | *p* | *% Var.* | *p* | *% Var.* | *p* | *% Var.* | *p* |
| *Sociodemographic* | | | | | | | | |
| Female | 1 | | 1 | | 1 | | 1 | |
| *Career* | | | | | | | | |
| Grad. inst. rating | 1 | -.02 | 1 | | 1 | | 3 | |
| Career age | 5 | | 8 | | 6 | | 4 | .04 |
| Assistant professor | 5 | | 9 | | 6 | | 5 | .00 |
| Associate professor | 6 | | 12 | | 9 | | 10 | |
| (Male full prof.) | | | | | | | | .00 |
| *Self-knowledge* | | | | | | | | |
| Self-competence | 16 | .02 | 15 | | 26 | .02 | 40 | .00 |
| Self-efficacy (infl.) | 17 | | 16 | | 26 | | 41 | |
| Ambit./compet./commit. | 17 | | 16 | | 26 | | 44 | |
| Research interest | 20 | | 23 | | 28 | | 46 | |
| Preference for research (% effort) | 35 | .00 | 48 | .00 | 47 | .00 | 62 | .00 |
| *Social knowledge* | | | | | | | | |
| Inst. pref. for research (% effort) | 37 | .00 | 52 | .01 | 47 | | 67 | .00 |
| Support services and colleagues | 38 | | 52 | | 47 | | 68 | .01 |
| Support, grant ($s) | 38 | | 53 | | 50 | .01 | 69 | |
| Credence to chair/dean | 38 | | 53 | | 50 | | 69 | -.03 |
| Colleague commitment to research | 39 | | 53 | | 51 | | 69 | |

*Source:* Blackburn, Bieber, Lawrence, and Trautvetter (1991).

*Regression Results*

Table 4.8 shows the results of the regression analysis with the outcome variable being percentage of effort given to research. First we see that the theoretical framework strongly predicts percentage of faculty effort given to research across all institutional types. The percentage of the explained variance in effort given to research ranges from 23 percent in LAC-II's—institutions that neither emphasize nor reward research—to 80 percent in Comp-II's, with an overall average above 50 percent.

However, not all variables turn out to be significant predictors. For example, the sociodemographic and career variables, the ones almost exclusively used in prior research on faculty productivity, rarely account for the effort given to research. Gender never does. The self-knowledge and social knowledge variables, however, do predict well. People who want to give

Table 4.8—*Continued*

| Comp-I | | Comp-II | | LAC-I | | LAC-II | | CC | |
|---|---|---|---|---|---|---|---|---|---|
| % Var. | p | % Var. | p | % Var. | p | % Var. | p | % Var. | p |
| 0 | | 4 | | 0 | | 2 | | 1 | |
| 1 | | 7 | | 1 | | 2 | | 1 | |
| 1 | | 13 | | 3 | | 4 | | 1 | |
| 2 | | 13 | | 4 | | 5 | | 2 | |
| 3 | | 13 | | 4 | | 5 | | 2 | |
| | .00 | | | | | | | | |
| 23 | .00 | 21 | | 18 | | 19 | .01 | 22 | .01 |
| 24 | | 25 | | 18 | | 20 | | 23 | |
| 25 | | 30 | .05 | 21 | | 20 | | 24 | |
| 31 | .00 | 40 | | 24 | | 20 | | 32 | |
| 41 | .00 | 74 | .00 | 35 | .01 | 20 | | 53 | .01 |
| 42 | .02 | 80 | .00 | 41 | | 23 | | 54 | |
| 42 | | 80 | | 42 | | 23 | | 54 | |
| 43 | .00 | 80 | | 42 | | 23 | | 54 | |
| 43 | | 80 | | 42 | | 23 | | 54 | |
| 44 | .01 | 80 | | 44 | | 23 | | 54 | |

time to research, feel that they are able researchers, and believe that research is a high institutional priority are the ones who allocate the most time to their research, a finding that is true across most college and university types (8 of 9, 6 of 9, and 5 of 9, respectively).

For example, we can see that the very high 80 percent explained variance in Comp-II's results principally from the faculty members' personal preference concerning how much time they wish to give to that role. The explained variance increased from 40 percent to 74 percent when that single variable entered the regression. Yet there are publication differences across institutional types, with faculty at Res-I's far outpublishing their counterparts along the Carnegie classes of institutions. Comp-II faculty's preferred effort, then, is not resulting in a proportionate number of publications. They must suffer frustrations.

These findings indicate that it is important for an institution to establish a climate conducive to what it values if it wishes to achieve its goals. If the organization wants increased faculty research output, there must be a clear message from above that such is the case. In addition, the institution must make it obvious that faculty research is being rewarded. Those who successfully serve this goal will receive visible honors, titles, raises. The scholarly record of new hires will be made public.

Turning to table 4.9, where the outcome variable is publications, the behavior variable effort given to research—now a predictor variable—significantly increases the amount of publication output accounted for in three institutional types (Res-I's, LAC-I's, and LAC-II's) but lowers it for two others (Doc-II's and Comp-II's). Self-competence and financial support through obtaining grants are the strong predictors of publishing. The former is significant in all institutional types and the latter in all but LAC-II's and Comp-II's. The entry of self-competence into the equation produces a significant percentage predictive increase for faculty in every college and university type. When grant support entered the regression, it produced a significant increase in the variance accounted for in six of the nine institutional types.

Of the sociodemographic and career variables, only two appear as significant predictors: career age (in three cases) and rating of institution granting the highest degree (two times). What is new here is that it is the younger faculty who are publishing more—the negative coefficient for significant career age means the opposite of older—an outcome different from all prior national surveys of faculty. At the same time, being a male full professor is a significant predictor of publication in five institutional types. It is also of interest that being a graduate of a non-Res-I predicts higher publications. What this discovery suggests is that if you have not graduated from a Res-I but you are a prominent publisher, research institutions will hire you. The finding also demonstrates that Res-I's are not necessarily the exclusive, snobbish clubs many accuse them of being. Faculty in Res-I's have not been growing appreciably for two decades now. These institutions are not hiring anywhere near the number of Ph.D.'s they graduate. Res-I's have been, and still are, the leading Ph.D. producers. They graduate many more than they can add to their staff. It would be a simple matter to have a faculty of 100 percent Res-I graduates, *if* that status was their goal. Here we see that Res-I's value performance over graduate school pedigree when it comes to whom they have on their staff.

We note that gender again fails to predict (except negatively in Comp-I's, meaning that males, coded the opposite of females, produce more there). Most earlier studies found that men published more than women. Also contrary to earlier expectations, interest in research did not predict actual output. We used this self-knowledge variable in a study on teaching (see chapter 5) and found it to be a strong predictor of effort given to teaching (Blackburn, Bieber, Lawrence, & Trautvetter, 1991). Self-efficacy, the ability to influence having one's work published, predicts only for faculty in Res-I institutions. Apparently faculty at the top believe that their status gives them the power to have a piece accepted for publication, a hegemony their colleagues in other institutions do not claim. As generally acknowledged researchers, their peers call on them to write chapters for books they are editing. They can influence the publication of their products. However, what proportion of their work effort they believe the institution wants them to give to research has no impact.

The strong role that having grants has in predicting faculty publication rate suggests that those institutions that want to increase this kind of output need to consider ways they can assist faculty members prepare acceptable proposals. Proposal writing requires skills and support for doing it. The task is about as difficult and complex as is writing up the research that flows from the grant support. Experts can teach others the fine points of grant writing, but they cannot do the writing for the faculty. The author has to know the subject and the state of the art, what research is needed, and how it can be creatively undertaken. Those outside the specialized field cannot design the research.

In addition to learning how to prepare grant proposals, the faculty member needs time and assistance. Relief from an assignment, help from advanced students who can locate key sources, and some seed money to gather critical pilot data and equipment are some of the things the institution can supply at a relatively low cost. If successful grant-getting senior faculty will pair themselves with upcoming researchers and show them the way, this is

Table 4.9   Predicting Publications

|  | Res-I | | Res-II | | Doc-I | | Doc-II | |
|---|---|---|---|---|---|---|---|---|
|  | % Var. | p | % Var. | p | % Var. | p | % Var. | p |
| *Sociodemographic* | | | | | | | | |
| Female | 1 | | 1 | | 1 | | 1 | |
| *Career* | | | | | | | | |
| Grad. inst. rating | 5 | -.01 | 1 | -.02 | 1 | | 3 | |
| Career age | 7 | -.01 | 10 | -.01 | 5 | | 4 | |
| Assistant professor | 10 | -.01 | 19 | -.01 | 6 | | 5 | |
| Associate professor | 17 | -.04 | 27 | | 13 | | 16 | |
| (Male full prof.) | | | | .01 | | | | |
| *Self-knowledge* | | | | | | | | |
| Self-competence | 41 | .00 | 37 | .05 | 34 | .01 | 47 | .00 |
| Self-efficacy (infl.) | 44 | .01 | 37 | | 34 | | 47 | |
| Ambit./compet./commit. | 44 | | 38 | | 36 | .04 | 49 | |
| Research interest | 44 | | 39 | | 36 | | 50 | |
| Preference for research (% effort) | 45 | .00 | 40 | | 38 | | 51 | |
| *Social knowledge* | | | | | | | | |
| Inst. pref. for research (% effort) | 45 | | 41 | | 39 | | 51 | |
| Support services and colleagues | 46 | .01 | 41 | | 39 | | 51 | |
| Support, grant ($s) | 55 | .00 | 44 | .04 | 47 | .00 | 57 | .00 |
| Credence to chair/dean | 55 | | 45 | .05 | 47 | | 57 | |
| Colleague commitment to research | 55 | | 45 | | 47 | | 57 | |
| *Behavior* | | | | | | | | |
| Effort given to research (% time) | 55 | | 48 | .02 | 48 | | 57 | |

*Source:* Blackburn, Bieber, Lawrence, and Trautvetter (1991).

an effective tactic to increase the number of faculty securing grants and subsequently publishing. Evidence shows that the size of the grant is not the critical condition. Even small amounts of money can induce faculty to pay back with a publication or two. Receiving support challenges them to deliver.

At the same time, the institution that chooses to have faculty increase their research output needs to be patient. Even after grant-writing skills have been mastered, it is several years from an idea, a submitted proposal, and funding to research carried out, written up, accepted for publication, and printed. Five years would be the typical minimum time lapse.

As for the outcome variable, namely, making presentations on campus and at conferences—activities that require preparation of research, but not

Table 4.9—*Continued*

| Comp-I | | Comp-II | | LAC-I | | LAC-II | | CC | |
|---|---|---|---|---|---|---|---|---|---|
| % Var. | p | % Var. | p | % Var. | p | % Var. | p | % Var. | p |
| 1 | -.02 | 5 | | 1 | | 1 | | 1 | |
| 1 | | 9 | | 3 | | 1 | | 1 | |
| 3 | | 18 | | 4 | | 3 | -.02 | 1 | |
| 5 | | 19 | | 4 | | 10 | | 1 | |
| 7 | | 19 | | 4 | | 10 | | 1 | |
| | .01 | | | | | | .01 | | .01 |
| 44 | .00 | 49 | .00 | 54 | .00 | 55 | .00 | 51 | .00 |
| 44 | | 49 | | 55 | | 56 | | 52 | |
| 44 | | 51 | | 55 | | 56 | | 52 | |
| 45 | | 52 | | 56 | | 57 | | 53 | |
| 46 | | 53 | | 56 | .01 | 57 | | 54 | .01 |
| 46 | | 53 | | 56 | | 58 | | 54 | |
| 46 | | 53 | | 57 | | 59 | -.05 | 55 | |
| 51 | .00 | 55 | | 59 | .03 | 59 | | 58 | |
| 51 | | 55 | | 59 | | 59 | | 58 | |
| 51 | | 55 | | 59 | | 59 | | 58 | |
| 51 | | 59 | .02 | 59 | | 59 | | 59 | .05 |

necessarily publications—the amounts of explained variance are still appreciable, much higher than they are in the typical faculty study, which most often used only sociodemographic and career variables. (See table 4.10.) The amounts are not, however, as high as they were for published articles, books, and the like. (Average is 32 percent vs. 55 percent.) The predictors are much the same. Self-competence is significant in six college and university types, and financial support (having grants) in four.

A new finding for this outcome measure is that in five institutional types, male full professors are the conference presenters, on campus and away. Conferences often include symposia and special presentations. These events favor the senior faculty who have earned a sound reputation for their research. They will also be on the program with their research papers, because

Table 4.10  Predicting Conference Presentations

|  | Res-I | | Res-II | | Doc-I | | Doc-II | |
|---|---|---|---|---|---|---|---|---|
|  | % Var. | p | % Var. | p | % Var. | p | % Var. | p |
| *Sociodemographic* | | | | | | | | |
| Female | 1 | | 1 | | 1 | | 1 | |
| *Career* | | | | | | | | |
| Grad. inst. rating | 1 | | 1 | | 1 | | 1 | |
| Career age | 6 | -.01 | 7 | | 3 | | 2 | |
| Assistant professor | 7 | | 7 | | 3 | | 2 | |
| Associate professor | 12 | -.04 | 10 | | 4 | | 11 | |
| (Male full prof.) | | .00 | | .03 | | .02 | | |
| *Self-knowledge* | | | | | | | | |
| Self-competence | 23 | .01 | 16 | | 14 | .04 | 25 | |
| Self-efficacy (infl.) | 25 | | 16 | | 14 | | 25 | |
| Ambit./compet./commit. | 25 | | 17 | | 14 | | 27 | |
| Research interest | 25 | | 17 | | 14 | | 27 | |
| Preference for research (% effort) | 25 | | 17 | | 15 | .04 | 28 | |
| *Social knowledge* | | | | | | | | |
| Inst. pref. for research (% effort) | 25 | | 17 | | 15 | | 29 | |
| Support services and colleagues | 25 | | 17 | | 15 | | 29 | |
| Support, grant ($s) | 29 | .00 | 18 | | 20 | .01 | 32 | .03 |
| Credence to chair/dean | 30 | | 19 | | 23 | .01 | 33 | |
| Colleague commitment to research | 30 | | 19 | | 23 | | 36 | .01 |
| *Behavior* | | | | | | | | |
| Effort given to research (% time) | 30 | | 20 | .02 | 24 | | 36 | |

*Source:* Blackburn, Bieber, Lawrence, and Trautvetter (1991).

most remain active throughout their career. Being a full professor predicts this activity.

Conference activity most often lies outside the institution. Regional and national meetings are beyond administrators' ability to influence, even if they wanted to. These are the professional disciplines at work—national, not in-house, operations. Administrators are welcome to participate in them and can be on the program, if they are active scholars. The organization can encourage faculty members' participation in disciplinary associations and can reward them by providing dollars for attendance, even sweetening the stimulus with additional amounts to those having their research papers accepted in a peer-review process.

Professional conferences are also the source of new ideas for faculty—

Table 4.10—*Continued*

| Comp-I | | Comp-II | | LAC-I | | LAC-II | | CC | |
|---|---|---|---|---|---|---|---|---|---|
| % Var. | p | % Var. | p | % Var. | p | % Var. | p | % Var. | p |
| 1 | | 3 | | 1 | | 2 | 0.04 | 1 | |
| 1 | | 3 | | 3 | | 2 | | 1 | |
| 3 | | 5 | | 1 | | 2 | | 1 | |
| 5 | | 9 | | 1 | | 4 | | 2 | |
| 6 | | 9 | | 1 | | 4 | | 5 | -.04 |
| | .00 | | | | | | .02 | | .05 |
| 18 | .00 | 15 | | 18 | | 32 | .00 | 23 | .00 |
| 18 | | 16 | | 20 | | 32 | | 25 | .05 |
| 18 | | 16 | | 20 | | 33 | | 26 | |
| 18 | | 21 | | 21 | | 34 | | 26 | |
| 18 | | 21 | | 21 | | 34 | | 27 | .01 |
| 19 | | 22 | | 23 | | 35 | | 27 | |
| 19 | | 22 | | 23 | | 35 | | 28 | |
| 21 | | 25 | | 23 | | 36 | | 31 | .00 |
| 21 | | 30 | | 25 | | 37 | | 32 | |
| 21 | | 30 | | 25 | | 37 | | 32 | |
| 22 | | 30 | | 28 | | 37 | | 32 | |

from the paper-presentation sessions and, even more important in the view of many, from the conversations faculty have with peers elsewhere who are doing related work, the talks that take place in the halls, bars, and restaurants. While making research presentations adds to the status of the individual faculty member, it also enhances the reputation of her or his department and college or university, goals the individual and the institution share.

The third outcome measure of research activity—collegial conversations and frequency of talking about your research with colleagues at professional conferences or by phone—produced unanticipated results. Besides providing a high percentage of the explained variance accounted for—38 percent, on the average, larger than for professional presentations—a broader assortment of predictor variables emerged. (See table 4.11.)

Table 4.11  Predicting Conversations Regarding Research

| | Res-I | | Res-II | | Doc-I | | Doc-II | |
|---|---|---|---|---|---|---|---|---|
| | % Var. | p | % Var. | p | % Var. | p | % Var. | p |
| *Sociodemographic* | | | | | | | | |
| Female | 1 | | 1 | | 1 | | 1 | |
| *Career* | | | | | | | | |
| Grad. inst. rating | 3 | | 1 | | 1 | | 1 | |
| Career age | 7 | -.01 | 6 | | 7 | -.02 | 3 | |
| Assistant professor | 8 | | 8 | | 9 | | 3 | |
| Associate professor | 13 | | 15 | | 11 | | 8 | |
| (Male full prof.) | | .03 | | | | .00 | | |
| *Self-knowledge* | | | | | | | | |
| Self-competence | 33 | .00 | 25 | | 27 | .01 | 24 | |
| Self efficacy (infl.) | 36 | .01 | 25 | | 27 | | 25 | |
| Ambit./compet./commit. | 38 | .00 | 27 | | 27 | | 31 | .02 |
| Research interest | 38 | | 27 | | 28 | .03 | 32 | |
| Preference for research (% effort) | 38 | | 27 | | 28 | | 32 | |
| *Social knowledge* | | | | | | | | |
| Inst. pref. for research (% effort) | 38 | | 28 | | 29 | | 32 | |
| Support services and colleagues | 39 | | 30 | | 29 | | 34 | |
| Support, grant ($s) | 40 | .01 | 30 | | 32 | .01 | 39 | .01 |
| Credence to chair/dean | 41 | | 35 | .01 | 32 | | 39 | |
| Colleague commitment to research | 41 | | 35 | | 33 | | 40 | |
| *Behavior* | | | | | | | | |
| Effort given to research (% time) | 41 | | 37 | | 33 | | 40 | |

*Source:* Blackburn, Bieber, Lawrence, and Trautvetter (1991).

Self-competence and financial support (grants) still dominated the explanations (in six and four of the institutional types, respectively). For the first time gender and ambition/competitiveness became significant predictors (in two and three institutional types, respectively). It may be that some people who are not part of the "old boy" network and are striving to improve their lot in the academic pecking order of institutions are using communication links to increase their publication output. For instance, a woman may have few female colleagues on her campus and so calls them elsewhere for a host of reasons. However, note that male full professors also engage in this activity, for they know how valuable colleague critiques and ideas are.

As private an enterprise as research is, in the end it is a social event. One shares what one has learned and benefits from the reviews one receives. As

154

Table 4.11—*Continued*

| Comp-I | | Comp-II | | LAC-I | | LAC-II | | CC | |
|---|---|---|---|---|---|---|---|---|---|
| % Var. | p | % Var. | p | % Var. | p | % Var. | p | % Var. | p |
| 1 | | 1 | | 1 | | 6 | .01 | 1 | .01 |
| 1 | | 2 | | 1 | | 7 | | 1 | |
| 4 | | 19 | -.01 | 5 | | 8 | | 1 | |
| 4 | | 22 | | 5 | | 8 | | 2 | |
| 4 | | 22 | | 6 | | 8 | | 2 | |
| | .00 | | .05 | | | | | | |
| 19 | .00 | 34 | | 31 | .01 | 24 | | 19 | .01 |
| 20 | .02 | 35 | | 32 | | 25 | | 22 | .05 |
| 20 | | 37 | | 32 | | 25 | | 26 | .00 |
| 20 | | 37 | | 36 | | 26 | | 26 | |
| 20 | | 42 | | 36 | | 29 | .01 | 31 | |
| 20 | | 43 | | 37 | | 29 | | 31 | |
| 20 | | 43 | | 37 | | 29 | | 31 | |
| 24 | | 45 | | 37 | | 30 | | 32 | .04 |
| 24 | | 47 | | 38 | | 32 | | 33 | |
| 24 | | 47 | | 38 | | 32 | | 34 | |
| 25 | .00 | 47 | | 40 | | 34 | | 34 | |

Storer (1966) argues, until expert peers judge a creation, nothing meaningful has been brought into the world. That ambitious, competitive, perseverant people are ones who talk with other experts is therefore not surprising. That women use phones to test ideas and obtain information also makes sense, in that sometimes it is easier to talk with people at a distance than at home if the environment is the chilly one many women say characterizes their department. Lincoln (1992) learned that a computer network may be especially advantageous for women. On line, neither their self nor their voice registers. As far as the correspondent on the Bitnet message system knows, they might even be male. Men's negative stereotypes of women as researchers do not have the same chance to emerge. Male faculty have found the computer network "efficient" (their words), whereas women praise its ability to link them with people they could not otherwise communicate and share research ideas and information with. Women want to succeed in this career, but they have not been doing so as well as men. Communicating with others pays dividends.

Administrative actions here are clear, simple, and inexpensive. The computer and modem have replaced the typewriter as standard equipment, in offices both on campus and at home. Some faculty still need to learn how to use them, or be converted. Today's typical university provides many ways for faculty to learn these skills. The cost-conscious and perceptive administrator will not try to save small amounts of money by restricting long-distance phone calls or cutting back on computing allocations. Rather, he or she will be looking for ways to motivate faculty who are not conversing with faculty elsewhere to do so.

### Discussion

In summary, then, the widespread strength of the explained variance argues powerfully for the usefulness of the theoretical framework. On several occasions self-knowledge and social knowledge variables significantly predicted behaviors and products, much more frequently than did socio-demographic or career variables.

We have also learned about how faculty behave and what they value. We see that they act quite autonomously. As far as their research effort and products are concerned, what they believe the institution wants them to do in this role, and particularly how much effort they should give to research, does not affect how much effort they give or how much they produce. Nor does their interest in research matter, at least in the way we measured it. It may be that the personal and professional satisfaction faculty receive from successful research effort would better explain what they produce other than books, chapters, and the like, constructs our data do not have. Percentage of effort preferred was a strong predictor and can be considered an indicator of personal valuation of the activity.

Still, research continues to be a lonely business on these campuses. Faculty do not believe they can influence the acceptance of their work to the degree they believe they can affect student learning. (See chapter 5.) Their lack of credence in their chairs' and deans' comments on their research suggests that administrators have little influence on their research success.[20] They do not even believe that having colleagues committed to research has anything to do with their own research accomplishments.

Finally, for the most part, research rewards lie outside the home institution. The organization can facilitate the faculty member's efforts but cannot guarantee them. Wise administrators will continue to support faculty research in the ways we have suggested, even if the faculty members do not recognize their important contributions.

## Sex Differences in the Sciences

Our analyses so far that involved regressions have treated sex as a dummy variable.[21] This is how studies of this kind typically proceed. However, treating the sex variable in this way limits the information acquired, because one cannot compare the relative strength of the constructs for the two sexes. The following study separates men from women and examines and contrasts the relative strengths of the predicting variables for each sex. We selected faculty in the sciences—biology, chemistry, and mathematics in our database—because of the current concerns regarding the need for more women in these disciplines. (See the discussion in chapter 2.)

Our data allow us to address selected gaps in this research. The specific question being addressed here is this: What are the relationships and differences for female and male full-time faculty in the natural sciences with regard to the predictive power of our framework's career, self-knowledge, social knowledge, and behavior variables regarding scholarly publication rate?[22]

Because of the small sample sizes for female scientists, we used a variation of the Carnegie system. We established the following three categories so as to obtain a larger sample size distribution: category 1, research universities I and II; category 2, doctoral universities I and liberal arts colleges I; and category 3, doctoral universities II and comprehensive universities and colleges I and II.[23] This procedure places together those institutions that are most alike in faculty research output and support for research. The three categories run from high to low and allow us to control for work environment and to test if place of work in part explains female and male productivity. The categories also tend to equalize the number of women in each collection. The subsamples of women in biology, chemistry, and mathematics and institutional categories are of sufficient size for the analyses being performed.

We used factor analyses and scaling when appropriate to increase the strength and reliability of some of the variables. The dependent variable was the number of articles published over the last two years. Appendix C lists the factor items.[24]

The data analyses proceeded through two stages. First, we ran descriptive and simple statistical tests to discern gender discrepancies within and among the three institutional categories and disciplines. Next, we employed separate stepwise multiple regressions by gender to observe the sex differences and the relationships among the constructs used for predicting publication rate. Since there were two independent samples, we can determine the significance of the differences in the variables' strengths. Furthermore, the regressions provide information about how much variance in publication rate the constructs explain for each sex.

Table 4.12 shows the similarities and differences in terms of some of the construct variables. The samples from each category are composed as follows: category 1, accounting for 28.9 percent of the study sample, is 88 percent male; category 2, 18.7 percent of the sample, is 81 percent male; and category 3, 52.4 percent of the sample, is 86 percent male.

Three general observations: (1) women are the minority in all three disciplines across the institutional categories, (2) more female faculty are found in biology than in the other two natural science disciplines, and (3) a higher percentage of assistant professors are women in all institutional categories.

A few sex differences exist in the three institutional categories. Career age in categories 1 and 2 is consistently lower for women. In Doc-I and LAC-I institutions (category 2), women in biology and math have a lower career age than men; however, women in chemistry have more faculty experience. In general, the men are more likely to be full professors.

In addition, male faculty members in the natural sciences are generally more likely to be graduates of Res-I institutions, to have the Ph.D. degree, and to produce more publications. The average two-year publication rates varied across institutional settings as well as disciplines. Res-I and -II (category 1) faculty have the highest rates, followed by Doc-I and LAC-I (category 2) faculty.

No sex differences exist in personal preference for effort allocated to research or actual effort allocated to research. Sex differences occur in perceived institutional preference for time allocated to research, but no pattern appears.

Table 4.13 shows the results for the separate regressions run against publication rate for each sex. The table contains a middle column of t-statistics. These are positive (female greater) or negative (male greater) numbers that test for the comparative strength of the predicting variables. When it is greater than 1.95 (either positive or negative), the difference is significant at $\leq .05$.

The explained variances in publication rate (last two years) for women and men in the two regressions were 71 percent and 62 percent, respectively. In addition, the constructs that predict these variances frequently differ for the two sexes.

Overall, professorial rank (assistant professors publish less), past publication experience (high past publishers publish more), and research self-competency account for female publication performance. The latter two produced the highest increase in explained variance for the women. Perceived research self-competence stands out as the major difference for female faculty members. The more competent female faculty believe themselves to be, the more they publish; if they do not have this valuation of themselves, they publish less.[25] Rank (assistant professors publish less), career age (less experienced faculty publish more), past publication experience (high past publishers publish more), and actual allocation to research effort (a behavior) account for the variance predicting male publication performance.[26] Career and self-knowledge variables produced the highest explained variance change for publication rate by the women.

We also calculated the differences between the variable strengths of the two independent samples. A positive t-statistic for a particular variable means that the variables had a stronger effect on women. There were only three significant variables that both regressions have in common. The effect that was stronger for women was research self-competency. However, being an assistant professor and past publication experience showed stronger effects for the men.

These strong findings require further elaboration. First, it is important to note that neither discipline nor place of work was a significant predictor. No matter which institutional category, and hence no matter which institutional type, the predictors were the same. Said another way, in the case of a woman's research efficacy, it matters not at all if she is in a rich, moderate, or weak research environment; those who believe they are competent researchers will be the higher publishers, and vice versa.

Furthermore, research self-competency remains significant even when we controlled for past publication rate. Prior publication rate, therefore, is not contributing to the impact of self-competence on current publications.[27] It is the current self-valuation, not earlier success, that matters. Like the successful composer with a blank score on the desk or the mathematician with a clean chalkboard on the wall, the researcher knows that the forthcoming creation may fall short. The symphony may receive negative reviews; the mathematician may flounder in the attempt to prove the theorem; nothing comes forth. Certainly earlier successes provide clues on how to proceed. However, the confidence to try something new depends upon current valuations of the self, on how the individual assesses her or his competence. With prior failures as well as successes, the past is not as strong an indicator as is the valuation of the moment.

The strength of the research-efficacy variable can also be seen by noting the variables that did not predict when all were in the regression. Highest

Table 4.12  Gender Characteristics by Institutional Category and Discipline, 1988

| | Category 1 | | | | | | Category 2 | | | | | | Category 3 | | | | | |
| | Biology | | Chemistry | | Math | | Biology | | Chemistry | | Math | | Biology | | Chemistry | | Math | |
| | F | M | F | M | F | M | F | M | F | M | F | M | F | M | F | M | F | M |
|---|---|---|---|---|---|---|---|---|---|---|---|---|---|---|---|---|---|---|
| *Number* | 19 | 98 | 6 | 96 | 10 | 67 | 19 | 49 | 9 | 51 | 8 | 55 | 30 | 156 | 18 | 131 | 28 | 173 |
| *Percent* | 16 | 84 | 6 | 94 | 13 | 87 | 28 | 72 | 15 | 85 | 13 | 87 | 16 | 84 | 12 | 88 | 14 | 86 |
| *Career age* | | | | | | | | | | | | | | | | | | |
| Mean | 11 | 18 | 12 | 20 | 19 | 20 | 15 | 20 | 24 | 18 | 15 | 20 | 13 | 20 | 16 | 20 | 12 | 19 |
| SD | 9 | 10 | 11 | 12 | 15 | 10 | 9 | 11 | 9 | 9 | 20 | 9 | 8 | 10 | 8 | 9 | 9 | 9 |
| *Rank* | | | | | | | | | | | | | | | | | | |
| Instructor | — | — | — | — | 10 | — | — | — | — | 2 | — | — | — | — | — | — | 4 | — |
| Assistant professor | 44 | 14 | 33 | 21 | 30 | 17 | 63 | 8 | 44 | 20 | 50 | 20 | 23 | 14 | 29 | 15 | 50 | 19 |
| Associate professor | 39 | 32 | — | 17 | 20 | 19 | 11 | 22 | 44 | 22 | 13 | 33 | 43 | 27 | 29 | 20 | 36 | 38 |
| Full professor | 11 | 53 | 67 | 63 | 40 | 65 | 26 | 69 | 11 | 57 | 38 | 47 | 33 | 59 | 41 | 65 | 11 | 43 |
| Lecturer | 6 | 1 | — | — | — | — | — | — | — | — | — | — | — | — | — | 1 | — | — |
| *Highest degree* | | | | | | | | | | | | | | | | | | |
| Bachelor's | — | — | — | — | 10 | — | — | — | — | — | — | — | — | — | — | — | — | — |
| Master's | 5 | 1 | — | — | 20 | — | 11 | — | 11 | — | 25 | 6 | 7 | 6 | 11 | 4 | 39 | 15 |
| Ed.D. | — | — | — | — | 10 | — | — | 2 | — | — | 13 | 6 | 3 | 1 | — | 3 | 11 | 11 |
| J.D. or M.D. | — | — | — | — | 10 | — | — | 2 | — | — | — | 2 | — | 1 | — | — | — | 1 |
| Ph.D. | 95 | 99 | 100 | 100 | 50 | 100 | 90 | 96 | 89 | 100 | 63 | 87 | 90 | 92 | 89 | 93 | 50 | 74 |
| *Graduated from Res-I* | | | | | | | | | | | | | | | | | | |
| inst. (%) | 74 | 75 | 50 | 71 | 56 | 72 | 63 | 47 | 50 | 62 | 38 | 47 | 27 | 44 | 39 | 55 | 44 | 47 |

| | | | | | | | | | | | | | | | | | | |
|---|---|---|---|---|---|---|---|---|---|---|---|---|---|---|---|---|---|---|
| **Preference for research (% effort)** | | | | | | | | | | | | | | | | | | |
| Mean | 46 | 44 | 43 | 44 | 36 | 39 | 30 | 31 | 28 | 31 | 22 | 23 | 25 | 23 | 22 | 22 | 17 | 16 |
| SD | 16 | 16 | 7 | 14 | 9 | 19 | 16 | 15 | 16 | 20 | 11 | 16 | 14 | 16 | 17 | 15 | 13 | 13 |
| **Inst. pref. for research (% effort)** | | | | | | | | | | | | | | | | | | |
| Mean | 39 | 41 | 40 | 38 | 42 | 42 | 20 | 24 | 22 | 29 | 17 | 23 | 24 | 20 | 15 | 21 | 17 | 20 |
| SD | 17 | 17 | 15 | 16 | 13 | 17 | 13 | 15 | 13 | 24 | 18 | 17 | 22 | 15 | 14 | 14 | 11 | 14 |
| **Research effort allocation (%)** | | | | | | | | | | | | | | | | | | |
| Mean | 31 | 34 | 37 | 35 | 28 | 25 | 18 | 16 | 18 | 22 | 14 | 14 | 14 | 14 | 11 | 13 | 8 | 10 |
| SD | 19 | 20 | 10 | 16 | 21 | 16 | 24 | 12 | 7 | 19 | 11 | 14 | 15 | 13 | 14 | 14 | 8 | 12 |
| **Number of prof. writings accepted in last two years (1985–87)** | | | | | | | | | | | | | | | | | | |
| Mean | 4 | 7 | 8 | 9 | 3 | 4 | 2 | 3 | 2 | 6 | 2 | 2 | 2 | 3 | 1 | 2 | 1 | 2 |
| SD | 4 | 6 | 5 | 7 | 3 | 3 | 4 | 4 | 3 | 11 | 2 | 3 | 2 | 6 | 1 | 4 | 1 | 3 |

Source: NCRIPTAL survey.

Note: Category 1 = Res-I and -II; category 2 = Doc-I and LAC-I; category 3 = Doc-II and Comp-I and -II.

Table 4.13  Regression Results for Female and Male Faculty Predicting Two-Year Publication Rate

|  | Female | | | | Male | | |
|---|---|---|---|---|---|---|---|
|  | R2 | p | Beta | t-stat. | R2 | p | Beta |
| **1. Career** | | | | | | | |
| x Career age | .58* |  | -0.05 | 0.25 | .56* | .009 | -0.06 |
| x Assistant professor |  | .005 | -2.13 | -0.71 |  | .031 | -1.43 |
| x Associate professor |  | .034 | -1.45 | -0.85 |  |  | -0.76 |
| x Inst. where one graduated |  | .040 | 0.99 | 0.58 |  |  | 0.64 |
| x Past publication experience |  | .000 | 2.19 | -2.15 |  | .000 | 2.83 |
| **2. Self-knowledge** | | | | | | | |
| Assistant professor | .69* | .024 | -1.57 | -0.03 | .59* | .019 | -1.54 |
| Past publication experience |  | .000 | 1.48 | -2.53 |  | .000 | 2.34 |
| x Research self-competency |  | .001 | 1.30 | 1.02 |  | .002 | 0.84 |
| **3. Social knowledge** | | | | | | | |
| Assistant professor | .71 |  | -1.61 | -0.07 | .59 | .021 | -1.54 |
| Past publication experience |  | .000 | 1.58 | -1.66 |  | .000 | 2.27 |
| Research self-competency |  | .002 | 1.46 | 1.28 |  | .007 | 0.79 |
| Personal disposition |  |  | -0.06 | -1.40 |  | .043 | 0.41 |
| x Perceived inst. pref. for res. |  |  | 0.00 | -1.73 |  | .008 | 0.04 |
| **4. Behavior** | | | | | | | |
| Assistant professor | .71 | .045 | -1.68 | -0.02 | .62* | .012 | -1.66 |
| Career age |  |  | -0.03 | 0.45 |  | .047 | -0.05 |
| Past publication experience |  | .000 | 1.60 | -1.48 |  | .000 | 2.22 |
| Research self-competency |  | .001 | 1.50 | 1.68 |  | .035 | 0.61 |
| x Effort allocated to research |  |  | -0.01 | -2.89 |  | .000 | 0.07 |

*Source:* Trautvetter and Blackburn (1990).

*Notes:* An asterisk indicates significant R2 change. x indicates the variables entered at each step. *p* is the significance level (*p* values ≤ .05 were recorded). Betas are unstandardized coefficients.

degree and rating of graduate school institution, along with discipline and institutional type (career variables); morale, disposition to conduct research, perceived career success, personal preference for research effort (self-knowledge); colleague support, having grants, perceived institutional preference for research effort (social knowledge)—while some of these variables were significant when first entered, none remained significant when all were present. Actual percentage of time given to research (behavior) had a small but significant strength. However, when comparing men with women, it produced the largest difference between the sexes (t = −.289, p ≤ .01). For men, effort was much stronger. Past publication experience (career) had the next largest t-value in the differences. Male scientists with stronger past publication records published more. Other current publication performance predictors that were stronger for men than for women before the behavior variable was added were perceived institutional preference for research and personal disposition (ambitious, competitive, perseverant)— attributes often associated with masculinity. These results tend to corroborate beliefs that men are more driven and competitive than women (Hamovitch & Morgenstern, 1977) and enjoy the research image more than their female colleagues do (Fulton & Trow, 1974).

These findings are also consistent with Bandura's (1982) explanations for why individuals may stop trying to achieve a given goal (in this case, publishing): (1) they lack a sense of personal control, (2) they expect their behavior to have no effect on an environment perceived to be unresponsive, and (3) they expect not to be rewarded for their efforts. Women may publish less because they feel a loss of personal control (efficacy) and receive less recognition and fewer rewards than men do.

Some previous studies that include natural scientists also show that female scientists do not think they are taken seriously and believe they are less competent than their male colleagues (Etaugh & Kasley, 1981; Frieze & Hanusa, 1984; Ramaley, 1978; Widom & Burke, 1978; Zuckerman & Cole, 1975). Linn and Hyde (1989) believe that sex differences in confidence may contribute to differential career access. Women interested in science and mathematics display lower confidence than men at early stages of the educational pipeline, generally during the high school years, even though their grades are high (Dossey, Mulles, Lindquist, & Chambers, 1988; Eccles, 1984). This lower perceived competence can easily continue through the years, even in the face of a strong academic record.

Many implications follow. What this study implies is that if one wants to understand better what explains the productivity of female academics, one must investigate female academics as female academics, not in comparison with men. It is time to set aside the notion that the existing, essentially male, model is the standard to measure women by. We urge a fresh line of inquiry. We have learned about what affects men. We have also learned that many male attributes do not predict for women.

We need to develop instruments grounded on the growing literature on what is distinctive about women. For example, we need to test variables such as support (e.g., a significant other, financial security, a mentor, a professional partner), networks (e.g., occupation of gatekeeper positions, off-campus professional activities, access to the power elite), available work time (e.g., good health, reduced family obligations), and career goals (e.g., success without vicious competitiveness, freedom from the constraints of traditional research).

So far we have said nothing about discrimination and harassment in the workplace. We trust that administrators are already increasing the likelihood of female success by eliminating the more blatant violations. The chilly climate for female academic scientists can be made warmer. Doing so may channel more women into science and into academe. (At the conclusion of this chapter we discuss in more detail management strategies for accomplishing individual and collective success in research.)

## Other Studies

Here we synoptically present findings from three other studies that used our framework but different databases. Two use data from the NSOPF88 national faculty survey conducted by the National Center for Educational Statistics, and one uses the 1989 national survey data collected by the Carnegie Foundation for the Advancement of Teaching. These are the two most recent available data banks.

Using the NCES database, Wenzel and Blackburn (1993) obtained percentage of explained variance in publication rate ranging from 15 percent for medical school faculty to 85 percent for nursing faculty (with 30 percent for engineering, 31 percent for natural sciences, and 35 percent for health sciences). In the main the strongest predictors were the same as those found above for arts and science faculty. For the most part these are lower values. Moreover, the variables often differ from those used in this chapter. The differences may result from the peculiar nature of these professional fields, and from the fact that the NCES database has very few of the theoretical framework's key variables in its questionnaire.

Wenzel, Crawley, and Blackburn (1993) used the 1989 Carnegie database. They accounted for 51 percent of the explained variance for business school faculty and 37 percent for engineering school faculty when publication in the last two years was the outcome variable.[28]

Crawley, Wenzel, and Blackburn (1993) used the NCES database to predict grant procuring as the output variable, a different dependent outcome. Twenty-four percent of the explained variance was accounted for. In the same way that prior publication rate was a strong predictor for current publications (number of scholarly articles in the last two years), so was prior proposal writing a strong predictor for grant getting. The lower value most likely resulted from the same limiting factors Wenzel and Blackburn found with this database.

Because they sampled faculty our NCRIPTAL survey did not, these databases were appreciably deficient in items that get at self-knowledge and social knowledge variables, yet they still obtained higher percentages than the earlier research on faculty did. Hence, the studies give indirect support to the basic structure of our framework. As Long (1987) pointed out so well, while researchers relish the large Ns needed for more sophisticated statistical analyses, if one has not tapped the critical variables, the sheer number of cases does not advance the ultimate research goal.

## An Institutional Case: Some Longitudinal Data

This longitudinal study employs interviews that allow the theoretical framework to account for what faculty tell us about their careers and how the university "works." While the number of respondents is small, the reported experiences supply new insights into why faculty behave as they do.

A research university's institutional prestige inextricably depends on faculty research accomplishments. Universities design their faculty selection and promotion processes to recruit and retain productive scholars. The reward systems provide ongoing incentives for faculty members to conduct research (Blau, 1973; Long & McGinnis, 1981). Yet despite these efforts, individual grant activity and publication output sometimes drop off or never quite attain institutionally desired levels (Fox, 1985b).

Here we focus on institutional incentives and on select career variables in order to examine their effects on faculty publication rates. We use longitudinal data to explore several questions. When an individual achieves the goal of becoming a full professor and academic promotion incentives no longer exist, do behavior and productivity change? Do faculty members from the humanities, social sciences, and natural sciences differ in their respective perceptions of the organization, their distribution of effort to research and administrative activities, and their rate of publication? Are there differences between career cohorts that may be the consequences of variations in their socialization by the university?

This analysis focuses on the productivity-feedback loop of the framework and on select career and self-knowledge variables that may influence its components (social knowledge, behavior, productivity, and environmental response). The higher-education literature suggests that (1) promotion and merit salary are highly correlated with publication in research universities, and (2) faculty from different disciplines and career cohorts may have different socialization experiences that lead to variations in behavior and productivity (Pfeffer, Leong, & Strehl, 1977; Tuckman & Leahey, 1975).

We collected data at two points in time, 1976 and 1986, from a panel of male faculty members in a Res-I university's liberal arts college.[29] Of the 75 individuals originally interviewed in 1976, 49 were reinterviewed in 1986.

Of these 49, 33 provided productivity data. These 33 comprise the panel set used in the longitudinal analysis. The subjects—16 humanists (from the disciplines of English, philosophy, classical studies, history, and romance languages and literature), 10 social scientists (economics, psychology, political science, anthropology, sociology, and speech), and 7 natural and physical scientists (biological sciences, computer science, and mathematics)— were appointed as assistant professors at the institution in one of three years: 1960, 1965, or 1970. There were both tenured and untenured respondents at the first time of data collection. By 1986 all 33 had been tenured, but not all had achieved the rank of full professor (full professor N = 27, associate N = 5, and assistant N = 1).

At both points in time, data were collected through in-depth interviews lasting approximately two hours and covering a range of issues. The interview questions elicited the respondents' perceptions of their department and college or university, including their explanations for key events that had occurred during the decade between interviews. They also talked about themselves (e.g., their values, interests, and competencies as researchers, teachers, and members of the "community"). They openly discussed their experiences with, and responses to, the merit and promotion systems of the institution.

Although the interview protocols used at the two points of data collection were not completely identical, they did include repeat measures on several variables, including those addressing the respondents' self-knowledge, social knowledge, and behavior. Responses to these repeat items and data from curriculum vitae constitute our data set.

We used the information collected in 1976 and 1986 to assess differences between faculty with dissimilar career experiences as well as individual change over time. We compared faculty from the three fields and from the three career cohorts at the two times with respect to their social knowledge, behavior, and productivity. In addition, we compared the publication rates of faculty members who were full professors in 1976 with that of assistant and associate professors in 1986. We also assessed individual changes in publication rate for two time periods: 1960–1976 and 1977–1986.

The repeat measures that are available permit assessments of faculty members' understanding of role expectations for the different ranks, criteria applied in tenure and promotion decisions, and degree of organizational consensus about these criteria (social knowledge). These measures are all scaled variables in which the respondent indicated the fraction of 100 percent allocated to each criterion or activity and the degree of consensus on a scale of 1 (low) to 6 (high). The distribution-of-effort indicator (behavior) is also a scaled variable. Individuals indicated how much of their full-time appointment they gave to teaching, research, and service. We used curriculum vitae to assess level of administrative responsibilities and publication output (productivity). We counted only those administrative responsibilities that involved assigned or reimbursed time (e.g., department chair, program director, dean, vice president). Publication output includes articles published in refereed journals, books authored and edited, chapters in books, and reviews. We used the rate of promotion—number of years in each rank—and number of promotions attained between 1960 and 1986 to define environmental response. We used other data available at the times of data gathering qualitatively to describe other framework constructs, primarily self-knowledge, that may contribute to variations in research effort and publication output.

To answer the questions posed, we divided respondents into several subgroups based on professorial rank, field, and year of initial appointment at the university. We calculated individual and collective publication rates in the first case by dividing a faculty member's total publications while in a given rank by the number of years the individual was in that rank. We defined the field and cohort publication rates, respectively, as the average for all respondents in the humanities, social sciences, or natural or physical sciences, and for all individuals appointed in 1960, 1965, or 1970. We calculated individual administrative responsibilities, like publication rates, as the number of assignments carried out by an individual during the time period of a particular rank; similarly, administrative responsibilities are also calculated for fields and career cohorts. We used frequency distributions and means to describe differences within and among faculty subgroups. In addition, t-tests evaluate the significance of differences between groups and the change in individual publication rate between 1976 and 1986.[30]

### Analysis by Point of Promotion

The first analysis sought to identify differences in productivity between faculty members who had achieved the rank of full professor and those who had yet to achieve this rank. By 1976, 20 assistant professors had been promoted to full professor. By 1986 seven more individuals had attained that rank. In 1976 full professors produced twice as many publications as the non–full professors. In 1986 full professors produced over three times as many publications as their non-full-professor counterparts.

Since the 1986 full-professor group includes both respondents that held this rank in 1976 and those who became full professors sometime between 1976 and 1986, we made additional comparisons. We compared the productivity rates, as measured in both 1976 and 1986, for individuals who were full professors at both times of data collection with those of individuals who became full professors after 1976. The productivity rate of the two groups was not significantly different. Furthermore, individuals who were full professors in 1976 did not decrease in productivity after the incentive of promotion was removed. There was no significant decrease in productivity among the seven faculty who achieved full-professor rank between 1976 and 1986. Last, at both times of data collection there was a significant difference in the productivity rate between the respondents who were full professors in 1976 and the group that had never been promoted to full professor.

### Analysis by Field

In 1976 and 1986 faculty in all fields—humanities, social sciences, and natural and physical sciences—generally agreed on the percentage of time they thought should be spent on research, teaching, and service for the tenure decision. For promotion to full professor, the natural and physical scientists preferred less emphasis on research and more on teaching and service than did the social scientists and humanists. However, these differences were not significant. With one exception there were no statistically significant differences among the fields in the percentage of time these faculty actually gave to research, teaching, and service in either 1976 or 1986. Also in 1976, for all three fields the percentage of time given to research and teaching decreased (not significantly), and the amount of time given to service increased, with the promotion from assistant to associate professor. With the move to full professor the percentage of time spent on research by the humanists and natural scientists also decreased, while the social scientists' time on research increased slightly. Similarly, time spent on teaching decreased for the humanists and social scientists and remained constant for the natural scientists.

The 1986 reports of behavior, however, do not replicate the 1976 reports. As faculty moved from the rank of associate to full professor, the time spent on research remained constant in the humanities and social sciences; it increased in the natural sciences. In all three fields faculty spent more time on research in 1986 than in 1976. In 1986 the humanists and social scientists also spent more time on service and less on teaching, while the natural scientists spent more on teaching and less on service.

Faculty reports of their perceptions of university expectations for distribution of effort (social knowledge) in 1976 and 1986 did not differ significantly among fields, with the exception of time given to teaching as an assistant professor. However, perceptions of expected effort did differ from reported behavior. Overall, faculty believed that the university expected them to spend a greater percentage of their time on research and a smaller percentage on service than they actually spent.

168

## Analysis by Cohort

### 1960

Nine individuals comprised the 1960 cohort—three natural and physical scientists, two social scientists, and four humanists. Their average number of publications per year decreased with each successive change in rank. Similarly, the range in publication rate decreased as rank changed. This indicates that over time these individuals' annual output became more homogeneous.

With respect to administrative involvement, the research productivity of those involved varied. Some increased; more decreased.

### 1965

The 1965 appointment cohort was the largest, with 20 faculty members: 4 natural and physical scientists, 7 social scientists, and 9 humanists. Productivity rates as assistant and associate professors were, on the average, not much greater for this group than for the 1960 cohort. However, the average time in rank was longer than the average for the 1960 cohort at both the assistant and associate levels.

Of the 16 full professors in the 1965 cohort who achieved that rank prior to 1986, 14 had some type of administrative responsibility during their time with the university. Of these 14, 11 held administrative responsibilities as associate professors. Comparatively, only one person in the 1960 cohort had any administrative responsibility as an associate professor. For the most part, those individuals who had played administrative roles as associate professors continued in those roles after being promoted.

Members of this cohort had been highly active administrators. Only 6 of the 20 individuals had had no administrative responsibilities. Of these six, three never achieved full professor. The three individuals who were non-administrator full professors (one from each field) were clearly "producers," averaging just short of 4.5 publications per year since their final promotion. Conversely, the 3 least productive (averaging only one publication every three years) of the 14 full-professor administrators all had administrative responsibilities at least three years prior to being promoted. This suggests that administrative contributions may have played a role in their final promotion.

### 1970

Of the four individuals who constituted the 1970 cohort, one was a social scientist and three were humanists. Three were full professors, while one of the humanists remained an associate professor. These four individuals spent more time in the rank of assistant professor than did the members of the other cohorts.

Among the three who were full professors in 1986, their average publication rate as associate professors was the highest of the three cohorts, while their time in rank as associate professors was the shortest. As full professors these three produced, on the average, 2.6 publications per year (again the highest).

The one associate professor never produced a scholarly publication and still achieved the rank of associate professor. The fact is an exception but lends credence to the faculty perception that the tenure decision is based on scholarly potential while the final promotion decision is based on actual productivity.[31]

*Discussion*

The comparison of faculty from different fields showed little variation in their personal values, perceptions of the institution's role expectations, and priorities in personnel decisions. It may well be, as Blau (1973) suggests, that the recruitment, retention, and reward processes have resulted in a faculty that, by and large, share a common set of values and beliefs emphasizing the importance of scholarship. The cohort analysis suggests, further, that the normative expectations with respect to publication rate may be escalating as each successive appointment cohort moves through the promotion process. The most recent cohort—individuals appointed in 1970—spent more time in rank as assistant professors when compared with the 1960 and 1965 cohorts. On the other hand, the publication rates of the 1970 cohort were higher for each of these time-in-rank periods. The question remains whether this heightened output is a result of social knowledge (the inferences about what was expected), or self-knowledge (the personal attraction to the research process among those hired and promoted), or environmental conditions (a conscious administrative decision to keep people in rank longer).

The evaluation of differences between faculty who are professors and those who are not suggests that the motivation to publish derives more from intrinsic factors than from the extrinsically mediated promotions and rewards. Some individuals exhibit definite spurts of productivity around the time of promotion. However, the statistical comparisons of groups indicate that the incentive value of further promotion may not be a factor in determining publication rate. The assessments of individual change in publication rate between 1976 and 1986 corroborate this interpretation, as output at the two times was similar.

The theoretical framework that frames this investigation provides possible explanations for the findings vis-à-vis promotion and publication output. Some of the respondents who had only recently been promoted to full professor in 1986 explained that when they became associate professors, they inferred from observing their predecessors that administrative performance would be taken into account in the promotion decision. However, when they were reviewed, they were told that their scholarly records were weak. Consequently, they reduced their administrative loads, increased their publications, and were promoted. In brief, their social knowledge was modified on the basis of an environmental response. Achieving the rank of full professor was important to them, and they changed their behavior so as to achieve it. Their publication rate increased, and they were promoted.

On the other hand, there were some individuals who were, in their own words, "unpromotable associate professors." The feedback on behavior and productivity they received led them to believe that the institution did not value their substantive areas of interest or the scholarly activities they preferred (social knowledge). Their affect and comments during the interviews suggested that the importance of becoming a full professor had diminished. They seemed to have decided to do things that were personally meaningful (self-knowledge) even though such activities did not fit with organizational priorities and often led to a negative environmental response (e.g., having no doctoral students as assistants or graduate courses to teach).

We quote from Bieber, Lawrence, and Blackburn (1992):

> In their interviews with University of Minnesota faculty, Clark, Corcoran, and Lewis (1986) coined the phrase "promotion-delayed" for a group of associate professors who had held this rank several years beyond their peers who had already been promoted to full professor. Our associate professors are also never likely to be promoted, as they attest, and primarily due to deficient research output. Declining productivity, coupled with the university's heightened emphasis on research, has exacerbated an increasingly "awkward" situation. By 1987–88, few faculty and administrators believed resuscitation possible and anxiety relievable.
>
> In 1976 and earlier, the associate professor whose rate of publication and grant acquisition declined, but did not stop altogether, would eventually be promoted, assuming a record of good teaching, active work with doctoral students, contribution to the department in curricular decisions, and/or overall service for the university. It might take 12 years (instead of five or six) but one would retire as a full professor. If the associate professor went into administration and continued to teach, but did not continue his program of scholarship, he would retire without the final promotion.
>
> By 1987–88, however, a department knew it could not send a candidate to the college's executive committee for promotion to full professor whose vita would not have qualified the same individual for promotion to associ-

ate professor (and tenure). Being turned down for promotion at the college level is more than losing face and reputation. A common understanding among faculty is that it endangers the department's ability to acquire future hiring funds. These delayed-promotion faculty receive below average raises each year. While their scholarly production is not likely to change, they continue to teach key courses, and students rate them and their courses highly. Discomfort with the situation, however, increases with each passing term.

Some full professors who jumped all the hurdles and are still on track question the wisdom of a single standard for the final promotion. Departments do not always have consensus on the issue even though they do agree on the criteria for tenure and promotion to associate professor. (Either an influential article in a top journal or a well-received book from an established press is the sine qua non and minimum requirement.) What is to be lost, some professors ask, from granting the promotion? Dollars do not have to accompany the new rank. Maintain the merit system, they urge, but remove the stigma of being "frozen in rank." This is not "softness" or an absence of standards; it simply would produce a better climate for everyone. After all, not promoting them does not change their behavior, and having them around as friends and peers who have "failed" is painful for all parties.

For the most part, the acerbity expressed in our conversations by these promotion-delayed individuals focused on the unidimensional character of the promotion process—significant publications in both quality and quantity. They acknowledge following the teaching and service route and knowing their preferences and decisions carried consequences—fewer chances for teaching advanced seminars, fewer strong doctoral students selecting them for dissertation chair, no promotion. Yet, despite some bitterness, these faculty were generally pleased they had the options they did—doing what they wanted with the security tenure provides. In addition, their departmental colleagues appreciate that their friends, many of whom joined the ranks at the same time with them and have close bonds from those initial experiences, carry the introductory courses and genuinely and conspicuously care about students.

Nonetheless, second-class citizenship status must carry some unpleasant consequences when one looks in the mirror every morning and anticipates the day's upcoming realities: knowing that the secretary will be too busy typing grant proposals for the coterie of research faculty to prepare your examination (so you will have to do by yourself that for which you used to have assistance); that you will not be dining at the faculty club with the prospective new faculty candidate now on campus; that you will still be teaching the introductory course even if the new candidate is hired so as to allow her or him time to develop a research program; and that there is a forthcoming announcement by the chair that extra dollars (still not enough) will be available for those presenting research papers at the national conference—but you will pay to attend out of your own pocket. They are like Professor Victor Jakob, who, while teaching Newtonian physics in the German university early in this century as quantum mechanics was winning the day (in Russell McCormmach's novel, *Night Thoughts of a Classical Physicist*, 1982), realizes his status when the custodian stops cleaning his chalkboard.

Longitudinal data allowed us to explore an important component of our theoretical framework that survey, cross-sectional data cannot—namely, the effects of environmental response. We see here that the changing—or perhaps more accurately, intensifying—university emphasis on research and making career success dependent upon it clearly became a part of the faculty's social knowledge. For most, their productivity went up, irrespective of the fact that no promotion reward was available. Some chose not to alter their research behavior and productivity, or they decided they could not. They remained associate professors.

We also witness the framework functioning well in the interview process and in the examination of the qualitative data this methodology produces. Career, self-knowledge, social knowledge, behavior, and productivity as constructs guided the interview protocol and interpretation of the responses. We now collect what has been learned in this chapter and interpret what it means for faculty and their colleges and universities.

## Fostering Success

As we have seen, faculty career success depends more and more on conducting and publishing research. As we noted earlier, the shift in emphasis has spread to faculty in all institutional types, including those primarily dedicated to instruction. More faculty have a higher interest in research than in teaching compared with 25 years ago. Interest and desire, however, do not by themselves lead to publishable products. Nor does effort expended. They may be necessary conditions, but they are not sufficient ones. Know-how and skills—expertise in the discipline and with methodologies—must also be in hand. These need to be learned and mastered. Not everyone can do it. In addition, there is the creative act, seeing something in a new and/or different way, a talent no one can be taught, nor can anyone predict who will have it.

How can would-be researchers and those responsible for providing the most supportive environment for successful research be helped? We return to the studies cited in chapters 2 and 3 that report correlates of faculty research and add them to what we have learned in this chapter. The correlates suggest some measures individuals and institutions can undertake to increase the likelihood of success.

Of course, some correlates are with unchangeable characteristics and past experiences. They are valueless when it comes to changing one's success. One's race or sex is a given, and so is where one went to graduate school, all of which correlate with publishing. Some contextual correlates also lie outside the individual's or administrator's ability to alter but still need to be recognized. For example, we have seen more than once the need to control for academic discipline. Academic specialties generally differ as to what they produce and how. Department demography also affects faculty standards and expectations (Pfeffer, 1981).[32] One can alter atypical age distributions only by hiring and firing or retiring staff. Larger departments are more productive than smaller ones (Gallant & Prothero, 1972; Wispe, 1969), but obviously one does not simply increase the number of faculty in a unit in order to make it more productive.

So we turn to factors that are changeable—faculty attributes and administrative strategies. One thing faculty can do is to fashion their research agenda to their advanced-course teaching, or vice versa, so that what their students deal with in class directly connects with what they themselves are researching and writing about. Students' questions and comments can trigger ideas, and the resulting new insights can enrich the course and the instruction.

Having gone to a less rigorous university, or to one where techniques or library resources were inadequate for doctoral work, does not mean one cannot update oneself. A sabbatical, leave, or postdoc year at a leading university can produce marked changes. Being in an environment where scholarly activity abounds not only sharpens research skills but also motivates one to engage in creative work. So can joining with a colleague; it leads to co-authorship. Simply making a contract with another faculty member to complete a piece of work by an established time sets right habits in motion and leads to finished products. In this vein, and contrary to advice from parents, it is more productive to be doing many things at once than to concentrate on a single one. Highly productive faculty have many irons in the fire, if for no other reason than that when you get stuck on one project— and paralysis always sets in somewhere along the way—you can turn to another and move it along until a good solution flashes across the brow.

Write every day, even if only a few sentences find their way to the page and even if you later alter or delete them. Make writing the highest priority, the activity that comes before all others, the first thing you do in the day, not something you save for the late evening hours. A blank sheet of paper can freeze the productive juices. Stop in the middle of a paragraph you know how to finish so that when you return tomorrow, the pen or the keyboard need not struggle to make its first marks. Like more mundane activities, creative work becomes more successful when it becomes habitual. A little success breeds satisfaction that in turn leads to more success. Wildavsky's (1989) *Craftways: On the Organization of Scholarly Work* opens many windows for the individual wanting to bring ideas to fruition.[33]

One also needs to have faith in the peer-review process. The top journals and presses, the ones everyone wants to have publish her or his work, have the leading scholars as their reviewers. They find the flaws you did not know were there. Develop a tough skin, for rejection occurs more often than acceptance. Improve what you have done. However, do not go to a vanity press. It is better not to publish anything at all than to have a review of your work that begins, "This is a bad book. It never should have been written," and then goes on for two pages to demonstrate why. Your work will probably be misjudged more than once in this business, but for the most part, the system sorts out for us what deserves reading and what does not. Keep faith in the system.

Turning from what individuals can do to how administrators can increase the publication output of their unit and assist individual faculty to do more and better work, the matter of course depends upon the current situation. The current faculty will normally search for and recommend candidates for hiring when the unit is in a position to add a new member either to fill a vacancy or because of planned expansion. However, the dean still has final control over the selection. The faculty choice may be an exciting young person full of ideas and well on the way to completing the dissertation—in short, one with strong potential. However, the evidence shows that past performance is the best predictor of future output. The already published individual with the Ph.D. is by far the better bet. The dean should act accordingly, especially today, with so many already productive individuals in the market.

The right start matters immensely for new faculty. Having the new assistant professor teach a seminar in her or his specialty rather than being assigned the large introductory course can make a tremendous difference. Add to that student assistance, critical equipment, and psychological support, and one can get the individual off on the right foot. Being sensitive to the differences between the underrepresented is also important. The minority or female faculty member is more likely to be the isolated one, not in on the important conversations, not learning how one does things in this place. Getting that person teamed with a senior colleague who is also sensitive to the special needs of women and minorities requires administrative knowhow, but that is not so very difficult to acquire.

Pelz and Andrews (1976) learned in their studies of scientists in organizations that units can become more productive when work groups compete with one another in healthy ways. They also learned that group membership needs to be changed from time to time if the good-spirited competition is to continue. If one group always wins, the others will stop playing the game, and total productivity goes down. (See also Andrews's [1979] edited book on work groups in European research centers.) Deans and chairs can facilitate work arrangements of these kinds. They can also support research output by felicitous scheduling. Creative work most often requires large blocks of time. Scheduling that results in no classes on some days and more on other days, rather than some every day, supports the research effort. While chancellor at the University of Wisconsin–Oshkosh, Birnbaum (1975) introduced a year-round academic calendar of optional short semesters and credits for preparing self-taught instructional packages that allowed entrepreneurial faculty to create blocks of time for themselves. The faculty members' efficacy, their ability to control their time—that most important element faculty continually fight for—clearly enhanced their output even more. They could determine their schedule and maximize it for their own ends.

Rewards also pay dividends. While intrinsic motivation must be high, faculty do respond to what they see and believe the organization honors. Tien and Blackburn (1993) learned that faculty publication rates rise as promotion time approaches. A higher status is a reward faculty work for. At the same time, the correlation between administrative leadership and faculty publications is zero, even negative (Hill & French, 1967). Faculty do not see the chair as having anything to do with their research success. So be it. Wise chairs will not attempt to dispel the untruth or try to take credit for what they nourished. Perhaps their dean will take note of what has been accomplished. Heydinger and Simsek's (1992) monograph contains many worthwhile suggestions for increasing faculty productivity.

Last, the wise dean will also evaluate chairs on the basis of their success in raising the unit's output and input (in the form of grants, awards, and the like). That dean, or higher-level administrator, will also pass judgment on those below on the basis of how many minority and female faculty succeed, and how well. For all faculty, but especially for the underrepresented people who are often isolated and alienated, the day of simply adding individuals to the unit and expecting them to survive alone—tossing them into the department and seeing if they sink or swim—is over. Research output is a collective enterprise. It needs not only to be seeded and cultivated; it needs nurturing.

Our theoretical framework continues to illuminate faculty productivity through a variety of inquiries—qualitative as well as quantitative. We turn next to research on the teaching role.

# 5

# FACULTY TEACHING

CONCEPTUAL COMPLICATIONS increase dramatically as we turn from predicting and explaining faculty research behavior and output to understanding academics in their teaching role. It is not that research is a simple matter. It is not. It is as complex as pedagogy is. Composing a musical score, designing the apparatus for conducting the crucial experiment, searching the archives for the critical evidence to illuminate a historical event, filling blackboards with assumed symbolic propositions that will prove a mathematical theorem—every discipline requires hours of mental effort that never get recorded in the product placed on display and judged successful. Research involves appreciably more intricacies than the visible scholarly article or other appropriate product that is typically used as a measure of output.

Difficulties in understanding faculty vis-à-vis their teaching arise for two important reasons. First, there are no clear products that result from teaching that can be measured, as can published articles in scholarly journals.[1] Second, faculty cannot obtain consensus on what constitutes high-quality teaching. While faculty rightly point out the incompleteness of published articles as an indicator of all that research involves, they do generally agree that an article in a leading journal demonstrates research performance. Faculty know the good presses and the vanity presses and can judge book publication on that basis alone. No parallels exist in the teaching domain. Instead, seemingly unsolvable issues dominate faculty discussion of the essence of good teaching.

Is excellent teaching to be assessed by student ratings of their instructors? Feldman (1976, 1977, 1986, 1989) identifies about 2,000 studies on what students like in an instructor and relates these characteristics and behaviors to the instructional context (class size, hour of the day, required or elective course, etc.). As we will see, some faculty heed these evaluations, and some change their behavior as a consequence of the comments they receive. More do not. While students tend to agree on the rating of an instructor, even the highest-scoring faculty member finds at least one student who judges her or his teaching to be a disaster. Similarly, the lowest-rated instructor always has at least one student who loves her or him. For the most part, though, faculty find student assessments less than definitive. In the same way that physicians respond to how their patients accept their prescriptions but do not consider them to be acceptable judges of their professional expertise, so do faculty believe that students are not in a position to assess their knowledge, the fundamental requisite faculty say is necessary for good teaching.[2]

Wayne Booth, George M. Pullman Distinguished Service Professor of English at the University of Chicago and the most noteworthy member of the American Association for Higher Education, writes on the subject of teaching as well as receiving awards for his scholarly publications in literature. In his autobiographical narrative *The Vocation of a Teacher* (1988) he describes his burning desire to be loved by his students. He gives undergraduates countless hours, even visiting them in the hospital when mononucleosis strikes them at the end of the term. At the same time, he keeps hearing about a colleague down the hall whom students rave about but whom he knows to be a fraud, a pretender to expertise that is both dated and false. New student ratings of the college faculty as teachers have just come out. As he casually enters the room where they are on file, he examines not only his own rating but also that of his nemesis. Devastating disaster: he receives lower scores. Students have shattered his faith in what he had believed most constitutes a good pedagogue, namely, what he does in the classroom.

There is some evidence (Choy, 1969; Maslow & Zimmerman, 1956; Sherman & Blackburn, 1975) that student ratings are determined principally by the instructor's personality, attributes such as being easily approachable and not distant—styles that are not readily changeable in adults. Furthermore, students' ratings may be biased by their personal selection of their instructor. The only two professors to win the award for outstanding teacher in the college at the University of Chicago differed from one another more than any other two colleagues on that faculty. Joseph Schwab, William Rainey Harper Professor of Biological Sciences and the founder of the great-ideas concept for the sciences in Chicago's Hutchins' College (*College Curriculum and Student Protest*, 1969), relentlessly cross-examined students in class until they had hopelessly contradicted and publicly embarrassed themselves. Norman Maclean (*A River Runs through It*, 1983) also conducted his English classes using the Socratic method to which the college subscribed, but with such loving care and kindness that students worshipped him. Many question student ratings as valid measures of faculty teaching.

Is high-quality teaching to be assessed by peer ratings? While peer ratings are much less common than student ratings, faculty not infrequently appraise one another's teaching. However, faculty most often form their judgment from student comments, not from direct observation. A few studies show a fair degree of agreement among students and faculty rating the same instructor (e.g., Blackburn & Clark, 1975). However, when Centra (1975) conducted a systematic inquiry of a group of qualified, same-discipline faculty rating new instructors, persons without established reputations, agreement among the faculty raters was so low that Centra estimated it would take at least 50 peer raters to get an error term low enough to have confidence in their collective judgment. Faculty obviously hold diverse views on the best way to teach topics in their specialty.

Is high-quality teaching to be assessed by administrators—by department chairs and deans? This practice is more prevalent than having colleagues conduct the evaluations, but it is rare in four-year institutions and universities. It most frequently takes place in community colleges and in institutions where faculty are unionized. (This procedure became a part of a negotiated contract.) Blackburn and Clark (1975) found the correlations between administrator and both student and faculty ratings to be much lower than between the two latter groups. Quite understandably, one would not expect administrators above the chair level to know all of the disciplines well enough to pass judgment on the adequacy of teachers in the classrooms they visited.

Is high-quality teaching to be assessed by the faculty themselves? Here the answer is clearly, "Not exclusively." While their personal assessments merit consideration, their agreement with their other constituencies— namely, students, faculty, and administrators—is essentially zero (Blackburn & Clark, 1975). Some higher-rated faculty judge themselves to be poor teachers, and vice versa. Moreover, faculty rate themselves higher than others rate them. Fifty percent place themselves in the top 10 percent, and 90 percent claim to be above average, a fact that haunts our analyses (see below). Faculty almost uniformly believe that they care more about good teaching than any of their colleagues do (Blackburn, Boberg, O'Connell, & Pellino, 1980), a fact that means that all faculty care very much about their teaching, as the Wayne Booth incident mentioned above testifies. Generally speaking, faculty believe they excel in the classroom.

Is high-quality teaching to be assessed by the products faculty produce? For example, some advocate student learning—a product—as the appropriate measure of effective teaching. Many concur. However, when it comes down to measuring student learning, agreement disappears both as to what constitutes and what causes any learning that takes place, and as to the problems that exist in measuring a student's gain in learning. At the minimum, every course would have to have a pretest to determine each student's knowledge level before the class began. In addition, one would need estimates of other factors that might affect learning in any course (e.g., mathematical ability in a beginning calculus course). Moreover, the final test would have to be the equivalent of the pretest so that "true" change in knowledge could be ascertained. Rarely do such data exist, save in a purposeful experiment here and there. But even if these conditions were met, issues remain as to how much of the estimated learning—the difference between post- and pretest scores—is attributable to the instructor. How much did students learn from one another? From a tutor? From other books? From television? Just from living? Is an instructor who started with a class of students who knew nothing and gained, say, 50 percent a more effective instructor than one who started with a class of knowledgeable students who gained only 25 percent? More questions exist than agreed-upon criteria.

Other teaching products could include detailed syllabi, self-help supplements for difficult topics, computer programs for self-testing—a variety of products to accompany the typical materials and activities of a course, namely, the text, the professor's lectures, responses to written assignments, counseling during office hours. However, as we will see below, there are no established relationships between these kinds of products and high-quality teaching.

In what ways and to what extent does our framework better inform us about faculty in the teaching role? From the preceding remarks we see that predicting teaching products is not going to be possible. This means that effort given to teaching (a behavior) will be our principal outcome indicator regarding teaching, along with sometimes specific teaching behaviors such as team teaching, changing syllabus regularly, and the like.

This is a regrettable limitation. We know from chapter 4 that effort given to research, while a strong predictor of published articles, does not perfectly predict research products. So even when we successfully predict what variables account for the percentage of time given to teaching-related activities, we still will not know that they necessarily lead to high-quality teaching, a construct for which there is no accepted measure. We have also seen that self-assessed teaching competence—unlike research self-competence, which did predict output, especially for women—will not predict here, since for us, as for others cited above, faculty rate their own teaching highly, and there is little variance on the measure. Constructs with no variance can contribute nothing to the percentage of variance accounted for. Still, we believe that our theoretical framework appreciably improves our knowledge about faculty and teaching. We entered this quagmire knowingly.

We report here selections from four teaching studies that utilized the framework. We presented each as a research paper at a national conference (Bieber, Blackburn, Lawrence, Okoloko, Ross, & Knuesel, 1988; Lawrence, Blackburn, & Hart, 1990; Blackburn, Lawrence, Bieber, & Trautvetter, 1988; Lawrence, Hart, Linder, Saulsberry, Dickman, & Blackburn, 1990).[3] The first comes from 111 interviews with faculty about their teaching, the preliminary work we did before developing the theoretical framework and constructing the questionnaire to collect the data to test it. The second is our test of the framework for accounting for faculty performance in the teaching role. The third uses our conceptually based NCRIPTAL national survey data and has effort given to teaching as the outcome variable, the next to last step in the theoretical framework. The last study uses an essential part of the framework and enlightens us about a large segment of higher-education faculty, namely, those who teach in community colleges.

## Interviews and the Quality of Teaching Effort

We begin with our pilot study. From it we learn about faculty teaching in four very different kinds of institutions and to what degree certain factors predict the kinds of teaching behaviors faculty report. We also witness how the NCRIPTAL questionnaire for the national survey was developed from the interview protocols that we taped, transcribed, and analyzed after our site visits at these four colleges and universities.

We tape-recorded structured interviews with 111 faculty from four institutions. The interviews lasted approximately one and a half hours. Ninety-eight respondents supplied all of the needed data. The institutions were a selective urban private liberal arts college in the Upper Midwest; a rural public regional university (Comp-I) in a central state; a public HBCU (Comp-II) on the outskirts of a city in the South; and a public community college in the rural Middle South. The institutions we used were selected to represent different organizational contexts. They were assumed to vary in mission, size, resources, student and faculty bodies, and so on.

At the regional Comp-I university we sampled full-time faculty at the assistant to full professor ranks in eight arts and science departments selected to represent the humanities (English and history), natural sciences (biology, chemistry, and math), and social sciences (political science, psychology, and sociology). We selected the subjects randomly, except that all

181

women were included, and the sample was stratified so as to contain, when possible, equal numbers of persons hired in the 1950s, 1970s, and 1980s. This procedure provided faculty of various ages and career stages. At the community college the sample was the entire faculty, including those in nursing and technology, since there were too few faculty in the arts and sciences. The final sample was distributed across the settings as follows: liberal arts college, N = 34; community college, N = 17; HBCU, N = 19; and regional Comp-I university; N = 28.[4]

In each instance we sent faculty a preinterview instrument consisting of demographic questions, questions about institutional priorities, and a series of items designed to elicit perceptions of the skills, values, and personality predispositions that characterized the valued professor on their campus.

In the interviews we asked professors to assess their capacity to influence institutional decisions and to explain why they rated that capacity as they did. We presented the faculty members with the list of characteristics they had ascribed to the valued professor. They explained why they had selected the attributes they had, and then assessed themselves with respect to each one. They also described the criteria and process applied in annual personnel evaluations. They told us how much they had changed their teaching, research, and service activities as a result of last year's evaluation feedback.

At the interview's conclusion we obtained a curriculum vita and gave the faculty member a postinterview questionnaire to complete and mail to us. Among other things, this instrument gathered data on faculty members' expectations that their actions would lead to desired outcomes—for example, the extent to which student learning depended upon what they did as teachers and the extent to which next year's merit salary increase depended upon their accomplishments this year—and on how much time they allocated to teaching, research, and service.

We performed a content analysis of faculty responses to the open-ended question on professional skills, values, and personality dispositions of the valued faculty member that resulted in clusters of adjectives and phrases for each of the three constructs. We then used the terms that best represented the main theme of each cluster to code the responses of each professor interviewed. We derived the self-efficacy indicator for the faculty members' responses to two questions: (1) To what extent does your next year's salary depend upon your accomplishments and contributions this year? (2) To what extent is student learning contingent on what you do as a teacher? Their ratings determined their self-competence assessment.

Table 5.1 displays selected data from our various sources. Frequency distributions are shown for the sociodemographic variables, each selected to serve as a general proxy for the time or era during which early career socialization activities occurred and skills and values were acquired. We

182

used date of highest degree as an indicator of career age and institution where faculty members completed their graduate education (Res-I or other) as a general proxy for the opportunities and professional values to which they were exposed.

The regional Comp-I university, liberal arts college, and HBCU faculty

Table 5.1    Distributions of Key Variables

| | Total Sample | Comp-I | LAC-I | CC | HBCU (Comp-II) |
|---|---|---|---|---|---|
| Number | 98 | 28 | 34 | 17 | 19 |
| | *1. Sociodemographic* | | | | |
| **Highest degree** | | | | | |
| Associate | 2 | 0 | 1 | 1 | 0 |
| B.A./B.S. | 3 | 0 | 0 | 3 | 0 |
| M.A./M.S. | 19 | 1 | 7 | 7 | 4 |
| Ed.D. | 8 | 1 | 2 | 4 | 1 |
| D.D.S./M.D. | 1 | 0 | 1 | 0 | 0 |
| Ph.D. | 59 | 23 | 21 | 2 | 13 |
| **Graduate institution** | | | | | |
| Res-I | 46 | 14 | 25 | 2 | 5 |
| Other | 44 | 11 | 7 | 15 | 11 |
| **Date of highest degree** | | | | | |
| 1949–59 | 10 | 3 | 5 | 0 | 2 |
| 1961–69 | 26 | 8 | 10 | 2 | 6 |
| 1970–79 | 32 | 8 | 9 | 8 | 7 |
| 1980–86 | 23 | 5 | 8 | 7 | 3 |
| **Academic rank** | | | | | |
| Instructor | 7 | 0 | 0 | 7 | 0 |
| Assistant professor | 18 | 5 | 9 | 1 | 3 |
| Associate professor | 30 | 9 | 8 | 4 | 9 |
| Professor | 37 | 11 | 15 | 5 | 6 |
| Dist. professor | 2 | 1 | 0 | 0 | 1 |
| **Sex** | | | | | |
| Female | 28 | 6 | 9 | 7 | 6 |
| Male | 64 | 20 | 22 | 10 | 12 |
| | *2. Distribution of Effort (means)* | | | | |
| Teaching (range 10–95%) | 58 | 37 | 61 | 73 | 67 |
| Scholarship (0–85%) | 16 | 36 | 13 | 5 | 9 |
| Service (0–80%) | 17 | 20 | 19 | 12 | 16 |
| Profess. growth (0–40%) | 8 | 8 | 7 | 11 | |
| Other (0–30%) | 1 | | | | |

*Continued next page*

Table 5.1—*Continued*

| | Total Sample | Comp-I | LAC-I | CC | HBCU (Comp-II) |
|---|---|---|---|---|---|
| | *3. Institutional Rewards (means)* | | | | |
| Teaching (0–99%) | 60 | 37 | 64 | 71 | 68 |
| Scholarship (0–100%) | 19 | 42 | 11 | 5 | 13 |
| Service (0–70%) | 18 | 19 | 15 | 21 | 15 |
| | *4. Change in Professional Activities Due to Evaluation (means)* | | | | |
| Teaching | 2.0 | 1.5 | 2.2 | 1.1 | 2.0 |
| Scholarship | 0.7 | 0.5 | 0.4 | 0.9 | 1.6 |
| Service | 0.4 | 0.2 | 0.6 | 0.3 | 0.8 |
| | *5. Self-Competence Ratings (means)* | | | | |
| Teaching | 3.3 | 3.1 | 3.4 | 3.4 | 3.4 |
| Scholarship | 3.1 | 3.0 | 3.0 | 2.5 | 3.7 |
| Communication | 3.5 | 4.0 | 3.3 | 3.5 | 3.5 |
| Organization | 3.3 | 3.5 | 3.0 | 4.0 | 3.5 |
| Interpersonal skills | 3.1 | 2.0 | 3.3 | 3.3 | 3.0 |
| Speaker/lecturer | 3.4 | 4.0 | 3.3 | — | 3.3 |

*Source:* NCRIPTAL interviews.

*Notes:* Because of missing data from individual faculty, the sum of the numbers in a category frequently will not add up to the Ns shown at the top. Those Ns are the maximum for each institution.

Both the distribution-of-effort and institutional-rewards measures were continuous variables, and the possible scores ranged from 0 percent to 100 percent.

The scales for change due to evaluation and self-competence ratings were four-point Likert scales, with 1 indicating a low assessment and 4 indicating a high assessment.

were similar in terms of distributions across degree and career-age categories. Compared with the other schools, a greater portion of the liberal arts college faculty completed their graduate work in Res-I institutions. The community college faculty typically held the M.A. or lower degree, while faculty in the three other schools had the Ph.D. The community college faculty were also more likely to have completed their graduate degree most recently. Men outnumbered women on all campuses.

The distribution-of-effort measures were in the anticipated direction, with the regional Comp-I faculty reporting the least time given to teaching and the most to research. The community college faculty said the opposite. Institutional rewards followed the same pattern. Faculty gave themselves high self-competence ratings. Their self-reports of changes in professional activities due to evaluation suggest that the likelihood that this feedback would lead to change was very small.[5]

The prototype valued faculty member is definitely an able teacher and scholar and one who is able to express herself or himself clearly to colleagues, administrators, and students (able communicator). This professor also has the ability to facilitate discussions, manage groups, and work with colleagues (interpersonal skills). Our subjects portrayed the valued faculty member as being organized and efficient, someone you can count on, committed. This professor is no nine-to-five person with routine tasks and responsibilities. In addition, he or she wants to be successful (will to achieve).

The questionnaire we left with faculty assessed the quality of effort they put forth on their teaching activities. We based the concept of quality of faculty effort on Pace's (1980) research on quality of student effort. We adapted Pace's work and developed a faculty instrument (Blackburn & Knuesel, 1987).[6] The quality of faculty effort (QFE) questionnaire provides data on how often faculty engage in activities considered to be representative of effective teaching.

Table 5.2 shows that the community college faculty are the principal readers of books and articles about teaching and every year consult with their colleagues about teaching. Everyone in this institution does (mean score of 5.0). In contrast, faculty in the regional Comp-I university read something about teaching every third or fourth year. Of the four groups, these university faculty also change their teaching method least frequently.

While faculty in all four institutions consult with colleagues about teaching techniques and problems nearly every year (the means are from 4.5 to 4.9 out of a possible 5), HBCU faculty do so least frequently. They also change their syllabi and texts least frequently. This may be the result of a number of factors. They spend more time teaching than do their counterparts in the other four-year institutions. Their very heavy teaching load leaves inadequate time to prepare new syllabi each year. Their institution is also the poorest. They have the least support staff help for typing new syllabus materials. Their student body has the least income. Secondhand texts cost appreciably less than the new books that would be required if the faculty member changed texts each year.

The liberal arts college faculty are at the pole. The liberal arts college has the wealthiest students. They can afford new books every year. These faculty change their texts almost annually. They most frequently change their method of teaching and engage in team teaching. Such behaviors suggest a strong commitment to teaching and a high affluence level. Teaching fewer courses allows them to team-teach, a procedure they value and believe has strong effects on students. Since normally there is no workload recognition for

Table 5.2    Teaching Activities

|  | Comp-I | | LAC-I | | CC | | HBCU (Comp-II) | |
|---|---|---|---|---|---|---|---|---|
|  | *Mean* | *SD* | *Mean* | *SD* | *Mean* | *SD* | *Mean* | *SD* |
| Change your course syllabus | 4.1 | 1.1 | 4.4 | 0.7 | 4.1 | 1.2 | 3.3 | 1.5 |
| Change texts | 3.5 | 1.6 | 3.5 | 1.1 | 2.6 | 0.9 | 2.5 | 1.1 |
| Read articles on teaching | 2.9 | 1.9 | 3.5 | 1.7 | 4.6 | 1.1 | 3.9 | 1.9 |
| Read books on teaching methods | 4.3 | 1.5 | 4.4 | 1.0 | 5.0 | 0.0 | 3.9 | 1.8 |
| Consult with colleague about teaching techniques/problems | 4.7 | 1.0 | 4.8 | 0.7 | 4.9 | 0.3 | 4.5 | 1.0 |
| Create/prepare supplemental text materials | 1.6 | 0.9 | 2.7 | 1.7 | 1.3 | 1.0 | 1.8 | 1.5 |
| Team-teach a class | 2.8 | 1.4 | 3.8 | 0.9 | 3.4 | 1.7 | 3.6 | 1.7 |
| Change teaching methods | 3.9 | 1.1 | 3.2 | 1.3 | 2.9 | 0.9 | 3.2 | 0.9 |

*Source:* NCRIPTAL survey.

*Note:* 5 - every year; 4 - every other year; 3 - every third year; 2 - every fourth year; 1 - rarely.

team teaching, one understands why others do it less frequently.

Table 5.3 shows that the regional Comp-I faculty most frequently attend a visiting lecturer's presentation on campus, present their ongoing work on campus, and supervise and direct student research activities. Each of these activities accompanies the research role more than the teaching one, but all are normally associated with good teaching. Most likely the other three institutions have fewer visiting scholars, fewer opportunities for faculty to present their own work—the institutions are not organized to do these things, even if they are highly valued, as they are at the liberal arts college—and fewer students engaged in research.

While this information is not presented in the table, we learned that the HBCU faculty rate themselves the most efficacious when it comes to believing that student learning is dependent upon what they do as a teacher. These faculty are clearly the most student-oriented of the four groups we interviewed. They have a clear mission to take in disadvantaged youths and move them into mainstream America. They have to believe that what they are doing matters.

Table 5.3    Scholarly Activities

| | Comp-I | | LAC-I | | CC | | HBCU (Comp-II) | |
|---|---|---|---|---|---|---|---|---|
| | *Mean* | *SD* | *Mean* | *SD* | *Mean* | *SD* | *Mean* | *SD* |
| Attended a visiting lecturer's presentation on campus | 3.8 | 1.1 | 3.2 | 1.2 | 2.9 | 1.0 | 3.2 | 0.9 |
| Presented ongoing work on campus | 1.9 | 1.0 | 1.7 | 0.8 | 1.4 | 0.7 | 1.3 | 0.5 |
| Supervised/directed student research activities | 3.6 | 1.5 | 3.0 | 1.4 | 1.7 | 0.9 | 2.9 | 1.3 |

*Source:* NCRIPTAL survey.

*Note:* 5 = every year; 4 = every other year; 3 = every third year; 2 = every fourth year; 1 = rarely.

As for table 5.4, the regional Comp-I faculty both teach the least and expect their future salary to be least affected by how well they do it. They know the point scale at their university and what it rewards. Teaching is not at the top.

We now turn to the three studies using our survey data and postpone our discussion of what we have learned from this first study and what its implications are.

Table 5.4    Teaching Effort Expended, Expected, and Rewarded

| | Comp-I | | LAC-I | | CC | | HBCU (Comp-II) | |
|---|---|---|---|---|---|---|---|---|
| | *Mean* | *SD* | *Mean* | *SD* | *Mean* | *SD* | *Mean* | *SD* |
| Percentage of weekly time given to teaching | 36.7 | 15.8 | 59.2 | 16.6 | 67.3 | 16.9 | 72.8 | 12.9 |
| Percentage of time you feel your institution expects you to spend teaching | 38.0 | 10.7 | 61.3 | 19.9 | 60.9 | 17.6 | 74.4 | 15.5 |
| Percentage of your merit raise dependent on how well you teach | 37.2 | 17.4 | 69.1 | 14.6 | 71.1 | 18.5 | 68.1 | 16.8 |

*Source:* NCRIPTAL survey.

187

## Teaching Outcome

The teaching outcome test of the framework becomes somewhat more complicated inasmuch as we now deal with behaviors, not products, and hence have no feedback loop as we did with the research test. Nonetheless, this less-than-perfect test remains an important one because it provides new insights into faculty teaching behaviors.

In the introduction to the chapter "Research on Teaching in Higher Education," Dunkin (1986, p. 754) notes three questions that dominate the literature on college instruction: "How do teachers behave? Why do they behave as they do? and What are the effects of their behavior?" Here we focus on the second question by examining how individual and institutional variables affect the teaching behavior of university faculty members.

The theoretical framework is based on process-outcome models of classroom teaching, the literature on college faculty, and the cognitive research on motivation, that is, our theoretical framework. Since the early 1960s, when Gage (1963) outlined his initial views on teaching processes and learning outcomes, many researchers have developed process-outcome models for research on teaching (Brophy & Good, 1974; Dunkin, 1986; Dunkin & Biddle, 1974; Shulman, 1986). The key components of those models include presage variables (characteristics of teachers and students that account for variations in teaching and learning processes), context variables (features of the institutional and community environments that may influence teaching and learning), process variables (the teaching behaviors and learning behaviors that instructors and students engage in during class), and outcomes (changes in learners). These models assume that teachers' and students' classroom behaviors are determined by their prior experiences, by individual differences in dispositions, abilities, activities, perceptions, and values, and by the environmental context within which instruction occurs.

Some researchers have explored the relationships among faculty members' sociodemographic characteristics, academic preparation, teaching values, and overall teaching effort (Blackburn, Lawrence, Okoloko, Bieber, Meiland, Ross, & Street, 1986). Others have focused on relationships between faculty goals and classroom practices (Bayer, 1973), faculty goals and course planning (Stark, Lowther, Ryan, Bomotti, Genthon, Havens, & Marten, 1986), classroom practices and faculty teaching effectiveness (Feldman, 1976), and faculty-student interaction outside the classroom (Wilson, Woods, & Gaff, 1974; Pascarella, Terenzeni, & Hibel, 1978). However, there has been little systematic inquiry into the relationships between these faculty presage variables and teaching behavior (Dunkin, 1986).

An extensive literature exists on institutional context and its impact on teaching (Peterson, Cameron, Mets, Jones, & Ettington, 1989; Dunkin, 1986). The general conclusions from this research are that variations in colleges' and universities' missions and resources affect teaching directly through the quality of laboratories, libraries, and the students and teachers they are able to recruit. Context also affects the teaching/learning process indirectly through the faculty and students. For example, a faculty member's perceptions of the promotion/tenure criteria may influence her or his decision about how much time to give to teaching. The faculty member's sense of the institution's norms regarding classroom behavior may also play a role in determining the teaching methods used.

Most investigators have concluded that faculty behavior is likely the product of such interactions between individual characteristics and institutional factors (Lawrence & Blackburn, 1985). Nevertheless, the process-outcome models that have guided the research on college teaching do not specify interactions between these different variable sets. Rather, the research tends to gather data on either the organization or else the individual.

Social psychology and cognitive science paradigms present alternative ways of modeling the process by which presage and contextual variables combine and influence teaching behavior. The research on social contingencies and self-efficacy (Bandura, 1977a, 1982; Schoen & Winocur, 1988) takes into account people's assessments of environmental expectations and their ability to meet these expectations. This research also posits that behavior depends on individuals' perceptions of their chances of success. Recent studies by cognitive scientists have extended this work by focusing on the strategies people use to enhance their chances of success in different situations (Fishbein & Ajzen, 1975; Linville & Clark, 1989; Snyder, 1981). In order to answer the question of why faculty behave as they do, we must consider both individuals' understanding of the environment in which they are teaching and their ability and desire to meet the expectations of that environment.

### Data and Analysis

The faculty population analyzed here is the same as that used in testing for research output. Our analysis utilized 3 measures of career (established faculty member, active scholar/grantsperson, and discipline);[7] 12 measures defining five theoretically distinct types of self-knowledge (organizational influence, control over career, values teaching, values cooperation/institutional commitment, and supportive/understanding); and 13 social knowledge factors that fell into four categories (personable teacher valued, faculty committed to teaching, faculty collegiality, and motivated students).

189

One factor was used to assess/measure environmental response (awarded promotion or tenure in last two years). In all, 41 factors were defined. Environmental conditions were estimated with seven dummy variables as proxies for the eight Res-I institutions that were surveyed. (See appendix D for details.)

The factor analysis of teaching behavior items identified two measures of teaching that we used as the outcome variables. The first measure, preparing undergraduates as scholars, is an eight-variable factor derived from a question that asked faculty members how often they engaged in certain teaching activities in an introductory course. The items that loaded were require a particular writing/lab format, supervise independent study, require annotated bibliographies/documented lab reports, design research internships, review drafts of papers/reports, have students do on-line searches/research projects, require research papers, and supervise tutorials (eigenvalue = 5.29). The second teaching behavior, work with advanced graduate students, is a four-item factor that indicates for the current and past year the number of dissertation committees served on and chaired and the number of comprehensive examinations/orals committees served on and chaired (eigenvalue = 3.28).

The theoretical framework that guided the analysis generates questions about both the direct and the indirect effects of faculty and institutional variables on teaching behavior. Multiple regression–based techniques were used to evaluate these effects and to describe the paths through which the different variables influence teaching.

We entered all factors, discrete measures (e.g., age, sex, race), and dummy variables into multiple regression analyses in separate steps in the order represented in the framework: sociodemographic, followed by career, self-knowledge, environmental conditions, environmental response, and social knowledge. In one analysis, preparing undergraduates as scholars was the teaching behavior that was predicted; in the other, work with advanced graduate students was the outcome variable.[8]

Analyses show that the correlations between the predictor variables and the teaching outcomes were small and insignificant. The theoretical framework variables entered into the regression framework accounted for 38.9 percent and 41.5 percent, respectively, of the overall variance in the teaching behaviors preparing undergraduates as scholars and work with advanced graduate students. The changes in the teaching behaviors for each step in the regression analyses are reported in tables 5.5 and 5.6 along with the standardized betas for the predictor variables.

The results indicate that a faculty member's discipline and perceptions of institutional values, faculty colleagues, and students (social knowledge)

Table 5.5    Regression Outcomes for Preparing Undergraduates as Scholars

| | 1 | 2 | 3 | 4 | 5 | 6 |
|---|---|---|---|---|---|---|
| *Sociodemographic* | | | | | | |
| Female | .111 | .075 | .081 | .082 | .086 | .089 |
| Asian | -.054 | -.044 | .000 | -.069 | -.071 | -.086 |
| Black | .028 | .036 | .011 | .023 | .043 | .043 |
| Age | -.023 | -.020 | .010 | -.021 | -.070 | -.070 |
| *Career* | | | | | | |
| Established faculty member | | -.004 | -.039 | -.039 | -.057 | .000 |
| Active scholar/grantsperson | | -.072 | -.052 | -.051 | -.046 | -.058 |
| Chemistry | | -.230 | .097 | .095 | -.072 | .044 |
| Mathematics | | **-.364** | -.324 | -.321 | -.314 | -.305 |
| English | | -.016 | -.004 | -.004 | -.004 | -.001 |
| History | | .094 | .085 | .083 | .086 | .107 |
| Political science | | -.006 | -.012 | -.011 | -.019 | -.019 |
| Psychology | | .042 | .054 | .050 | -.065 | .072 |
| Sociology | | -.056 | -.054 | -.063 | -.051 | -.052 |
| *Self-knowledge* | | | | | | |
| Organizational influence | | | -.053 | -.021 | -.041 | .015 |
| Control over career | | | -.086 | -.081 | -.080 | -.072 |
| Values teaching | | | -.020 | -.021 | -.021 | -.022 |
| Values coop./inst. commit. | | | .050 | .058 | .055 | .080 |
| Understanding/supportive | | | .026 | .019 | .019 | .013 |
| *Institutional context* | | | | | | |
| A | | | | -.150 | -.152 | -.155 |
| B | | | | -.036 | -.038 | -.038 |
| C | | | | -.021 | -.024 | -.025 |
| D | | | | -.023 | -.022 | .021 |
| E | | | | -.043 | -.045 | -.046 |
| F | | | | -.036 | -.036 | -.038 |
| G | | | | -.050 | -.050 | .051 |
| *Environmental response* | | | | | | |
| Recent promotion | | | | | -.030 | -.037 |
| *Social knowledge* | | | | | | |
| Personable teacher valued | | | | | | *.165* |
| Faculty collegiality | | | | | | *-.145* |
| Faculty committed to teaching | | | | | | *-.171* |
| Motivated students | | | | | | *.175* |
| *Percentage of explained variance* | 19.0 | *18.6* | 21.7 | 22.1 | 22.7 | *38.9* |

*Source:* NCRIPTAL survey.

*Notes:* Standardized betas: only those variables that entered a path analysis in which each variable was regressed against all possible antecedents. Bold, italicized numbers are at $p \leq .05$ for betas and change in variance explained.

Table 5.6    Regression Outcomes for Work with Advanced Graduate Students

| | 1 | 2 | 3 | 4 | 5 | 6 |
|---|---|---|---|---|---|---|
| *Sociodemographic* | | | | | | |
| Female | -.075 | -.062 | -.050 | -.056 | -.059 | -.061 |
| Asian | .009 | .013 | .035 | .039 | .040 | .044 |
| Black | .051 | .027 | .027 | .026 | .024 | .021 |
| Age | .115 | .145 | .161 | .158 | .150 | .151 |
| *Career* | | | | | | |
| Established faculty member | | -.046 | .083 | -.084 | -.084 | -.087 |
| Active scholar/grantsperson | | *.188* | *.201* | *.195* | *.174* | *.163* |
| Chemistry | | *.272* | *.248* | *.240* | *.220* | *.216* |
| Mathematics | | -.037 | -.035 | -.085 | -.098 | -.105 |
| English | | -.023 | -.023 | -.029 | -.051 | -.062 |
| History | | .056 | -.055 | -.047 | -.041 | -.037 |
| Political science | | .142 | .119 | .108 | .092 | .088 |
| Psychology | | .210 | .171 | .162 | -.140 | .135 |
| Sociology | | .154 | .152 | .118 | .082 | .057 |
| *Self-knowledge* | | | | | | |
| Organizational influence | | | .063 | .071 | .078 | .084 |
| Control over career | | | *.174* | .121 | .117 | .106 |
| Values teaching | | | .018 | .023 | .027 | .030 |
| Values coop./inst. commit. | | | .023 | .040 | .040 | .042 |
| Understanding/supportive | | | *.162* | *.162* | *.162* | *.165* |
| *Institutional context* | | | | | | |
| A | | | | -.110 | -.112 | -.114 |
| B | | | | *.201* | *.209* | *.209* |
| C | | | | .038 | .040 | .040 |
| D | | | | .160 | .160 | .161 |
| E | | | | -.048 | -.050 | -.051 |
| F | | | | -.123 | -.124 | -.124 |
| G | | | | -.062 | -.063 | -.065 |
| *Environmental response* | | | | | | |
| Recent promotion | | | | | .021 | .021 |
| *Social knowledge* | | | | | | |
| Personable teacher valued | | | | | | -.087 |
| Faculty collegiality | | | | | | *-.082* |
| Faculty committed to teaching | | | | | | *.091* |
| Motivated students | | | | | | -.126 |
| *Percentage of explained variance* | 2.6 | *17.8* | *24.0* | *31.8* | 32.6 | *41.5* |

*Source:* NCRIPTAL survey.

*Notes:* Standardized betas: only those variables that entered a path analysis in which each variable was regressed against all possible antecedents. Bold, italicized numbers are at $p \leq .05$ for betas and change in variance explained.

192

directly affected how often he or she engaged in teaching behavior that prepares undergraduates as scholars. The regressions for work with advanced graduate student show that perceptions of the work environment (social knowledge) were important in predicting variance in this teaching behavior. The direct effects of one's discipline, being an active scholar/ grantsperson, and the context of the employing institution persisted through the final step in the analysis.

Social knowledge appears to mediate the impact of other variables on teaching behavior that emphasizes individualized attention and encourages systematic inquiry into the subject matter by undergraduates. The particular institution where one works, rather than perceptions of the workplace, seems to have more bearing on level of involvement with graduate students. (Recall that all eight institutions were Res-I's.)

We used a path analysis to examine how the individual and institutional variables combined to influence teaching behavior. We regressed each variable against all the antecedent variables in the theoretical framework. Figure 5.1 diagrams the relationships.

To read this complex figure, start, for example, with the socio-

Figure 5.1   Variables with Direct and Indirect Effects on Teaching

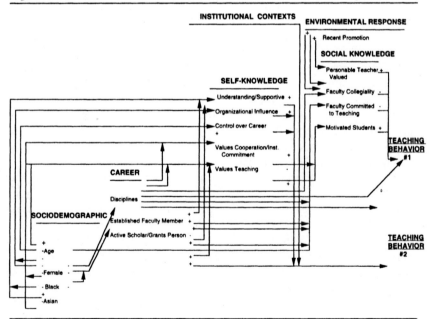

*Source:* Blackburn, Lawrence, Hart, and Dickman (1990).

demographic variable age (the minus sign means younger). A line runs straight left to right parallel to the bottom of the figure and then turns 90 degrees upward. Along the way, arrows from the career variables of discipline, established faculty member, and active scholar/grantsperson have effects on the outcome "teaching behavior #1" (preparing undergraduates as scholars). However, no self-knowledge variables end on the line, which now turns 90 degrees right to the social knowledge variable of belief that the faculty at one's institution are committed to teaching (the minus sign means a belief that they are not). This then leads to a prediction of "teaching behavior #1."

The factors classified as context variables in process-outcome models of teaching impact (i.e., institutional context, environmental response, and discipline) exerted both direct and indirect influences on teaching behavior. Institutional context directly affected work with advanced graduate students and indirectly influenced preparing undergraduates as scholars. Performance feedback to a faculty member (environmental response) had an indirect effect on the measure of graduate teaching behavior that was transmitted through the faculty member's perceptions of institutional norms and sense of collegiality among faculty members (social knowledge). An individual's discipline had direct and indirect effects on both teaching behaviors. In two instances influence was exerted through self-knowledge; in two other cases it came through social knowledge. The context variables overall had greater direct effects (larger betas) on work with advanced graduate students.

The presage variables (i.e., sociodemographic, career other than discipline, self-knowledge, and social knowledge) were more likely to influence the teaching behavior preparing undergraduates as scholars. A faculty member's general background and career-specific experiences had the greatest impact on the person's self-concept as a faculty member. This self-knowledge, in turn, affected the individual's view of the work environment (social knowledge) and, ultimately, teaching behavior.

If, as suggested by the cognitive scientists, one frames the question of why faculty engage in a certain teaching behavior as a problem-solving endeavor, certain strategies are implied by the findings. The data suggest a dispositional strategy by indicating that individuals who are active scholars and grantspersons, and who believe they are not particularly understanding and supportive, are less likely to be involved with graduate students. (Of course, it may also be the graduate students' strategy not to become involved with those individuals.) A values-and-beliefs strategy is suggested by the findings that older professors as well as active researchers, who also value teaching highly and believe students are motivated, are more likely to work with undergraduates in ways that prepare them as scholars. Established faculty members who tend to believe they can influence organizational decisions may be less inclined to teach in ways that encourage scholarship among undergraduates because they do not perceive collegial support for this behavior, an efficacy strategy. On the other hand, those individuals who have just been promoted and infer from this decision that teachers are valued by their universities will more likely engage in this kind of undergraduate instruction.

In addition to testing our framework with teaching variables, we held another goal—namely, to begin identifying the processes through which faculty characteristics and institutional factors influence how one teaches. The findings are consistent with the results of correlational studies and show that the subject matter being taught (discipline) as well as individual career and self-knowledge variables are related to teaching behavior. The results also underscore the importance of faculty members' perceptions of their work environments as predictors of teaching behavior. In some instances, professors' views of the priorities within their universities and their perceptions of colleagues and students strengthened the impact of their background experiences, values, and other individual variables on their teaching behavior; in others, the effects were reduced.

### Discussion

The findings indicate ways in which institutional variables interact with individual characteristics and result in differences in teaching. The data indicate that institutional context and institutional rewards (e.g., promotion) may not shape teaching behavior through reinforcement but instead influence a faculty member's understanding of the institution. It is this understanding that ultimately affects how one teaches. On the other hand, the findings imply that some aspects of institutional context, not measured explicitly in this analysis, directly influence one's work with graduate students. Clearly some organizational factors—for example, the student-faculty ratio in a department—can affect how often one is called upon to evaluate and work with graduate students on their research.

The results also provide evidence that it may be appropriate to model interactions between faculty members' understanding of themselves and their organization as elements of a problem-solving process with effective teaching behavior as the goal. Survey respondents were not asked to describe teaching tasks and the strategies they used to complete these tasks. However, the path analysis suggests individuals may have different strategies that they use in teaching situations. The basic components of the strategies appear to be thoughts, feelings and effort sometimes directed toward

195

the self and other times descriptive of others or of the task context itself (Langstom & Cantor, 1989).

## Effort Given to Teaching

The annals of higher education express a recurring concern about the quality of college and university teaching. The discussion began in the late 1950s and has continued unabated. Today's debates appear more heated and certainly are more prolonged. Even those who do not believe that the quality of teaching is in as serious disrepair as many claim it to be—even they agree that pedagogy and curricula need upgrading.

Faculty improvement depends upon motivation. Critics assume that faculty could teach better if only they would try harder. Colleges and universities have responded by employing a number of strategies. Incentives sometimes come in the form of rewards—if not merit raises and promotions, then public recognition and prizes for outstanding teacher of the year. Colleges and universities engage external experts who give workshops to stimulate interest. They also set up instructional improvement centers to offer consulting assistance and to award monetary grants for faculty with worthy pedagogical projects.

These strategies, however, rarely take into account faculty self-valuations of teaching and their individual perceptions of what the organizational environment desires and supports.[9] This inquiry investigates the degree to which our theoretical cognitive motivation framework accounts for faculty teaching behavior.

Compared with studies on faculty research output, studies of faculty in the teaching role remain sparse. Most researchers empirically examine the relationship between indicators of teaching effectiveness (almost always student ratings) and contextual variables (e.g., class size, whether or not a particular course is required).[10] Less frequent are correlation studies with student learning (see P. Cohen, 1981). Few if any published studies predict teaching behavior (e.g., effort given to teaching) or productivity (e.g., creating a new course).

Our NCRIPTAL questionnaire has self-evaluation indicators of commitment to instruction, faculty self-assessments of their teaching competence, impact of their teaching on student outcomes (efficacy), degree of interest in teaching, and percentage of effort they desire to give to teaching. As for perceptions of the teaching environment, faculty have told us the degree of consensus there is about the curriculum, the support they experience, how committed their colleagues are to teaching, and what percentage of their work effort they believe the administration wants them to give to instructional matters. We also asked faculty members to indicate (1) how concerned they were as teachers about a set of student outcomes, (2) how strongly they agreed with a series of assumptions about undergraduates' approaches to learning and about optimal teaching/learning conditions, and (3) how frequently they engaged in certain teaching activities. These responses enriched our insight into what motivates faculty vis-à-vis their teaching.

We analyzed responses from faculty in CCs, Comp-I's, and Res-I's. We selected these three Carnegie types for the following reasons. First, they represent the extremes of the percentage of time given by faculty to teaching: CCs are at one end (about 70 percent) and Res-I's at the other (about 35 percent), with an intermediate allocation at Comp-I's (60 percent). Second, these institutional types have the largest number of faculty. Third, they span the spectrum of faculty role expectations, from no research and medium-sized classes with no graduate student teaching assistants in CCs to a significant research effort and graduate seminars mixed with large lecture classes and supervising TAs in Res-I's. We took the largest departments in each of the three fields: English for the humanities, chemistry for the natural sciences, and psychology for the social sciences.[11]

As for the sociodemographic variables we used, we dropped race because the numbers in any ethnic group except Caucasian were too small to permit analyses. We used career age rather than chronological age for the reasons given in chapter 4. Sex/gender serves as a surrogate for psychological need differences related to sex as well as opportunity and role expectations. (See chapter 2.)

We used rank, discipline, where faculty obtained their highest degree (Res-I vs. any other type of institution), and career age (number of years as a faculty member at any type of institution) for career variables.

We employed a number of self-knowledge variables—self-competence, self-efficacy, interest, and instructional commitment. (The survey items that constitute each factor are listed in appendix E.) We take the two constructs interest in teaching and instructional commitment as being sufficiently distinct from one another that including both is justified. For example, a professor could be more interested in research than in teaching (interest variable) yet still have a commitment to teaching (instructional commitment variable). In addition, we take both indicators as being different from preferred percentage of time given to teaching. Two professors could have the same interest in teaching, but one could prefer to teach less and the other more.

There were three social knowledge variables—institutional preference for effort given to teaching, colleague commitment to teaching, and consensus and support.

The outcome (dependent) variable is the actual percentage of effort faculty allocated to teaching. We instructed respondents to include in their estimated effort not only actual time spent in class but also time given to preparation, grading, working with students, and other activities that constitute instruction.

We ran descriptive statistics to display the characteristics of the sample.[12] Regressions were run to test the strength of the predictor variables and to determine the percentage of the variance for which each variable was accountable.

### Descriptive Results

Tables 5.7 and 5.8 display the sociodemographic, career, self-knowledge, social knowledge, and behavior variables by institutional type and by discipline.

The Comp-I's and the Res-I's show a heavy proportion of faculty at the top ranks and very few at the assistant professor level. (There are none at the instructor level, a disappearing rank that in the past was the first appointment a new faculty member typically received.) These data agree with the evidence for an aging professoriate and a marketplace cramped by economic constraints. There has been little hiring at the entry level (see, e.g., Bowen & Schuster, 1986). Almost identical average number of years as a college teacher (career age) exists across the three institutional types—19.3 for two-year colleges, 19.5 for comprehensive colleges and universities, and 18.5 for the research universities. (See table 5.8.) There is also little variation across disciplines. Since the average age at receiving the Ph.D. is in the late 20s in the natural sciences and the early 30s in the humanities, the average age of the sampled faculties is between 44 and 52, well within the range

Table 5.7    Descriptive Data on the Sample and on the Variables Entered into the Regression (Percent)

|  | Two-Year Public | | | Comprehensive I | | | Research I | | |
|---|---|---|---|---|---|---|---|---|---|
|  | *Engl.* | *Chem.* | *Psych.* | *Engl.* | *Chem.* | *Psych.* | *Engl.* | *Chem.* | *Psych.* |
| Number | 186 | 42 | 51 | 199 | 104 | 131 | 87 | 72 | 80 |
| Full prof. | 38.7 | 48.8 | 46.0 | 53.8 | 60.6 | 54.2 | 43.8 | 72.2 | 0.6 |
| Assoc. prof. | 27.6 | 22.0 | 30.0 | 26.1 | 23.1 | 29.8 | 37.9 | 12.5 | 0.2 |
| Assist. prof. | 11.1 | 2.4 | 8.0 | 19.6 | 15.4 | 16.0 | 16.1 | 15.3 | 0.2 |
| Instructor | 21.5 | 26.8 | 16.0 | 0.0 | 0.0 | 0.0 | 0.0 | 0.0 | 0.0 |
| Lecturer | 1.1 | 0.0 | 0.0 | 0.9 | 0.9 | 0.0 | 2.2 | 0.0 | 0.0 |
| Female % | 42.6 | 22.8 | 29.7 | 34.3 | 12.4 | 16.9 | 31.0 | 26.6 | 0.3 |

*Source:* NCRIPTAL survey.

198

Table 5.8    Descriptive Data on the Sample and on the Variables Entered into the Regression

| | *Engl.* | | *Chem.* | | *Psych.* | |
|---|---|---|---|---|---|---|
| | *Mean* | *SD* | *Mean* | *SD* | *Mean* | *SD* |
| | *Two-Year Public* | | | | | |
| Career age | 18.10 | 7.50 | 19.70 | 6.20 | 19.70 | 7.20 |
| % allotted to teaching | 69.70 | 16.30 | 75.30 | 16.30 | 65.90 | 19.10 |
| % preferred by institution | 66.40 | 16.60 | 74.70 | 12.40 | 67.30 | 17.70 |
| % preferred to teach | 60.50 | 15.60 | 68.20 | 16.70 | 59.50 | 17.30 |
| Competence factor[a] | 0.20 | 0.86 | 0.30 | 0.86 | 0.24 | 0.95 |
| Self-efficacy factor[a] | 0.04 | 0.94 | 0.49 | 0.97 | −0.01 | 1.10 |
| Interest in teaching[a] | 0.91 | 0.28 | 0.95 | 0.22 | 0.92 | 0.27 |
| Instructional commitment[a] | 0.31 | 0.71 | 0.49 | 0.47 | 0.20 | 0.82 |
| Colleague commit. to teaching[a] | 0.55 | 0.63 | 0.79 | 0.54 | 0.73 | 0.54 |
| Consensus and support[a] | 0.10 | 1.00 | 0.37 | 0.92 | 0.07 | 0.96 |
| | *Comprehensive I* | | | | | |
| Career age | 21.00 | 9.70 | 18.70 | 8.70 | 17.50 | 7.90 |
| % allotted to teaching | 61.60 | 18.00 | 63.30 | 17.50 | 54.20 | 17.80 |
| % preferred by institution | 52.10 | 19.50 | 55.70 | 16.50 | 52.20 | 18.80 |
| % preferred to teach | 53.00 | 16.00 | 55.00 | 15.50 | 46.50 | 16.40 |
| Competence factor[a] | 0.05 | 1.00 | −0.07 | 1.06 | −0.02 | 1.00 |
| Self-efficacy factor[a] | −0.20 | 1.10 | 0.24 | 0.88 | −0.09 | 0.93 |
| Interest in teaching[a] | 0.75 | 0.43 | 0.81 | 0.40 | 0.67 | 0.47 |
| Instructional commitment[a] | 0.09 | 0.98 | 0.27 | 0.65 | −0.12 | 1.04 |
| Colleague commit. to teaching[a] | 0.19 | 0.63 | 0.30 | 0.69 | 0.22 | 0.71 |
| Consensus and support[a] | −0.26 | 1.10 | 0.19 | 1.00 | −0.06 | 0.88 |
| | *Research I* | | | | | |
| Career age | 17.90 | 10.50 | 19.90 | 11.90 | 20.50 | 10.10 |
| % allotted to teaching | 43.70 | 20.90 | 28.90 | 17.10 | 31.80 | 13.90 |
| % preferred by institution | 33.30 | 15.60 | 31.30 | 12.20 | 27.90 | 12.30 |
| % preferred to teach | 37.30 | 12.90 | 28.00 | 9.50 | 26.00 | 12.90 |
| Competence factor[a] | −0.09 | 1.00 | −0.48 | 1.10 | −0.34 | 1.10 |
| Self-efficacy factor[a] | −0.01 | 0.98 | −0.02 | 0.93 | −0.14 | 1.10 |
| Interest in teaching[a] | 0.34 | 0.48 | 0.13 | 0.33 | 0.15 | 0.36 |
| Instructional commitment[a] | −0.31 | 1.10 | −0.81 | 1.24 | −0.81 | 1.24 |
| Colleague commit. to teaching[a] | −1.11 | 0.68 | −1.36 | 0.69 | −1.60 | 0.60 |
| Consensus and support[a] | −0.21 | 1.10 | 0.81 | 0.89 | −0.07 | 0.85 |

*Source:* NCRIPTAL survey.

a. Scaled score with mean = 0 and SD = 1 (range from −3 to 3).

reported in other national surveys (e.g., in Lawrence, Blackburn, & Yoon, 1987).

The numbers of female faculty are misleading. Within the humanities, English has more female faculty than does history; within the social sciences, psychology has a higher percentage than do political science and sociology. The number of female academics has increased in the last decade (see chapter 2), but since we selected disciplines with above-average percentages of women, the actual overall numbers are not as high as the data show.

Striking differences appear in the percentage of time allocated to teaching across institutional types. Differences in time distributions across disciplines are smaller within institutional types. We reported these in chapter 3 and do not repeat them here.

As for the remaining variables in table 5.8, all but one are factors and are scored in such a manner as to have a mean of 0 and a standard deviation of 1. This procedure means that approximately 58 percent of the means will be between plus and minus 1 and 95 percent between plus and minus 2.[13] Interest in teaching is not a factor but rather is a single item turned into a dummy variable with higher interest in teaching coded as 1 and higher interest in research coded as 0.

We note a number of differences. When it comes to competence in teaching, CC faculty rate themselves above average, Comp-I faculty at about the mean, and Res-I faculty a little below it. By itself, however, the phrase "below the mean" is misleading. The means for the items that constitute the teaching self-efficacy factor for two-year and research university faculty are, respectively, 3.73 and 3.45 (where the maximum is 4) for "teaches effectively"; 3.52 and 3.39 for "communicates well"; 3.51 and 3.23 for "works skillfully with students"; and 3.30 and 3.18 for "is an excellent lecturer." All of the differences are small. Faculty everywhere and in every discipline rate themselves as competent teachers. The self-efficacy scores are all close to the mean, the exception being chemists in CCs. These faculty believe they make a real difference both in what students learn and in their career achievement.[14]

As for interest in teaching, which turns out to be strongly correlated with preferred allocation of effort given to teaching, community college faculty have, on average, the highest interest (0.9 out of a possible 1), with comprehensive college and university faculty somewhat lower (about 0.75) but still very high. Research university faculty respond with the general reputation they have, namely, more interested in research than in teaching. The instructional-commitment indicator maintains the same differences across institutional types, but the means shift downward, to less than 0.5 for two-

200

year faculty, around 0 for the comprehensive university faculty, and below 0 for the research university faculty. On both those variables the differences tend to be small, and no consistent pattern appears. The perception-of-the-environment factors—colleague commitment to teaching and institutional consensus and support—follow a similar pattern.

### Regression Results

We ran regressions with percentage of time given to teaching as the outcome variable. Table 5.9 displays the results of the regressions by institutional type, discipline, and predictor variable.

In general, the sociodemographic and career variables, as well as the self-efficacy variables from the self-knowledge category, do not predict percentage of time allocated to the teaching role. The amount of variance they account for is not significant. The exceptions are for two career variables—having received the highest degree from a Res-I university and being an assistant professor—for English faculty in Comp-I's.

Second, when the remaining self-knowledge variables—instructional commitment, interest in teaching, and percentage of time the faculty member prefers to give to teaching—are taken into consideration, the percentage of explained variance increases noticeably and becomes statistically significant at $\leq .05$ for all faculty except those in English and chemistry in Res-I universities and in psychology in CCs. The dominant predictor in every instance, except English in Comp-I's, is the fraction of their time faculty members would like to give to the pedagogical role. That is, their personal valuations influence how much time they give to this activity.

Adding the percentage of time faculty believe their institution wants them to give to teaching increases the percentage of the variance accounted for even more, and in many instances it becomes a significant predictor itself—except in the case of all faculty in the Res-I institutions, where there is no significant change in the percentage of explained variance.

The remaining social knowledge variables have little consequence in Res-I's. Moreover, with the exception of chemistry faculty in CCs, these two variables have little effect in the other institutional types and disciplines.

Having run the planned regressions and found which variables did and did not predict when discipline/department was controlled, we ran another regression for all faculty within each institutional type but without control for discipline. The last row in table 5.9 uses the same variables, only this time for all faculty in each of the three institutional types. All the percentages of variance accounted for are significant, including the one for Res-I's.

The percentage of variance accounted for and the multiple correlations are high, especially for predicting such a complex phenomenon as effort

Table 5.9  Summary of Regression Outcomes Predicting Time Given to Teaching

| | CC | | | Comp-I | | | Res-I | | |
|---|---|---|---|---|---|---|---|---|---|
| | Engl. | Chem. | Psych. | Engl. | Chem. | Psych. | Engl. | Chem. | Psych |
| *Sociodemographic* | | | | | | | | | |
| Gender | | * | | | | | | | |
| *Career* | | | | | | | | | |
| Career age | | * | | | | | | | |
| Graduate school rating | | | | * | | | | | |
| Rank | | * | | * | | | | | |
| *Self-knowledge* | | | | | | | | | |
| Efficacy | | | | | | | | | |
| Interest in teaching | | * | | | | | | | |
| Preferred % time for teaching | * | * | | * | * | * | | | |
| *Social knowledge* | | | | | | | | | |
| Perceived % time institution prefers | * | | | * | | * | | | |
| Consensus and support | | * | | | | | | | |
| Colleague commitment | | | | | | | | | |
| *Behavior* | | | | | | | | | |
| Percentage of explained variance | 38 | 86 | 68 | 49 | 59 | 46 | 34 | 25 | 27 |
| Percentage of explained variance when disciplines are combined | | 44 | | | 46 | | | 32 | |

*Source:* Blackburn, Lawrence, Bieber, and Trautvetter (1991).

*Notes:* Asterisks signify when the variable was significant at $p \leq .05$. All of the explained variance results are significant for the combined disciplines.

given to teaching. Wahba and House's (1981, p. 122) examination of studies based on the concepts of expectancy (subjective probability) and valence (anticipated value) found multiple regression coefficients for predicting job performance ranging from .11 to .72, with the majority being around .30. Our related constructs of efficacy and value, in conjunction with other predictors, produced generally higher percentages of variance and hence give overall support to our conceptual framework.

The sociodemographic and career correlates of behavior generally failed to contribute to the explained variance. The interest-in-teaching variable (self-knowledge) as well as the consensus-and-support and colleague-commitment-to-teaching variables (social knowledge) were strongly correlated with percentage of time respondents preferred to give to teaching (e.g., .5 in Res-I's and Comp-I's). This may be why these variables fail to appear as significant in the regressions. One's current reading of oneself and of what the environment will reward—cognitive processing of a variety of clues—seems to be a much stronger motivator than one's past is.

That both personal preference for time given to teaching (self-knowledge) and perceived institutional preference (social knowledge) were strong predictors suggests that a fit between the two variables is what matters. Said another way, if faculty members believe they have the ability to achieve personal and institutionally valued goals, then they are more likely to believe that their teaching will have an effect on students. In addition, if they believe they can influence student learning, their teaching is more likely to be efficacious.

The second self-efficacy factor, career achievement, did not add to the explained variance. We think the flaw was in the questions asked. They were not situation-specific. Unlike more global concepts such as self-esteem, self-efficacy is task-specific. Asking faculty the degree to which they influence student career achievement is too global. The respondents answered truthfully, saying for the most part that they really do not know the extent to which they exert influence. They recognize that a student will have 30 or 40 other instructors in the course of a college career, and that their own individual influence most likely cannot be very great. If we had instead asked faculty to estimate their influence on students' learning how to conduct, for example, specific chemical experiments, the predictive power of the career-development factor might have increased.

The self-efficacy factor also did not contribute to the explained variance (except for chemistry faculty in CCs). One reason is that the factor has very little variation. Faculty rated themselves high on all four items constituting the factor in the comprehensive and two-year institutions.

The virtual absence of gender predicting allocation of effort given to teaching is both interesting and important. (Gender is significant only for chemistry faculty in two-year publics.) Earlier studies (for a summary, see Blackburn, Behymer, & Hall, 1978) find that women do more teaching, and less publishing, than men. The inference has been that women prefer teaching to research, that they have a socialized preference for nurturing activities (teaching) and a learned avoidance of competitive situations (research). Others have explained the heavier teaching load for women as a consequence of the biased assignment of duties by (typically male) administrators. Whatever the reasons, the good news here may be equity in role effort. Women are as interested as men are in research (and are now publishing as much, as we saw in chapters 2 and 4). Moreover, men are as interested as women are in teaching.

Neither rank nor career age predicted percentage of time given to teaching.[15] The studies that found positive relationships between these variables are most often concerned with student judgment of teaching effectiveness (e.g., Centra, 1977) or with faculty interest in teaching (e.g., Baldwin & Blackburn, 1981). For example, Baldwin and Blackburn found that beginning assistant professors and full professors near the end of their career show a higher degree of interest in teaching. Our results do not support the earlier research finding that there is a positive relationship between age and effectiveness, interest, or effort in teaching (or research). As a surrogate for a faculty member's psychological needs, age is not a good predictor.

The finding that graduate school preparation in other than a Res-I university is not related to effort given to teaching is contrary to what was expected. Supposedly the socialization received in Res-I institutions is not merely toward research but purposively away from teaching, including interest in teaching. The nonrelationship also shows that being a graduate of a Res-I university does not ipso facto stamp that individual as one who disdains teaching.

In conclusion, faculty are saying this: I am very good at teaching (self-efficacy) (self-knowledge). If I am also genuinely interested in teaching (self-knowledge), and if I believe that my institution cares (social knowledge), I will give a lot of time to teaching. If I am not very interested or do not believe that my institution cares, I will not give much time to teaching. All of this is irrespective of where I work (what type of college or university), what field I am in, how long I have been an academic, what rank I hold, what my specialty is (all career variables), whether my department or institution supports teaching, or whether my colleagues care about teaching (both social knowledge variables).

## Implications

The principal findings carry implications for administrative leadership. Since faculty are responding to current motivations, and especially to perceived institutional rewards for greater effort in teaching, sincere deans can make their wishes known and expect to see an increased effort. Unfortunately, however, the matter is more complicated than simply making known what the institution wishes. We also learned that faculty believe they are excellent teachers. Faculty rate their teaching competence very high, a fact observed in other studies and corroborated by student rating scores (e.g., see McKeachie, 1979a). Why should I participate in faculty development activities when I know I am a good pedagogue? My time can be better spent reorganizing a course or designing a new one—a whole host of things I do not require "experts" to tell me how to do. In addition, I have a long agenda of academic things to do that have a higher priority than doing better what I already do well. I know there is no financial reward for trying harder. Someone, perhaps the department chair, is going to have to convince me that there will be increased personal satisfaction, greater intrinsic rewards, before I direct my already overcommitted time to improving my teaching competence.

We saw that a combination of teaching self-efficacy, personal valuation of teaching, and perceived institutional valuation of teaching is what led to variation in teaching effort. There are points of entry to effect faculty change, such as workshops to enhance teaching efficacy and organizational incentives and support. We return to these at the end of the chapter.

A second implication is somewhat easier to manage. That interest in teaching varies among individuals but is not predictable by career age implies that one's interest fluctuates over time, an outcome that Baldwin and Blackburn (1981) found. Most likely the teaching interest rises and declines and is not systematic for most individuals. The cycle is not predictable except in some gross way, with too little certainty on which to base long-range plans for individuals. The sensitive administrator would be wise to set aside her or his "fairness" rule of having everyone, irrespective of rank and stature, teaching the same number of credit hours every term. What would be more effective for the individual faculty member and for the organization would be to have faculty teach more when that is their interest and desire and to teach less when other activities hold a higher value. Equity would be achieved over the long run, but variation would be an option in the shorter time spans. Simultaneously, flexible workloads mean that faculty are accountable for the products they say they will deliver. Obviously planning is involved, for courses need to be taught for student schedules. Annual conferences with faculty regarding their career plans and their teaching and research interests can allow chairs to introduce flexibility into faculty and institutional lives and simultaneously to foster a more effective and productive organization.

## Ph.D. Faculty in Community Colleges

Next we view teaching faculty in community colleges and examine one variable in particular, namely, what difference having a Ph.D. makes. Twenty years ago a community college Ph.D. faculty member was a rare individual. When the community college movement spread in the late 1950s and early 1970s, the original offerings tended to be primarily late-afternoon and evening classes taught in the district's high school. The K–12 superintendent took on the additional title of dean. The faculty were senior high school teachers with master's degrees and with a good reputation as teachers. As the community college movement expanded and as districts and counties passed bond issues to build separate institutions, offer classes day and night, and have a board of their own, the existing faculty went along. When it was necessary to increase the staff, high school teachers along with young people with master's degrees from the neighboring university were hired. So were a few Ph.D.'s, but not many then, for they could get positions in four-year colleges, the initial ambition for the vast majority. As for the Ph.D.'s who were hired, the trouble they caused was frequently greater than the benefit their additional education brought to the institution. They wanted to raise entrance standards, increase requirements for graduation, or expand the institution into a four-year college offering the bachelor's degree—all goals contrary to the community college mission. Administrators stopped hiring Ph.D.'s.

Now the number of community college faculty with doctorates is around 30 percent nationwide. The increase has come about for multiple reasons. Some master's-degree faculty went back to the university, usually on a part-time basis, and earned the doctorate simply because they liked learning; others saw the degree as a way to an administrative post; some would gain financially from the negotiated salary schedule that paid a higher salary to a Ph.D. While these trends were going on, the market collapsed for new Ph.D.'s in four-year institutions in some fields, especially the humanities. Ph.D.'s were available. Some administrators thought adding pedigreed individuals to their staff would increase their institution's status. In addition, some Ph.D.'s had developed a genuine commitment to the community college's special mission. A community college was where they sought their career. This combination of factors has changed the composition of community college faculty. It is important to find out what effects Ph.D. faculty are having on the institution.

We identify differences between community college faculty members who have earned doctorates and those who have not with respect to their (1) educational beliefs and values, (2) personal efficacy, (3) career satisfaction, (4) perceptions of their employing institution, and (5) professional behaviors. Furthermore, we examined (a) whether the impact of graduate preparation persists when field of preparation and timing of graduate study (Ph.D. before employment or during employment) are taken into account, and (b) whether the influence of doctoral preparation on behavior is greater than that of individual beliefs and values, personal competence, satisfaction, and organizational perceptions. In our theoretical framework, (1) and (2) are self-knowledge variables, (3) is in the career category, (4) is social knowledge, and (5) contains behaviors.

We created measures for each of the five variable categories through factor analysis. A total of 42 factors emerged: career has 2 for satisfaction; under self-knowledge, 11 represented beliefs and values, and 6 were personal competence; social knowledge had 10 for perceptions of the organizational environment; and behavior had 13 different activities. Appendix F contains the items that composed the factors, the eigenvalues, and the names we gave to each factor.[16]

We divided the sample into several subgroups based on respondents' field of teaching, doctoral preparation, and the time when the Ph.D. was earned. We used one-way analyses of variance and t-tests to identify significant differences between faculty members with and without doctorates, between those who had obtained the degree before and during their current appointment at their community college, and between Ph.D.'s and non-Ph.D.'s within academic field groups. We ran hierarchical multiple regression analyses (1) to assess the effects of field and doctoral preparation on beliefs/values, personal efficacy, sense of satisfaction as a community college faculty member, perceptions of the organizational environment, and teaching behaviors, and (2) to evaluate the impact of the educational efficacy, satisfaction, and other perceptual variables on the faculty member's teaching, research, and service behavior. Here we report only teaching behaviors.

## Sample

Among the 857 respondents to our NCRIPTAL survey of 55 community colleges, 795 had no missing data with respect to their highest degree and being in one of the eight departments used here. Of the 795, 216 (27.2 percent) had the Ph.D. degree, and 66 (8.3 percent) had another earned doctorate—Ed.D., D.A. (doctor of arts), J.D., or M.D.—for a combined 35.5 percent having earned a doctoral degree.[17] Of the doctoral holders, 73 percent had earned their degree before beginning to teach at their current community college. In addition, one-third of all of the faculty had earned their highest degree—B.A. (only 5), M.A. (the most frequent highest degree), Ph.D.—from a Res-I university. The 795 faculty were distributed across the disciplines as follows: English, 240 (35 percent with doctorates); history, 82 (52 percent with doctorates); biology, 107 (28 percent with doctorates); chemistry, 59 (37 percent with doctorates); mathematics/ statistics, 160 (21 percent with doctorates); political science, 35 (49 percent

207

with doctorates); psychology, 63 (56 percent with doctorates); and sociology, 49 (33 percent with doctorates).

### Differences between Faculty Subgroups

Table 5.10 summarizes the faculty beliefs, competence, satisfaction, environment, and behavior data from the three different fields, for faculty members who completed the Ph.D. before and after joining their present institution, and for those from the same field with and without the Ph.D.

When there is no asterisk in a category's column, there is no significant difference between the different classes. For example, factor 2, concern for personal/social development, does not differ between faculty in the humanities, social sciences, and natural sciences; between those who hold the Ph.D. and those who do not; between those who earned the Ph.D. before and those who earned it during employment at their community college; or between holders and nonholders of the Ph.D. in each of the three fields. When there is a single, double, or triple asterisk in a column, there is a significant difference. For example, with respect to factor 1, the belief that students are motivated, Ph.D.'s in the natural sciences believe significantly more strongly than do non-Ph.D.'s that this is true. The triple asterisk means the significance of the differences is at the .001 level; two asterisks are at the .01 level; and a single asterisk is at the .05 level.

Faculty in different fields varied in their beliefs. Natural science faculty are more committed to teaching (5, the factor number in table 5.10) and less to research (10) than are humanities and social science faculty. Humanists are the most devoted to the goal of intellectual development for students and dedication to the liberal arts (5), and they value individualized instruction (4) more than natural scientists do.

Field differences also emerged in faculty members' assessments of their own efficacy. Natural scientists believe more strongly than humanists and social scientists in their ability to affect student outcomes (14), whereas the beliefs reverse themselves when it comes to the ability to influence a variety of department or unit-level decisions (16). These faculty differed by field as well in overall satisfaction with their careers (general feelings about the institution, likelihood of choosing the faculty career again, and self-assessment of success compared with like faculty). Humanists were more satisfied than natural scientists (18).

Further, with respect to perceptions of the organizational environment, differences emerged among the three fields in faculty members' overall view of the organizational climate (20, their trust that the administration and faculty groups act in good faith, and that the institution encourages them to work for the collective good of the unit). Natural scientists believe this more strongly than do social scientists. Humanists more than either of the other groups discern that rewarded faculty are those oriented primarily toward professional accomplishments (24) and research (28). On the other hand, natural scientists more than the other two groups say there is consensus in curricular matters and support for teaching on their campus (25).

Statistical tests revealed field differences in teaching behavior. Humanists placed stronger emphasis on requiring student writing and research activities (30) than did social and natural scientists, whereas the latter two groups gave more effort to individualizing instruction (32). Both humanists and natural scientists spent more time developing their courses (35). Further, they differed on the balance they struck between scholarship/professional growth (34, time spent enhancing one's knowledge that does not necessarily result in a publication, social scientists doing the most) and teaching dissemination activities (33, publishing chapters in books, writing for the popular press, humanists doing more than natural scientists).[18]

Tests showed differences between faculty with the Ph.D. and their non-Ph.D. colleagues. With respect to self-knowledge beliefs about teaching and research, Ph.D. faculty were less committed to teaching (6), less personally devoted to teaching (7), but more devoted to intellectual development and the liberal arts (5). They reported higher research efficacy (15) and greater overall career satisfaction (18, general positive feelings about the institution, likelihood of choosing the faculty career again, and self-assessment of career success).

Regarding teaching behaviors, Ph.D.'s indicated less time spent on course development (35) and more on teaching dissemination activities (33). With respect to research behaviors, Ph.D. faculty engaged more in editorial involvement (39), journal publishing (38), and active grant-getting (36), but less in association activity (40).

Three differences existed when the Ph.D.'s were subdivided into groups based on the timing of their doctoral study. As indicated by their perception of their effect on student outcomes, faculty who received the degree before they were hired at the current institution indicated more teaching efficacy (14), assessed their environment as less supportive of scholarship (29), and had less involvement in professional association activity (40).

When we compared Ph.D. faculty with their non-Ph.D. colleagues within the fields of knowledge, tests indicated 11 significant differences among the humanists. Ph.D. respondents revealed more commitment to and efficacy in research (10 and 15), greater overall career satisfaction (18), and assessments that the environment values research (28) but does not support scholarship (29). Regarding teaching behavior, Ph.D. faculty indicated they are

Table 5.10 Differences between Community College Faculty Subgroups on Predictor and Outcome Measures

| | Field | | | Ph.D. | | Ph.D. during Appointment | | Humanities | | Social Sci. | | Natural Sci. | |
|---|---|---|---|---|---|---|---|---|---|---|---|---|---|
| | Hum. | Soc. Sci. | Nat. Sci. | No | Yes | Yes | No | No Ph.D. | Ph.D. | No Ph.D. | Ph.D | No Ph.D. | Ph.D. |
| **Beliefs** | | | | | | | | | | | | | |
| 1 Students are motivated | -.006 | .151 | -.017 | .062 | -.061 | -.040 | -.097 | .071 | -.162 | .238 | -.030 | -.019 | .045*** |
| 2 Concern for personal/ social development | .021 | .062 | -.057 | -.007 | -.014 | .115 | -.080 | .030 | -.003 | .024 | .113 | -.055 | -.129 |
| 3 Values teacher control | -.056 | -.071 | .070 | -.002 | -.028 | .028 | -.109 | -.033 | -.128 | -.124 | .027 | .077 | .059 |
| 4 Values individualized instruction | .095 | .068 | -.110 | .005 | -.015 | .112 | -.136 | .109 | .073 | .073 | .055 | -.106 | -.187 |
| 5 Devotion to intellectual development/lib. arts | .367 | -.243 | -.291 | -.114 | .181*** | .084 | .262 | .316 | .484 | -.339 | -.047 | -.361 | -.029* |
| 6 Personal commitment to teaching | -.135 | -.122 | .200 | .068 | -.152** | -.250 | -.131 | -.111 | -.223 | -.181 | -.014 | .316 | -.172** |
| 7 Devotion to teaching | -.058 | -.152 | .140 | .090 | -.221*** | -.237 | -.147 | -.018 | -.159 | -.068 | -.343 | .242 | -.203*** |
| 8 Favor student competition | -.218 | -.140 | .240 | .001 | -.044 | -.156 | .011 | -.290 | -.065 | .014 | -.410 | .225 | .281 |
| 9 Concern for content/ process | -.265 | -.030 | .318 | .039 | -.027 | -.104 | .081 | -.199 | -.398 | -.007 | -.078 | .268 | .496* |
| 10 Commitment to research | .303 | .143 | -.272 | -.191 | .622*** | .709 | .484 | .112 | .757*** | -.116 | .638*** | -.472 | .428*** |
| 11 Commitment to service/institution | -.054 | .049 | .025 | .013 | -.046 | -.145 | .057 | -.088 | .006 | .103 | -.079 | .051 | -.094 |
| **Efficacy** | | | | | | | | | | | | | |
| 12 Teaching competence | .045 | .041 | -.055 | -.033 | .110 | .179 | .018 | .017 | .129 | -.035 | .188 | -.076 | .023 |
| 13 Dealing with difficult classes | -.051 | -.025 | .058 | -.024 | .052 | -.065 | .170 | -.049 | -.037 | -.018 | -.020 | .001 | .233 |

| | c1 | c2 | c3 | c4 | c5 | c6 | c7 | c8 | c9 | c10 | c11 | c12 | c13 |
|---|---|---|---|---|---|---|---|---|---|---|---|---|---|
| 14 Effect on student outcomes | -.063 | -.134 | .172 | .049 | -.057 | -.294 | .200** | -.036 | -.132 | -.051 | -.282 | .155 | 222 |
| 15 Research competence | .249 | .026 | -.180 | -.120 | .442*** | 550 | .339 | .052 | .704*** | -.134 | .349** | -.276 | .128** |
| 16 Department decision influence | -.095 | .032 | .097 | .002 | .015 | .116 | -.050 | -.134 | -.010 | -.034 | .140 | .131 | -.053 |
| 17 Academic decision influence | -.021 | -.074 | .039 | -.018 | -.005 | -.164 | .088 | .005 | -.107 | -.060 | -.100 | -.021 | 228 |
| **Satisfaction** | | | | | | | | | | | | | |
| 18 Career satisfaction | .110 | .045 | -.093 | -.082 | .254*** | 227 | .299 | .018 | .301* | -.015 | .196 | -.188 | .233*** |
| 19 Salary satisfaction | -.003 | -.038 | .012 | .022 | -.066 | -.138 | -.039 | .014 | -.033 | .041 | -.207 | .013 | -.002 |
| **Environment** | | | | | | | | | | | | | |
| 20 View of org. climate | -.035 | -.151 | .095 | .042 | -.138* | -.134 | -.181 | -.051 | -.022 | -.113 | -.246 | .187 | -.224* |
| 21 View of governance/support | .067 | -.070 | -.091 | -.021 | -.025 | .057 | -.081 | .007 | .164 | .037 | -.265 | -.075 | -.118 |
| 22 Environment values involvement | .109 | -.074 | -.036 | .008 | .044 | -.021 | .134 | .069 | .181 | -.074 | -.075 | -.018 | -.065 |
| 23 Support for teaching | -.035 | -.061 | .071 | -.019 | .070 | .081 | .100 | -.062 | .075 | -.089 | -.011 | .046 | .126 |
| 24 Discipline impacts teaching | .030 | -.048 | -.054 | -.026 | -.037 | -.004 | -.125 | .062 | -.065 | -.038 | -.039 | -.096 | -.004 |
| 25 Curriculum consensus/support | -.118 | -.087 | .176 | .043 | -.092 | -.021 | -.092 | -.095 | -.197 | -.046 | -.174 | .191 | .123 |
| 26 Environmental commitment to teaching | -.177 | .097 | .115 | -.017 | .047 | -.023 | .048 | -.249 | -.003 | .133 | .073 | .117 | 099 |
| 27 Environmental pressure on teachers | .036 | -.084 | .038 | .032 | -.016 | .035 | -.009 | .042 | .008 | -.022 | -.175 | .043 | 070 |
| 28 Environment values research | .183 | -.187 | -.051 | -.051 | .165*** | 316 | .082 | .088 | .368* | -.243 | -.131 | -.089 | .092 |
| 29 Environment supports scholarship | -.041 | -.100 | .088 | .087 | -.258*** | -.076 | -.386* | .043 | -.246* | -.014 | -.288 | .175 | -.254*** |

Continued next page

Table 5.10—Continued

| Behavior | Field | | | Ph.D. | | Ph.D. during Appointment | | Humanities | | Social Sci. | | Natural Sci. | |
|---|---|---|---|---|---|---|---|---|---|---|---|---|---|
| | Hum. | Soc. Sci. | Nat. Sci. | No | Yes | Yes | No | No Ph.D. | Ph.D. | No Ph.D. | Ph.D. | No Ph.D. | Ph.D. |
| 30 Research activities | .696 | -.180 | -.659 | -.079 | .079 | .110 | .110 | .712 | .651 | -.086 | -.354* | -.751 | -.336*** |
| 31 Exchanging expertise | .037 | -.057 | .027 | .002 | .046 | .104 | .059 | .023 | .041 | -.142 | .099 | .037 | .011 |
| 32 Individualizing instruction | -.169 | .166 | .061 | .001 | -.032 | -.076 | -.075 | -.165 | -.208 | .205 | .091 | .047 | .106 |
| 33 Dissemination | .213 | -.024 | -.214 | -.101 | .236*** | .287 | .168 | .033 | .637*** | -.104 | .123 | -.210 | -.212 |
| 34 Preference for professional growth | .102 | .387 | -.233 | .006 | .055 | .088 | .043 | .116 | .098 | .450 | .199 | -.271 | -.120 |
| 35 Course development | .037 | -.328 | .151 | .062 | -.118* | -.136 | -.078 | .128 | -.158* | -.329 | -.334 | .170 | .113 |
| 36 Active grantsperson | .085 | .165 | -.075 | -.065 | .283*** | .273 | .283 | -.037 | .319* | .118 | .268 | -.166 | .248* |
| 37 Scholarly | .102 | .107 | -.120 | -.038 | .144 | .208 | .086 | .085 | .137 | -.030 | .356 | -.148 | .002 |
| 38 Journal publisher | .148 | -.013 | -.200 | -.159 | .317*** | .416 | .172 | .017 | .471** | -.029 | .355** | -.281 | .088*** |
| 39 Editorial involvement | .106 | -.111 | .050 | -.071 | .303*** | .256 | .348 | -.079 | .481*** | -.228 | .102* | .007 | .212 |
| 40 Association activity | .144 | -.155 | -.118 | .065 | -.239*** | .023 | -.466*** | .264 | -.100* | -.094 | -.261 | -.036 | -.406*** |
| 41 Active scholar | .134 | .199 | -.214 | .002 | -.022 | -.056 | .042 | .033 | .278 | .454 | -.245* | -.197 | -.255 |
| 42 Campus committee work | .021 | .028 | -.006 | -.018 | -.073 | .147 | .085 | -.012 | .072 | -.006 | .094 | -.028 | .056 |

Source: NCRIPTAL survey.
Note: * $p \leq .05$. ** $p \leq .01$. *** $p \leq .001$.

involved in fewer course development activities (35) and more written (e.g., book chapters) teaching dissemination activities (33) than the nondoctoral faculty. They were also more likely to be active grantspersons (36), publishers (38), and participants in editorial activities (39).

Among the social scientists, six differences distinguished those with Ph.D.'s from those without. Like the humanists, these Ph.D.'s showed stronger commitment to and efficacy in research (10 and 15). They required writing and research activities for students more than those without the degree did (30). On three research behaviors, Ph.D.'s indicated more traditional journal publication (38) and editorial involvement (39) but less involvement in scholarly activities (41).

Ph.D. natural scientists differed more frequently from their non-Ph.D. counterparts. Differences emerged on six beliefs. The natural science Ph.D.'s had less commitment to teaching (6), less personal devotion to teaching (7), and less concern for students' intellectual development and the liberal arts (5). On the other hand, they were more concerned about discipline content and process (9), viewed student motivation more positively (1), and were more personally committed to research (10). The doctoral faculty expressed greater research competence (15) and overall career satisfaction (18) than did their colleagues without that degree. On two environment factors, Ph.D. faculty held a less positive view of the organizational climate (20) and a less positive perception of the institution's support for scholarship (29).

The Ph.D. natural scientists exhibited differences in four behaviors: in their teaching, they were less likely to require student writing and research activities (30), but they were also more likely to be active grantspersons (36) and journal publishers (38) but not to be involved in professional associations (40).

### Predicting Faculty Behavior and Effort

In the final hierarchical multiple regression analysis, we used the belief, efficacy, satisfaction, and organizational environment perceptions along with the field, degree held (Ph.D. or not), and timing of degree (before or during appointment) variables as predictors of teaching behaviors among community college faculty. We entered the new factors into the regression after these variables' effects had been taken into account. This order of entry allowed us to evaluate the separate and combined effects of career socialization (field, degree held, timing of doctoral study) and individual differences in beliefs, competence, satisfaction, and organizational perceptions on faculty behavior.

When we ran the regressions for the teaching behavior outcomes, more

213

than 20 variables had a significant effect. The percentage of explained variance ranged from 13 percent to 54 percent. Rather than showing the regression data for each of the seven outcome variables, table 5.11 summarizes the findings.

The respondents' disciplinary field (top row of the table) influenced their teaching in every instance except for the outcome "exchanging expertise." Having the Ph.D. degree (second row) was significant in only two instances—positively for dissemination of their knowledge and negatively for percent effort given to teaching. Doctorate holders gave less effort to teaching. The time of earning the degree was significant only when the outcome was "individualizing instruction." Faculty who had earned their degree after their appointment at the community college rather than having it before starting to teach there were significantly more likely to individualize their teaching.

The remainder of the table contains the numbers of the factors that were significant in their category. (See table 5.10.) For example, in the category of beliefs regarding teaching, factors 5 (devoted to student intellectual development and the liberal arts), 7 (devoted to teaching), and 9 (concern for course content and process) each significantly predicted having students engage in research activities. Overall, the self-knowledge variables of beliefs regarding teaching and the social knowledge variables of environment for teaching had the greatest number of factors predicting several of the teaching behaviors.

Several of the belief/perception variables that had significant effects on the teaching behaviors were not affected by field or doctoral preparation measures. Clearly, factors other than those in the framework were affecting the faculty members' perceptions of themselves and their work environments. The number of respondents from each community college was not of sufficient size to allow us to control for institution and see if there were differences among campuses in faculty beliefs, perceptions, and behaviors. However, the data set includes other variables such as years of teaching experience, age, and gender that could be taken into account.[19]

## Discussion

As is typical in a commentary on findings, the differences between the groups discussed here receive more attention than the similarities. We need to recognize that these community college faculty have many characteristics in common with their colleagues in different specialties as well as with those in four-year colleges and universities. Humanists everywhere—not just those in community colleges—are more committed to intellectual development and to the liberal arts. Natural scientists everywhere are more con-

Table 5.11  Predicting Teaching Behaviors among Community College Faculty

| | Research Activity | Exchanging Expertise | Individualizing Instruction | Dissemination | Preference for Professional Growth | Course Development | Percent Effort to Teaching |
|---|---|---|---|---|---|---|---|
| Field | Hum. & soc. sci. | | Nat. sci. | Hum. | Soc. sci. | Nat. sci. | Nat. sci. |
| Have Ph.D. | | | | | | | |
| When earned Ph.D. | | | During appt. | | | | |
| *Self-knowledge* | | | | | | | |
| Beliefs re teaching | 5, 7, 9[a] | | | | | -6 | 3, 6, 7, 9 |
| Beliefs re research | | | 10 | | -10 | | -11 |
| Beliefs re service | -11[b] | | | | | | |
| Competence re teaching | 14 | 12 | 12, 14 | | | -13 | |
| Competence re research | | | | 15 | | 15 | -15 |
| Competence re service | | | | -16 | | 17 | -16, -17 |
| Career satisfaction | 19 | | | | | | |
| *Social knowledge* | | | | | | | |
| General environment | | | | | | | 20, 22 |
| Environment for teaching | 27 | 24–26 | 24 | | | 24, 25, 26 | 23, 26 |
| Environment for research | | | | | | | |
| Environment for service | | | | | | | |
| *Behavior* | | | | | | | |
| Percentage of explained behavior | 47 | 13 | 16 | 18 | 35 | 16 | 54 |

*Source:* NCRIPTAL survey.

*Note:* These are the 29 variables (1–29) that remain in the seven regressions for teaching behaviors that are at $p \leq .05$.

a. Factor numbers (see table 5.10).

b. Minus sign means opposite of factor (here, not committed to service).

215

cerned about course content and transferring information from themselves to their students (process).

In some respects the similarities between Ph.D. and non-Ph.D. faculty, and also between Ph.D. faculty earning the degree before and during appointment, are more informative than the differences. By way of illustration, there are no differences between Ph.D. and non-Ph.D. faculty on their concern for the social development of students. Ph.D.'s are not supposed to possess that value, but the traditional community college faculty member does. Both groups also value teacher control and individualized instruction, are concerned about course content, are committed to their institution, and are committed to teaching.

Of the 42 factors, only 2 showed a difference between those who earned their Ph.D. before taking a position in the community college and those who earned the degree after their appointment began. Still, the degree matters, for the Ph.D.'s are significantly the more satisfied faculty members. The Ph.D. faculty, irrespective of the career point at which they earned the degree, have a much greater investment in being an academic, a college teacher.

The M.A. is a comparatively easy degree to earn. One takes 30 to 35 semester hours, 10 to 12 courses. There is no comprehensive examination. Only a few disciplines require a short thesis (history frequently does). The thesis reduces the number of course credit hours required. For the most part there is little difference between work at this level and the senior year of the bachelor's degree. At times it can be even less demanding. The degree can be earned in a calendar year. On the other hand, the Ph.D. requires 50-plus semester hours beyond the bachelor's, a highly demanding qualifying examination, advanced research methodology, seminar papers, and a dissertation that itself can take several years. The time from the bachelor's degree to the Ph.D. ranges from a minimum of 5 years in the natural sciences to 12 years in the humanities, with the average being a little over 8 years. As we saw, Ph.D. faculty do differ from M.A. faculty, and most often in positive ways.

Without recounting the significant outcomes we found in the various analyses of these data, when we concentrate on the regression findings for percentage of effort given to teaching, our strongest behavioral outcome (with 54 percent of the variance explained) and the one we believe to be most important, three principal conclusions are warranted. (They are essentially the same for predicting requiring research activities of students, an outcome that also had a high percentage of its variance accounted for, 47 percent; see table 5.11.)

First, personal beliefs matter, especially commitment to teaching (personal preference for teaching and scholarship), dedication to teaching (concern for students), and the importance of content and process (transmitting the discipline and demonstrating a scholarly process). Second, these faculty express low efficacy when it comes to their research competence and their ability to influence organizational matters like curricular decisions or admission requirements. Said positively, they are teachers, not academic politicians. Third, these teachers have a positive view of the organization (they trust their administrators to act in good faith and believe they also value teaching), perceive that their college values their involvement, and believe that their colleagues are also committed to teaching.

### Implications

Some consequences for administrators flow from these findings. It is not easy to change less committed teachers into dedicated ones, which is what one might wish to do, especially in an institution whose primary function is teaching. People who select the academic career have a strong desire to teach, but some make this a more exclusive goal than do others. The administrative trick occurs first in the hiring process, to find ways to select individuals who can demonstrate this high level of commitment and devotion. Demonstrated experience provides better evidence than self-professed desire, a condition one can obtain with Ph.D. candidates, for they are quite likely—especially in the humanities—to have had experience as a teaching assistant. A newly minted M.A. graduate is less likely to have taught anywhere.

A second administrative problem arises with the Ph.D. faculty. For the most part it appears that Ph.D. faculty are a positive, not negative, addition to a community college staff. Ph.D. faculty add a dimension that had been lacking, and they are teachers as well. Their expertise is going to be more up-to-date than that of their master's-degree colleagues, who may even be falling behind and most likely do not have the knowledge that the teaching assistant in the university has. These Ph.D.'s who also have a research interest could be lonely individuals in need of colleagues in their discipline. On average, the study's 55 community colleges have less than two Ph.D.'s on their staff in any one field, and less than one in the social sciences. Administrators could assist their selected Ph.D. faculty to make and maintain relationships with faculty—and their libraries and laboratories—in neighboring universities and thereby satisfy healthy desires the community college is not designed to meet.

With a national effort to have more community college (especially minority) students go on to four-year institutions and earn baccalaureate degrees, institutional articulation between the community college courses and their counterparts at the four-year college or university becomes essential. Ph.D.

faculty are well positioned to play an important role in this transition.

In light of these findings, it seems for the most part that the generalizations about the negative consequences of hiring doctorally prepared faculty are not supported. Although doctoral preparation did influence teaching behavior, the effects were usually indirect. The changes in behavior due to (either or both) highest degree earned and timing of graduate study were statistically significant in only two instances—engaging in scholarly teaching-related behavior and time spent on teaching. Field of expertise and individual beliefs and perceptions accounted for the most variance. In fact field, along with highest degree, predicted how much time one gave to teaching. Consequently, analysts' concern about the level of teaching effort among doctorally prepared faculty may be justified. At the same time, these critics need to be aware that people in some fields spend more time on teaching than people in others spend.

The data on career satisfaction suggest that doctorally prepared individuals are not dissatisfied with their careers as community college faculty members. Although the amount of satisfaction accounted for was small (the explained variance was 3 percent), the significant effects of field and level of preparation were positive. It may well be, as London (1978) suggests, that these professors have resolved any disappointment they may have experienced by redefining themselves and their careers in ways that bring them more in line with the expectations of the community colleges that employ them.

## Themes in the Literature

That the results here are not as robust as they were for the research outcomes is not surprising. As we noted at the outset, there is appreciably less consensus among students, faculty, and administrators regarding what constitutes "good teaching." The teaching construct contains a large qualitative component. Measures and indicators are more difficult to come by. We have found no studies with which to compare our findings in either quality or quantity (the amount of variance explained). What we have accounted for may be very good.

In sum, we desired to be more successful than we have been. At the same time, our belief is that the upper limit for explained variance in teaching will remain comparatively low. While our theoretical framework can be improved by introducing other measures of good teaching, we believe its overall structure to be sound.

Since improved teaching has received the extensive attention it has, we close this chapter by briefly noting some themes and key players in the literature that address teaching and learning issues even though they do not have direct connections to our framework or to predicting faculty teaching behaviors. Bill McKeachie (*Teaching Tips*, 8th ed., 1986) has used his own research findings along with the best of others' to touch on the many dimensions of the art of teaching, in a book that is especially helpful for the beginning faculty member. Joseph Katz and Mildred Henry (*Turning Professors into Teachers*, 1988) have spent the major portion of their careers interviewing faculty and working with them on ways to create environments that facilitate student learning. A few researchers (e.g., Centra, 1973; Cohen, 1980; Erickson & Erickson, 1979; Marsh & Roche, 1993) have experimented with intervention techniques and shown that faculty who receive feedback from experts and peers during the conduct of a course they are teaching receive higher student ratings at the end of the term than those who do not. For the most part, however, the massive literature on college teaching is restricted to finding correlations between student course evaluations and some aspect of the course (required, size, time of day—an almost endless list) that neither inform us very much about why faculty do what they do nor lead to any kind of improvement, even in student satisfaction.

A second thread in this larger domain of teaching improvement revolves around an organization called POD—Professional and Organization Development. The individuals who compose this comparatively recently formed organization are directors and staff members of faculty development units on their campuses—nearly 2,000 of them at one point in time. Their role is to assist faculty with many kinds of professional and organizational problems. They take their principal professional development activity to be in the teaching domain. These people run and organize workshops, videotape a faculty member's teaching (if that is her or his desire), supply written materials, bring in specialists, and in general lend their expertise to satisfy faculty desires and needs. Many of these campus units publish regular newsletters about latest developments, and one can be on their mailing list almost always without charge. The effectiveness of Faculty Development Centers is yet to be assessed.

K. Patricia Cross and Thomas Angelo (*Classroom Assessment Techniques: A Handbook for Faculty*, 1988) and Thomas Angelo ("A Teachers Dozen," 1993) interconnect with the POD people (and many of the persons named here fall into more than one category). Their work teaches faculty how to design teaching and learning experiments in their own classrooms; that is, it turns them into researchers with regard to pedagogy quite irrespective of their academic specialty. The idea behind this movement is that not only would we all learn things that work, and do not work, with regard to learning and teaching, but a corporate body of knowledge would also be generated upon which theory could be built. This comparatively recent innovation is yet to prove its merit.

Ernest Boyer (1990) has championed more strongly linking scholarship with teaching. Still another related strand of current activity with respect to faculty development in the teaching role is provided by Patricia Hutchings' work ("Introducing Portfolios," 1993; *The Teaching Portfolio,* 1991, with Russell Edgerton as first author), Martin Finkelstein's New Jersey Institute for Collegiate Teaching and Learning, and Maryellen Wiemer and Robert Menges's program in the National Center on Postsecondary Teaching, Learning, and Assessment. See Wiemer's 1994 release of papers from a Princeton conference on the topic. See also the Features section of the Nov./Dec. 1993 issue of *Change* (vol. 25, no. 6) for case descriptions of current developments on teaching around the country. The interested faculty member or administrator can tap any of these sources and easily connect to ongoing activities regarding teaching and learning.

Changes require resources—people and, most often, money. Administrators are key persons when it comes to improving the workplace and helping faculty to grow. The remainder of this chapter examines a few selected strategies and practices colleges and universities can use to accomplish personnel and institutional goals. The immediate faculty supervisor receives the major attention in this discussion—most often the department chair in a large institution, the dean of faculty in a smaller one. If these supervisors do not have the resources, they are still the key contact for aiding faculty and changing the immediate work environment. They have access to the next higher level.

Creswell, Seagren, Wheeler, Vavrus, Grady, Egly, and Wilhite's (1987) study of chairs documents the importance of their role. Central to every strategy chairs employ is their caring. Faculty have to believe that the chair's interest in them is sincere. They have to believe that the feedback they receive has credence before they will act to make changes.[20] Administrators must have good interpersonal skills. Even then, the outcomes are not always positive. Many faculty tend to react negatively to assessment of their work. One strategy used by a few colleges is performance contracts, a practice Blackburn and Pitney (1988) recommend as the best of the array of alternatives they examined.

The chair can arrange and support a mentor relationship between an established senior faculty member and junior assistant professor, a practice that has met with some success. Unfortunately, this notion receives considerable endorsement but little supporting evidence as to its outcomes. In addition, when the institution is small the danger exists that the supporter may also be the judge when it comes to promotion and tenure decisions, a situation that involves a conflict of interest. To circumvent this problem, the Great Lakes College Association (GLCA), a consortium of 12 private liberal arts colleges in Indiana, Michigan, and Ohio, paired new assistant professors with full professors in the same discipline and specialty at a neighboring school.[21] The beginners now have a senior colleague to whom they can confess teaching and research failures without being judged stupid and incompetent. Williams and Blackburn (1988) learned that senior nursing school faculty could launch a new assistant professor's research career, but only if they worked on a project as full partners. Praise, encouragement, tips, how-to advice, and the like did not accomplish the goal. We expect that the same holds for dealing with teaching issues. One needs more than being told what to do; co-teaching with the mentor and visiting each other's classes provide the needed experience.

We (Lawrence, Blackburn, Hart, Mackie, Dickman, & Frank, 1991) conducted a pilot study to learn what kinds of things, people, time, and money would be required for a faculty person to convert her or his regular undergraduate class from the good one it is to a perfect one. Next to smaller classes and brighter, more self-motivated students, time turned out to be the most significant element. Faculty needed time to reconstruct the course. They wanted more flexibility in the scheduling of the class—a time problem. Time, of course, costs money, but there are inexpensive ways of changing assignments that provide relief from some duties to free up time for a creative revision of a course. Most important, faculty wanted assurances that they would not be penalized in terms of promotions or raises if their innovation failed, that the dean would stand behind them. Boice (1992) and Braskamp and Ory (1994) provide helpful advice for administrators working with faculty.

Chapter 6 tests the theoretical framework on the third faculty role, service. It also examines the framework's ability to inform us about faculty "scholarship," a term that lacks a clear and agreed-upon meaning within academe but one on which our NCRIPTAL data set collected information.

# 6

# FACULTY SERVICE AND SCHOLARSHIP

## Service

SERVICE IS THE CATCHALL name for everything that is neither teaching, research, nor scholarship. Performing "for the good of the organization" is one kind of service. Meeting with a board committee, speaking to an alumni association gathering, arranging a visiting-lecturer series, sponsoring a student organization, entertaining advisees at your home—almost anything that casts the college in a favorable light among its many constituencies falls under the heading we call "internal" service.

Committee assignments catch nearly all faculty and are the most common form of internal service. Faculty describe committees in expletives. For many, frustrations mount from seemingly countless hours that produce minimum results. For a few, committees are their lifeblood. These individuals earn the title of campus politicos. The give and take, the compromises, the sense of power in shaping rules and regulations—this is a rich diet for these faculty, who give every free hour to the role.

From one perspective, faculty committees are governance bodies. They do the work of administrators in bureaucratic organizations. In colleges and universities, which are bureaucracies though structurally flatter ones than corporations, faculty want to have a strong say regarding the conditions of work. They do not fully trust their administrators, not even those they selected, to make the best decisions. They believe they know better than their administrators what is good for the institution. As one illustration, the faculty's "right" to set the requirements for graduation is not in the institution's charter. It has been passed down from the board to the president and then entrusted to them. Faculty did not have such rights in the past. Obtaining them has been a long struggle. Faculty do not want to lose the powers they now have. In order to retain their voice, they reluctantly play the service role.

Committees function for nearly every facet of the institution. There is a curriculum committee, an admissions committee, a finance committee, a grievance committee, and many more. They differ appreciably in their status and importance. Parents' weekend committees are for the untalented. Executive committees that advise the dean and the promotion and tenure committees play in high-stakes games. Respected faculty get elected or appointed to them.

Faculty also perform service functions outside their college or university. Three kinds capture most of the wide assortment of activities we call "external" service. One is consulting—selling personal services to parties that believe they need the professor's specialized knowledge. Business, industry, and government hire faculty for their expertise. Colleges and universities also hire faculty, usually from other institutions, and more rarely from within their own, to assist them with problems—for example, setting up a computer network or assisting faculty to improve their teaching. *Consulting* is what this is called by some; *moonlighting* is the name others give to it.

Schools and colleges value consulting differently. More arts and science faculty tend to agree with the moonlighting position. They see consulting basically as a means of fattening one's income. In their view, faculty who consult are detracting from the status of the department. Their consulting time could have been spent on research that would bring prestige to the unit. Consulting is like writing textbooks. If you are a genuine scholar, you do not waste your energy in simply passing on information when you could be creating knowledge. On the other hand, professional school faculty value consulting and argue that this kind of activity is professional development. It keeps the faculty in touch with "real world" problems, increases the likelihood of research support, and enhances the reputation of the organization by showing off how many "important" people are on the staff.

Paid consulting raises ethical issues. Just how much time is the professor giving to work that clearly requires hours and days away from the chief faculty roles of teaching, research, and internal service? How much of the institution's resources are being used by the consultant? Beyond what point is the return to the institution negative? Colleges and universities struggle with these questions and take quite different stands. Some have no limitations. Others have a rule of one day per week, but rarely are procedures in place to monitor how and where faculty spend their time. Still other institutions prohibit consulting activity outright. For example, in the case of a music professor wanting to give private lessons to some gifted individuals, the college may require that the student enroll in the college, irrespective of age and eligibility, and pay the institution, not the professor. The college then makes the activity a part of the professor's assigned workload.

Educational organizations like accrediting agencies also pay faculty for doing work for them. We label this activity "professional" consulting, work done for the sake of the profession overall (e.g., the North Central Association) or for a special subgroup such as the one that accredits chemistry departments for the American Chemical Society. One is helping higher education maintain standards of excellence and telling the world that a graduate from an accredited organization carries a guarantee of being qualified. The professor doing this work typically receives an "honorarium," a token number of dollars far less than what the professional consultant within industry commands. Faculty who serve on panels in Washington (NIH, NSF, OERI) or who review proposals for foundations generally receive a modest stipend for their work.

Ethical issues also arise in this, especially for reviewers of research proposals. The activity bestows status on the individual. It also affords the reviewer an opportunity to learn of new techniques that are yet to be tested. It provides ideas and can involve projects that may be very close to the reviewer's own research. It gives one an advantage of being on the inside, of coming to know what others will not learn about for several years. There can be genuine temptations to plagiarize.

A second external service type is much like consulting, only it is done pro bono, without remuneration. A law school faculty member aids the local school board without a fee or does volunteer work with the American Civil Liberties Union. A medical school professor becomes the local high school's team physician. A biology professor helps the city water department examine its supply for pollutants. A business school faculty member lends her expertise to the Community Chest drive. A music school professor directs the choir at his church. A faculty member from any school or college sits on the local school board. These "good citizen" activities build rapport between town and gown and mitigate a not infrequently strained relationship. Administrators applaud faculty who perform such service, even if they do not visibly reward it.

The third type of external service is that which faculty give to their disciplinary specialty, their "professional associations." Associations require officers, committees, and so on. They have all of the trappings of an academic organization. Regional and national meetings are planned and conducted almost exclusively with volunteer faculty help. Conference organizers schedule presentations of research papers that faculty need to review.

They chair sessions and serve as critics of the scholarship presented. Association journals require faculty board members and a host of experts to review manuscripts submitted for publication. Serving in these roles carries professional recognition. Peers elect their most scholarly colleagues to serve their association. Journal editors recruit the most highly valued experts in a subspecialty of the discipline to review submitted manuscripts. Participating faculty spend an appreciable number of non-dollar-remunerated hours in these activities—the most honorable of the service roles, in the eyes of many faculty.

Like serving on review panels, this role provides status awards. It locates the faculty member at the cutting edge of what research has discovered. By accepting and rejecting manuscripts, the faculty member serves as a gatekeeper to the discipline and determines the directions it takes. Being an insider has the rewards of knowing before others what has been discovered, invented, developed. The role bestows status. It also raises essentially the same ethical-responsibility issues that confront those serving on review panels.

No agreement exists on how to assess a faculty member's service performance. Consequently, the activity essentially passes unrewarded when it comes to matters of promotion, tenure, or merit pay. Unless there is intrinsic pleasure and satisfaction with service activities, frustration mounts. Faculty may be penalized if they do not serve on any committee, and a few may be rewarded for conducting an absolutely crucial and time-consuming task "for the good of the organization." For most, however, institutional service takes time away from preferred other roles and activities.

In contrast to the vast literature on faculty research activity and related issues, there is almost no research on faculty in service roles. The exception is Boyer and Lewis (1985), who have made a genuine contribution by providing an excellent review of what is known from studies on faculty consulting.

Our survey respondents reported both internal service (institutional committees, senates) and external service (professional associations). There are but minor differences across institutional types on the percentage of effort faculty prefer to give to service and the percentage they believe administrators want them to give. (See table 6.1.) With but one exception faculty members' personal preference is slightly higher than what they think their institutions want. The one exception was in community colleges, where personal preference was a single percentage point lower.

We used our theoretical framework and NCRIPTAL data to examine the service roles in more depth. We employed the following variables:

Table 6.1   Preference for Service: Self-Valuation, Perception of the Environment, and Behavior (Percent)

|  | Res-I | Res-II | Doc-I | Doc-II | Comp-I | Comp-II | LAC-I | LAC-II | CC |
|---|---|---|---|---|---|---|---|---|---|
| Personal pref. | 14 | 16 | 13 | 13 | 15 | 16 | 15 | 15 | 10 |
| Institution pref. | 10 | 12 | 11 | 10 | 11 | 11 | 10 | 11 | 11 |
| Effort given | 20 | 19 | 19 | 16 | 17 | 18 | 16 | 16 | 14 |

*Source:* NCRIPTAL survey.

## SELF-KNOWLEDGE

Self-competence factor (two items): How characteristic of you communicating well and responding to requests are.

Self-efficacy (one item): How much influence you have vis-à-vis departmental curriculum committee decisions.

Commitment to service/supportive personality factor (two items): How characteristic of you being a team player and being devoted to the institution are.

Interest (one item): How characteristic of you being supportive is.

Personal preference (one item): The percentage of time you personally prefer to spend on service activities.

## SOCIAL KNOWLEDGE

Credence (one item): How much credence you give to your chair's or dean's comments on your service activities.

Consensus and support (one item): The extent to which it is true that you are encouraged by your institution to work for the collective well-being of your unit.

Institutional preference (one item): The percentage of time you believe your institution would prefer that you spend on service activities.

We had three service outcome variables:

Public service was a single item asking the subject how often during the last year he or she had served as a guest on a local radio or television program.[1]

Professional service was a factor consisting of four items: How often in the last two years the subject had (1) reviewed articles for a professional journal, (2) organized a professional meeting, (3) edited the proceedings of a professional meeting, or (4) served on an editorial board of a professional journal.

Institutional service was a factor consisting of four items: How often during the past five years the subject had (1) participated in campuswide committees dealing with major issues, (2) chaired a campus or unit committee, (3) played a role in the unit's curriculum revision, or (4) conducted a study to help solve a unit problem.

In analyzing each of the three outcome components of the study, we first treated the percentage of effort the faculty member gave to service as the dependent variable. This procedure allowed us to ascertain the degree to which the sociodemographic, career, self-knowledge, and social knowledge variables contributed to the explained variance of the faculty service behavior. The behavior variable consisted of one item: the percentage of time the subject actually devoted to service activities. Table 6.2 shows these results.[2] We then used the service behavior variable as an independent variable for predicting the three specific service behaviors.

Table 6.2 shows the percentage of variance for effort given to service to be high: an average of 50 percent, the same as effort for research—an unexpected result for this ambiguous role. What constitutes service and what rewards it have received appreciable discussion in faculty lounges, but empirical evidence with respect to the role is nonexistent. What is clear is that personal preference for service and the perceived institutional expectation for the activity dominate the predictor variables—in all institutional types for both variables. Both variables produced a significant increase in the percentage of explained variance in time given to service for all institutional types. The other predictors never enter in more than two institutional types. Conclusion: Those who have a high preference for the service role and think their department desires it give the most effort to it. Those who have a low personal preference for the role and perceive a low institutional preference for it give the least.

We divided service activities into three kinds of behaviors: public (dealing with the nonacademic outside world), professional (e.g., working with disciplinary associations), and campus (committees, etc.).

With respect to professional service, as can be seen in table 6.3, the final percentages of explained variance were significant in the nine institutional types, but only twice was more than 20 percent of the explained variance accounted for (in Res-II's and LAC-I's). Being a male full professor was a significant predictor for professional service in all colleges and universities. This finding supports the often-heard statement that it is the senior oligarchy that controls the flow of information—what gets published. The result is not surprising, for this kind of contributed time typically falls to those who have established a national reputation on the disciplinary scene. What

Table 6.2    Predicting Percent Effort Given to Service

|  | Res-I | | Res-II | | Doc-I | | Doc-II | |
|---|---|---|---|---|---|---|---|---|
|  | % Var. | p | % Var. | p | % Var. | p | % Var. | p |
| *Sociodemographic* | | | | | | | | |
| Female | 1 | | 2 | | 1 | | 1 | |
| *Career* | | | | | | | | |
| Grad. inst. rating | 2 | .05 | 6 | | 1 | | 3 | |
| Career age | 5 | | 8 | | 2 | | 3 | |
| Assist. prof. | 7 | | 12 | | 2 | | 6 | |
| Assoc. prof. | 8 | | 18 | | 2 | | 6 | |
| (Male full prof.) | | −.02 | | | | −.01 | | |
| *Self-knowledge* | | | | | | | | |
| Competency for service | 9 | | 21 | | 6 | .05 | 7 | |
| Efficacy (influence curriculum) | 13 | | 22 | | 7 | | 10 | |
| Commitment to institution | 16 | .00 | 26 | | 9 | | 10 | |
| Supportive person | 16 | | 26 | | 9 | | 11 | |
| Preference for service (% effort) | 33 | .00 | 45 | .00 | 38 | .00 | 45 | .00 |
| *Social knowledge* | | | | | | | | |
| Chair's comments on service | 33 | | 47 | .04 | 39 | | 46 | |
| Encouraged to work for the unit | 34 | | 48 | | 39 | | 46 | |
| Inst. pref. for service (% effort) | 39 | .00 | 52 | .01 | 40 | .00 | 50 | .00 |

*Source:* Blackburn, Bieber, Lawrence, and Trautvetter (1991).

is not clear from these results is why the variable less-than-average career age also predicts time given to professional service. It may be that the newly promoted full professors are the ones who are called upon to carry on this type of professional work, or that younger people see the career importance of being engaged in their professional societies.

The percentages of explained variance for service on campus (internal service) are all significant and larger than anticipated for such an unvalued activity. Faculty seldom describe serving on a campus committee, being involved in curriculum revision, chairing a committee of one's unit, or solving a unit's problem as desired activities. However, as table 6.4 shows, in Res-II's over 50 percent of the variance in service effort was accounted for by two variables.

The self-efficacy indicator—believing that one has influence on curricular decisions within the unit—was significant in seven of the institutional

Table 6.2—*Continued*

| Comp-I | | Comp-II | | LAC-I | | LAC-II | | CC | |
|---|---|---|---|---|---|---|---|---|---|
| % Var. | p | % Var. | p | % Var. | p | % Var. | p | % Var. | p |
| 1 | | 2 | | 1 | | 0 | | 1 | |
| | | | | | | | | | |
| 1 | | 5 | .03 | 1 | | 1 | | 1 | |
| 1 | | 5 | | 1 | | 3 | | 1 | |
| 2 | -.03 | 7 | | 3 | | 3 | -.04 | 2 | |
| 3 | | 8 | | 3 | | 4 | | 3 | |
| | | | | | | | | | |
| 4 | | 10 | | 3 | | 4 | | 3 | |
| 7 | .01 | 10 | | 9 | | 4 | | 4 | |
| 8 | | 10 | | 14 | | 4 | | 6 | .03 |
| 8 | | 10 | | 14 | | 5 | | 7 | |
| 34 | .00 | 29 | .02 | 24 | .00 | 58 | .00 | 52 | .00 |
| | | | | | | | | | |
| 35 | .01 | 30 | | 25 | | 58 | | 53 | |
| 35 | | 30 | | 25 | | 58 | | 53 | |
| 40 | .00 | 62 | .00 | 43 | .00 | 65 | .00 | 58 | .00 |

types. In every instance it produced a significant percentage of explained variance increase. This is the first time efficacy emerged as a strong and widespread predictor. A number of other variables entered in more than one institutional type—being older (career age), being a team player and devoted to the institution (commitment/supportive personality), and institutional preference for this kind of service. (The assistant professor $p$ values are almost all negative, indicating again that it is the senior members who are most engaged.) A chair's comments on a professor's service work (credence) also entered in three cases. Faculty in a few institutions are influenced by the boss. What this says to department chairs is that faculty who believe they can affect the outcomes of work-related decisions will give time and effort to service activities. At the same time, those who believe they have little influence on outcomes are less likely to participate in institutional service.

Table 6.3    Predicting Percent Effort Given to External Service

| | Res-I | | Res-II | | Doc-I | | Doc-II | |
|---|---|---|---|---|---|---|---|---|
| | % Var. | p | % Var. | p | % Var. | p | % Var. | p |
| *Sociodemographic* | | | | | | | | |
| Female | 0 | | 1 | | 1 | | 0 | |
| *Career* | | | | | | | | |
| Grad. inst. rating | 1 | | 2 | | 1 | | 2 | |
| Career age | 2 | -.01 | 2 | -.01 | 1 | -.01 | 2 | -.02 |
| Assist. prof. | 5 | -.01 | 8 | -.01 | 4 | -.01 | 4 | -.01 |
| Assoc. prof. | 7 | -.01 | 21 | -.01 | 11 | -.01 | 11 | -.01 |
| (Male full prof.) | | .00 | | .00 | | .00 | | .00 |
| *Self-knowledge* | | | | | | | | |
| Competency for service | 15 | | 21 | | 12 | .03 | 11 | |
| Efficacy (influence curriculum) | 16 | | 21 | | 12 | | 12 | |
| Commitment to institution | 17 | | 23 | | 12 | | 13 | |
| Supportive person | 18 | | 23 | | 14 | .03 | 13 | |
| Preference for service (% effort) | 18 | | 24 | | 15 | | 13 | |
| *Social knowledge* | | | | | | | | |
| Chair's comments on service | 18 | | 24 | | 15 | | 14 | |
| Encouraged to work for the unit | 18 | | 24 | | 15 | | 14 | |
| Inst. pref. for service (% effort) | 18 | | 24 | | 15 | | 16 | |
| *Behavior* | | | | | | | | |
| Effort given to ext. service (% time) | 19 | | 25 | | 15 | | 18 | .05 |

*Source:* Blackburn, Bieber, Lawrence, and Trautvetter (1991).

What inferences might administrators draw from these findings? It is difficult to tell. Maybe faculty complaints about committee time are the result of how administrators run the committee. If the dean devotes most of the time to announcements and pronouncements from the chair, faculty rightfully moan. The meeting has been an insulting show of indifference to the fact that time is their most precious commodity. More than that, here is a table of talented individuals who delight in solving problems, a rich human resource that the chair has not capitalized on to solve an important problem.

The department chair or dean has few ways to reward committee service, especially with dollars (merit raises). Faculty can be rewarded with words and sometimes with special little honors—for example, representing the chair or dean in an honorific setting. Departments and schools might also imitate what many professional societies do at their annual meetings. In

Table 6.3—*Continued*

| Comp-I | | Comp-II | | LAC-I | | LAC-II | | CC | |
|---|---|---|---|---|---|---|---|---|---|
| % Var. | p | % Var. | p | % Var. | p | % Var. | p | % Var. | p |
| 1 | | 6 | .05 | 0 | | 1 | | 1 | |
| | | | | | | | | | |
| 1 | | 6 | | 1 | | 1 | | 2 | |
| 1 | | 6 | | 1 | | 3 | | 2 | |
| 1 | -.03 | 8 | | 1 | | 4 | | 4 | .00 |
| 2 | | 8 | | 1 | | 4 | | 6 | |
| | .00 | | .03 | | .00 | | .04 | | .00 |
| | | | | | | | | | |
| 2 | | 10 | | 2 | | 8 | .01 | 6 | |
| 3 | .01 | 12 | | 2 | | 9 | | 6 | |
| 3 | | 13 | | 4 | -.02 | 9 | | 7 | |
| 3 | | 14 | | 6 | | 10 | | 7 | |
| 4 | .00 | 14 | .02 | 6 | | 10 | | 10 | |
| | | | | | | | | | |
| 4 | .01 | 18 | | 7 | | 11 | | 10 | |
| 4 | | 18 | | 8 | | 11 | | 10 | |
| 4 | .00 | 18 | .00 | 20 | .02 | 11 | | 10 | |
| | | | | | | | | | |
| 4 | | 20 | | 21 | | 15 | .02 | 11 | |

addition to presenting plaques to the outstanding researcher of the year, they do the same for an individual who has given much that matters to the maintenance and good health of the organization, a recognition all applaud. They know what it takes to make an association effective. They are delighted that someone other than themselves has put in so many hours of groveling work.

We now turn to that activity euphemistically labeled scholarship and see to what degree the framework can illuminate it. In doing so we do not infer a close link between service and scholarship. In fact, if scholarship has an intimate relationship with any of the three principal faculty roles, we suspect it is closest with teaching.

Table 6.4    Predicting Percent Effort Given to Internal Service

|  | Res-I | | Res-II | | Doc-I | | Doc-II | |
|---|---|---|---|---|---|---|---|---|
|  | % Var. | p | % Var. | p | % Var. | p | % Var. | p |
| *Sociodemographic* | | | | | | | | |
| Female | 1 | | 1 | | 1 | .05 | 1 | |
| *Career* | | | | | | | | |
| Grad. inst. rating | 1 | | *4* | | 1 | | 1 | |
| Career age | 6 | | 19 | .01 | 9 | | 8 | |
| Assist. prof. | *9* | -.03 | 23 | | 15 | -.01 | 11 | |
| Assoc. prof. | 10 | | 23 | | 15 | | 11 | |
| (Male full prof.) | | | | | | | | |
| *Self-knowledge* | | | | | | | | |
| Competency for service | *14* | | 26 | | 18 | | 18 | |
| Efficacy (influence curriculum) | 25 | .00 | 35 | .01 | 27 | .01 | 22 | .03 |
| Commitment to institution | 29 | .04 | *40* | | 29 | .05 | 27 | .01 |
| Supportive person | 29 | | 40 | | 31 | | 28 | |
| Preference for service (% effort) | *31* | | 41 | | 35 | .04 | *31* | |
| *Social knowledge* | | | | | | | | |
| Chair's comments on service | 32 | .01 | 42 | | *36* | .05 | 33 | |
| Encouraged to work for the unit | 33 | | 42 | | 36 | | 33 | |
| Inst. pref. for service (% effort) | 33 | | 42 | | 36 | | 34 | |
| *Behavior* | | | | | | | | |
| Effort given to int. service (% time) | *36* | .01 | 53 | .00 | 37 | | 35 | |

*Source:* Blackburn, Bieber, Lawrence, and Trautvetter (1991).

## Scholarship

The term *scholarship* has a long history. Its meaning has changed considerably during that time, especially since World War II. At one time *scholarship* and *research* were essentially synonymous, although the former was more often employed when talking about what humanists do and the latter when describing what scientists engage in. Both did creative work and contributed to knowledge. However, the nature of their activities and their language differed. Today academic artists—painters, for example—talk about their work on the canvas as *research,* using the word in the same way biologists do in describing an experiment in their laboratory. Neither typically identifies with *scholar.*

In our national survey we gave the respondents specific "definitions" of

Table 6.4—*Continued*

| Comp-I | | Comp-II | | LAC-I | | LAC-II | | CC | |
|---|---|---|---|---|---|---|---|---|---|
| % Var. | p | % Var. | p | % Var. | p | % Var. | p | % Var. | p |
| 1 | | 3 | | 1 | | 1 | | 2 | |
| 1 | | 3 | | 3 | -.02 | 1 | | 2 | |
| 1 | | 7 | | 18 | | 2 | | 2 | |
| 3 | -.01 | 16 | .03 | 21 | | 4 | | 4 | .00 |
| 3 | | 17 | | 21 | | 4 | | 6 | |
| | | | .05 | | | | .01 | | .00 |
| 7 | .01 | 18 | | 26 | | 4 | -.05 | 7 | |
| 19 | .00 | 23 | | 32 | | 10 | .01 | 12 | |
| 20 | | 24 | | 34 | | 11 | | 12 | |
| 21 | | 25 | | 34 | | 11 | | 12 | |
| 23 | | 25 | | 35 | | 11 | | 15 | |
| 25 | .01 | 25 | | 35 | | 11 | | 15 | |
| 25 | | 27 | | 36 | | 16 | .01 | 16 | |
| 26 | .03 | 28 | | 48 | .01 | 18 | | 16 | |
| 30 | .00 | 28 | | 50 | | 19 | | 21 | |

the two terms. We defined research as an activity that leads to a concrete product—for example, an article, report, monograph, book, grant proposal, software program. (See appendix H, question 13.) We linked scholarship to professional growth, enhancing one's knowledge or skill in ways that may not necessarily result in a concrete product—for example, library work, reading, exploratory inquiries, computer use. We drew this particular distinction not because of some philosophical position we hold but simply because we wanted information about both kinds of activities. Respondents had to know what we meant when we used *research* and when we used *scholarship*.

Ernest Boyer (1990) has recently pleaded for colleges and universities to recognize and reward "scholarship" and not just "research." Boyer considers *research* much as we have, but *scholarship* for him carries an even

Table 6.5    Preference for Scholarship: Self-Valuation, Perception of the Environment, and Behavior (Percent)

|  | Res-I | Res-II | Doc-I | Doc-II | Comp-I | Comp-II | LAC-I | LAC-II | CC |
|---|---|---|---|---|---|---|---|---|---|
| Personal pref. | 13 | 11 | 13 | 12 | 12 | 12 | 12 | 11 | 11 |
| Institution pref. | 20 | 17 | 18 | 17 | 18 | 17 | 17 | 17 | 17 |
| Effort given | 15 | 11 | 13 | 12 | 13 | 11 | 11 | 12 | 11 |

*Source:* NCRIPTAL survey.

broader connotation. For him it includes teaching, an activity we took to be a separate faculty role. We do not imply that creativity is not a part of teaching; it certainly is.

At the same time, teaching and research both demand continuous growth. Keeping abreast of new discoveries in one's specialty, a minimum scholarly requisite, has become a seemingly endless, impossible task. As we saw in chapter 4, the knowledge explosion inundates everyone, teacher as well as researcher. I cannot enter a classroom without knowing what happened this morning that relates to what the class is discussing. As much as I

Table 6.6    Predicting Percent Effort Given to Scholarship

|  | Res-I | | Res-II | | Doc-I | | Doc-II | |
|---|---|---|---|---|---|---|---|---|
|  | % Var. | p | % Var. | p | % Var. | p | % Var. | p |
| *Sociodemographic* | | | | | | | | |
| Female | 1 | | 1 | | 1 | | 1 | |
| *Career* | | | | | | | | |
| Grad. inst. rating | 1 | | 1 | | 2 | | 1 | |
| Career age | 1 | | 1 | | 3 | | 1 | |
| Assist. prof. | 1 | | 1 | | 3 | | 2 | |
| Assoc. prof. | 1 | | 1 | | 3 | | 2 | |
| (Male full prof.) | | | | | | | | |
| *Self-knowledge* | | | | | | | | |
| Keeps abreast of discipline | 2 | | 1 | | 6 | .01 | 3 | |
| Efficacy re scholarship | 2 | | 5 | | 6 | | 4 | .01 |
| Preference for schol. (% effort) | 17 | .00 | 26 | .01 | 13 | | 22 | .00 |
| *Social knowledge* | | | | | | | | |
| Support services and colleagues | 17 | | 28 | | 13 | | 24 | |
| Inst. pref. for schol. (% effort) | 31 | .00 | 31 | .00 | 38 | .00 | 39 | .00 |

*Source:* Blackburn, Bieber, Lawrence, and Trautvetter (1991).

234

desire to be a generalist—one who knows what is essential about everything and is capable of linking the overlaps and contradictions into a sensible whole—I know I am incapable of it. In addition, I do not believe anyone can be a generalist today, even those much brighter than I. Cut my specialty in half—that is my research survival message. But for teaching, reading, learning new techniques, and the like, "faculty development" (in the argot of the day) is close to what Boyer and we mean by *scholarship*. For now we retain the distinctions we made between research and scholarship and report our findings on the latter.[3]

In contrast to the vast literature on faculty research activity and related issues, virtually nothing exits on scholarship. Table 6.5 displays faculty members' percentage of effort with respect to scholarship—personal preference, perceived institutional preference, and actual effort given. There is virtually no difference across institutional types on each of the three variables. Faculty appear to allocate the time they give to scholarly activities as they wish to. (Note the close relationship of the percentages in rows one and three for each institutional type.) In addition, the amounts preferred and given consistently fall below the amount faculty believe their administrators want them to spend.

Table 6.6—*Continued*

| Comp-I | | Comp-II | | LAC-I | | LAC-II | | CC | |
|---|---|---|---|---|---|---|---|---|---|
| % Var. | p | % Var. | p | % Var. | p | % Var. | p | % Var. | p |
| 1 | | 3 | | 1 | | 1 | | 1 | |
| 1 | | 3 | | 3 | | 1 | | 1 | |
| 3 | | 3 | | 6 | | 1 | | 1 | |
| 3 | | 6 | | 6 | | 1 | | 2 | |
| 3 | | 7 | | 6 | | 1 | | 2 | |
| | -.02 | | | | | | | | |
| 4 | | 8 | | 7 | | 3 | | 6 | |
| 5 | | 10 | | 7 | | 3 | | 6 | |
| 8 | .01 | 28 | .01 | 13 | | 15 | .01 | 12 | |
| 8 | | 28 | | 13 | | 15 | | 13 | |
| 32 | .00 | 32 | | 42 | .02 | 21 | .01 | 31 | |

Table 6.7   Predicting Percent Effort Given to Attending Lectures/Talks/Meetings

|  | Res-I | | Res-II | | Doc-I | | Doc-II | |
|---|---|---|---|---|---|---|---|---|
|  | % Var. | p | % Var. | p | % Var. | p | % Var. | p |
| *Sociodemographic* | | | | | | | | |
| Female | 2 | .01 | 1 | | 1 | | 1 | |
| *Career* | | | | | | | | |
| Grad. inst. rating | 2 | | 1 | | 1 | | 1 | |
| Career age | 3 | .00 | 5 | .00 | 1 | | 3 | |
| Assist. prof. | 5 | .00 | 6 | .03 | 1 | | 3 | |
| Assoc. prof. | 7 | -.01 | 9 | | 1 | | 7 | |
| (Male full prof.) | | .00 | | .00 | | .00 | | |
| *Self-knowledge* | | | | | | | | |
| Keeps abreast of discipline | 13 | .00 | 12 | .02 | 7 | .01 | 17 | |
| Efficacy re schol. | 13 | | 13 | | 7 | | 17 | |
| Preference for schol. (% effort) | 13 | .00 | 14 | | 9 | | 18 | |
| *Social knowledge* | | | | | | | | |
| Support services and colleagues | 13 | | 15 | | 9 | | 23 | |
| Inst. pref. for schol. (% effort) | 13 | .00 | 15 | .00 | 9 | | 23 | |
| *Behavior* | | | | | | | | |
| Effort given to attending lectures (% time) | 13 | | 16 | | 10 | | 23 | |

*Source:* Blackburn, Bieber, Lawrence, and Trautvetter (1991).

Next, we used our framework and NCRIPTAL data to examine the scholarly role in more depth. We employed the following independent variables:

SELF-KNOWLEDGE

Self-competency (one item): How characteristic of you keeping abreast of your discipline is $(r = .73)$.[4]

Self-efficacy (one item): How much influence you have vis-à-vis pursuing the personal interests you wish to pursue $(r = .48)$.

Personal preference (one item): The percentage of time you personally prefer to spend on your scholarship $(r = .68)$.

SOCIAL KNOWLEDGE

Physical/collegial support (one item): The extent to which it is true that the support services for teaching at your institution—lab facilities,

Table 6.7—*Continued*

| Comp-I | | Comp-II | | LAC-I | | LAC-II | | CC | |
|---|---|---|---|---|---|---|---|---|---|
| % Var. | p | % Var. | p | % Var. | p | % Var. | p | % Var. | p |
| 1 | | 1 | | 1 | | 4 | | 1 | |
| 1 | | 1 | | 2 | | 4 | | 1 | |
| 2 | | 9 | -.01 | 3 | | 5 | | 1 | |
| 2 | | 10 | | 3 | | 5 | | 1 | |
| 2 | | 10 | | 4 | | 5 | | 2 | |
| | .00 | | .00 | | .00 | | .02 | | .00 |
| 4 | .01 | 13 | | 10 | .02 | 16 | .00 | 6 | .01 |
| 4 | | 14 | | 11 | | 17 | | 6 | |
| 4 | | 15 | | 11 | | 18 | | 6 | |
| 4 | | 18 | | 12 | | 18 | | 6 | |
| 5 | | 22 | .03 | 12 | | 18 | | 7 | |
| 5 | | 23 | | 13 | | 18 | | 8 | |

computers, libraries, clerical assistance, audiovisual aids, student assistance—help you to teach what you would like, as you would like $(r = .41)$.

Institutional preference (1 item): The percentage of time you believe your institution would prefer you to spend on your scholarly activities $(r = .55)$.

In analyzing the data, we again first treated the percentage of effort the faculty member gave to scholarship as the dependent variable. This procedure allowed us to ascertain the degree to which the sociodemographic, career, self-knowledge, and social knowledge variables accounted for the explained variance in scholarly behavior. Table 6.6 displays these results. We then used the scholarly behavior variable as an independent variable for predicting one specific scholarly behavior.

The behavioral variable consisted of one item: the percentage of time the subject actually devoted to scholarly activities $(r = .65)$.

The specific dependent variable was a scaled score consisting of three items: how often during the last year you attended a visiting lecturer's presentation on campus ($r = .73$), had telephone conversations with colleagues to discuss scholarly work ($r = .77$), or went off campus to attend a meeting on the teaching of your discipline ($r = .72$). The regression results are shown in table 6.7.

While the average explained variance percentages for effort given to scholarship are appreciably lower than they were for effort given to research (30 percent vs. 50 percent), they are all statistically significant. (See table 6.6.) Personal preference and perceived institutional preference for time given to scholarship are the most frequent predictors (six and seven institutional types, respectively). Both produced a significant percentage of the explained variance increase in every institutional type. They are, in fact, essentially the only two variables in the framework that appear more than once.

Table 6.7 shows the regression results for predicting attending on-campus lectures, having phone conversations regarding scholarship, and going to off-campus meetings (behaviors, not products). While the percentages of explained variance are statistically significant, they are lower than any of the above regression results. Keeping abreast of the discipline, the competency measure, yielded a significant percentage of explained variance increase in every instance. Either the predictor variables need additions or the outcome variable lacks validity. We believe that the latter is the principal culprit. Our instrument had not been specifically designed to secure multiple measures of scholarship. These are what we had; they are but a small piece of what the construct denotes.

What inferences might administrators draw from these findings?

Professors' scholarly activities are even less easily discernible than their service contributions. Indirectly, chairs and deans know which faculty are alive and growing and which are listing, maybe even sinking. However, there are no good ways publicly to acknowledge those deserving individuals as good scholars.

Fortunately, doing so is not really necessary. Being an active scholar has its own rewards. People who chose this career love to learn. Even in their darkest moments they confess to leading the best lives that exist. They are able to earn a living doing exactly, or almost exactly, what they like doing— reading, sculpting, experimenting, solving puzzles, writing. No wonder such an overwhelming proportion respond positively to the repeated survey question, "If you had the opportunity to begin a career all over again, would you select the academic one?" The response? "You betcha."

The professorial life, however, is not a perfect one. Like other employed people, faculty have to deal with the organization and its seemingly absurd regulations and behaviors. Chapter 7 displays how perceptions of the work environment are not always the same when you query management and worker.

# 7

# ADMINISTRATIVE AND FACULTY VIEWS OF THE WORKPLACE

ACADEME PROVIDES opportunities for a variety of career paths, even for the same individual over the course of 40 or so years. The simplest and cleanest path is the professorial one. A fairly typical sequence of events, especially in the arts and science disciplines, is for the individual to have been a teaching assistant during the doctoral program, perhaps having a couple of postdoctoral years (particularly in the sciences), taking a position as an assistant professor, and then enjoying two promotions on the way to becoming a full professor. For most, two or three institutional changes will occur along the way—the postdoc being at a different university and the first full appointment at still another. One might eventually return to one's alma mater.

Academic administrative careers follow no regular pattern, except for almost always starting down the academic line.[1] Still, very few become professors with the clear intention of becoming a college president. More often faculty back into administrative posts. They may become an assistant departmental chair for a few years, then move back into a full-time academic position. Some will make a career of that assistant position and yearly acquire more and more power as chairs and deans above them change. They become the living history of the organization and know what can and cannot be accomplished. Or they may become the chair, perhaps at another institution. The hierarchy of assistant/associate/chair/dean/provost/vice president/president/chancellor can be shown on a chart, but rarely does it go step by step in real life. A fair number of today's administrators never had a faculty position but rather entered an administrative post directly.

People jump over the stages, move sideways to another college or university, go up or down the institutional status levels, return to the faculty, go back into administration at the same or a different place. For most, however, after some number of years and at a high enough level, the option to return to a professorship in the department of initial expertise essentially ends. One has been too long removed from the growth of disciplinary knowledge and methodological developments. It simply takes too long to catch up. The department does not want you back. You have even lost friends along the way, for the longer you have been doing administrative work, the more times you have had to deny requests. Faculty don't love you anymore.

With few exceptions the administrator learns everything he or she knows on the job. The American Council on Education has had intern fellowships over the years, a program that takes promising potential administrators into an academic office—most often at another university—to show them how things are done at headquarters. Some universities have Centers for the Study of Higher Education that provide not only intellectual and practical education leading to a doctoral degree but also opportunities for postdoctoral fellows—often department chairs who want to become deans—to study and intern in university central offices. Most administrators do not believe in this approach. You learn by doing, not by studying. After all, they learned this way, and they are good at their job.

We briefly described these two principal academic careers not so as to judge which is better, or to determine whether the follower of one or the other has a more successful career. We simply want to prepare the reader with some minimum background against which to consider the studies we are about to present. As will be seen, faculty and administrators often judge the quality of the work environment quite differently.

Chief academic administrators from a number of the colleges and universities in the NCRIPTAL survey supplied information about themselves and their views of their institutions and their faculty. These data provided the base for two research conference papers (Blackburn, Pitney, Lawrence, & Trautvetter, 1989; Lawrence, Blackburn, Pitney, & Trautvetter, 1988) and a monograph (Blackburn, Lawrence, Hart, & Dickman, 1990). This chapter merges selections from these three documents, with slight modifications. We close with some reflections on the administrative career.

## Congruence between Administrator and Faculty Views

Some say that post-1970 economic constraints combined with interactions between colleges and universities, on the one hand, and external agencies, on the other, to transfer power from faculty to central administration and to encourage bureaucratized growth. Many faculty believe that vice presidents, provosts, and deans manage, rather than lead, our higher-education institutions. Administrators have become business executives and have lost their sensitivity to those in the trenches. Not only are administrators now more removed from faculty, but increasingly they have not even had the academic preparation or the teaching career that would allow them to experience and hence understand faculty values and behaviors. Low faculty morale is the consequence, or so the story goes (Austin & Gamson, 1983; Bowen & Schuster, 1986; Rice & Austin, 1988).

Our data allow us to address portions of these undocumented contentions. We investigate the extent to which the degree of administrators' socialization into faculty norms is related to their congruence with faculty values and behaviors.

Within our career category, socialization theory predicts that the norms and values faculty hold with regard to who makes what kinds of decisions within their institution are acquired principally from their experiences in graduate school. While there are variations by discipline, it is during this critical time just prior to launching an academic career that they are sensitized to the fundamental importance of academic freedom. It is at this point that the desire to control the conditions of the work environment—who their clients (students) will be, the selection of their co-workers (colleagues) and bosses (department chair and dean), and the conditions of the job (what to teach and when)—and the importance of maintaining that control are instilled. Some periods in history give a special emphasis to certain matters that leaves an indelible mark on successive cohorts (e.g., the civil rights movement and the questioning of authority). However, control of the curriculum, degree requirements, and matters of academic freedom remain in the faculty domain. They are not directly taught; they are passed on by example and almost unconsciously absorbed. Furthermore, these basic values, beliefs, and attitudes endure throughout the academic career. Some administrators have had socialization experiences essentially identical to those that faculty have had; others have not. One expects that the congruence between administrators' and faculty members' beliefs and behaviors will be related to the former's degree of prior academic work experience. (See, e.g., Bayer & Dutton, 1977; Bayer & Folger, 1966; Blackburn, 1985; McCain, O'Reilly, & Pfeffer, 1982.)

We know little about the backgrounds and careers of academic administrators. Moore and Sagaria (1982) and Moore (1983) have conducted the most extensive studies on top-level administrator careers, including a national survey. Austin and Gamson (1983, p. 57) have reviewed the literature on middle-level administrators. There is, however, little research on (1) what administrators think faculty believe about students, (2) how administrators wish faculty to allocate their time to their different roles, and (3) how administrators perceive the faculty view of the work environment on their campus, including faculty views on the competence of administrators.

We prepared and tested an administrator survey (reproduced in appendix I). It was sent in March 1988 to presidents of the 181 postsecondary institutions that participated in the faculty survey (appendix H). The president was asked to choose five to seven academic-area administrators from a list that included vice presidents, deans, and directors who were responsible for academic matters (e.g., admissions, libraries, institutional research). We received completed survey instruments from 500 administrators distributed across 103 institutions (57 percent of all institutions). (N = 454 for this report, since we dropped institutions when there were three or fewer administration respondents from the college or university.)

The administrator questionnaire was a modified version of the faculty instrument. In brief, the respondents were asked about their perceptions of their institution, their self-competence and efficacy, and their beliefs (as well as their perceptions of faculty concerns) about teaching. They also reported separately for faculty members in the humanities, social sciences, and natural sciences concerning how they would like professors to allocate their effort across teaching, research, scholarship, and service. In sum, we have data from academic administrators and faculty on identical or similar survey items and can match them by institution.

The background and career (independent) variables selected for administrators were their gender; ethnicity (black, white, or other);[2] the field in which they received their highest degree (natural science, humanities, social science, education, professional, or other); their highest degree (bachelor's, master's, Ed.D., D.A., M.D., J.D., or Ph.D.); their administrative level in the organization (upper [president/vice president], middle [dean], or lower [director]); the number of years they have been an administrator at all colleges and universities; career age (defined as total number of years as either a faculty member or an administrator in higher education); years of experience; experience as a faculty member; whether they held a concurrent faculty appointment; whether they had a tenured appointment; and whether they were teaching and/or engaged in research at the time of the survey.

A few categorical differences exist. For faculty, discipline is the field in which they are teaching (not necessarily the field in which they received their highest degree, as was the case for administrators). Faculty ranks are reported where administrators were categorized by level within the organization. Data are also reported on whether faculty are currently in an administrative position (e.g., department chair).[3] For those faculty who were not tenured, the percentage who are on a tenure track is reported. Last, the percentage of those faculty who had a higher interest in research than in teaching is shown.

Tables 7.1 and 7.2 display the sociodemographic characteristics and the career features (graduate school, prior experience, and current experience) of the administrator and faculty samples by institutional type. The sociodemographic percentages for each institutional category are similar for both samples, namely, predominantly white and male across all institutional categories.

In general, most administrators in research, doctoral, and comprehensive institutions have earned a Ph.D. The percentage of faculty having earned Ph.D.'s is also higher in these institutions than in the other institutional types. The administrator sample has fewer Ph.D. respondents in the LAC-II and CC categories. The faculty sample also has fewer respondents who had earned a Ph.D. in the CCs. Those respondents' highest degree was more likely to be the master's. Additionally, there is a surprisingly large number of administrators who earned a degree in education in all college and university types.

Both samples are senior in career age. The mode of the total number of years as either a faculty member or an administrator in higher education is 16–20 years. The average career age is almost identical across all institutional categories for both samples.

In addition, the faculty are a highly tenured group. This heavy concentration in the top ranks agrees with the evidence on an aging professoriate (Bowen & Schuster, 1986). A majority of the administrators in research, doctoral, and comprehensive institutions hold academic appointments. The administrators in research and doctoral institutions are more likely to have tenured appointments than administrators in liberal arts and community colleges. Most administrators in all institutional categories have had faculty experience at one time. More than half of the administrators in Res-I and Doc-I institutions were engaged in research, while many administrators in Res-II, Comp-II, and CC institutions were teaching. Roughly 20 percent of the respondents in the faculty sample were currently in an administrative position (most often as a department head).

Faculty had responded to three sets of 10 items each on the (1) skills/ abilities, (2) beliefs/attitudes/values, and (3) personality characteristics of what they believed was the valued faculty member on their campus. Administrators responded to the same items, expressing how characteristic these 30 items are of the faculty members they (the administrators) value on their campus. Each of the three sets of 10 was factor-analyzed to reduce the data and strengthen the reliability.

The first eight variables come from one section of the faculty questionnaire (question 11 of appendix H) dealing with attributes of a valued faculty member on their campus (social knowledge). When faculty data were factor-

Table 7.1    Administrator Demographics and Career Data (N = 454)

|  | Res-I | Res-II | Doc-I | Doc-II | Comp-I | Comp-II | LAC-I | LAC-II | CC |
|---|---|---|---|---|---|---|---|---|---|
| Percent in sample | 3.3 | 4.2 | 5.1 | 4.8 | 17.2 | 5.3 | 7.7 | 14.8 | 37.7 |
| Gender (%) | | | | | | | | | |
| Male | 73 | 84 | 61 | 68 | 82 | 88 | 69 | 77 | 71 |
| Female | 27 | 16 | 39 | 32 | 18 | 13 | 31 | 22 | 29 |
| Race (%) | | | | | | | | | |
| White | 87 | 100 | 91 | 100 | 86 | 83 | 94 | 91 | 94 |
| Black | 7 | 0 | 5 | 0 | 13 | 13 | 6 | 8 | 5 |
| Other | 6 | 0 | 4 | 0 | 1 | 4 | 0 | 1 | 1 |
| Highest deg. earned (%) | | | | | | | | | |
| Baccalaureate | 0 | 0 | 0 | 0 | 0 | 8 | 6 | 11 | 2 |
| Master's | 7 | 21 | 13 | 9 | 21 | 25 | 31 | 33 | 44 |
| Ed.D. or D.A. | 7 | 0 | 13 | 9 | 9 | 17 | 3 | 14 | 25 |
| M.D., J.D., etc. | 0 | 10 | 0 | 0 | 0 | 0 | 0 | 2 | 0 |
| Ph.D. | 87 | 68 | 74 | 82 | 70 | 50 | 60 | 40 | 29 |
| Field (%) | | | | | | | | | |
| Natural science | 27 | 16 | 5 | 15 | 19 | 17 | 9 | 8 | 11 |
| Humanities | 20 | 37 | 27 | 15 | 28 | 13 | 31 | 30 | 15 |
| Social science | 13 | 21 | 36 | 15 | 12 | 13 | 26 | 14 | 11 |
| Education | 27 | 16 | 27 | 35 | 23 | 44 | 20 | 30 | 47 |
| Professional | 13 | 10 | 5 | 15 | 11 | 13 | 8 | 14 | 13 |
| Other | 0 | 0 | 0 | 5 | 7 | 0 | 6 | 5 | 3 |
| Status (%) | | | | | | | | | |
| Upper level | 53 | 47 | 65 | 45 | 24 | 21 | 27 | 28 | 17 |
| Middle level | 20 | 37 | 17 | 32 | 41 | 46 | 35 | 34 | 47 |
| Lower level | 27 | 16 | 18 | 23 | 35 | 33 | 38 | 38 | 36 |
| Career age (years) | | | | | | | | | |
| Mean | 22 | 22 | 20 | 23 | 20 | 20 | 23 | 19 | 20 |
| SD | 6 | 7 | 7 | 9 | 9 | 8 | 12 | 12 | 8 |
| Career age | | | | | | | | | |
| 0–5 years | 0 | 0 | 0 | 5 | 1 | 9 | 3 | 8 | 4 |
| 6–10 years | 0 | 0 | 9 | 5 | 9 | 9 | 16 | 16 | 6 |
| 11–15 years | 13 | 21 | 9 | 9 | 21 | 4 | 9 | 18 | 14 |
| 16–20 years | 40 | 32 | 43 | 27 | 25 | 26 | 19 | 18 | 34 |
| 21–25 years | 33 | 26 | 17 | 27 | 21 | 35 | 16 | 20 | 22 |
| 26+ years | 4 | 21 | 22 | 27 | 23 | 17 | 37 | 20 | 20 |
| Years as administrator | | | | | | | | | |
| Mean | 15 | 13 | 13 | 16 | 13 | 13 | 18 | 13 | 13 |
| SD | 12 | 7 | 7 | 11 | 10 | 8 | 13 | 14 | 9 |

*Continued next page*

Table 7.1—*Continued*

| | Res-I | Res-II | Doc-I | Doc-II | Comp-I | Comp-II | LAC-I | LAC-II | CC |
|---|---|---|---|---|---|---|---|---|---|
| **Years as faculty member** | | | | | | | | | |
| Mean | 10 | 12 | 10 | 11 | 9 | 10 | 10 | 11 | 8 |
| SD | 9 | 10 | 10 | 9 | 8 | 9 | 10 | 24 | 7 |
| Faculty experience (%) | 67 | 79 | 82 | 81 | 80 | 77 | 71 | 57 | 80 |
| Academic appt. (%) | 67 | 67 | 78 | 76 | 67 | 75 | 53 | 54 | 30 |
| Tenure appt. (%) | 67 | 61 | 56 | 62 | 54 | 46 | 21 | 22 | 22 |
| Tenure track (%) | 17 | 0 | 9 | 0 | 10 | 0 | 0 | 9 | 4 |
| Currently teaching (%) | 7 | 44 | 35 | 24 | 7 | 44 | 35 | 24 | 39 |
| Currently doing research (%) | 50 | 39 | 61 | 29 | 37 | 29 | 37 | 28 | 21 |

*Source:* NCRIPTAL survey.

analyzed, the items under skills of the valued faculty member produced three strong factors—pedagogical, research, and social. The items under beliefs also produced three factors—virtues of hard work, being a team player, and being committed to research. The personality items yielded two factors—understanding and ambitious/competitive. Since there is not a common number of items per factor, leading to incomparable summation scores across factors, each factor score was normalized with a mean set at zero and a standard deviation of one. Table 7.3 presents this set of variables by institutional type.

From the next set of variables there emerged four factors concerning self-efficacy, the degree to which people believe they have influence on matters important to their work (self-knowledge); two concern factors dealing with assumptions faculty make with regard to their role as a teacher (self-knowledge); and four teaching factors dealing with beliefs faculty hold with regard to how students best learn (self-knowledge). These were normalized and treated like the first set. They are shown in table 7.4.

The third variable set is a collection of items about which both groups expressed their degree of agreement with assertions about different aspects/features of the environment (social knowledge). The first five are single items, while the sixth—support—is the addition of two items. The possible means range from 4 (strongly agree) to 1 (strongly disagree).[4] The last five variables in this set are time allocations expressed as percentages. In the faculty survey, respondents indicated how much time they believed the institution prefers them to give to teaching, and how much time they themselves would prefer to give to the four roles of teaching, research, scholarship, and service (social knowledge). In the administrative survey, respon-

Table 7.2    Faculty Demographics and Career Data (N = 2,370)

|  | Res-I | Res-II | Doc-I | Doc-II | Comp-I | Comp-II | LAC-I | LAC-II | CC |
|---|---|---|---|---|---|---|---|---|---|
| Percent in sample | 10.9 | 10.3 | 9.4 | 8.8 | 19.7 | 2.5 | 5.1 | 6.6 | 26.5 |
| Gender (%) | | | | | | | | | |
| Male | 79 | 77 | 79 | 80 | 77 | 82 | 72 | 69 | 67 |
| Female | 21 | 23 | 21 | 20 | 23 | 16 | 28 | 31 | 33 |
| Race (%) | | | | | | | | | |
| White | 96 | 36 | 95 | 95 | 90 | 92 | 97 | 93 | 96 |
| Black | 3 | 1 | 1 | 0 | 4 | 3 | 2 | 1 | 2 |
| Other | 1 | 3 | 4 | 5 | 6 | 5 | 1 | 6 | 2 |
| Highest deg. earned (%) | | | | | | | | | |
| Baccalaureate | 0 | 0 | 0 | 1 | 0 | 0 | 0 | 0 | 1 |
| Master's | 1 | 1 | 4 | 6 | 10 | 17 | 13 | 24 | 62 |
| Ed.D. or D.A. | 1 | 0 | 2 | 0 | 4 | 3 | 2 | 5 | 4 |
| M.D., J.D., etc. | 0 | 0 | 1 | 0 | 0 | 0 | 0 | 0 | 0 |
| Ph.D. | 90 | 97 | 91 | 93 | 86 | 80 | 85 | 71 | 29 |
| Field (%) | | | | | | | | | |
| Natural science | 16 | 12 | 12 | 43 | 42 | 48 | 33 | 41 | 41 |
| Humanities | 26 | 29 | 36 | 31 | 30 | 33 | 32 | 38 | 43 |
| Social science | 36 | 39 | 32 | 26 | 28 | 19 | 35 | 21 | 16 |
| Rank (%) | | | | | | | | | |
| Instructor | 0 | 0 | 0 | 0 | 0 | 0 | 0 | 4 | 14 |
| Assistant professor | 16 | 36 | 17 | 26 | 20 | 23 | 26 | 22 | 10 |
| Associate professor | 24 | 35 | 30 | 32 | 31 | 22 | 30 | 32 | 28 |
| Professor | 59 | 35 | 51 | 42 | 49 | 55 | 43 | 41 | 46 |
| Lecturer | 1 | 0 | 1 | 0 | 0 | 0 | 0 | 2 | 2 |
| Career age (years) | | | | | | | | | |
| Mean | 19 | 17 | 18 | 17 | 18 | 19 | 17 | 16 | 18 |
| SD | 10 | 10 | 9 | 10 | 9 | 10 | 10 | 9 | 7 |
| Career age | | | | | | | | | |
| 0–5 years | 10 | 16 | 11 | 13 | 8 | 13 | 14 | 15 | 5 |
| 6–10 years | 14 | 16 | 11 | 26 | 12 | 7 | 15 | 22 | 9 |
| 11–15 years | 13 | 18 | 15 | 19 | 15 | 13 | 17 | 13 | 14 |
| 16–20 years | 22 | 17 | 25 | 29 | 28 | 15 | 18 | 20 | 34 |
| 21–25 years | 19 | 13 | 23 | 16 | 21 | 35 | 13 | 14 | 26 |
| 26+ years | 22 | 21 | 14 | 17 | 14 | 16 | 22 | 16 | 11 |
| Years as faculty member | | | | | | | | | |
| Mean | 19 | 17 | 18 | 18 | 19 | 19 | 19 | 17 | 18 |
| SD | 10 | 11 | 9 | 11 | 9 | 9 | 10 | 9 | 7 |

*Continued next page*

Table 7.2—*Continued*

|  | Res-I | Res-II | Doc-I | Doc-II | Comp-I | Comp-II | LAC-I | LAC-II | CC |
|---|---|---|---|---|---|---|---|---|---|
| **Years as administrator** | | | | | | | | | |
| Mean | 3 | 3 | 3 | 2 | 4 | 6 | 2 | 3 | 3 |
| SD | 5 | 5 | 5 | 4 | 6 | 9 | 4 | 6 | 5 |
| **Currently in admin.** | | | | | | | | | |
| position (%) | 20 | 21 | 25 | 18 | 20 | 26 | 20 | 21 | 11 |
| Tenure appt. (%) | 85 | 71 | 78 | 74 | 81 | 78 | 78 | 68 | 84 |
| Tenure track (%) | 84 | 72 | 79 | 73 | 82 | 77 | 78 | 79 | 85 |
| Commit. to teaching (%) | 24 | 32 | 63 | 49 | 76 | 87 | 77 | 85 | 94 |
| Commit. to research (%) | 76 | 68 | 47 | 51 | 24 | 13 | 23 | 15 | 6 |

*Source:* NCRIPTAL survey.

dents indicated how much time they thought faculty thought their institution wants them to give to teaching, and how much time they thought faculty preferred to give to each role. These data are presented in table 7.5.

Rather than describe and display each of the 30 outcomes from these tables, we present representative findings from our monograph (Blackburn, Lawrence, Hart, & Dickman, 1990). Our key findings fall into four general categories: (1) attributes of the valued faculty member, (2) faculty members' influence on matters important to their work, (3) beliefs about teaching and learning, and (4) perceptions of the campus environment. For each finding we provide the question we asked and a graphic representation of the results. Some findings represent results from an individual question item, while others are factors, sets of items that grouped together conceptually and statistically.

Each figure shows the results for the individual item or factor for both faculty (solid black) and administrators (shaded) from the different institutional types. We have indicated when differences between faculty and administrators are significant by placing one, two, or three asterisks beside the appropriate institutional label. One asterisk means that the differences are significant at the $\leq .05$ level; two, significance at the $\leq .01$ level; and three, significance at the $\leq .001$ level.

We selected the beginning and end points of each graph so as to run close to the lowest and highest means. For example, in figure 7.1, instead of plotting the data to run from 1 to 4 (the possible range of the scale), we went from 3 (all faculty and administrative means are above 3) to 3.75 (none exceeded that mean). The overall average (3.43 in this case) is therefore approximately at the midpoint of the chart. The Res, Doc, and CC institutions differ significantly (see the asterisks). The visible differences in the

Table 7.3 Skills, Beliefs, and Personality Characteristics of Valued Faculty Members: Comparison of Faculty and Administrators (Faculty, Administrators)

| | Res-I | Res-II | Doc-I | Doc-II | Comp-I | Comp-II | LAC-I | LAC-II | CC |
|---|---|---|---|---|---|---|---|---|---|
| Skill 1 | -.55, .17 * | -.47, .49 *** | -.18, .51 ** | -.22, .66 *** | .00, .38 | .07, .36 | .14, .12 | .18, .25 | .22, .39 * |
| Skill 2 | 1.14, .74 ** | .84, .48 * | .64, .91 ** | .61, .28 | .01, -.07 | -.56, -.49 | -.33, -.39 | -.32, -.41 | -.73, -.75 |
| Skill 3 | -.08, -.51 | .04, -.57 ** | .18, -.55 *** | .10, -.22 | .15, -.53 *** | -.06, -.67 * | .03, -.74 *** | .06, -.68 *** | .14, -.37 *** |
| Belief 1 | -.48, .34 *** | -.50, .64 *** | -.24, .62 *** | -.32, .56 *** | -.11, .56 *** | -.02, .65 *** | .27, .55 * | .24, .57 *** | .14, .46 *** |
| Belief 2 | -.59, -.37 | -.25, -.36 | .02, .14 | -.02, .03 | .09, .10 | .25, .26 | .29, .16 | .48, .23 | .01, .03 |
| Belief 3 | 1.23, .75 ** | .72, .42 | .52, .90 *** | .55, .20 * | -.07, -.11 | -.36, -.45 | -.34, -.26 | -.32, -.39 | -.67, -.69 |
| Personality 1 | -.62, .23 *** | -.56, .51 *** | -.17, .54 *** | -.34, .52 *** | -.09, .47 *** | .10, .61 ** | .20, .36 | .23, .50 * | .22, .53 *** |
| Personality 2 | .53, .00 * | .36, -.11 * | .25, .13 | .32, .07 | .00, -.21 | -.30, -.21 | -.23, -.25 | -.22, -.27 | -.22, .29 |

Source: NCRIPTAL survey.

Notes: When the number differences are significant, one, two, or three asterisks appear under the higher number.

Skill factors: (1) dealing with students (teaching effectively, excellent lecturer, communicates well, responds to requests); (2) obtaining grants and publications; (3) knowing how to work the system (the system being the organization).

Belief factors: (1) virtue of hard work, holds high standards, has integrity, dedicated to the liberal arts, accepts liberal arts values; (2) team player and devoted to institution; (3) highly committed to research.

Personality factors: (1) understanding, open, candid, dedicated, personable; (2) ambitious, competitive, perseverant.

* $p \leq .05$.  ** $p \leq .01$.  *** $p \leq .001$.

249

Table 7.4  Self-Efficacy, Concerns, and Teaching Beliefs: Comparison of Faculty and Administrators (Faculty, Administrators)

| | Res-I | Res-II | Doc-I | Doc-II | Comp-I | Comp-II | LAC-I | LAC-II | CC |
|---|---|---|---|---|---|---|---|---|---|
| Self-efficacy 1 | -.21, .83 *** | -.25, .77 *** | -.08, .71 *** | .02, .94 *** | -.02, .71 *** | -.16, .43 ** | .31, .90 | .03, .42 * | -.22, -.44 *** |
| Self-efficacy 2 | .83, .31 | .38, .19 | .11, .41 | .15, .06 | -.09, -.04 | -.44, -.08 | -.14, .00 | -.36, -.27 | -.28, -.18 |
| Self-efficacy 3 | -.05, .49 *** | -.19, .80 *** | -.07, .66 ** | -.17, .50 *** | -.21, .42 * | .17, .79 *** | -.02, .72 *** | .01, .96 *** | -.10, .36 |
| Self-efficacy 4 | -.36, -.32 | -.31, .01 | -.27, .16 | -.02, .39 | -.05, .25 * | .11, .66 ** | .31, .25 | .11, .41 * | -.10, .24 |
| Concern 1 | -.48, -.90 | -.22, -.95 *** | -.14, -.69 * | -.10, .05 | .15, .44 *** | .35, .22 | .02, -.60 *** | .28, .12 | .41, -.36 *** |
| Concern 2 | .08, .12 | .02, -.15 | .03, -.02 | .04, .17 | .07, -.20 * | .00, .23 | .14, .09 | -.01, .02 | -.06, -.26 * |
| Teaching beliefs 1 | .07, .45 | -.10, .53 * | .04, .48 | -.16, .11 | -.04, .11 | -.14, .35 * | .23, .57 | .02, .32 | -.07, -.03 |
| Teaching beliefs 2 | .01, -.30 | -.03, -.09 | .01, -.70 *** | .18, -.18 | .19, -.25 *** | .02, -.33 | .26, -.33 ** | -.10, -.32 | .04, -.50 *** |
| Teaching beliefs 3 | -.24, -.02 | -.29, .00 | -.04, -.28 | -.10, .50 ** | -.04, .06 | .01, .23 | .11, .27 | -.04, .18 | .06, .45 *** |
| Teaching beliefs 4 | -.09, .41 * | -.09, .54 ** | -.02, .82 *** | .06, .60 * | -.04, .33 ** | .40, .48 | .15, .36 ** | -.08, .36 ** | -.12, .30 *** |

Source: NCRIPTAL survey.

Notes: When the number differences are significant, one, two, or three asterisks appear under the higher number.

Self-efficacy factors: (1) influence departmental curriculum and department chair; (2) influence their salary increases, acceptance of publications, and decisions to secure more resources to maintain important programs; (3) influence institutional requirements; (4) influence student learning and career achievements.

Concern factors: (1) helping to improve students' lives (personal, social); (2) transmitting principles and demonstrating processes.

Teaching beliefs factors: (1) expect students to think for themselves, share work cooperatively; (2) course content determined cooperatively by faculty and students; (3) students need to be challenged and need feedback; (4) students are competitive.

* p ≤ .05.   ** p ≤ .01.   *** p ≤ .001.

Table 7.5 Perception of the Environment: Comparison of Faculty and Administrators (Faculty, Administrators)

| | Res-I | Res-II | Doc-I | Doc-II | Comp-I | Comp-II | LAC-I | LAC-II | CC |
|---|---|---|---|---|---|---|---|---|---|
| Encouraged to work for collective good | 2.5, 3.0 ** | 2.5, 2.5 | 2.6, 3.0 ** | 2.7, 3.1 *** | 2.7, 3.2 | 3.0, 3.3 * | 2.9, 3.3 *** | 3.0, 3.2 * | 2.8, 3.1 *** |
| Institutional commitment to teaching | 1.8, 1.7 | 2.3, 2.6 | 2.6, 2.7 | 2.7, 3.2 ** | 3.2, 3.5 *** | 3.5, 3.8 * | 3.2, 3.4 | 3.5, 3.7 *** | 3.7, 3.8 *** |
| Trust administration | 2.3, 3.3 *** | 2.3, 3.1 *** | 2.2, 3.2 *** | 2.3, 3.2 *** | 2.4, 3.3 *** | 2.6, 3.2 *** | 2.6, 3.0 ** | 2.6, 3.3 *** | 2.4, 3.2 *** |
| Trust faculty | 2.7, 2.8 | 2.6, 2.9 | 2.7, 3.1 ** | 2.7, 3.2 *** | 2.7, 3.2 *** | 2.9, 3.2 | 3.0, 3.2 * | 3.0, 3.2 | 2.9, 3.1 |
| Some units are favored, get more money | 3.1, 2.9 | 3.2, 2.7 ** | 3.2, 2.6 *** | 3.2, 2.9 | 2.9, 2.5 *** | 2.7, 2.5 | 2.6, 2.3 ** | 2.7, 2.4 *** | 2.7, 2.4 |
| Collegial resources and support services | 5.6, 6.1 *** | 5.5, 5.6 | 5.3, 5.8 | 5.4, 6.1 *** | 5.4, 6.1 *** | 5.5, 6.0 ** | 5.6, 6.2 *** | 5.4, 5.7 ** | 5.6, 6.1 *** |
| Teaching effort preferred by inst. | 31.1, 33.7 | 37.4, 42.4 ** | 40.2, 44.0 | 44.6, 53.1 * | 53.4, 56.8 * | 63.7, 64.5 | 59.0, 56.2 | 64.2, 62.6 | 69.0, 69.1 |
| Teaching effort preferred by faculty | 30.9, 31.5 | 35.5, 42.0 ** | 41.9, 45.5 | 43.2, 53.0 * | 51.7, 60.1 *** | 59.5, 64.5 | 54.1, 57.8 | 58.4, 63.1 * | 62.9, 71.7 *** |
| Scholarship effort preferred by faculty | 19.4, 23.3 | 16.9, 18.0 | 17.3, 18.9 | 17.1, 15.1 | 17.9, 16.0 | 15.3, 13.6 | 16.5, 17.4 | 16.2, 14.0 | 16.6, 13.9 ** |
| Research effort preferred by faculty | 39.4, 34.2 | 36.0, 29.5 * | 28.5, 25.2 | 30.1, 21.1 * | 19.8, 14.4 *** | 15.5, 9.5 * | 19.0, 15.2 | 14.8, 11.3 ** | 10.0, 5.7 *** |
| Service effort preferred by faculty | 10.4, 11.1 | 11.6, 10.5 | 12.2, 10.4 | 9.5, 10.8 | 10.7, 9.5 | 9.7, 12.4 | 10.4, 9.6 | 10.6, 11.6 | 10.6, 8.6 *** |

Source: NCRIPTAL survey.

Notes: When the number differences are significant, one, two, or three asterisks appear under the higher number.

* $p \leq .05$. ** $p \leq .01$. *** $p \leq .001$.

Figure 7.1   The Valued Faculty Member Deals Effectively with Students

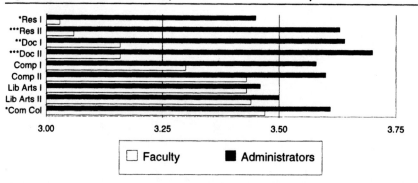

*Note:* Response scale: 1 = not at all characteristic; 2 = slightly characteristic; 3 = somewhat characteristic; 4 = highly characteristic (3.43 = average, faculty + administrators). *Source:* Blackburn, Lawrence, Hart, and Dickman (1990).

length of the bars alone do not determine the degree of significance. The significance also depends on the number of subjects who responded. The smaller the number, the larger must be the difference in order for it to be statistically significant.

### Attributes of the Valued Faculty Member

*Finding 1: The Valued Faculty Member Deals Effectively with Students*

Overall, administrators and faculty say that dealing effectively with students is about halfway between "somewhat" and "highly" characteristic of valued faculty members on their campus. However, in the research and doctoral universities, administrators believe significantly more strongly than their faculties do that dealing effectively with students characterizes the valued faculty member. In the comprehensive, liberal arts, and two-year public institutions, administrators and their faculties agree that the valued faculty member teaches effectively, is an excellent lecturer, communicates well, and responds to requests.

*The question:* Below is a set of words and phrases that faculty have used to describe the valued faculty members on their campuses. The set below has to do with skills and abilities of these faculty members.

To what extent is the word or phrase not at all characteristic, slightly characteristic, somewhat characteristic, highly characteristic of the faculty members you believe are valued on your campus?

1. Teaches effectively
2. Keeps abreast of developments in the discipline
3. Obtains grants
4. Communicates well
5. Publishes
6. Is organized
7. Works skillfully with students
8. Responds to requests
9. Is an excellent lecturer
10. Knows how to work the system

Responses 1, 4, 7, and 9 grouped together to form a factor called "deals effectively with students."

### Finding 2: The Valued Faculty Member Believes in the Academic Work Ethic

In every institutional type, administrators believe significantly more strongly than faculty do that the valued faculty member on their campus subscribes to the virtue of hard work, holds high standards, has integrity, and is dedicated to the liberal arts.

*The question:* Below is a second set of words and phrases that faculty have used to describe the valued faculty members on their campuses. The set below consists of values and attitudes ascribed to these people.

To what extent is the word or phrase not at all characteristic, slightly characteristic, somewhat characteristic, highly characteristic of the faculty members you believe are valued on campus?

BELIEFS, ATTITUDES, AND VALUES

1. Is highly committed to teaching
2. Is concerned about students
3. Believes in the virtue of hard work
4. Is highly committed to research
5. Holds high standards
6. Has integrity
7. Respects others
8. Is dedicated to the liberal arts

9. Is a team player

10. Is devoted to the institution

Responses 3, 5, 6, and 8 grouped together to form a factor called "believes in the academic work ethic."

*Finding 3: The Valued Faculty Member Is Understanding, Open, Candid, Dedicated, and Personable*

In every institutional type, administrators believe more strongly than faculty do that the valued faculty member is understanding, open, candid, dedicated, and personable.

*The question:* Below are sets of words and phrases that faculty have used to describe the valued faculty members on their campuses. The set below contains personality characteristics respected faculty members are said to possess.

To what extent is the word or phrase not at all characteristic, slightly characteristic, somewhat characteristic, highly characteristic of the faculty members you believe are valued on your campus?

PERSONALITY CHARACTERISTICS

1. Is supportive

2. Is understanding

3. Is open

Figure 7.2 The Valued Faculty Member Believes in the Academic Work Ethic

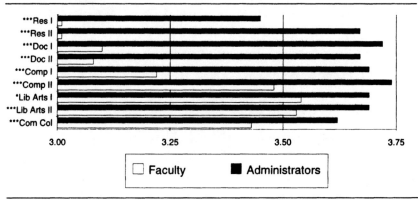

*Note:* Response scale: 1 = not at all characteristic; 2 = slightly characteristic; 3 = somewhat characteristic; 4 = highly characteristic (3.46 = average, faculty + administrators).
*Source:* Blackburn, Lawrence, Hart, and Dickman (1990).

4. Is candid

5. Has a sense of humor

6. Is personable

7. Is dedicated

8. Is ambitious

9. Is competitive

10. Is perseverant

Responses 2, 3, 4, 6, and 7 grouped together to form a factor called "understanding, open, candid, dedicated, and personable."

### Faculty Influence on Matters Important to Their Work

*Finding 1: Perception of Faculty Influence on Departmental Matters*

In all institutional types, faculty believe they have significantly less influence in such departmental matters as determining the curriculum, selecting the next chair of their unit, and choosing the next faculty member to be hired in their unit than the administrators in their institutions believe faculty have.

*The question:* Below are some outcomes that depend to varying degrees on faculty efforts. How much influence do you think faculty have on each of the following? Choices: really no influence at all, minor influence, some

Figure 7.3   The Valued Faculty Member Is Understanding, Open, Candid, Dedicated, and Personable

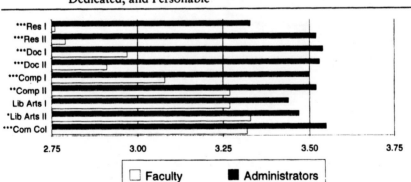

*Note:* Response scale: 1 = not at all characteristic; 2 = slightly characteristic; 3 = somewhat characteristic; 4 = highly characteristic (3.28 = average, faculty + administrators).
*Source:* Blackburn, Lawrence, Hart, and Dickman (1990).

influence, substantial influence. [On the faculty questionnaire the question asked how much influence they thought they had.]

1. Departmental curriculum decisions

2. Selecting the next chair of their unit

Items 1 and 2 grouped together to form a factor called "faculty influence on departmental matters."

*Finding 2: Perception of Faculty Influence on Institutional Requirements and Policies*

Except in Res-I universities, administrators believe that faculty have more influence on setting admissions and graduation requirements and establishing criteria for the annual review of faculty than the faculty believe they have. No differences between the two constituencies were statistically significant.

*The question:* Below are some outcomes that depend to varying degrees on faculty efforts. How much influence do you think faculty have on each of the following? Choices: really no influence at all, minor influence, some influence, substantial influence. [On the faculty questionnaire the question asked how much influence they thought they had.]

1. Establishing student admissions requirements

2. Setting requirements for graduation

3. Establishing criteria for annual review of faculty members

Figure 7.4   Perception of Faculty Influence on Departmental Matters

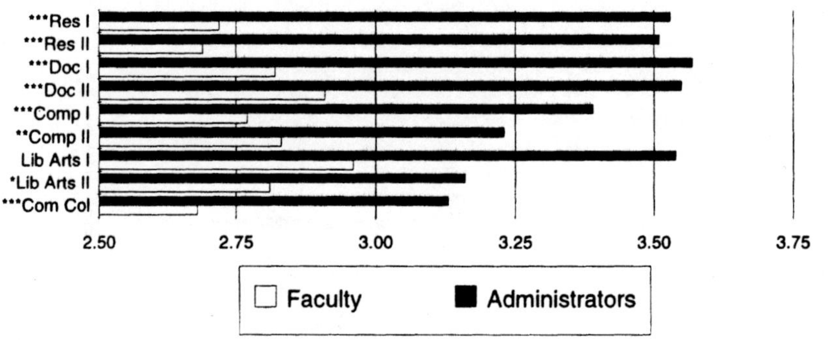

*Note:* Response scale: 1 = really no influence at all; 2 = minor influence; 3 = some influence; 4 = substantial influence (3.10 = average, faculty + administrators).
*Source:* Blackburn, Lawrence, Hart, and Dickman (1990).

Figure 7.5  Perception of Faculty Influence on Institutional Requirements and Policies

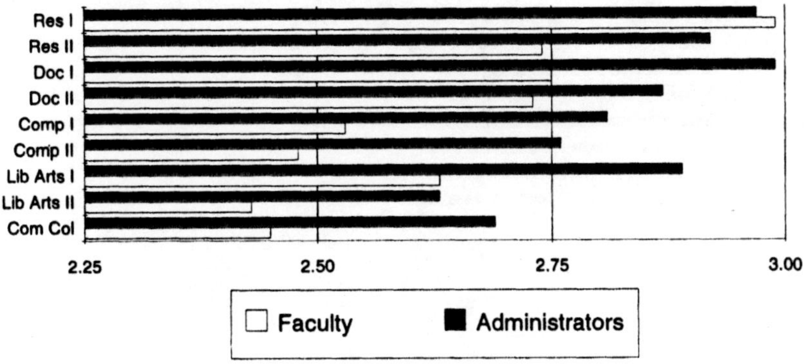

*Note:* Response scale: 1 = really no influence at all; 2 = minor influence; 3 = some influence; 4 = substantial influence (2.74 = average, faculty + administrators).
*Source:* Blackburn, Lawrence, Hart, and Dickman (1990).

Items, 1, 2, and 3 grouped together to form a factor called "faculty influence on institutional requirements and policies."

### Beliefs about Teaching and Learning

*Finding 1: Students Learn Best through Competition*

Faculty and administrators generally agree in their expectations about how students learn and about the conditions that best foster learning. However, administrators seem to believe more strongly than faculty do that competition among students promotes student learning. Faculty believe that more cooperative learning environments, where students share ideas with one another and where faculty and students determine course content and grades together, lead to better student learning. Note, however, that the average response is almost exactly between agree and disagree. This indicates a split between the two groups.

*The question:* Indicate whether you strongly disagree, tend to disagree, tend to agree, strongly agree with the statement below:

I assume undergraduates learn best when competition among students is fostered.

Figure 7.6    Students Learn Best through Competition

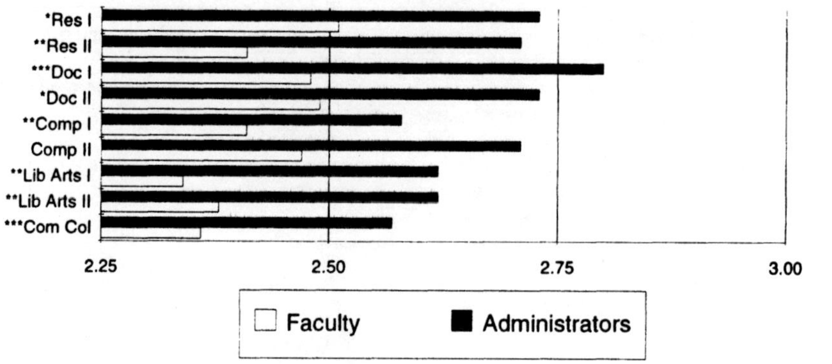

*Note:* Response scale: 1 = strongly disagree; 2 = tend to disagree; 3 = tend to agree; 4 = strongly agree (2.55 = average, faculty + administrators).
*Source:* Blackburn, Lawrence, Hart, and Dickman (1990).

### Perceptions of the Campus Environment

#### Finding 1: Administrators Can Be Trusted to Act in Good Faith

Administrators believe they can be trusted to act in good faith for the betterment of their institutions. Faculty, however, indicate a lower level of faith in their administrators. The average institutional administrator score is above 3, whereas the faculty average is less than 2.5. The differences are significant at $p \leq .001$ for every institutional type.

*The question:* Indicate whether you strongly disagree, tend to disagree, tend to agree, or strongly agree with the statement below:

Faculty can trust the administration to act in good faith for the betterment of the institution.

#### Finding 2: Faculty Groups Can Be Trusted to Act in Good Faith

Administrators appear to have more faith in faculty groups (e.g., senates, governance committees) than the faculty themselves do.

*The question:* Indicate whether you strongly disagree, tend to disagree, tend to agree, or strongly agree with the statement below:

Faculty can trust established faculty groups (e.g., governance committees) to act in good faith for the betterment of the institution.

Figure 7.7   Administrators Can Be Trusted to Act in Good Faith

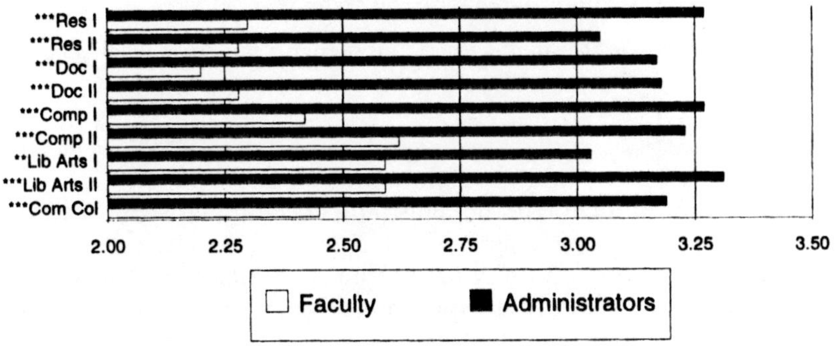

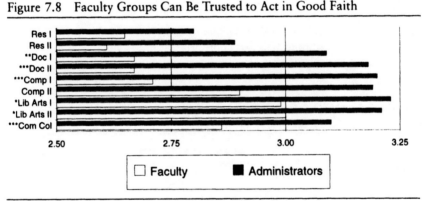

*Note:* Response scale: 1 = strongly disagree; 2 = tend to disagree; 3 = tend to agree; 4 = strongly agree (2.80 = average, faculty + administrators).
*Source:* Blackburn, Lawrence, Hart, and Dickman (1990).

Figure 7.8   Faculty Groups Can Be Trusted to Act in Good Faith

*Note:* Response scale: 1 = strongly disagree; 2 = tend to disagree; 3 = tend to agree; 4 = strongly agree (2.94 = average, faculty + administrators).
*Source:* Blackburn, Lawrence, Hart, and Dickman (1990).

### *Finding 3: Some Units Get More Than a Fair Share of Institutional Resources*

Faculty believe that some units on their campus receive more than a fair share of the central administration's allocation of resources. Administrators agree that there is inequity in funding, but concur less strongly.

*The question:* Indicate whether you strongly disagree, tend to disagree, tend to agree, or strongly agree with the statement below:

Some units on this campus receive more than a fair share when it comes to the central administration's allocation of resources.

### Finding 4: Adequate Collegial Resources and Support Services Are Available

In every institutional type, administrators believe that support services for teaching (laboratory facilities, computers, libraries, clerical assistance) and collegial resources (faculty to contribute to each other's classes and persons with whom to discuss appropriate topics) are more available or more plentiful than the faculty believe they are.

*The question:* Indicate whether you believe the following statements are true. Choices: little or no truth, generally not true, generally true, very high degree of truth.

1. The support services for teaching (lab facilities, computers, libraries, clerical assistance, audiovisual aids, student assistance, etc.) help faculty teach what and how they would like.

2. The collegial resources (faculty to contribute to each other's class, persons with whom to discuss appropriate topics) available at my institution help enrich teaching.

Figure 7.9    Some Units Get More Than a Fair Share of Institutional
Resources

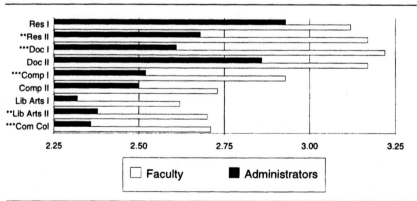

*Note:* Response scale: 1 = strongly disagree; 2 = tend to disagree; 3 = tend to agree; 4 = strongly agree (2.75 = average, faculty + administrators).
*Source:* Blackburn, Lawrence, Hart, and Dickman (1990).

260

Statements 1 and 2 added together to form a measure called "availability of collegial resources and support services." As a "scale" rather than a "factor," its range runs from the sum of its lowest possible score to its highest, in this case, from 2 to 8 (1 to 4 on each element).

## Discussion

If the valued faculty member in professors' eyes is the successful one—namely, the person who is rewarded by the institution (administration)—they paint her or him more negatively than do the administrators, especially in the doctoral and research universities. Faculty recognize research skills, but otherwise their response carries a touch of the cynical when it comes to who is valued and on what grounds. The differences among the Comp-II through CC institutions appear to be more of degree than of kind.

Taking the ability to influence departmental and institutional requirements as a matter of faculty governance, faculty are saying that they are relatively impotent. Either administrators err when they judge how much power faculty have or else faculty fail to see, or refuse to acknowledge, the influence they wield. The discrepancy in perceptions can contribute to lowered faculty morale. Faculty are not having the work environment control that they seek and that they believe they should have.

With respect to the factors on teaching goals, expectations about student behavior, and the learning conditions believed to be best, a high consensus

Figure 7.10    Adequate Collegial Resources and Support Services Are Available

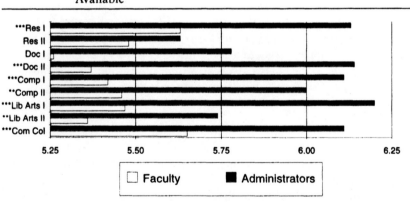

*Note:* Response scale: 2 = little or no truth; 4 = generally not true; 6 = generally true; 8 = very high degree of truth (5.72 = average, faculty + administrators).
*Source:* Blackburn, Lawrence, Hart, and Dickman (1990).

261

generally exists between the two constituencies—a not especially surprising outcome when one recalls that the majority of the administrators had been faculty and a number were teaching at the time of the survey. While neither group had been taught how to teach—some with degrees in education no doubt had, but those with Ph.D.'s in the liberal arts are highly unlikely to have been taught—they had seen a variety of teaching styles and learning situations and made decisions on how to behave with regard to these expectations and assumptions. The varied strategies tend to balance out in both groups, so that consensus may be a statistical artifact resulting from disagreements within both constituencies.

The exception to this generalization is the administrators' stronger belief that learning will be improved when students try to outperform one another. Maybe administrators see a more competitive world "out there"; or alternatively, perhaps they themselves are more competitive individuals, since they are the ones who moved into administration.

CCs have the most discrepancies between administrator and faculty perspectives. One explanation for the greatest number of disagreements occurring in the CC sector, and the least number in the Res-I's, is the smaller number of CC faculty having Ph.D.'s. They have spent less time in graduate schools and have not worked closely with professors on research projects and dissertations, where the mentor constantly expresses values about students and teaching as well as transmitting scholarly skills.

Another explanation is that the CC efficacy scores were consistently lower. (See finding 1 under "Faculty Influence on Matters Important to Their Work.") Faculty feel they are almost completely unable to affect the work environment. They experience an all-powerful administration, one more removed from them than from faculty in the other types of institutions. Moreover, unionized faculty—as CCs have, and as no Res-I's and -II's in our sample have—sometimes separate themselves from administrators and have fewer occasions to assess how things are going. In many instances the primary reason for CC faculty moving to collective bargaining was their dissatisfaction with their administration, its inability to be sensitive to their work concerns.

In general, the faculty and administration do not see identical work environments. Administrators uniformly picture the faculty work environment as much richer and stronger than the faculty do. We know from another study that perceived social support and morale are highly associated among faculty (Lawrence, Blackburn, Pitney, & Trautvetter, 1988). We do not know how this perceptual difference in the robustness of the work environment affects faculty performance. It is highly unlikely that it enhances morale.

We offer two overall observations. First, our proposition based on socialization theory—common background, ergo common values and beliefs, and therefore, presumably, common perceptions of the work environment—has been called into question. Perhaps times have changed enough that current faculty members' views of what characterizes valued faculty on the campuses are genuinely different from the views of their peers who are now administrators. But that is not what the data indicate. Faculty and administrator career ages are the same. Besides, some administrators are still teaching.

A more likely explanation for the lack of congruence is resocialization into the administrative role, new social knowledge that calls for a strong dedication to the institution. While faculty care about their institution's academic reputation, administrators' concerns are more multifaceted. They care about academic reputation too, but they also attend to social and financial matters as well. Administrators are working hard for the institution's good name. They see it more positively than faculty do. They care. They are fair. Certainly they can be trusted to do what is best for the institution—but faculty do not think so.

Second, there are a large number of disagreements about the work environment. Academe is populated by at least two cultures—not necessarily C. P. Snow's humanists and scientists, but rather faculty and administrators. They work in the same place, but they hold different perceptions of what it is like.

## Consensus between Administrators and Faculty on Teaching-Related Issues

In a related study (Lawrence, Blackburn, Pitney, & Trautvetter, 1988), researchers pursued the degree of consensus between administrators and faculty on teaching-related issues. The study then examined the relationship between the degree of their agreement and faculty morale.

We have seen that differences in values and beliefs exist between faculty and administrators. These differences, it is assumed, can affect the work performance of professors and hence the quality of students' educational experiences. However, there have been very few empirical studies of the issues around which such polarization occurs and the consequences for faculty, students, and administrators (Gross & Grambsch, 1968; Pellino, Blackburn, & Boberg, 1984; Rice & Austin, 1988).

The two general questions to be addressed are these:

Do academic administrators and faculty members (1) have similar values regarding the goals of undergraduate education, (2) make the same assumptions about optimal classroom learning conditions, (3) have similar perceptions of the adequacy of instructional resources and their institution's role expectations for faculty, and (4) share a common understanding about how professors ought to distribute their time to teaching?

Does the degree of agreement affect faculty members' morale?[5]

The quality of undergraduate education is a national concern. Although the specific issues that predominate vary from time to time, two questions are central to the ongoing debate: how should professors teach, and to what extent and in what ways do college administrators support faculty teaching efforts? The literature is rich with studies of teaching methods and student outcomes (McKeachie, Pintrich, Lin, & Smith, 1986) as well as research on how teaching behavior is affected by faculty perceptions of institutional support and encouragement of effective teaching (Blackburn, Lawrence, Okoloko, Bieber, Ross, Street, & Knuesel, 1987). Very little has been done, however, to connect the areas of inquiry—to see, for example, if on campuses where faculty and administrators agree on how professors should teach, both groups believe teaching is supported by the institution and faculty morale is high.

Theory and research in organizational behavior and management provide the conceptual framework for this study, especially perspectives drawn from the behavioral sciences. Considerable research has examined the connections between specific facets of work settings and employee morale, a somewhat imprecise concept that describes a complex phenomenon.

Bowen and Schuster (1986, p. 139), acknowledging that morale is "perhaps the most elusive dimension of the faculty condition," equate morale to one's mood or state of spirits. They suggest that the low faculty morale they report is the result not only of several specific campus or work environment conditions (e.g., level of compensation) but also of general unfavorable developments in higher education.

Rice and Austin (1988) define morale as a measure of faculty members' overall well-being at a college, as expressed in their enthusiasm for the institution, mutual trust and respect among them, their confidence in the administration, and their involvement in college functions. Not surprisingly, organizational climates that are cohesive tend to produce good employee morale. Conversely, competing sets of beliefs, values, and expectations in an organization are likely to result in conflict and disharmony. They can have a negative impact on individual morale and productivity (Austin & Gamson, 1983; Fisher & Gitelson, 1983).

Person/environment-fit theorists have increasingly begun to consider the importance of goal congruence within work environments (Moos, 1987). Simply put, the degree to which the goals of two interacting groups are compatible or conflicting can have multiple effects on an organization and its members. Gross and Grambsch (1968) conducted the first large-scale investigation of faculty-administrator goal congruence. They found that a high level of agreement existed between the two groups on their institution's goals. Both constituencies valued and worked toward essentially the same ends. Existing disagreements centered around institutional management issues rather than mission. Gross and Grambsch's investigation stopped short of considering the relationship between administrator-faculty goal congruence and faculty morale. Even if they had addressed this relationship, the tremendous changes in and pressures on American higher education in the last 25 years require that the question be addressed anew.

Rice and Austin (1988) found that the morale of faculty in small liberal arts colleges was generally higher than had been anticipated. In identifying the factors and conditions that promote and sustain high faculty morale, Rice and Austin cite a congruence of individual faculty values with organizational goals and missions. High-morale colleges, they say, are those in which faculty and administrators hold similar views about the academic workplace.

The main conclusion of recent findings on faculty members' morale is that it has been declining (Anderson, 1983; Bowen & Schuster, 1986; Boyer, 1987). Since morale has implications for faculty productivity and student learning, colleges and universities rightly show concern. Faculty reactions to their work settings can carry over to the classroom and ultimately impact on student outcomes. Faculty who lack support from colleagues and administrators and who do not have a sense of shared purpose with others in their institution may not only be demoralized; they may also find it difficult to establish a supportive learning environment for their students.

Our analysis departs in two ways from previous endeavors. First, it focuses on values, beliefs, and expectations relative to one particular activity, namely, undergraduate teaching and learning. Some writers could argue that consensus about only one facet of the faculty role will not predict well to overall morale. We selected colleges and universities where undergraduate education is to varying degrees a key component of mission, but where the assumed importance and consensus about teaching might differ. In brief, the hypothesis is that agreement between administrator and faculty opinions about teaching should be more closely associated with overall morale on teaching-oriented campuses.

The second departure is in our definition of morale. We define morale in terms of the faculty member's sense of both collective and personal well-being. Collective well-being includes, for example, the feeling that colleagues and administrators can be trusted. Personal well-being, on the other hand, is the individual's sense that he or she has made a sound career choice and is employed by a compatible institution. Our conceptualization of morale was an outgrowth of person/environment-fit theory and previous research on faculty, and therefore we thought both types of well-being should be included. Data came from the administrator and faculty surveys described above.

The general question that guided the analysis was, "To what extent is faculty morale affected by the organizational climate (degree of consensus about organizational goals and faculty role expectations)?" Specifically, we were interested in knowing if agreement within and between faculty and administrator groups regarding (1) the goals of undergraduate education and optimal learning conditions (beliefs—self-knowledge), (2) institutional role expectations for faculty members (expectations—social knowledge), and (3) institutional support for teaching (support—social knowledge) would be associated with higher morale.

The belief measures were items probing respondents' assumptions about undergraduate students' learning attitudes and behaviors, their views of the teaching environment, their level of concern about student learning outcomes, and their perceptions of their institution's goals for undergraduate instruction. Role expectations were taken to be (1) faculty members' understanding of how their institutions want them to spend their time and the types of behaviors that are rewarded on their campuses, and (2) administrators' responses to questions about how they believe professors should distribute their effort. The measures of institutional support were assessments of the instrumental (e.g., library, lab, clerical) and collegial (e.g., faculty with common interests) resources on their campuses. Morale was defined as faculty members' sense of the general well-being at their college or university, the goodness of fit between themselves and their institution, and their overall satisfaction with their careers.

We ran descriptive analyses to identify differences across institutional types and within faculty and administrator samples. A comparison of the means for the belief, expectation, and support items (predictor variables) indicated that the institutional samples from each of the nine Carnegie classifications should be treated separately. In addition, the data showed that there might be different perceptions among the faculty respondents who differed in discipline, career age, and rank as well as among administrators who differed in position, discipline, career age, and faculty experience.

With controls on institutional type, we ran separate correlations using first all faculty and then all administrator responses to the predictor and morale (outcome) items. The matrices revealed moderate intercorrelations among the belief items and among the role expectation and support items. We therefore created three separate scales. The *belief scale* consists of 15 items that assess respondents' (1) concern with students' personal and cognitive development and social advancement and (2) assumptions about students' motivation and ability to work independently, as well as desired teacher and student control of course content and pace. Faculty responded in terms of personal concerns and assumptions; administrators indicated both their perceptions of the faculty's level of concern and their own assumptions about teaching and learning.

The *expectation scale* includes identical items about institutional pressures and faculty commitment to teaching. In addition, the faculty indicated their perceptions of institutional preferences for faculty distribution of effort to teaching (faculty survey), and administrators noted their own preferences for faculty distribution of effort to teaching (administrator survey).[6]

The *support scale* is composed of two items measuring perceptions of support services (laboratory, library, etc.) and collegial resources that enrich teaching.

The faculty *morale scale* has five items about trust in administrators and colleagues, sense of equity in the allocation of institutional resources, personal fit within the employing institution, and satisfaction with the professorial career.

Intercorrelations among items on each scale were .45 or higher ($p \leq .05$), and between the individual belief, expectation, support, and morale items the correlation coefficients were at least .45 ($p \leq .05$). Hence, we used the sum of the mean scores as indicator of each theoretical component of organizational climate.

We measured consensus in several ways. We examined the differences within and between the faculty and administrator samples in terms of their teaching-related beliefs, role expectations, and sense of institutional support. We also assessed their overall agreement on all three scales (e.g., a lack of significant differences between groups on mean scores on any of the scales represents the highest-consensus campus).

Responses from faculty and administrators in Comp-I's, LAC-II's, and CCs were analyzed. The selection was based in part on the distribution of the data (the numbers of faculty and administrator respondents) and on the knowledge that these types of institutions vary greatly in mission. For example, there is more emphasis on research in the Comp-I's than in the LAC-II's and CCs. Therefore, we predict that low consensus on teaching-related goals and support has less impact on morale in the Comp-I's.

In all, 19 campuses were selected for study. The sample consisted of faculty and administrators from five Comp I's, five LAC-II's, and nine CCs. Tables 7.6 and 7.7 summarize the distribution of respondents across institutions and career variables.

The small samples in some of the institutions accurately reflect the num-

Table 7.6 Distribution of Faculty Samples on Career Variables (Percent)

| | Career Age | | | | | | | Discipline | | | | | | | | Rank | | | |
|---|---|---|---|---|---|---|---|---|---|---|---|---|---|---|---|---|---|---|---|
| | 0-5 | 6-10 | 11-15 | 16-20 | 21-25 | 26-30 | 31+ | Bio. | Chem. | Math. | Engl. | Hist. | Poli. Sci. | Psy. | Soc. | Instr. | Assist. Prof. | Assoc. Prof. | Full Prof. |
| **Comprehensive I** | | | | | | | | | | | | | | | | | | | |
| A (N = 74) | 6 | 6 | 8 | 31 | 24 | 13 | 12 | 18 | 16 | 11 | 15 | 8 | 8 | 14 | 10 | 0 | 3 | 8 | 89 |
| B (N = 42) | 6 | 17 | 14 | 31 | 26 | 6 | 0 | 5 | 13 | 19 | 19 | 14 | 17 | 12 | 5 | 0 | 14 | 55 | 31 |
| C (N = 28) | 0 | 8 | 15 | 46 | 19 | 8 | 4 | 14 | 7 | 4 | 21 | 21 | 11 | 14 | 7 | 0 | 0 | 57 | 43 |
| D (N = 53) | 2 | 14 | 9 | 33 | 23 | 9 | 9 | 8 | 23 | 19 | 9 | 8 | 4 | 26 | 4 | 0 | 6 | 13 | 81 |
| E (N = 13) | 0 | 0 | 11 | 33 | 33 | 11 | 11 | 15 | 15 | 15 | 23 | 8 | 7 | 15 | 0 | 0 | 39 | 8 | 54 |
| **Liberal arts II** | | | | | | | | | | | | | | | | | | | |
| F (N = 5) | 20 | 20 | 20 | 20 | 20 | 0 | 0 | 20 | 0 | 20 | 0 | 20 | 0 | 0 | 40 | 0 | 20 | 60 | 20 |
| G (N = 4) | 25 | 25 | 25 | 0 | 25 | 0 | 0 | 25 | 25 | 25 | 25 | 0 | 0 | 0 | 0 | 0 | 25 | 25 | 50 |
| H (N = 4) | 0 | 25 | 0 | 0 | 75 | 0 | 0 | 25 | 25 | 0 | 25 | 25 | 0 | 0 | 0 | 0 | 25 | 50 | 25 |
| I (N = 14) | 14 | 29 | 14 | 14 | 14 | 14 | 0 | 7 | 14 | 21 | 29 | 14 | 0 | 7 | 7 | 5 | 24 | 41 | 29 |
| J (N = 5) | 0 | 20 | 0 | 20 | 20 | 20 | 20 | 20 | 0 | 20 | 20 | 20 | 0 | 0 | 20 | 0 | 33 | 67 | 0 |
| **Two-year college** | | | | | | | | | | | | | | | | | | | |
| K (N = 6) | 0 | 0 | 0 | 50 | 50 | 0 | 0 | 0 | 17 | 33 | 17 | 0 | 17 | 17 | 0 | | missing data | | |
| L (N = 14) | 0 | 7 | 7 | 36 | 7 | 29 | 14 | 7 | 0 | 14 | 36 | 21 | 0 | 77 | 14 | 0 | 14 | 21 | 64 |
| M (N = 5) | 20 | 20 | 20 | 60 | 0 | 0 | 0 | 0 | 20 | 20 | 0 | 40 | 0 | 20 | 0 | | missing data | | |
| N (N = 31) | 10 | 13 | 10 | 23 | 26 | 16 | 3 | 26 | 10 | 20 | 26 | 7 | 3 | 7 | 3 | | missing data | | |
| O (N = 7) | 17 | 17 | 33 | 17 | 17 | 0 | 0 | 0 | 0 | 29 | 29 | 14 | 0 | 14 | 14 | 14 | 29 | 14 | 43 |
| P (N = 2) | 50 | 0 | 0 | 50 | 0 | 0 | 0 | 50 | 0 | 50 | 0 | 0 | 0 | 0 | 0 | 100 | 0 | 0 | 0 |
| Q (N = 14) | 0 | 20 | 20 | 10 | 40 | 10 | 0 | 21 | 14 | 21 | 36 | 7 | 0 | 0 | 0 | 7 | 21 | 36 | 36 |
| R (N = 15) | 0 | 0 | 27 | 33 | 20 | 0 | 20 | 27 | 13 | 0 | 40 | 7 | 7 | 7 | 7 | | missing data | | |
| S (N = 5) | 0 | 20 | 0 | 60 | 0 | 0 | 20 | 24 | 10 | 5 | 29 | 14 | 10 | 5 | 5 | 0 | 5 | 19 | 26 |

Source: NCRIPTAL survey.

Note: The distributions are reported as percentages of all respondents from each individual institution.

Table 7.7 Distribution of Administrator Samples on Career Variables (Percent)

| | Career Age | | | | | | | Discipline | | | | | Administration Level | | | Fac. Exp.[a] | |
|---|---|---|---|---|---|---|---|---|---|---|---|---|---|---|---|---|---|
| | 0-5 | 6-10 | 11-15 | 16-20 | 21-25 | 26-30 | 31+ | Nat. Sci. | Hum. | Soc. Sci. | Edu. | Other | High | Middle | Low | Yes | No |
| Comprehensive I | | | | | | | | | | | | | | | | | |
| A (N = 6) | 0 | 0 | 0 | 50 | 50 | 0 | 0 | 17 | 17 | 17 | 17 | 33 | 40 | 20 | 40 | 100 | 0 |
| B (N = 5) | 0 | 0 | 25 | 25 | 25 | 0 | 25 | 0 | 40 | 0 | 40 | 20 | 20 | 20 | 60 | 67 | 33 |
| C (N = 6) | 0 | 20 | 20 | 20 | 0 | 0 | 20 | 0 | 33 | 33 | 17 | 17 | 0 | 50 | 50 | 80 | 20 |
| D (N = 6) | 0 | 20 | 0 | 20 | 40 | 20 | 0 | 20 | 20 | 0 | 60 | 0 | 60 | 40 | 0 | 60 | 40 |
| E (N = 4) | 0 | 25 | 0 | 25 | 25 | 25 | 25 | 25 | 50 | 0 | 0 | 25 | 25 | 0 | 75 | 75 | 25 |
| Liberal arts II | | | | | | | | | | | | | | | | | |
| F (N = 4) | 0 | 25 | 0 | 25 | 0 | 25 | 25 | 0 | 75 | 25 | 0 | 0 | 20 | 40 | 40 | 60 | 40 |
| G (N = 3) | 0 | 0 | 33 | 0 | 67 | 0 | 0 | 0 | 0 | 0 | 67 | 33 | 50 | 25 | 25 | 100 | 0 |
| H (N = 5) | 0 | 0 | 33 | 33 | 33 | 0 | 0 | 0 | 0 | 0 | 33 | 67 | 25 | 25 | 50 | 50 | 50 |
| I (N = 5) | 0 | 0 | 20 | 20 | 40 | 0 | 20 | 0 | 40 | 20 | 40 | 0 | 40 | 40 | 20 | 40 | 60 |
| J (N = 2) | 0 | 0 | 0 | 50 | 0 | 0 | 50 | 50 | 0 | 0 | 50 | 0 | 0 | 100 | 0 | 100 | 0 |
| Two-year college | | | | | | | | | | | | | | | | | |
| K (N = 5) | 20 | 0 | 0 | 20 | 20 | 40 | 0 | 60 | 20 | 0 | 20 | 0 | 0 | 60 | 40 | 100 | 0 |
| L (N = 2) | 0 | 0 | 0 | 50 | 0 | 0 | 50 | 50 | 50 | 0 | 0 | 0 | 0 | 100 | 0 | 100 | 0 |
| M (N = 5) | 0 | 0 | 0 | 80 | 0 | 20 | 0 | 0 | 0 | 0 | 60 | 40 | 20 | 20 | 60 | 100 | 0 |
| N (N = 4) | 0 | 0 | 0 | 50 | 0 | 50 | 0 | 0 | 0 | 0 | 75 | 25 | 0 | 50 | 50 | 100 | 0 |
| O (N = 6) | 17 | 17 | 17 | 17 | 17 | 17 | 0 | 33 | 33 | 0 | 33 | 0 | 0 | 40 | 60 | 67 | 33 |
| P (N = 5) | 0 | 20 | 20 | 20 | 20 | 0 | 20 | 20 | 0 | 0 | 60 | 20 | 20 | 60 | 20 | 80 | 20 |
| Q (N = 6) | 0 | 0 | 20 | 40 | 40 | 0 | 0 | 17 | 17 | 0 | 17 | 50 | 0 | 83 | 17 | 100 | 0 |
| R (N = 5) | 0 | 0 | 40 | 40 | 20 | 0 | 0 | 0 | 0 | 0 | 80 | 20 | 40 | 40 | 20 | 60 | 40 |
| S (N = 2) | 0 | 0 | 0 | 100 | 0 | 0 | 0 | 0 | 50 | 0 | 50 | 0 | 50 | 50 | 0 | 100 | 0 |

Source: NCRIPTAL survey.

Note: The distributions are reported as percentages of all respondents from each individual institution.

a. Administrators who had a minimum of one year's experience (yes) or no experience (no).

ber of faculty members in the liberal arts disciplines. For example, institution O has only seven faculty in the sampled disciplines, and this was a 70 percent response rate (7 out of 10 surveys sent were returned). The average faculty response rate for the Comp-I's was 45 percent, for the LAC-II's it was 45 percent, and for the CCs it was 48 percent. With a few exceptions (e.g., institutions G and P) the faculty respondents were distributed across the disciplines, and the administrators were from different disciplines and levels in the administrative structure.[7] The two samples were, however, senior in career age, and the faculty were highly tenured.

### Consensus among Faculty

The range of possible scores on the belief scale was 15 to 60 (15 indicated low concern or degree of agreement). An individual could score between 2 and 108 on the expectation scale. (The reason for the larger score was that one item asked for a percentage-of-time estimate.) The scores on the support scale could range from 2 to 8. On both these last two scales the higher scores indicated greater encouragement and support for teaching. The scores on the morale scale could range from 5 to 19, with a higher score representing a greater sense of personal and faculty well-being.

We examined agreement about teaching goals and activities and perceptions of role expectations. Institutional support was investigated for faculty in each institution by running anovas on each of the scale means by discipline, rank, and career age. Few significant differences (the most, three, occurred within the Comp-I's) appeared, and in these instances the amount of explained variance was small (average = 3.5 percent). Anovas were also run for morale with the same end results.

Correlations between the belief, expectation, and support scores and faculty morale indicated that perceived institutional support for teaching was most often associated with morale. (See table 7.8.)

### Consensus among Administrators

Analysis of variance with the career variables—discipline, career age, administrative level, and faculty experience—revealed few significant differences among administrators. (The greatest number, three, were found among administrators in CCs.) In those instances when the small institutional Ns precluded meaningful analyses, inspection of the data showed that the variance in means was very small.

### Consensus between Faculty and Administrators

We assessed consensus between faculty and administrators on each of the 19 campuses by using t-tests for the significance of the differences on each of

Table 7.8    Correlations between Faculty Scores on Organizational Context Scales and Faculty Morale

|  | Beliefs | Expectations | Support |
|---|---|---|---|
| *Comprehensive I* | | | |
| A | .167 | -.038 | .434* |
| B | .139 | .168 | .574* |
| C | .404* | .118 | .690* |
| D | .044 | .036 | .366* |
| E | .093 | -.201 | .519* |
| *Liberal arts II* | | | |
| F | .174 | -.349 | .196 |
| G | -.850 | -.571 | .405 |
| H | .866* | .037 | .939* |
| I | .393 | .093 | .417* |
| J | -.084 | -.126 | .358 |
| *Two-year college* | | | |
| K | .791* | -.104 | .420 |
| L | .142 | -.209 | .429 |
| M | .648 | .560 | .716 |
| N | .159 | .019 | .237 |
| O | .091 | .484 | .224 |
| P | -.607 | .221 | .293 |
| Q | -.344 | .105 | .497* |
| R | .453* | .502* | .551* |
| S | .462 | 1.000 | .776* |

*Source:* NCRIPTAL survey.

* $p \leq .05$.

the organizational context scales. (See table 7.9.) The two groups differed most often in their perceptions of institutional support for teaching and next most often in their understanding of role expectations. This was true when the institutional samples were both large (e.g., faculty $N = 74$ and administrator $N = 6$) and small (faculty $N = 5$ and administrator $N = 5$).

To see if consensus affected morale, we gave institutions scores representing overall consensus based on the number of significant t-tests (3 = no significant differences, 2 = significant differences on one scale, and 1 = significant differences on two of the three scales). Almost two-thirds of the institutions with scores of 3 (greatest consensus), one-third of the campuses with scores of 2 (moderate consensus), and half of the schools with scores of 1 (lowest consensus) had faculty morale scores of 14 or higher (after round-

Table 7.9 Consensus on Organizational Context Scales and Faculty Morale

| | Beliefs | | | | | Expectations | | | | | Support | | | | | Faculty Morale | |
|---|---|---|---|---|---|---|---|---|---|---|---|---|---|---|---|---|---|
| | Faculty | | Admin. | | | Faculty | | Admin. | | | Faculty | | Admin. | | | | |
| | Mean | SD | Mean | SD | t | Mean | SD | Mean | SD | t | Mean | SD | Mean | SD | t | Mean | SD |
| **Comp-I** | | | | | | | | | | | | | | | | | |
| A | 44.1 | 3.20 | 42.5 | 4.40 | 0.80 | 64.2 | 16.70 | 56.4 | 8.80 | *1.78* | 5.2 | 1.20 | 6.3 | 0.95 | *2.67* | 13.0 | 2.40 |
| B | 44.5 | 3.70 | 43.6 | 2.40 | 0.68 | 58.8 | 16.90 | 60.7 | 14.10 | 0.66 | 5.6 | 1.30 | 6.5 | 0.84 | 0.47 | 13.4 | 2.20 |
| C | 44.5 | 3.80 | 41.8 | 3.40 | 1.47 | 55.0 | 18.80 | 55.2 | 6.10 | 0.05 | 5.2 | 1.10 | 5.8 | 1.20 | 1.04 | 13.2 | 2.50 |
| D | 46.6 | 4.20 | 39.0 | 6.00 | *2.49* | 54.3 | 17.50 | 59.3 | 10.80 | 0.75 | 5.5 | 1.30 | 6.0 | 0.00 | 0.07 | 12.8 | 2.40 |
| E | 46.6 | 2.80 | 45.3 | 0.58 | 1.43 | 76.9 | 18.60 | 68.8 | 9.00 | 1.11 | 4.9 | 1.40 | 5.3 | 0.96 | 0.59 | 11.6 | 2.10 |
| **LAC-II** | | | | | | | | | | | | | | | | | |
| F | 43.6 | 3.20 | 47.2 | 4.60 | 1.38 | 76.4 | 10.90 | 60.3 | 14.60 | *1.76* | 4.4 | 1.30 | 6.0 | 0.63 | *2.26* | 13.4 | 3.00 |
| G | 45.8 | 2.60 | 44.0 | 3.60 | 0.73 | 78.8 | 19.40 | 74.1 | 16.20 | 0.32 | 4.3 | 2.10 | 5.0 | 1.20 | 0.50 | 13.3 | 3.10 |
| H | 45.9 | 1.80 | 44.0 | 3.60 | 0.87 | 83.0 | 7.90 | 66.0 | 11.90 | *2.27* | 5.4 | 1.40 | 5.0 | 0.82 | 0.56 | 15.0 | 3.00 |
| I | 46.1 | 3.20 | 46.0 | 6.10 | 0.03 | 75.4 | 14.60 | 72.5 | 6.00 | 0.58 | 4.9 | 1.70 | 6.2 | 1.10 | *2.69* | 12.4 | 2.80 |
| J | 49.6 | 2.40 | 51.0 | 5.70 | 0.24 | 59.4 | 6.70 | 64.5 | 10.60 | 0.47 | 5.0 | 0.93 | 6.0 | 1.40 | 0.69 | 13.1 | 2.60 |
| **Two-year** | | | | | | | | | | | | | | | | | |
| K | 45.9 | 2.00 | 43.4 | 7.30 | 0.67 | 84.5 | 12.00 | 80.9 | 5.30 | 0.60 | 5.9 | 3.80 | 5.4 | 1.80 | 0.55 | 14.9 | 2.00 |
| L | 45.0 | 3.70 | 40.0 | 2.80 | *2.12* | 83.3 | 17.10 | 78.0 | 0.00 | 0.98 | 5.4 | 1.20 | 6.0 | 0.00 | *1.94* | 13.3 | 2.60 |
| M | 45.2 | 3.10 | 44.0 | 5.10 | 0.37 | 75.0 | 9.80 | 85.8 | 6.90 | *1.94* | 5.0 | 1.70 | 5.8 | 1.10 | 0.85 | 14.2 | 1.20 |
| N | 46.1 | 4.10 | 41.8 | 5.10 | 1.43 | 79.9 | 13.70 | 78.9 | 2.00 | 0.33 | 5.8 | 0.93 | 6.3 | 0.50 | 1.54 | 13.7 | 2.00 |
| O | 44.6 | 4.50 | 41.3 | 2.60 | 1.52 | 77.2 | 8.20 | 75.7 | 10.40 | 0.25 | 6.0 | 0.58 | 5.3 | 1.20 | 0.84 | 14.4 | 2.60 |
| P | 44.5 | 3.70 | 44.4 | 2.50 | 0.04 | 81.8 | 17.40 | 84.0 | 15.50 | 0.17 | 4.5 | 1.00 | 6.0 | 1.20 | *1.61* | 12.8 | 1.70 |
| Q | 44.7 | 4.20 | 44.5 | 4.40 | 0.09 | 72.7 | 15.40 | 72.3 | 9.30 | 0.06 | 5.0 | 1.50 | 6.2 | 0.75 | *2.34* | 12.2 | 2.80 |
| R | 46.3 | 2.90 | 49.6 | 3.20 | *1.90* | 80.3 | 15.20 | 77.5 | 6.80 | 0.58 | 5.9 | 1.40 | 7.8 | 0.45 | *5.01* | 14.3 | 1.80 |
| S | 43.2 | 3.30 | 43.0 | 2.80 | 0.06 | 79.0 | 5.70 | 79.5 | 3.50 | 0.07 | 4.6 | 1.10 | 5.0 | 1.40 | 0.26 | 13.6 | 2.90 |

Source: NCRIPTAL survey.

Note: $p \le .05$ when t value shown in bold and italics.

ing up). The major outcome was as we expected: colleges with high consensus were more likely to have higher faculty morale.

Consensus between the faculty and administrator respondents on the 19 campuses was generally strong. In 9 of the 19 institutions (47 percent) no significant differences existed on the three measures of organizational climate. The two groups varied most often on the institutional support scale. Administrators in these instances always gave higher ratings of support for teaching. In contrast, administrators seemed to have a good sense of faculty teaching goals—for example, whether they were most highly concerned with transmitting facts or with encouraging students' overall personal development—and they tended to make similar assumptions about undergraduate students' learning behavior and optimal teaching conditions. Faculty and administrators also tended to have a common understanding of teaching-related role expectations. In those cases when faculty and administrators did not agree, the faculty had higher mean scores on the measure of faculty commitment to teaching and administrator preferences for distribution of effort to teaching.

The data suggest that faculty morale was "middling" (the midpoint of the scale was 12.5). In the majority of institutions the mean was 13 or better, but it was never greater than 16. Although the results are not directly comparable to those from the Bowen and Schuster (1986) or Rice and Austin (1988) studies, our measure of morale was more similar to Rice and Austin's. As was the case in their study, we found that faculty sense of well-being was quite strong in the LAC-II's. In addition, we found that morale was generally strong in both the Comp-I's and the CCs.

Inspection of the data suggests a relationship between overall faculty-administrator consensus and faculty morale. We have no ready explanation for why two of the low-consensus institutions (two-year colleges L and R) had higher morale. Even in the Comps-I's, where we thought agreement on teaching-related matters might have less to do with overall morale, the trends in three of the five institutions indicate that higher faculty morale existed on campuses with greater consensus. We found that among the faculty, perceived institutional support for teaching and morale were positively correlated. We anticipated, therefore, that on those campuses where correlations were significant, consensus between faculty and administrators on this scale might be more likely to have an effect on morale. In the Comp-I's the correlations were all significant, and there was only one instance where faculty and administrators varied significantly in their perceptions (institution A). In this case faculty morale was just above the scale mean. Among the LAC-II's morale was highest for the school where there was faculty-administrator agreement (H) and lowest where there was not agreement about support (I). Within the two-year institutions the findings were mixed. In two cases, Q and R, where there were significant differences, and in institution S, where there was agreement, morale was just above the scale mean.

## Implications for Practice

Clues emerge from the wide assortment of studies reported in chapters 2–3, and from our own studies presented in chapters 4–6 and here, as to how individuals might change and how the work environment might be altered so that faculty could become more effective in all of their roles. They would be happier, their research and scholarship richer and more abundant, their teaching more stimulating, and their service to society, the professions, and their institution more effective.

By way of illustration, consider the first study on teaching described in chapter 5, the one dealing with the interviews on four campuses and the use of our quality of faculty effort (QFE) instrument for predicting teaching behavior. These data and results pose a considerable challenge to higher and postsecondary educators. On the one hand, it seems apparent that by setting the expectation of improved teaching and rewarding those who follow through, one can ensure that faculty will teach well. Similarly, by logical extension, it would appear that to entice faculty to engage in activities aimed at improving their teaching, the expectation needs to be set and appropriate rewards provided. To get faculty to become truly engaged with their teaching to such a degree that they find it personally rewarding without regard to institutional incentives and expectations, however, is another issue.

Moreover, this issue cannot be directly addressed by the data. The QFE instrument does not ascertain whether faculty participate in such activities because they find them inherently attractive or because they know they must become better teachers if they hope to reap the benefits of the reward system. It is disconcerting that faculty behavior, for whatever reason, does not indicate a sense of commitment to teaching in these four institutions whose primary mission is teaching.

Viewed from another perspective, however, these data, and especially the lack of positive correlations, may indicate that faculty have positive feelings about themselves as teachers and, as such, do not find the approaches or activities included in the questionnaire to represent the types of things they engage in for the purpose of becoming better teachers. In addition, for those items that proved to have significant relationships for at least one institution, all but four allowed the respondents to indicate only whether they had participated in the activity. It may be the case that respondents participated in one activity several times and chose not to participate in others. After all, professors may believe that faculty development programs or books or even colleagues cannot really help them improve their teaching. And to the extent that they, like the professoriate all across the country, are getting older, they have seen faculty development programs come and go as regularly as they have seen how-to-teach fads enter and leave. Through learned skepticism, they may place little credence in them.

Except for the regional university, these institutions are small, their cultures well developed, and their missions more narrowly focused on teaching. It might not take new, younger faculty long to realize that the older faculty do not place much stock in the more structured forms (e.g., workshops, books) of learning how to become better teachers. In such small institutions new faculty could be quickly socialized into thinking this way. At the larger regional university the younger faculty are coming increasingly from research universities and are being socialized via their graduate programs to place less emphasis on teaching. In turn, when they arrive on campus as new faculty, they do not experience the priority given by administrators to teaching enhancement programs or workshops, nor do they see them as having priority among the existing faculty. Besides, the new hires at the regional university were recruited for their research potential, with the clear message that research is what will be rewarded. Whatever the reason, having a sense that one can make a difference in the classroom without participating in specific structured activities—which is what the data presented in this study show—does not necessarily spell doom for college teaching.

In general, administrators have higher salaries than faculty with comparable experience. They have access to more funds for travel and conference attendance, for they often represent the organization at important meetings. They have a 12-month job, whereas the normal faculty one is for 9 to 10 months. They have control of the budget. They have power. They are trying to take the institution where they believe it should be headed. They enjoy high external status, for most outsiders believe a vice presidency represents the same kind of career success in academia as it does in the world of business and industry.

Administrators also put in long hours. Their life seems to be a continuous succession of crises. There is never enough money to do what has to be done. The college's many constituencies are at odds with one another. Demands for accountability from Washington require responses. New lawsuits arrive daily. Outside forces make impossible demands. Visits must be made to potential large donors across the country. The governing board divides on a crucial issue—fully recognizing homosexuals, for example. Job security is

275

threatened. Mistakes are made. The positions at the top are a long distance from the excitement and hesitancy of walking into that first classroom in early September some 20 years ago. Did I follow the right path?

Are there some ways to mix the two career paths and enjoy the fruits of each? A few institutions and a few individuals seem to have found satisfactory resolutions. For example, deans at the University of Chicago are selected without regard to past administrative experience. They're doing service for their colleagues. The appointment is a nonrenewable one—five years. They maintain their research agendas, for they are going back to it full-time when their stint of duty is over. They may teach less, but they will be in the classroom to some extent. They are not changing careers.

James Bryant Conant did not assume the presidency of Harvard each morning until nine o'clock, no matter what emergencies awaited him. From six until nine he was the scientist he had been educated to be. If he was not in his laboratory, he was translating Lavoisier's *Elements of Chemistry* for a case study he was preparing for the freshman general education science course he taught. A former Colgate president spent his first hours every day in his library carrel writing his famous history volumes on Lafayette. Nan Keohane, now president of Duke, took the presidency of Wellesley only on the condition that she would have a full sabbatical after six years. She spent it back at her alma mater, Stanford, in the political science department.

We do not know how realistic these examples are. We suspect that the new administrators' good intentions of keeping abreast with their discipline are not likely to succeed if the scheduled reading and writing times are set for evenings, weekends, or school breaks. Students who leave to take positions before completing their dissertations rarely succeed in completing them with strategies of this kind. The scholarly effort must have the first priority of the day, every day, if it is to work.

It's important that it work. Administrators who are intellectually alive will be better administrators. They will know what faculty are going through. They will more likely understand what faculty care about, and what they gripe about. They are more likely to be respected as administrators.

# PART THREE

# What We
# Learned

# 8

# FINDINGS, THEORIES, AND NEXT STEPS

THIS CONCLUDING CHAPTER summarizes what the studies with our theoretical framework and a national data set have to say about faculty at work. It examines how the outcomes relate to the other theories that lie—sometimes explicitly but more often implicitly—behind the studies reported in the introduction and in chapters 2 and 3, and to our theory in particular. We close by arguing for the importance of things that need to be done next to expand our knowledge and deepen our understanding of academic life. Appendix G discusses some of the technical and practical limitations of our efforts as well as the design choices confronting us.

## The Findings

Table 8.1 contains a simple frequency count of the number of times the different institutional types appeared in the studies we presented. We used some more than others. That Res-I's occur most often results in part from our decision to test the framework first where data were richest. (See chapter 4.) While not every institutional type entered every inquiry, each construct did at least five times. Our findings, then, apply, but not always in the same way, throughout the different kinds of colleges and universities in this country—a small but not unimportant finding.

Table 8.2 also displays a simple frequency count of the number of times variables in each of the framework's principal categories remained as a significant predictor after we entered all independent variables into the final regression analyses. We briefly discuss the variables within a category that appear most frequently. Keep in mind that we did not use all variables in every study, so the frequency of any one variable (say, gender) is not a direct measure of its potency. We comment on what we see to be important. We

Table 8.1    Institutional Types in the Studies

| College or University Type | Frequency |
|---|---|
| Res-I | 9 |
| Res-II | 6 |
| Doc-I | 7 |
| Doc-II | 6 |
| Comp-I | 8 |
| Comp-II | 5 |
| LAC-I | 6 |
| LAC-II | 5 |
| CC | 6 |

*Source:* NCRIPTAL survey.

then make inferences as to what the framework has taught us about what motivates faculty to do what they do while at work.

The sociodemographic variables make rare appearances—age and race/ethnicity but once each. Remember, however, that we often excluded race/ethnicity because of the small Ns. About the only time gender predicted was when the research outcome was conversations regarding research. Women talked more with colleagues about their research. Gender frequently had a direct effect on career and self-knowledge. However, when we entered social knowledge and behaviors, its effect almost always disappeared. In sum, the variables most often used in other studies—sociodemographics—turn out to be poor and weak predictors when one takes self-knowledge and social knowledge variables into account.

As for career variables, career age accounted for nearly half the entries, appearing 15 times. Senior faculty were both the higher publishers and the persons who gave the greatest effort to teaching, an outcome that is partly

Table 8.2    Variables in the Final Regressions

| Variable Category | Frequency |
|---|---|
| Sociodemographic | 8 |
| Career | 33 |
| Self-knowledge | 46 |
| Social knowledge | 49 |
| Behavior | 16 |
| Institutional response | 0 |

*Source:* NCRIPTAL survey.

an artifact of their having survived.[1] That is, because they have published, they are still on the job. They have higher ranks, the second most frequently occurring career variable. Quality of graduate school, a frequently used variable in earlier studies, remains a predictor in only three instances, although we used it in nearly every study.[2] A kennel club pedigree may initially locate one at a more highly regarded university. Today's success, however, depends upon performance, not prejob credentials.

Both our self-knowledge and social knowledge categories dominated the framework's contribution to the explained variance. As for self-knowledge, self-efficacy—as a researcher, pedagogue, committee member—in the corresponding outcome domain mattered more than any other variable in any category. It was significant in 26 instances at one time or another in every institutional type and academic discipline. Interest in the activity, percentage of preferred effort to give to it, feeling that one can influence outcomes, and being dedicated, ambitious, competitive, and perseverant round out the other more frequently occurring variables. As we saw in chapter 4 in the third study, comparing female and male science academics, self-efficacy was the predictor for women's scholarly output.

Social knowledge contained the greatest number of predictors, in total and in scope. The two that occurred most often, each more than a dozen times, were support and the effort faculty believed their institution desired. Grants—that is, dollars and cents—predicted behavior the largest number of times. However, support as estimated by having credible colleagues, having a credible department chair, and believing there is consensus among one's peers also remained in final regression runs. The work environment of important people and of physical and fiscal resources has genuine effects on faculty performance at work.

Behavior variables were strong predictors, as would be consistent with our theory. Faculty do what they believe they are good at (self-competence), devote energy to what interests them (interest and percentage of effort preferred), engage in activities in which they can influence outcomes (efficacy). It is not surprising, then, that the corresponding behavior—say, doing research—results in publications.

Of course, all is not quite that simple. We are dealing with complex individuals engaged in complex social relations in complex environments.[3] At the same time, effort (time) given to research, grant activity, applying for fellowships, dissertation involvement, communicating with fellow researchers—all appeared in one or more of the final regressions.

Institutional response, however, did not. We tried it at the outset. It did not work. Recall that our data are not longitudinal, and the evidence did not support our attempt to introduce a time dimension by noting what might have happened to individuals—for example, receiving a promotion or being given additional assistance—as a consequence of their publications. Cause and effect here are tenuous to begin with, and the timing all but impossible to control. There are lags, sometimes of years, between the completion of a research effort and its appearance in print. There can also be time lapses in institutional response. If one has just been promoted, a second accomplishment will not lead to another immediate promotion. After all, two promotions are all there are in the career, and few come after age 40 (on the average). Once one is a full professor, that is it. Rank can no longer be a motivator, if it ever directly was. Said another way, we are not convinced that institutional response is not a motivator. However, survey data may never be able to test this component of our framework adequately.

## Theories

While we have been building and testing a motivation-based framework to account for why faculty do what they do at work, we are but a part of a larger body of inquiry that looks at professionals at work in organizations. Pelz and Andrew's (1976) study of scientists in organizations (industry, research laboratories, and universities) and Freidson's (1973) research on physicians are good examples. Most studies are sociologically based. To date, the most theoretically sound studies of faculty are Wilson's (1942), Lazarsfeld and Thielens's (1958), Parsons and Platt's (1968), and Blau's (1973).

Before turning to sociological and psychological faculty studies, the ones closest to our framework, we briefly look over related social scientific theories used in research on faculty. Had we covered other relational studies of academics we would have found a variety of disciplinary theories underpinning the inquiries.[4] Researchers have borrowed from a wide assortment of conceptual frameworks—a natural thing to do, since no conclusive framework exists for understanding this occupational group. We assess their strengths and weaknesses and indicate their relationship to our framework.

### *Political Scientists and Sociologists*

A small, influential mix of political scientists and sociologists directed the early large-faculty surveys. Lazarsfeld and Thielens (1958) surveyed 2,451 social scientists on their responses to the McCarthy era, a mammoth undertaking in the days before computerized data processing. Parsons and Platt (1968) systematically gathered data on faculty in diverse settings. Ladd, Lipset, Trow, and Bayer controlled the 1969, 1972, and 1975 national surveys sponsored by the Carnegie Commission and the American Council on Education. They designed the instruments and provided the early data analyses.

One set of studies that emerged from those data sets revolved around faculty values and beliefs about social issues—student freedoms, faculty unionization, the Vietnam War. Faculty responses to statements made on the topical issues allowed political scales of liberalism and conservatism to be created. Like studies on voter behavior and liberal/conservative viewpoint, faculty liberal/conservative scales were looked at with respect to place of work, publication output, salary, age, and family background. They revealed that liberals were concentrated in the elite institutions. Liberals earned more and published more frequently in prestigious journals.

A second set of studies using the same databases took the sociodemographic data and linked them with the same outcome variables—place of work, salary, and publications, all of which highly intercorrelate. Religion raised—not necessarily current faith—correlated with these outcomes. Out of proportion to their numbers in the U.S. population, faculty brought up in Jewish homes worked at the elite universities (not colleges), earned more, and published more. Those raised as Catholics fell at the other end of the scales.

The data analyses in these studies are statistically quite simple. They report percentages of faculty in different categories. Seldom are there correlations and regressions for predicting and accounting for the variance. Their mode of inquiry does not, or at least did not at the time (1960s and early 1970s), use these statistical techniques. We know now that their variables are weak predictors.

Of relevant theoretical interest is the persistent employment of these sociodemographic, and single-personal-characteristic, variables in the national surveys. NSOPF88 had them. The 1990 UCLA Higher Education Research Institute survey had them. They were being asked again by NCES in 1993. Such inquiries do, like census data, make possible the comparison over time of shifts in the academic population. However, they only occasionally inform us on faculty self-knowledge and social knowledge, the variables that most strongly predict faculty behavior. The political science and sociodemographic theorists provide some scintillating information fixed in time on a group of people they feel are worth knowing about. They do not tell us why faculty behave as they do.

### Extrinsic and Intrinsic Motivation—Economics and Psychology

Extrinsic-motivation theorists (economists, in this case) believe that people are "rational" (their term). People always act to maximize rewards. Rewards come in many forms, but dollars are pervasive. Whether it is a promotion, a public recognition of good work, or extra resources, faculty will do what the organization wants when they believe their behaviors will be rewarded. Extrinsic factors are the motivators. Faculty may claim they are doing research because that is what interests them most; in reality they are conducting experiments and publishing because the rewards are higher in this role than they are in teaching. So economists claim. (See Tuckman [1976] and the studies cited in chapters 2 and 4.)

Intrinsic-motivation theorists (psychologists) say behavior follows from internal drives and interests and responds only minimally to external rewards. Faculty may compete for prizes, but if they enjoy the activity, their enthusiasm/motivation persists even if they do not win. Offering faculty more money to give more attention to an activity holding a lesser value for them does not change their behavior. They continue to spend their time on what they want to do. They fulfill their obligations, certainly, but when time allocations are theirs to make, internal motivations predict what they will do. McKeachie (1979b) and Staw (1983), from somewhat different principles, argue that rewarding faculty for improving their teaching becomes dysfunctional. Furthermore, organizationally it is impractical; no one can manage it.

Existing evidence fails to settle the ongoing debate. That faculty continue to publish after being promoted to full professor no more proves the intrinsic-motivation theory than the positive correlation between publications and salary proves that extrinsic motivation determines faculty activities. The aging professor may be continuing to publish in the hope of securing higher-than-average raises, and professors who do not change their behavior when offered rewards to do so may balk not because of an internal drive to do what they have been doing but rather for fear that they will fail at the new task. Settling the intrinsic/extrinsic debate requires a sophisticated set of experiments, ones never likely to be launched. Neither theory alone can adequately account for faculty behavior. One again suspects that there are interactions involved, and that faculty call on one or the other reward system depending on factors and circumstances neither theory alone adequately takes into account.

### Biological/Genetic Theories—Sociobiology

Sociobiology (biological determinism) offers intriguing explanations for observed academic sex differences in Western European and American societies. By way of illustration, Hudson and Jacot (1991) use marriage patterns of academic humanists and scientists and the mathematical performance differences between the sexes as evidence for a biological foundation. Men and women not only have different biological genitalia; their brains are biologically different.[5]

It is the raising of girls and boys that explains why men think as they do, and differently from the way women think.[6] Hudson and Jacot argue for what they call the "male wound," the psychological separation of the boy from his mother in early childhood. Once experienced, "the wound generates needs and tensions in the male mind for which there is no direct female equivalent" (p. viii). Their account then becomes more psychological (and cultural). Depending upon the kind and degree of successful separation from the mother, men function somewhat differently. In general, men treat human beings as inanimate objects to be studied and assign human behaviors to inanimate objects. In addition, the male wound creates an extraordinary drive in men—just the kind needed for success in the sciences, but one that also leads to frightening forms of violence rarely witnessed in women.

At this stage biological determinism, even when accompanied by psychological and cultural explanations, raises more questions than it answers, and understandably so. Despite its inability to predict, one needs to entertain its possibilities rather than dismiss it outright and endorse the belief that all sex differences stem from cultural and societal practices. If there are basic biological sex differences directly linked to aptitudes and abilities, one must recognize and deal with them.

We now turn to two noncognitive motivation theories that we presented in chapter 1, namely, socialization and life course.

### Socialization Theory

As Blau (1973, pp. 249–280) elaborates in his closing chapter, "differentiation" is a basic construct in sociological theory. On the basis of both human resources (student and faculty intellectual talents) and material resources (money and equipment), U.S. higher education displays a highly stratified set of colleges and universities. Carnegie named what already existed. At the gross organizational level, our and others' findings on differential research output as a function of institutional type support Blau's sociological assertions.

Within the differentiation construct is what sociologists term "socialization." New members are taught what to do and how to behave. After the norms are inculcated, the compliance process essentially acts automatically and sometimes unconsciously on individuals. In the same way that families and organized religious bodies transmit accepted values and behaviors to children, so are graduate schools—one of our career variables—predicated to socialize their Ph.D. recipients with attitudes regarding such matters as faculty governance, academic freedom, and the habits of what it takes to be successful on the job, namely, conducting and publishing research. Socialization theory has these values lasting indefinitely. New professors carry them into the new setting, irrespective of where it is. More socialization from the discipline and from senior professors takes place on the job.

Socialization theory receives weaker support at the level of the individual faculty member. Graduate school effects weaken and most often disappear when self-knowledge and social knowledge variables come into play. We suspect, but did not test, that new socialization takes place on the job as the actual faculty career commences.[7] Just as different religious denominations instill different values, so do different universities socialize their doctoral students selectively for the academic career. In the case of graduates of Res-I universities, the vast majority find themselves in another stratum of the system, either by choice or because they were not able to secure an appointment in a Res-I institution. Norms and expectations differ across the strata. Teaching or committee work may be more highly valued at one level or the other. New faculty must adjust their values and behaviors if they are to succeed. New socialization, or resocialization, takes place.

We also suspect, but did not test, that resocializations occur along the career path as the faculty member moves through the ranks and accumulates experiences that reshape/resocialize the original and previously revised values and behaviors. For example, obligations to one's department and the academic discipline may take on greater importance, and former activities less, as colleagues implicitly champion the new obligations. In addition, new structures and practices require changes in behavior.

What we suggest, then, is that socialization is a recurring, if not continuous, phenomenon. The further one travels along the career path, the weaker the original effects become (unless, perhaps, one stays in the same institutional type). Socialization theory has been expanded to include such considerations into its conceptual framework. However, it still does not include the cognitive motivation processes. We witnessed some of its shortcomings in chapter 2 on hypotheses advanced to explain a relationship between age and productivity.

### Life Course

We gave the life-course theoretical perspective extended treatment in chapter 2 when we examined age and productivity research outcomes. The theory's strength lies in its taking into consideration both psychological and sociological factors. At the same time, it requires a determined pattern of change dependent only upon age. One passes through an inevitable sequence of plateaus and crises, events anchored to age. No one escapes them, a claim that raises the eyebrows of everyone who studies this and related phenomena.

Blackburn and Havighurst's (1979) data from retired social science faculty on events that significantly affected their careers showed that such events bore but a minor relationship to steps on the life cycle. These highly successful academics identified an unexpected honor, a sabbatical leave, the favorable reception of an article or book, the death of a spouse, or the move to a different university as their principal career determinants. Their careers were altered by what happened, not by when it happened. Critical events, not a life stage, led to new pursuits, to early departure, or to prolonged scholarly activity.

There may be inevitable life-course stages between birth and death, but the pattern appears anything but universal. This theory takes into account interactions between the individual and the environment but has no way to incorporate the immense diversity in both individuals and their worlds.

### Needed Extensions to Our Framework

As we noted in chapter 1, prior research on academics fell principally into one of two categories: organizational/contextual or personal. That is, researchers tested faculty behavior either (1) to establish the degree to which organizational variables such as resources, rewards, structures, climate, and the like correlated with faculty productivity, or else (2) to establish the degree to which personal attributes such as age, sex/gender, race/ethnicity, interests, satisfactions, and the like served as the predictors of scholarly output. In the main, neither avenue took into account interactions between the environment and the individual. Both failed to consider how individual behaviors change organizations and how an individual's perceptions of the work environment rationally affect behavior. Blau (1973) demonstrates the consequences of resources—human, material, institutional—and how they lead to differentiation across institutions, departments, and subunits. However, his purely sociological approach cannot explain the wide array of behavior exhibited by faculty within the same setting. At the same time, a purely intrinsic interest in an activity—say, McKeachie's (1979b) psychological approach—is difficult to demonstrate, because one is unable to obtain both pre- and post-test measures of intrinsic motivation.

We designed our framework to overcome the major shortcomings we saw in the research on faculty up to this point. Consequently, we included variables related to cognitive rationality. Still, our framework is a framework. It is not a theory.

Were our framework a theory in the strictest sense of the word, we would proceed as Blau did in his analysis of his and the Parsons and Platt (1968) survey data. In his concluding chapter he deduced consequences from status differentiation—essentially a noncognitive motivational theory—and placed them up against his findings. Theory and results were not always in accord.

What we have demonstrated is that the strongest predictors of faculty products include self-judged competence, preferred effort to give to a role, and perceived institutional expectation of effort given to the role. The first two are personal self-assessments (self-knowledge); the last is an environmental perception (social knowledge). The findings strongly suggest that it is the interaction between the two that determines faculty behavior. Faculty behavior is a dynamic process, not a static set of conditions. Of the motivation theories examined in chapter 1, our findings are most in accord with the cognitive ones, especially with efficacy and information processing.

## Next Steps

The framework, of course, is not perfect. Here we comment on how we would conduct a future survey. In addition to what we have in our instrument, we would collect pertinent data on the three cells that were essentially vacant, namely, environmental conditions, environmental response, and social contingencies.

Environmental conditions might more easily and reliably be collected from the institutions where the surveyed faculty work. NCES's NSOPF-88 did that, even though the data have not been used in conjunction with faculty behaviors. That survey had an 88 percent response rate from the colleges and universities in its sample. Its procedure adds nothing to the faculty instrument because the two instruments cannot be linked, a not unimportant consideration.

Environmental response information will continue to be difficult to obtain in large data sets. As we noted earlier, there are problems of delays between a faculty accomplishment and an institutional reward. It will also be difficult to link the one to the other because prizes and major awards most often recognize a history of accomplishments, not a single contribution. There are also many fewer visible recognitions an institution can bestow on young scholars who have made important contributions to their discipline and institution. For example, the institution cannot make an appointment to an honorific body.

Social contingencies can be added to surveys.[8] These include the faculty member's health, extent of obligations to significant others (spouse, children, parents), financial strains, pregnancy—the host of real-life factors that alter an emotional state and make demands on time that might have been given to the faculty role. Contingencies can be expected to affect behavior and product.

Turning to the variables within our self-knowledge and social knowledge categories, published faculty studies and our own continuing interviews with faculty about their work and their perceptions of their work environment suggest that other important dimensions relate to faculty productivity. In the self-knowledge domain, one is the faculty member's intentions, her or his career goals, both short term and long range. Another is the depth of commitment the individual has to the career. Still another is what constitutes success for the individual.[9] There is also some evidence that such personal characteristics as self-esteem, body cathexis, and self-confidence mitigate stress that detracts from productivity. (See, e.g., Blackburn, Horowitz, Edington, & Klos, 1987.) We would add information on these personal traits.

As for social knowledge, we would extend the work environment from the campus to include the home. For example, social support has also been shown to reduce dysfunctional stress. We would add items to assess the degree to which a faculty member believes he or she has social support. Our social contingency information does this in part. We also want to find ways to corroborate faculty perceptions of the environment with the actual conditions. While faculty will first respond to their perceptions, knowing the reality can suggest ways institutions might create conditions more conducive to productive work.

We do not extend our approach to other professionals working in organizations, such as physicians in hospitals, lawyers in firms, economists in large corporations or in government agencies, scientists in industry—all achievement-laden environments. At the same time, were the appropriate idiosyncratic individual and environmental characteristics factored in, our adapted framework might prove fruitful for better understanding why other professionals at work in their organizations do as they do.

Having indicated some ways in which we would amend our framework, we remain stymied when it comes to testing it. Said another way, our problems rest more with the data available than with conceptualizations and the underlying theoretical constructs. If we are right, even if only approximately, the consequences of behaviors and products for the individual and the organization lead to new behaviors and products. There are also consequences for the individual's perceptions of herself or himself and of the environment. That is, there is an ongoing cycle of interactions and altered cognitions, values, beliefs, preferences, and behaviors.

Since survey data provide a snapshot in time—an instantaneously developed photograph, not a movie—we cannot infer what will happen next. As we noted, our abbreviated attempt to test environmental response fell short. We explained why, but adding more items to a survey instrument will most likely not help. We need to be able to monitor faculty on some regular basis over an extended period of time. We need a longitudinal study.

Without speculating on the time intervals between data collections, the sample size, the number of institutions and types, the choice of disciplines and professional schools and colleges—the entire array of decisions that must be made in order to be able to generalize—the temptation to select cohorts, perhaps by career age, must be set aside. Those at work already have a past we cannot fully recover. We need to begin the longitudinal study with graduate students, probably beginning doctoral candidates (some of whom will select an academic career while others will not, or will change their minds).

Even this most ambitious agenda has its limitations. The environment changes in unpredictable ways. A cohort starting doctoral programs 10 years after our proposed 40-year study will most assuredly have a different set of experiences. Witness the differences between those earning their Ph.D.'s in the late 1960s, the influential faculty of today who created radical criticism as a rebuke to authority, and those graduates of the early 1980s who exhibit a much more corporate view of the university. Still, the first study would illuminate much, and would make a second (and others) appreciably easier and better.

We urge the launching of a longitudinal study.

# EPILOGUE

Our book has not been a defense of U.S. higher education and its faculty. However, now that we have fulfilled our purposes, we find it obligatory to comment, in the light of what we learned about faculty at work, on the highly publicized critics—those who see in higher education a complete abandonment of standards, a fatal capitulation to multiculturalism, a fiscal rape of parents and the public treasury, a suicidal rejection of the roots of Western civilization, the indoctrination of a single point of view (political correctness), and more. These disasters are said to be the consequence of inept and weak administrators and radicalized, entrepreneurial faculty who do not earn their inflated salaries. We therefore turn to this acerbic prose and see how it accords with what we know about academia and academics.

The current critics[1] are not the first to hurl bricks at faculty and higher education. When a flurry of critical attacks on faculty joined students' blasts on the curriculum and on the quality of pedagogy in the late 1960s, one of us examined the historical record for the foundation of these allegations (Blackburn, 1970). The following quickly surfaced.

As associate editor of *Harper's* in 1970, John Fischer wrote:

What [today's students] want is . . . what used to be called a "liberal education". As recently as twenty years ago they might have found it in most good American universities. Today their chances are close to zero.

As we searched backwards in time, to the late 1940s, we found complaints about liberal arts education that were the same as Fischer's. This seemed reason enough to retreat a few more decades. There the record repeated itself again. Back even further, a 1912 copy of the *Nation* had this statement:

Probably nearly everyone will admit that the spot where our educational institutions have suffered most deterioration from loss of [outstanding teachers] is at the heart of them—in the colleges of liberal arts. . . . Vast classes of 500 to 1,000 are vaguely lectured at wholesale, or cut up into small sections and turned over to a battalion of teething assistants and instructors, who are not infrequently far below the level of the average high school teacher [in effectiveness] and in general intelligence.[2] Between the graduate school above, with its emphasis on investigation, and the "slave-labor" below . . . the high calling of the teacher is belittled.

291

A different author in the same magazine in 1909 declared:

> The mass of students in the major part of their college course come in
> contact only with callow, inexperienced, and (often through sheer excess of
> zeal) inefficient teachers. The leading professors are, in the main, accessible
> only to the few who have had perseverance to continue . . . for several years;
> or if the younger students ever see the head professor at all, the distinguished
> man merely harangues or lectures.

The year 1900 yields this:

> It is at least a curious coincidence that the development of the modern
> science of pedagogy, with its array of physiological and psychological data,
> should have been accompanied by a distinct decline in the prominence of
> the teacher. No one, we suppose, will question that the number of great
> teachers is decidedly less now than it once was, and the depleted ranks are
> not being adequately filled up. . . . Perhaps in no single respect, indeed,
> does the average college of the present day contrast more sharply with the
> college of a generation or two ago.

With this injunctive we stopped.[3] It appears we have uncovered a rare
verity: an unchanging fashion. Like complaints about institutional food,
trenchant prose on pedagogy seems to be the penchant of the savant.

What is new about the current set of ambushers? In some respects, not
much. Their methods remain unchanged. They target isolated instances of
extreme divergence from the norms, next either ridicule them or erro-
neously report them (or both) and fail to supply acceptable supporting
evidence, and then repeat them—what Byrne (1993) refers to as the "Snark
Syndrome" (repeat anything three times, and it becomes true).[4] Having
assumed that everyone agrees that their claims are true, the critics quickly
supply the reasons for their political position. And, of course, they generalize their selected atypical examples to be true—if not everywhere, then
almost everywhere. Or as Michael Bérubé writes:

> Journalists, disgruntled professors, embittered ex–graduate students, and
> their families and friends now feel entitled to say anything about the acade-
> my without fear of contradiction by general readers. The field is wide open,
> and there's no penalty for charlatanism (quite the contrary), since few gener-
> al readers are informed enough to spot even the grossest form of misrepre-
> sentation and fraud. (Cited in Edmundson, 1993, p. 6)

In other respects, the current attacks are different from the old ones in
some important ways. Whereas the earlier critics came more from within
the academy, or were at least associated with highbrow publications and the
nation's intellectuals, the current critics, and often their presses as well, are

from the right, even the far right. They are on the lecture circuit.[5] Their books sell. (Even a university press has printed one of them.) They are getting away with a grand hoax and, as they say, laughing all the way to the bank.

Supposedly they too will pass. Smears, however, have wider and longer-lasting effects than do successful demonstrations of their falsehood. People seem inclined to believe one guilty until proven innocent. Sensationalism penetrates more deeply than calm truth.

So it is with our muckrakers. While several of the current set hold, at best, weak credentials for asserting their claims, the structure of U.S. higher education prevents any respected spokesperson from rebutting them. In addition, a wise person knows the futility of even trying. That person's book not only would not sell; it would become new fodder for the mudslingers. The few who have tried to respond to these critics—for example, two collections of essays, one edited by Edmundson (1993) and the other by Gless and Smith (1992)—have sold little in comparison with D'Souza's *Illiberal Education* (1991). They are to be thanked for their effort. Their effect, however, has to be minimal. Even when Ernest Boyer (1990), a most respected national figure, writes on a new view of scholarship and argues for greater emphasis on pedagogy, not only does he not receive strong endorsement from within the academy; probably only a few even read his book.

We do not engage here in a counterattack, a losing game. Rather, we present some matters for reflection.

What can be said of the quality of faculty work today?[6]

With respect to the teaching role, no nationwide indicator exists for assessing how good faculty are in that role. However, reported studies of student ratings show scores well above "average." For example, we have seen that research university faculty judge their effectiveness lower than faculty in other institutions do. In addition, these faculty enjoy the reputation of being the worst teachers. Yet at the University of Michigan, the mean student rating of faculty teaching is above 4 (excellent) on a five-point scale (McKeachie, 1979a). Curricular revision is widespread across the country, with special attention given to pedagogy. Experimentation with computer-aided instruction expands yearly. More colleges and universities claim they are giving increased weight to faculty teaching when they make tenure, promotion, and merit pay decisions (Edgerton, 1993).

With respect to engagement in research, the critics' claim that faculty write nothing but trash and trivia is far from its mark. Many journals are indeed highly specialized. They consequently are inaccessible to the average reader, even to scholars in related fields. The so-called fragmentation of knowledge, however, is a consequence of the explosion of knowledge and its division into smaller units. Between 1978 and 1988, 29,000 new scholarly journals were founded to accommodate the transmission of new knowledge and make it publicly available to everyone—even to business and industry, at no cost to them. The proliferation of publications is not simply faculty playing pad-the-curriculum-vitae game.

Journal rejection rates of submitted papers are one indicator of the high and rising quality of faculty research. The strongest and most highly regarded journals in the social sciences publish, on average, only 15 percent of the manuscripts they receive. Today's methodologies are more sophisticated, analytical procedures more powerful, and databases appreciably larger. Interactions among colleagues across the country and across the world are now a daily event. While no study exists to verify our belief, we think journals today would accept less than 10 percent of the articles published 25 years ago. Moreover, we suspect that most would not even be submitted for consideration today, or if they were, they would not be sent out for review. American research universities are the envy of the world, with scholars from every nation flocking to them. No other segment of the U.S. economy has a foreign trade balance that approaches that of higher education.

With respect to matters above and beyond the traditional roles of teaching and research, the critics frequently charge faculty with a lack of loyalty and dedication to their college or university. Faculty look out only for themselves. They take, but they do not give back in return. Their students are a burden, a distraction from the tasks that matter most to them. Personal career advancement is all they care about. Increased interactions with faculty elsewhere could be taken as proof of these charges.

It seems to us, however, that fallacious inferences have been drawn. Loyalty to a scholarly professional body does not mean disloyalty, or even less loyalty, to one's unit and institution. Our ambassador to the United Nations has not shed or lessened her or his loyalty to the United States. Rather, the individual has simply expanded her or his concerns to embrace a larger corpus of people.

Faculty care very much about the academic reputation of their place of work. They know that their own local and national status depends upon how others judge the quality of their department and institution. They can be almost cruel with colleagues who, by eliciting student criticism of their teaching or failing to make scholarly contributions, are not holding up their end of the enterprise.

Faculty display their loyalty in other ways as well. At home they verbally chastise their administrators for stupid decisions and failures to correct obvious absurdities. However, once they leave campus, they proudly declare their institutional loyalty. Their jogging pants and sweats display the institution's seal and logo. They boast about the good things at home—the placement of their students, the new faculty member they enticed away from a first-rate place, the computer facilities they have available.

We have seen the long hours they put in every week. That is not their complaint, however. What bothers them the most is that they do not have enough time to accomplish all that is on their agenda. They cherish the flexibility they have in how they allocate their efforts. They are hooked on ideas. They know that not many people can get paid for doing what they like best. They like ideas and books and the arts, and these are available to them. When asked would they become a professor again were the opportunity offered, they overwhelmingly say yes. Indeed, it is a good life.

Louis Menand (1991), of the English faculty at Queens College and the Graduate Center of the City University of New York, gives a more balanced view of the "debate" between the critics and the defenders. We close with his words:

> The contention that the current problems in the academy are the natural outcome of the Sixties radicalism is common to many of the recent attacks on higher education—it can be found in Bloom's, Kimball's, and D'Souza's books. . . . I think the claim is basically false, and that . . . the humorless ethos of the politically correct humanities department could not be more antithetical to the spirit of the 1960s. Even the most callow radicalism of that era has nothing to do with the sort of doctrinaire political attitudes critics of the contemporary academy complain about. Are the people who are so eager to censor "fighting words" on campus today the same people who went around in 1968 calling anyone wearing a uniform or necktie a "pig"? If they are the same people, they have left their radicalism behind.
>
> There is one thing, however, that the present situation does owe to the 1960s, and that is the belief that the university is a miniature reproduction of the society as a whole. That idea dominates, for example, the Port Huron Statement . . . endorsed by the Students for a Democratic Society in 1962. But it is not only a leftist idea; for the postwar university has always been eager to incorporate every new intellectual and cultural development that has come its way.
>
> The university is, in fact, expressly designed to do this: It can accommodate almost any interest by creating a new course, a new program, a new studies center. It has managed, for instance, to institutionalize activities like painting and creative writing, not traditionally thought to require academic preparation, by devising M.F.A. programs—which, in turn, provide a place

on university faculties for practicing painters and writers. When new scholarly movements emerged—Third World Studies, Women' Studies—the university was quick to establish research centers and institutes to house [them]. Degrees are now offered in almost everything. There are few intellectual activities left that do not have an academic incarnation. (P. 54)

No wonder many are envious of college and university professors. They simultaneously are always at work—and never at work.

# Appendix A

# THE CARNEGIE CLASSIFICATION SYSTEM

The 1987 Carnegie classification includes all colleges and universities in the United States listed in the 1985–86 *Higher Education General Information Survey of Institutional Characteristics*. It groups institutions into categories on the basis of the level of degree offered—ranging from prebaccalaureate to the doctorate—and the comprehensiveness of their missions. The categories are as follows:

*Research Universities I:* These institutions offer a full range of baccalaureate programs, are committed to graduate education through the doctorate degree, and give high priority to research. They receive annually at least $33.5 million in federal support[1] and award at least 50 Ph.D. degrees each year.[2]

*Research Universities II:* These institutions offer a full range of baccalaureate programs, are committed to graduate education through the doctorate degree, and give high priority to research. They receive annually between $12.5 million and $33.5 million in federal support for research and development[1] and award at least 50 Ph.D. degrees each year.[2]

*Doctorate-Granting Universities I:* In addition to offering a full range of baccalaureate programs, the mission of these institutions includes a commitment to graduate education through the doctorate degree. They award at least 40 Ph.D. degrees annually in five or more academic disciplines.[2]

*Doctorate-Granting Universities II:* In addition to offering a full range of baccalaureate programs, the mission of these institutions includes a commitment to graduate education through the doctorate degree. They award annually 20 or more Ph.D. degrees in at least one discipline or 10 or more Ph.D. degrees in three or more disciplines.[2]

*Comprehensive Universities and Colleges I:* These institutions offer baccalaureate programs and, with few exceptions, graduate education through the masters degree. More than half of their baccalaureate degrees are awarded in two or more occupational or professional disciplines such as engineering or business administration.[3] All of the institutions in this group enroll at least 2,500 students.[4]

*Comprehensive Universities and Colleges II:* These institutions award more than half of their baccalaureate degrees in two or more occupational or profes-

Reprinted from the 1987 edition of *A Classification of Institutions of Higher Education* (Princeton, N.J.: Carnegie Foundation for the Advancement of Teaching), pp. 7–8.

sional disciplines, such as engineering or business administration, and many also offer graduate education through the masters degree.[3] All of the colleges and universities in this group enroll between 1,500 and 2,500 students.[4]

*Liberal Arts Colleges I:* These highly selective institutions[5] are primarily undergraduate colleges that award more than half of their baccalaureate degrees in arts and science fields.[3]

*Liberal Arts Colleges II:* These institutions are primarily undergraduate colleges that are less selective[5] and award more than half of their degrees in liberal arts fields.[3] This category also includes a group of colleges . . . that award *less* than half of their degrees in liberal arts fields but, with fewer than 1,500 students, are too small to be considered comprehensive.

*Two-Year Community, Junior, and Technical Colleges:* These institutions offer certificate or degree programs through the Associate of Arts level and, with few exceptions, offer no baccalaureate degrees.

*Professional Schools and Other Specialized Institutions:* These institutions offer degrees ranging from the bachelor's to the doctorate. At least 50 percent of the degrees awarded by these institutions[2] are in a single specialized field. Specialized institutions include:

> *Theological seminaries, Bible colleges, and other institutions offering degrees in religion:* This category includes institutions at which the primary purpose is to offer religious instruction or train members of the clergy.
>
> *Medical schools and medical centers:* These institutions award most of their professional degrees in medicine. In some instances, their programs include other health professional schools, such as dentistry, pharmacy, or nursing.[6]
>
> *Other separate health profession schools:* Institutions in this category award most of their degrees in such fields as chiropractory, pharmacy, or podiatry.
>
> *Schools of law:* The schools included in this category award most of their degrees in law. The list includes only institutions that are listed as separate campuses in the *Higher Education General Information Survey.*
>
> *Schools of engineering and technology:* The institutions in this category award at least a bachelor's degree in programs limited almost exclusively to technical fields of study.
>
> *Schools of business and management:* The schools in this category award most of their bachelor's or graduate degrees in business or business-related programs.
>
> *Schools of art, music, and design:* Institutions in this category award most of their bachelor's or graduate degrees in art, music, design, architecture or some combination of such fields.
>
> *Teachers colleges:* Institutions in this category award most of their bachelor's or graduate degrees in education or education-related fields.

*Other specialized institutions:* Institutions in this category include graduate centers, maritime academies, military institutes without liberal arts programs, and institutions that do not fit any other classification category.

*Corporate sponsored institutions:* These institutions are accredited, degree-granting colleges and universities established by profit-making corporations.[7]

## Notes on Definitions

1. The years used in calculating average federal support were 1983, 1984, and 1985.

2. The academic year for determining the number of degrees awarded by institutions was 1983–84.

3. The *Liberal Arts* disciplines include area studies, biological science, the fine arts, foreign languages, letters, mathematics, physical sciences, psychology, the social sciences, and interdisciplinary studies. *Occupational/pre-professional* disciplines include agriculture, the natural sciences, architecture and environmental design, business and management, communications, computer and information science, education, engineering, the health professions, home economics, law, library science, public affairs, and theology.

4. The years used for calculating average student enrollment were 1982, 1983, and 1984.

5. An index developed by Alexander W. Astin at the University of California at Los Angeles is used to determine the selectivity of liberal arts colleges.

6. This category lists only institutions that appear in the *Higher Education General Information Survey* as separate campuses. Those seeking a complete listing of accredited professional schools should consult publications of the separate professional associations such as the annual report on medical education published by the American Medical Association.

7. Our list of corporate colleges and universities is taken from Eurich, Nell P., *Corporate Classrooms: The Learning Business* (Princeton, N.J.: The Carnegie Foundation for the Advancement of Teaching, 1985). Since that report was published some of the institutions it included have become independent or part of other institutions.

# Appendix B

# VARIABLES USED IN THE REGRESSION ANALYSES: TABLE 4.6

Sociodemographic

*Sex* was coded 0 = male and 1 = female.

*Race* was coded as dummy variables: DBlack where 1 = black and 0 = all others; DAsian where 1 = Asian and 0 = all others; and DOther where 1 = not black, white, or Asian and 0 = all others.

*Age* was chronological age as of 1987.

Career

The eight disciplines were coded as dummy variables, with biology as the constant.

### Research I

*Active publisher/grantsperson:* This is a two-item factorially derived measure including total publications prior to 1985 (.750) and number of grant proposals submitted prior to 1985 (.546). (Eigenvalue = 1.29.)

*Educational preparation:* This two-item factor includes the highest degree earned (.666) and the type of graduate institution attended, i.e., research university or other (.704). (Eigenvalue = 1.08.)

### Comprehensive I

*Active publisher/grantsperson:* This is a three-item factorially derived measure including total publications prior to 1985 (.737), number of grant proposals submitted prior to 1985 (.548), and number of books published prior to 1985 (.673). (Eigenvalue = 1.50.)

### Doctoral I

*Active publisher/grantsperson:* This is a three-item factor including total publications prior to 1985 (.794), number of grant proposals submitted prior to 1985 (.696), and number of books published prior to 1985 (.505). (Eigenvalue = 1.53.)

*Established faculty member:* This is a three-item factor consisting of career

300

age (years since highest degree awarded) (.878), tenure status prior to 1985 (.828), and current academic rank (.723). (Eigenvalue = 2.47.)

## Self-Knowledge

### Research I

*Committed to teaching:* This measure includes the following items: personal interest in teaching (.850), high commitment to teaching (.690), high commitment to research (−.667), personal preference for time spent on teaching (.817), and personal preference for time spent on research (−.733). (Eigenvalue = 4.22.)

*Values discipline-focused teaching:* This factor is composed of assumptions about the teacher's role in the teaching-learning process: transmitting facts and principles (.725), demonstrating an intellectual/artistic/scientific process (.698), enhancing students' abilities to reason and communicate (.525), and assisting students who demonstrate an interest in learning (.586). (Eigenvalue = 1.41.)

*Values cooperation/institutional commitment:* This two-item factor consists of self-ratings indicating the value one places on being a "team player" (.750) and one's devotion to the employing institution (.780). (Eigenvalue = 1.21.)

*Values scholarship:* This variable is a single-item measure of personal preference for giving time to activities that enhance one's knowledge or skill in ways that may not result in publication (−.925). (Eigenvalue = 1.05.)

*Competent researcher:* This factor includes self-evaluations in three areas: keeping abreast of developments in the discipline (.540), obtaining grants (.809), and publishing (.744). (Eigenvalue = 1.66.)

### Doctoral I

*Committed to teaching:* This measure includes the following items: personal interest in teaching (.889), high commitment to teaching (.593), high commitment to research (−.789), personal preference for time spent on teaching (.848), and personal preference for time spent on research (−.854). (Eigenvalue = 4.09.)

*Responsible faculty member:* This four-item factor consists of self-appraisals indicating the extent to which the individual is organized (.551), works well with students (.527), responds to requests (.799), and knows how to "work the system" (.555). (Eigenvalue = 1.58.)

### Comprehensive I

*Committed to teaching:* This measure includes the following items: personal interest in teaching (.881), commitment to research (−.829), personal preference for time spent on teaching (.716), and personal preference for time spent on research (−.874). (Eigenvalue = 4.03.)

*Values discipline-focused teaching:* This two-item factor consists of assumptions about the teacher's role in the teaching-learning process: transmitting facts and principles (.771) and demonstrating an intellectual/artistic/scientific process (.653). (Eigenvalue = 1.27.)

*Competent researcher:* This three-item factor consists of self-appraisals in three areas: keeping abreast of developments in the discipline (.571), obtaining grants (.765), and publishing (.822). (Eigenvalue = 1.50.)

Environmental Responses

*Research I*

No factors entered the regression.

*Doctoral I*

*Journal editorial work:* This two-item factor indicates how often the faculty member reviews articles for a professional journal (.803) and serves on the editorial board of a journal (.826). (Eigenvalue = 1.52.)

*Comprehensive I*

*Journal editorial work:* This two-item factor also consists of levels of involvement in reviewing articles (.838) and editorial work (.835). (Eigenvalue = 1.38.)

Social Knowledge

*Research I*

*Credible colleagues:* This measure emerged from a factor analysis of a question about how much credence respondents gave to several forms of performance feedback. The scores ranged from 1 (never received) to 5 (great deal of credence). The two variables that loaded were your colleagues' evaluation of your teaching (.826) and your colleagues' comments on your scholarly work (.662). (Eigenvalue = 1.17.)

*Doctoral I*

*Faculty committed to teaching:* This is a two-item factor created from respondents' assessments of their faculty colleagues' commitment to teaching their discipline rather than adding to their discipline's knowledge base (.876) and their commitment to teaching rather than research in their disciplinary domain (.869). (Eigenvalue = 2.25.)

*Students are motivated:* This five-item factor includes respondents' perceptions of undergraduate students, specifically the extent to which they think for themselves (.704), share ideas and work cooperatively (.610), learn only what is required (−.668), lack interest in the subject matter (−.678), and work on their own (.736). (Eigenvalue = 3.17.)

*Teacher control needed:* This three-item factor consists of respondents' assumptions that undergraduates learn best when course content is determined cooperatively by students and the teacher ( −.589), course content is determined by the teacher (.859), and pace is set for the group by the teacher (.827). (Eigenvalue = 2.26.)

*Course relevance important:* This two-item factor is also extracted from the survey question about faculty perceptions of undergraduates and represents the expectation that they learn best when course content is perceived to have immediate relevance to students' lives (.780) and course content is determined cooperatively by students and the teacher (.524). (Eigenvalue = 1.54.)

*Credibility of alumni:* This single-item factor measures credence of feedback from alumni about faculty members' impact on them as students (.681). (Eigenvalue = 1.17.)

*Students are competitive:* This factor is the expectation that students seek to outperform one another (.810). (Eigenvalue = 1.01.)

*Well-rounded teacher valued:* This 18-item measure emerged from factor analysis of a question that asked respondents to indicate the skills, beliefs/values, and personality traits they believed characterized the valued faculty member on their campus. The scores ranged from 1 (not at all characteristic) to 4 (highly characteristic). The following characteristics loaded on this factor: teaches effectively (.565), communicates well (.616), is organized (.527), works skillfully with students (.674), responds to requests (.679), is an excellent lecturer (.567), is highly committed to teaching (.690), is concerned about students (.742), holds high standards (.585), has integrity (.764), respects others (.859), is dedicated to the liberal arts (.643), is supportive (.830), is understanding (.861), is open (.879), is candid (.799), has a sense of humor (.784), and is personable (.654). (Eigenvalue = 11.9.)

*Ambition/dedication valued:* This five-item measure emerged from the same question about the institutionally valued faculty member. It consists of several disposition and belief characteristics: believes in the virtue of hard work (.588), is dedicated (.597), is ambitious (.717), is competitive (.713), and is perseverant (.763). (Eigenvalue = 4.80.)

*Salary equity:* This two-item factor is derived from faculty perceptions of how fair their salaries are in comparison with those of peers in their institution (.787) and how their salaries compare with those of peers at other institutions (.787). (Eigenvalue = 1.34.)

*Institution values scholarship:* This factor indicates what percentage of their total work effort faculty thought their colleges or universities wanted them to give to scholarship (e.g., self-enhancement but not publication) (.865). (Eigenvalue = 1.14.)

Behavior

*Research I*

*Grant preparation:* This two-term factor includes the number of external grant proposals submitted within the last two years (1985–1987) (.763) and the number of research proposals submitted to a government or private agency within the last two years (.817). (Eigenvalue = 2.08.)

*High research effort:* This factor consists of two items: percentage of time given to research (.675) and to teaching during the current term (.831). The possible responses ranged from 0 percent to 100 percent. (Eigenvalue = 1.38.)

*Communicates/works hard:* This three-variable factor includes two items that assess the number of times during the last year the respondent conversed informally about research with colleagues at professional meetings (.541) or on the telephone (.535). The responses ranged from 1 (never) to 5 (more than 10 times). The third variable indicated whether the previous estimation was more time than five years ago, the same, or less (−.653). (Eigenvalue = 1.09.)

*Applying for fellowship:* This variable indicates the number of fellowship applications submitted within the last two years (1985–1987) (.698). (Eigenvalue = 1.09.)

### Doctoral I

*High research involvement:* This six-item factor includes the number of times during the last year the respondent conversed informally about research with colleagues on the telephone (.588), submitted articles for publication in an academic or professional journal (.626), submitted research proposals to a government or private agency (.715), or submitted external grant proposals within the last two years (1985–1987) (.649). Percentage of time given to research (.769) and to teaching (−.697) during the current term also loaded on this factor. The possible responses ranged from 0 percent to 100 percent. (Eigenvalue = 3.45.)

*Dissertation work:* This four-item factor indicates, for the current and past year, the number of dissertation committees served on and chaired (.777, .723) and the number of comprehensive examinations/orals committees served on and chaired (.731, .736). (Eigenvalue = 2.25.)

# Appendix C

# VARIABLES USED IN THE REGRESSION ANALYSES: TABLE 4.13

Sociodemographic

*Gender*

Career

*Career age:* Total number of years as a faculty member
*Highest degree received:* Bachelor's, master's, Ed.D., D.A./M.D./J.D., or Ph.D.
*Current rank in organization:* Lecturer, instructor, assistant professor, associate professor, or full professor
*Type of graduate institution attended:* Res-I university or other
*Past publication experience:* Number of articles published during career minus number of articles published over last two years (1985–87) divided by the career age

Self-Knowledge

*Efficacy:* A two-item scale of a respondent's perception of the amount of individual influence he or she has on getting something accepted for publication and in obtaining money for travel to professional association meetings beyond the standard institutional allocations
*Personal interest in research:* A dummy coded variable where 1 = more interested in research than teaching
*Personal preference for research:* Preferred percentage of effort allocated to research
*Self-competency in research:* A factor (eigenvalue = 1.59 for natural sciences, 1.41 for humanities, and 1.44 for social sciences; cronbach alpha = .74) consisting of two skill items that evaluate the characteristics of publishing (loading = 0.89 for natural sciences, 0.84 for humanities, and 0.85 for social sciences) and obtaining grants (loading = 0.89 for natural sciences, 0.84 for humanities, and 0.85 for social sciences)
*Personal disposition for research:* A three-item factor (eigenvalue = 1.96 for natural sciences, 1.92 for humanities, and 1.98 for social sciences; cronbach

alpha = 0.73) with the following characteristics: ambitious (loading = 0.73 for natural sciences, 0.88 for humanities, and 0.88 for social sciences), competitive (loading = 0.72 for natural sciences, 0.86 for humanities, and 0.84 for social sciences), and perseverant (loading = 0.51 for natural sciences, 0.64 for humanities, and 0.71 for social sciences)

## Social Knowledge

*Nonfinancial (institutional) research support:* A two-item scale of the perception of whether there are available support services for scholarship and support from colleagues to assist and critically review respondent's scholarly work

*Financial research support (grants) from any source:* A scale of six items that include support from institutional or departmental funds, federal agencies, state or local governmental agencies, private foundations, private industry, or other sources

*Institutional or departmental commitment to research:* A two-item scale that registers the degree to which a department and unit are committed to research versus teaching

*Morale:* A five-item scale that includes faculty trust for administrators and established faculty groups, perceived fair allocation of resources on campus, a sense of whether a respondent believes he or she has a good institutional fit, and career satisfaction

*Perceived institutional preference for the allocation of research effort*

## Behavior

*Percentage of effort allocated to research*

## Current Publication Output (Dependent Variable)

*Number of professional writings published or accepted for publication in the last two years*

# Appendix D

# VARIABLES USED IN THE REGRESSION ANALYSES: TABLES 5.5 AND 5.6

## Sociodemographic

*Female* was coded as a dummy variable: $0 =$ male and $1 =$ female.
*Asian:* DAsian where $1 =$ Asian and $0 =$ all others.
*Black:* DBlack where $1 =$ black and $0 =$ all others.
*Age* was chronological age as of 1987.

## Career

*Established faculty member:* This is a four-item factorially derived measure including career age (years since highest degree award), tenure status (prior to 1985), administrative experience (before 1985), and current academic rank. (Eigenvalue $= 2.94$.)

*Active scholar/grantsperson:* This factor consists of the following four items: total publications, total chapters authored, and numbers of grant proposals and fellowship applications submitted, all prior to 1985. (Eigenvalue $= 1.29$.)

*Discipline:* This is a discrete measure indicating the academic department in which the respondents have teaching appointments. There are eight dummy variables: Dhistory, DEnglish, Dpsychology, Dsociology, Dpolitical science, Dchemistry, and Dmath/statistics. Dbiology is the null dummy variable.

## Self-Knowledge

*Organizational influence:* This five-item factor assesses personal influence on departmental curriculum committee decisions, the next chair of the unit, the next faculty member hired in the unit, securing the resources to maintain ongoing programs faculty members consider important, and establishing criteria for annual review of faculty members. (Eigenvalue $= 3.92$.)

*Control over career:* This is a four-item factor indicating personal influence on decisions that have a direct impact on one's career: having something you have written accepted for publication, the salary increase you will receive next year, obtaining money for travel to professional association meetings (beyond standard institutional allocations), and the personal interests you wish to pursue. (Eigenvalue $= 1.42$.)

*Values teaching:* This factor consists of four items on which the respondents indicated the extent to which they personally were highly committed to teaching, concerned about students, dedicated to the liberal arts, and highly committed to research (the last item has a negative factor loading); and two other items assessing the extent to which they valued teaching over research and the amount of time they would prefer to spend on teaching, research, and service. (Eigenvalue = 4.30.)

*Values cooperation/institutional commitment:* This two-item factor consists of self-ratings indicating the value one places on being a "team player" and being "devoted to the institution." (Eigenvalue = 1.16.)

*Supportive/understanding:* This factor consists of self-ratings on three traits: supportiveness, being understanding, and personableness. (Eigenvalue = 2.09.)

## Institutional Context

Dummy variables were created to represent each of the eight universities where the respondents were employed.

## Environmental Response

*Recent promotion/tenure:* This measure consists of two items (date of tenure and last promotion) indicating that tenure or promotion was awarded between 1985 and 1987. (Eigenvalue = 1.78.)

## Social Knowledge

*Personable teacher valued:* This 14-item measure emerged from factor analysis of a question that asked respondents to indicate the skills, beliefs/values, and personality traits they believed characterize the valued faculty member on their campus. The scores ranged from 1 (not at all characteristic) to 5 (highly characteristic). The following characteristics loaded on this factor: teaches effectively, communicates well, works skillfully with students, responds to requests, is an excellent lecturer, is highly committed to teaching, respects others, is dedicated to the liberal arts, is supportive, is understanding, is open, is candid, is personable, and has a sense of humor. (Eigenvalue = 10.57.)

*Faculty committed to teaching:* The two items that loaded on this factor indicated that the respondent thought faculty in her or his institution and unit were committed to teaching. (Eigenvalue = 1.60.)

*Faculty collegiality:* The four items loading on this factor indicated that established faculty groups could be trusted, and that within units, colleagues agreed on the curriculum, could critique one another's scholarly work, and could cover courses for one another. (Eigenvalue = 2.24.)

*Motivated students:* This measure evolved from factor analysis of a question on which faculty indicated how strongly they agreed with nine assumptions about undergraduate students. The scores ranged from 1 (strongly disagree) to 4 (strongly agree). Three assumptions had positive loadings: students think for themselves, share ideas/cooperate, and work on their own. Three others had negative loadings: learn only what is required, lack interest, and feel overwhelmed by course requirements. (Eigenvalue = 2.83.)

# Appendix E

# VARIABLES USED IN THE REGRESSION ANALYSES: TABLE 5.9

For each item listed below, faculty were asked to indicate "how characteristic the skills, the beliefs/attitudes/values, and the personality characteristics are for you," where 1 = not at all characteristic, 2 = slightly characteristic, 3 = somewhat characteristic, and 4 = highly characteristic. The following items comprised the factors:

*INSTRUCTIONAL COMMITMENT*

Highly committed to teaching

Concerned about students

*SELF-COMPETENCE*

Teaches effectively

Communicates well

Works skillfully with students

Is an excellent lecturer

For the *self-efficacy* factor, faculty were asked to identify the option that "best corresponds to how much influence you think you have on each of the following," where 1 = really no influence at all, 2 = minor influence, 3 = some influence, and 4 = substantial influence. The following items comprised the factor:

*SELF-EFFICACY*

Student learning

Student career achievements

For the *interest-in-teaching* item, faculty were asked whether their "interests lie primarily in teaching or in research," where 1 = very heavily in research, 2 = in both, but leaning toward research, 3 = in both, but leaning toward teaching, and 4 = very heavily in teaching.

For the next set of factors, faculty were asked to "indicate the degree of truthfulness [each item] has for you," where 1 = little or no truth, 2 = generally not true, 3 = generally true, and 4 = very high degree of truth. The following items comprised the factors:

### CONSENSUS AND SUPPORT

There is a high degree of agreement among my unit's colleagues about the content of our curriculum.

The support services for teaching (lab facilities, computers, libraries, clerical assistance, audiovisual aids, student assistance, etc.) help me teach how and what I would like.

### COLLEAGUE COMMITMENT TO TEACHING

The faculty in my *unit* are more committed to the teaching of their discipline than they are to adding to their discipline's knowledge base.

The faculty in this *institution* are more committed to teaching than they are to doing research in their disciplinary domain.

For the following items, faculty were asked to respond in actual percentages:

My institution's preferences for how much time I spend on teaching (institutional preference)

My personal preferences for how much time I spend on teaching (personal preference)

The actual amount of time I spend on teaching (outcome variable)

# Appendix F

# VARIABLES USED IN THE REGRESSION ANALYSES: TABLE 5.10

Beliefs, Assumptions, and Values

### Beliefs: Teaching

FACTOR 1: STUDENTS ARE MOTIVATED (eigenvalue = 3.5566)

| | |
|---|---|
| Students think independently | .7153 |
| Students share ideas | .6336 |
| Students work on their own | .6207 |
| Students will feel overwhelmed by requirements | −.5077 |
| Students lack interest in the subject | −.6905 |
| Students learn what's required | −.7108 |

FACTOR 2: CONCERN FOR PERSONAL/SOCIAL DEVELOPMENT (eigenvalue = 2.3936)

| | |
|---|---|
| Goal is improving students' social roles | .7636 |
| Goal is students' personal development | .7287 |
| Goal is advancing students' socioeconomic status | .6645 |

FACTOR 3: VALUES TEACHER CONTROL (eigenvalue = 2.3245)

| | |
|---|---|
| Teacher controls course content | .8486 |
| Teacher sets pace of course | .8351 |
| Teacher and students set content cooperatively | −.5214 |

FACTOR 4: VALUES INDIVIDUALIZED INSTRUCTION (eigenvalue = 1.8187)

| | |
|---|---|
| Students need frequent feedback | .6707 |
| Students will be appropriately challenged by course requirements | .6008 |
| Conditions allow students to discover new principles | .5756 |
| Course content is relevant to students' lives | .5278 |

312

*FACTOR 5: DEVOTION TO INTELLECTUAL DEVELOPMENT/LIBERAL ARTS* (eigenvalue = 1.5280)

| | |
|---|---|
| Goal is developing reasoning and communication | .6832 |
| Goal is helping interested students | .6029 |
| Dedicated to the liberal arts | .5502 |

*FACTOR 6: PERSONAL COMMITMENT TO TEACHING* (eigenvalue = 1.4072)

| | |
|---|---|
| Personal preference for teaching | .8800 |
| Personal preference for scholarship | −.8249 |

*FACTOR 7: DEVOTION TO TEACHING* (eigenvalue = 1.2841)

| | |
|---|---|
| Committed to teaching | .8292 |
| Personal preference for scholarship | .6988 |

*FACTOR 8: FAVOR STUDENT COMPETITION* (eigenvalue = 1.1579)

| | |
|---|---|
| Fostering competition improves learning | .7392 |
| Students learn by outperforming one another | .7171 |

*FACTOR 9: CONCERN FOR CONTENT/PROCESS* (eigenvalue = 1.0822)

| | |
|---|---|
| Concern about transmitting discipline | .7781 |
| Concern about demonstrating a process | .7328 |

**Beliefs: Research**

*FACTOR 10: COMMITMENT TO RESEARCH* (eigenvalue = 2.2680)

| | |
|---|---|
| % time preference for research | .8561 |
| Highly committed to research | .8511 |
| Interests lie primarily in teaching | −.8760 |

**Beliefs: Service**

*FACTOR 11: COMMITMENT TO SERVICE/INSTITUTION* (eigenvalue = 1.1321)

| | |
|---|---|
| Devotion to the institution | .7524 |
| % time preference for service | .7524 |

Competence, Efficacy

### *Competence: Teaching*

FACTOR 12: TEACHING COMPETENCE (eigenvalue = 2.1102)

| | |
|---|---|
| Teaches effectively | .7647 |
| Excellent lecturer | .7520 |
| Works well with students | .5624 |

FACTOR 13: DEALING WITH DIFFICULT CLASSES (eigenvalue = 1.2971)

| | |
|---|---|
| Underprepared students affect teaching negatively | .8186 |
| Wide range of abilities most difficult to teach | .8096 |

FACTOR 14: EFFECT ON STUDENT OUTCOMES (eigenvalue = 1.0442)

| | |
|---|---|
| Influence on student achievement | .8102 |
| Influence on student learning | .7296 |

### *Competence: Research*

FACTOR 15: RESEARCH COMPETENCE (eigenvalue = 1.6410)

| | |
|---|---|
| Publishes | .7813 |
| Obtains grants | .6888 |
| Influence on own work being published | .6282 |

### *Competence: Service*

FACTOR 16: DEPARTMENT DECISION INFLUENCE (eigenvalue = 3.0434)

| | |
|---|---|
| Influence on choice of new faculty | .7516 |
| Influence on department curriculum decisions | .6976 |
| Influence on choice of next chair | .6779 |
| Influence on criteria for review of faculty | .6217 |
| Influence on allocation of resources | .5538 |

FACTOR 17: ACADEMIC DECISION INFLUENCE (eigenvalue = 1.0014)

| | |
|---|---|
| Influence on admission requirements | .8663 |
| Influence on graduation requirements | .8126 |

## Career Satisfaction

*FACTOR 18: CAREER SATISFACTION* (eigenvalue = 1.8764)

| | |
|---|---|
| General feeling about institution | .7833 |
| Would choose faculty career again | .7584 |
| Self-assessment of success positive compared with like faculty | .6966 |

*FACTOR 19: SALARY SATISFACTION* (eigenvalue = 1.1454)

| | |
|---|---|
| Salary comparison with peers at other institutions | .8170 |
| Salary comparison within institution | .7918 |

## Environment

### Environment: General

*FACTOR 20: VIEW OF ORGANIZATIONAL CLIMATE* (eigenvalue = 2.3488)

| | |
|---|---|
| Faculty can trust administration to act in good faith | .7720 |
| Institution encourages work for collective good of unit | .7272 |
| Faculty can trust established faculty groups to act in good faith | .6152 |
| Rewarded faculty are oriented primarily toward professional accomplishments | .5750 |

*FACTOR 21: VIEW OF GOVERNANCE/SUPPORT* (eigenvalue = 1.2239)

| | |
|---|---|
| Institution's goals are more toward careers | .6675 |
| Some units get more than their share of resources | .5648 |
| Institution values devotion to the liberal arts | −.6182 |

*FACTOR 22: ENVIRONMENT VALUES INVOLVEMENT* (eigenvalue = 1.0893)

| | |
|---|---|
| Institution values knowing how to work the system | .7770 |
| Institution values devotion to institution | .7256 |

### Environment: Teaching

*FACTOR 23: SUPPORT FOR TEACHING* (eigenvalue = 3.8357)

| | |
|---|---|
| Institution values commitment to teaching | .8841 |
| Institution values concern for students | .8704 |
| Institution values effective teaching | .8592 |

Institution values working well with students      .8502

Institution values an excellent lecturer      .7071

FACTOR 24: DISCIPLINE IMPACTS TEACHING
(eigenvalue = 1.1725)

Changes in discipline necessitated changes in teaching method      .8508

Changes in discipline necessitated changes in courses      .8491

FACTOR 25: CURRICULUM CONSENSUS/SUPPORT (eigenvalue = 1.5708)

Collegial resources support teaching efforts      .7054

Services support teaching efforts      .6649

Agreement in unit about the curriculum      .5666

FACTOR 26: ENVIRONMENTAL COMMITMENT TO TEACHING
(eigenvalue = 1.4209)

Faculty in the unit more committed to teaching than to adding
to discipline      .8543

Faculty in institution more committed to teaching than
to research in discipline      .8638

FACTOR 27: ENVIRONMENTAL PRESSURE ON TEACHERS
(eigenvalue = 1.1242)

Pressure from colleagues to teach certain way      .8598

Pressure from institution to grade certain way      .8411

**Environment: Research**

FACTOR 28: ENVIRONMENT VALUES RESEARCH (eigenvalue = 2.0484)

Institution values publishing      .8550

Institution values commitment to research      .8030

Institution values getting grants      .7444

FACTOR 29: ENVIRONMENT SUPPORTS SCHOLARSHIP
(eigenvalue = 1.4085)

Support services for scholarship enhance my scholarship      .7177

Colleagues assist and review my scholarly work      .7032

Institution values keeping up in one's discipline      .6741

Behavior

### *Behavior: Teaching*

FACTOR 30: RESEARCH ACTIVITIES (eigenvalue = 5.7727)

| | |
|---|---|
| Require a research paper | .8257 |
| Require annotated bibliographies | .7560 |
| Review rough drafts of students' papers | .7526 |
| Require style manual/proper writing format | .7205 |
| Require on-line searches for projects | .6932 |

FACTOR 31: EXCHANGING EXPERTISE (eigenvalue = 1.9501)

| | |
|---|---|
| Attended presentation of colleague on campus | .7170 |
| Attended presentation of visiting lecturer on campus | .6919 |
| Attended campus workshops on teaching | .6718 |
| Attended off-campus workshop on teaching discipline | .5956 |

FACTOR 32: INDIVIDUALIZING INSTRUCTION (eigenvalue = 1.3386)

| | |
|---|---|
| Supervise independent studies | .7246 |
| Supervise tutorials | .6862 |
| Design research internships for students | .5742 |

FACTOR 33: DISSEMINATION (eigenvalue = 1.2156)

| | |
|---|---|
| Has published chapters in a book | .7069 |
| Has written for the popular press | .6837 |

FACTOR 34: PREFERENCE FOR PROFESSIONAL GROWTH (eigenvalue = 1.0844)

| | |
|---|---|
| % time to scholarship | .8654 |
| % time to teaching | −.7398 |

FACTOR 35: COURSE DEVELOPMENT (eigenvalue = 1.0066)

| | |
|---|---|
| Develop new materials for course/lab | .6850 |
| Team teaching | .5711 |

### *Behavior: Research*

FACTOR 36: ACTIVE GRANTSPERSON (eigenvalue = 4.8937)

| | |
|---|---|
| Submitted a research proposal | .8367 |

Number of grant proposals submitted in past two years      .7376

Wrote a research report      .6158

*FACTOR 37: SCHOLARLY* (eigenvalue = 1.8494)

Attended presentation by campus colleague      .7506

Attended lecture on campus      .6939

Presented own work on campus      .6589

Had conversations with colleagues at professional meetings      .5222

*FACTOR 38: JOURNAL PUBLISHER* (eigenvalue = 1.3483)

% time to research      .6910

Number of publications (or pieces accepted for publication) in past two years      .6308

Published a scholarly article      .5394

Submitted a scholarly article for publication      .5325

*FACTOR 39: EDITORIAL INVOLVEMENT* (eigenvalue = 1.2778)

Served on journal editorial board      .7902

Reviewed articles for professional journal      .7055

*FACTOR 40: ASSOCIATION ACTIVITY* (eigenvalue = 1.0938)

Edited conference proceedings      .8271

Organized professional meeting      .7706

*FACTOR 41: ACTIVE SCHOLAR* (eigenvalue = 1.0189)

Fellowship application in past two years      .7202

% time to scholarship      .6816

**Behavior: Service**

*FACTOR 42: CAMPUS COMMITTEE WORK* (eigenvalue = 2.6150)

Chaired a campus/unit committee      .8033

Participated in campus committees on issues      .7704

Conducted a study to help solve a unit problem      .7616

Played a role in unit's curriculum revision      .7604

# Appendix G

# SOME LIMITATIONS OF
# THE THEORETICAL FRAMEWORK ·

Chapter 2 calls attention to possible errors in the data we have used and to the limitations of some measures of our constructs. Chapters 1 and 8 examine theoretical concerns involving our framework. Here we include additional reasons to be cautious when asserting truths about faculty behaviors. There are practical and technical restrictions, and there are consequences that result from our design and methodology.

## Practical and Technical Limitations

One practical limitation was the amount of money that was available for staff, questionnaires, mailing, coding—everything it takes to design, collect, and analyze data. A larger sample—say, five times as large—would have allowed us to run more analyses and test more subgroups for their similarities and differences vis-à-vis the overwhelmingly white, heterosexual, male majority group. The dearth of minority and female faculty in some disciplines in some institutional types made it impossible to test our framework with them. Had we had more money, we could, among other things, have increased our response rate and felt more confident about our findings.

A second practical limitation is instrument length, and hence the amount of information collected. A questionnaire can be only so long before hardly anyone will respond to it (unless he or she is paid a fair hourly wage—the money business again). We judged our survey to be about as long as it could be without jeopardizing the response rate. We decided not to get information on two constructs in the framework—social contingencies and environmental conditions. As seen, we made a small effort to get indicators of environmental response. Others of our constructs had fewer items for estimating them than we desired. Two- and three-item factors have lower reliabilities.

In this real and finite world, trade-offs always enter research. Constraints of money and time have their consequences.

## Design and Methodology

There are two important consequences of our design and methodological choices. First, one both gains and loses when one chooses the method of data collection—interviews versus questionnaires, in most instances. We chose the latter. We needed data from many people in order to test our framework. Questionnaires, however, cannot penetrate to the level that skillful interviewers can attain. Intensive interviewing can bring forth deep feelings and subtle motivations. Such subtleties are unlikely to surface through checked-off responses to statements on a sheet of paper or with open-ended written responses.

We had more than 100 lengthy, taped interviews with faculty in different settings. They served as the foundation for designing our questionnaire. We believe we tapped important dimensions of our framework. However, we also know that our knowledge was limited by the questionnaire's inability to probe the complexities of motivations, their competing nature, their intensity, how they change over time, and the like. These sacrifices are a consequence of our choice of the questionnaire survey as our principal data collection device.

Second, we have a static design. Faculty told us about themselves and their workplace at one point in time—a snapshot taken on one day of their life. In order to determine how reliable the responses were, we randomly sent portions of the questionnaire again to groups of 50 faculty about six weeks after we received their completed questionnaires. Over 80 percent returned the instrument, and we correlated their initial responses with the later ones. (See Blackburn & Mackie, 1992.) Our retest demonstrated that what faculty revealed was quite reliable, stable in this case. However, that was six weeks later, not a year or two afterward. Ours is not a longitudinal design, nor can it become one. We have cross-sectional data, as have the other national surveys. Speculations about the causes of changes between data collection times are highly dubious. We have noted where behaviors and conditions differ at different points in time (e.g., female and male productivity rates over the past two decades). However, we do not have evidence as to the causes of the changes. These limitations are why we argue as strongly as we do in chapter 8 for a longitudinal study.

# Appendix H

# FACULTY SURVEY

Faculty at Work: A Survey of
Motivations, Expectations, and Satisfactions

### General Directions

1. This survey is concerned with your teaching of *undergraduates* (even if you do not happen to be teaching undergraduates this term). Keep *this in mind* when you are responding to questions about classes and instruction.

2. Several questions deal with your *immediate area of work*. In many institutions that will be a department; in others it can be a division; in still others it could be a center or other organization. Because of the diverse possibilities, we have used the term unit as a generic term for all the organizational labels that exist. Simply read in your own situation when you see the word unit.

3. The terms teaching, scholarship, research, and service have a range of definitions. For the purpose of this survey, please use these:

   *Teaching*: Class preparation, scheduled classroom and laboratory instruction, grading, working with students in your office.

   *Research*: Activity that leads to a concrete product (an article, report, monograph, book, grant proposal, software development).

   *Scholarship*: Professional growth—enhancing your knowledge or skill in ways which may not necessarily result in a concrete product (library work, reading, exploratory inquiries, computer use).

   *Service*: Work in college/university meetings, community activities, professional association involvements.

4. We have tried to design the questionnaire so the greatest number of individuals can respond. Some questions, however, may be inappropriate for your own situation. Answer all the questions as well as you can.

5. You'll enjoy the questions more if you take each at its most obvious intention and avoid making subtle (even when valid) distinctions.

Robert T. Blackburn, Project Director
Janet H. Lawrence, Associate Director
Virginia Polk Okoloko, Research Associate
Jeffery P. Bieber, Research Assistant
Judith Pitney, Research Assistant
Kwang Suk Yoon, Research Assistant

The Center is funded by the University of Michigan and the U. S. Department of Education's Office of Educational Research and Improvement under OERI grant number G008690010.

---

### Response Instructions

Most of the questions below can be answered by simply filling in the circle ● which identifies what you consider the most appropriate response.

It does not matter what type of pen or pencil you use.

If you change your mind or mark the wrong space, cross it out ✗ and fill in the space you wish.

---

1. Below are several statements about the environment in which you work. They can affect your ability to do what is expected and/or achieve your goals. For each statement, indicate the degree of truthfulness it has for you by filling in the appropriate circle.

Very high degree of truth
Generally true
Generally not true
Little or no truth

a. My institution's goals for students tend to be more oriented toward careers and professionalism than toward the liberal arts. ① ② ③ ④

b. As a result of changes in my discipline in the past decade, I have had to make significant changes in my teaching methods. ① ② ③ ④

c. The most highly rewarded faculty members at my institution are those oriented primarily toward their professional accomplishment. ① ② ③ ④

d. The support services for teaching (lab facilities, computers, libraries, clerical assistance, audio-visual aids, student assistance, etc.) help me teach what and how I would like. ① ② ③ ④

e. The support services available at my institution for my scholarship help me conduct the kind of inquiry I desire. ① ② ③ ④

f. The collegial resources (faculty to contribute to my class, persons with whom I can discuss appropriate topics) available at my institution help enrich my teaching. ① ② ③ ④

g. There is a high degree of agreement among my unit's colleagues about the content of our curriculum. ① ② ③ ④

h. As a result of changes in my discipline in the past decade, I have had to make significant changes in the content of my courses. ① ② ③ ④

i. I am encouraged by my institution to work for the collective good of my unit. ① ② ③ ④

*(continued in next column)*

*(continued from previous column)*

Very high degree of truth
Generally true
Generally not true
Little or no truth

j. I feel pressure from my colleagues to teach in a particular way. ① ② ③ ④

k. I feel pressure from my institution to grade in a particular way. ① ② ③ ④

l. A class with a wide range of student abilities is most difficult for me to teach. ① ② ③ ④

m. Faculty can trust the administration to act in good faith for the betterment of the institution. ① ② ③ ④

n. Faculty can trust established faculty groups (e.g., governance committees) to act in good faith for the betterment of the institution. ① ② ③ ④

o. The faculty in my *unit* are more committed to the teaching of their discipline than they are to adding to their discipline's knowledge base. ① ② ③ ④

p. The faculty in this *institution* are more committed to teaching than they are to doing research in their disciplinary domain. ① ② ③ ④

q. My unit's colleagues know my specialty well enough to assist and critically review my scholarly work. ① ② ③ ④

r. A class composed primarily of under-prepared students negatively affects my teaching. ① ② ③ ④

s. Some units on this campus receive more than a fair share when it comes to the central administration's allocation of resources. ① ② ③ ④

t. An ineffective/unproductive colleague at my institution can be changed into a contributing member of this organization. ① ② ③ ④

2

2. A faculty member's activities may influence what happens to others as well as to herself or himself. Below are some outcomes that depend to varying degrees on your efforts. Fill in the circle that best corresponds to how much influence you think you have on each of the following.

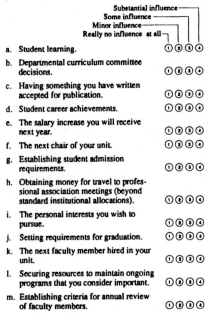

Substantial influence ——
Some influence ——
Minor influence——
Really no influence at all ⌐

a. Student learning. ① ② ③ ④

b. Departmental curriculum committee decisions. ① ② ③ ④

c. Having something you have written accepted for publication. ① ② ③ ④

d. Student career achievements. ① ② ③ ④

e. The salary increase you will receive next year. ① ② ③ ④

f. The next chair of your unit. ① ② ③ ④

g. Establishing student admission requirements. ① ② ③ ④

h. Obtaining money for travel to professional association meetings (beyond standard institutional allocations). ① ② ③ ④

i. The personal interests you wish to pursue. ① ② ③ ④

j. Setting requirements for graduation. ① ② ③ ④

k. The next faculty member hired in your unit. ① ② ③ ④

l. Securing resources to maintain ongoing programs that you consider important. ① ② ③ ④

m. Establishing criteria for annual review of faculty members. ① ② ③ ④

3. Consider a *basic introductory* course you teach on a regular basis. Fill in the response which corresponds to how frequently you do each of the following.

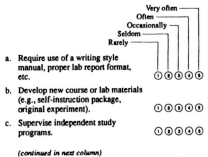

Very often ——
Often ——
Occasionally ——
Seldom ——
Rarely ——

a. Require use of a writing style manual, proper lab report format, etc. ① ② ③ ④ ⑤

b. Develop new course or lab materials (e.g., self-instruction package, original experiment). ① ② ③ ④ ⑤

c. Supervise independent study programs. ① ② ③ ④ ⑤

*(continued in next column)*

*(continued from previous column)*

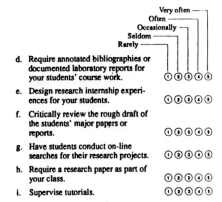

Very often ——
Often ——
Occasionally ——
Seldom ——
Rarely ——

d. Require annotated bibliographies or documented laboratory reports for your students' course work. ① ② ③ ④ ⑤

e. Design research internship experiences for your students. ① ② ③ ④ ⑤

f. Critically review the rough draft of the students' major papers or reports. ① ② ③ ④ ⑤

g. Have students conduct on-line searches for their research projects. ① ② ③ ④ ⑤

h. Require a research paper as part of your class. ① ② ③ ④ ⑤

i. Supervise tutorials. ① ② ③ ④ ⑤

4. Fill in the circle that most closely indicates how often you have done the following during the *last year*.

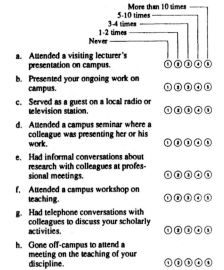

More than 10 times ——
5-10 times ——
3-4 times ——
1-2 times ——
Never ——

a. Attended a visiting lecturer's presentation on campus. ① ② ③ ④ ⑤

b. Presented your ongoing work on campus. ① ② ③ ④ ⑤

c. Served as a guest on a local radio or television station. ① ② ③ ④ ⑤

d. Attended a campus seminar where a colleague was presenting her or his work. ① ② ③ ④ ⑤

e. Had informal conversations about research with colleagues at professional meetings. ① ② ③ ④ ⑤

f. Attended a campus workshop on teaching. ① ② ③ ④ ⑤

g. Had telephone conversations with colleagues to discuss your scholarly activities. ① ② ③ ④ ⑤

h. Gone off-campus to attend a meeting on the teaching of your discipline. ① ② ③ ④ ⑤

3

5. Fill in the circle that most closely indicates how frequently you have done each of the following during the *prior two years*.

More than 10 times
5-10 times
3-4 times
1-2 times
Never

a. Submitted an article for publication in an academic or professional journal. ① ② ③ ④ ⑤

b. Made a presentation at a professional conference. ① ② ③ ④ ⑤

c. Written for the popular press. ① ② ③ ④ ⑤

d. Published chapters in a book. ① ② ③ ④ ⑤

e. Reviewed articles for a professional journal. ① ② ③ ④ ⑤

f. Organized a professional meeting. ① ② ③ ④ ⑤

g. Edited the proceedings of a professional meeting. ① ② ③ ④ ⑤

h. Submitted a research proposal to a governmental or private agency. ① ② ③ ④ ⑤

i. Written a research report for an agency, institution, or other group. ① ② ③ ④ ⑤

j. Served on an editorial board of a journal. ① ② ③ ④ ⑤

k. Published scholarly articles. ① ② ③ ④ ⑤

6. Consider the *past five academic years*. Fill in the circle that indicates how many times you have done each of the following.

More than 10 times
5-10 times
3-4 times
1-2 times
Never

a. Team taught a class. ① ② ③ ④ ⑤

b. Participated in campus-wide committees dealing with major issues. ① ② ③ ④ ⑤

c. Chaired a campus or unit committee. ① ② ③ ④ ⑤

d. Played a role in your unit's curriculum revision. ① ② ③ ④ ⑤

e. Conducted a study to help solve a unit problem. ① ② ③ ④ ⑤

7. Faculty implicitly or explicitly make some assumptions about teaching-learning processes. Use the scale below to fill in the blank in the sentence "As a teacher, I am _____ with . . ."

Very highly concerned
Moderately concerned
Somewhat concerned
Slightly or not concerned

*As a teacher, I am* _____ *with:*

a. transmitting facts, principles, and theories of my discipline. ① ② ③ ④

b. helping students to improve and make the most of their roles in society. ① ② ③ ④

c. demonstrating an intellectual, artistic, or scientific process. ① ② ③ ④

d. encouraging students' overall personal development. ① ② ③ ④

e. enhancing students' abilities to reason and communicate their thoughts. ① ② ③ ④

f. assisting students who demonstrate an interest in learning. ① ② ③ ④

g. having students advance their socio-economic status. ① ② ③ ④

8. The following questions are about your background. Fill in the appropriate circle or write the response in the appropriate blanks. (If you have a joint appointment, answer from the perspective of the academic unit that is most important to you.)

a. List the highest academic degree you have earned, the institution granting it, and the year in which it was obtained.

Degree _____ Year _____

Institution _____

b. In what unit (e.g., natural sciences, history) is your principal teaching appointment?

_____

c. What is your area of specialization (e.g., sociology, chemistry)?

_____

d. How many colleagues do you have on campus who either can teach your courses if you need to be elsewhere or can give a constructive critique of your scholarly work? _____

*(continued on next page)*

4

324

*(continued from previous page)*

e. How many years have you been at
this institution (not including this year)? \_\_\_\_
(total years)

As a faculty member \_\_\_\_ (years)

As an administrator \_\_\_\_ (years)

f. Are you currently appointed to an administrative
position?

① Yes   ② No  (If no, skip to letter h.)

g. If yes, what percentage of your time does
this administrative appointment represent? \_\_\_\_%

h. How many years have you been at
other colleges and universities? \_\_\_\_ (total years)

As a faculty member \_\_\_\_ (years)

As an administrator \_\_\_\_ (years)

i. What is your gender?

① Female   ② Male

j. In what year were you born? 19\_\_\_\_

k. What is your present rank? (Fill in one only.)

① Instructor                ⑤ Lecturer
② Assistant Professor        ⑥ There are no ranks at
③ Associate Professor           my institution.
④ Professor                  ⑦ Other

l. How many years have you held your
current rank (not including this year)? \_\_\_\_ (years)

m. What kind of appointment do you now hold? (Fill in
one only.)

① Regular with tenure        ④ Visiting
② Regular without tenure      ⑤ Other
③ Yearly term appointment

n. If not tenured, are you in a tenure track position?
(Leave blank if tenured.)

① Yes   ② No

o. How fair is your salary in comparison with that of
your peers at your institution?

① More than I deserve
② About as much as I deserve
③ Somewhat less than I deserve
④ Much less than I deserve
⑤ I don't know.
⑥ I don't care.

p. How does your salary compare with those of your
colleagues at peer institutions?

① Appreciably higher
② Somewhat higher
③ About the same
④ Somewhat lower
⑤ Appreciably lower
⑥ I don't know.
⑦ I don't care.

*(continued in next column)*

*(continued from previous column)*

q. What percentage of your raise
for this year was based on merit? \_\_\_\_ %

(E.g., if the institution's salary program called for an
average or total raise of 6%, and 4% of this was
"across-the-board," you would enter "2%.")

r. Into approximately how many dollars
does that percent merit raise translate? $ \_\_\_\_

s. Your race or ethnic group is:

① White/Caucasian
② Black/Negro/Afro-American
③ Native American/American Indian
④ Mexican American/Chicano
⑤ Puerto Rican
⑥ Hispanic
⑦ Oriental
⑧ Other Asian
⑨ Other

t. Comparing yourself with other academic persons of
your age and qualifications, how successful do you
consider yourself in your career?

① Very successful
② Fairly successful
③ Fairly unsuccessful
④ Very unsuccessful

u. In general, how do you feel about this institution?

① It is a very good place for me.
② It is a fairly good place for me.
③ It is not the place for me.

v. If you were to begin your career again, would you still
want to be a faculty member?

① Definitely yes
② Probably yes
③ Probably no
④ Definitely no

w. Do your interests lie primarily in teaching or in
research?

① Very heavily in research
② In both, but leaning toward research
③ In both, but leaning toward teaching
④ Very heavily in teaching

x. In the past 12 months, did you (or your project) have
research support from any of the sources listed below?
Fill in "yes" or "no" for *each* possible response.

| | Yes | No |
|---|---|---|
| (1) Institutional or departmental funds | ① | ② |
| (2) Federal agencies | ① | ② |
| (3) State or local government agencies | ① | ② |
| (4) Private foundations | ① | ② |
| (5) Private industry | ① | ② |
| (6) Other | ① | ② |

*(continued on next page)*

5

325

*(continued from previous page)*

y. How many external grant proposals have you submitted within the *last two years* (best estimate)? _____

z. How many external fellowship applications have you submitted within the *last two years* (best estimate)? _____

aa. Over your career, how many external grant proposals have you submitted (best estimate)? _____

bb. Over your career, how many external fellowship applications have you submitted (best estimate)? _____

cc. How many of your professional writings have been published or accepted for publication in the *last two years*? _____

dd. Over your career, how many articles have you published in academic or professional journals (best estimate)? _____

ee. Over your career, how many books or monographs have you published or edited, alone or in collaboration (best estimate)? _____

9. Faculty receive feedback on their work in a variety of ways and from different people. Fill in the circle that best corresponds with the degree of credence you give to each of the following :

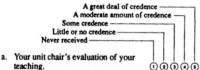

A great deal of credence  
A moderate amount of credence  
Some credence  
Little or no credence  
Never received

a. Your unit chair's evaluation of your teaching. ① ② ③ ④ ⑤

b. Your colleagues' (faculty members in your unit) evaluation of your teaching. ① ② ③ ④ ⑤

c. Student responses on teaching evaluation forms. ① ② ③ ④ ⑤

d. Your chair's or dean's comments on your scholarly activities. ① ② ③ ④ ⑤

e. Your colleagues' (faculty members in your unit) comments on your scholarly work. ① ② ③ ④ ⑤

f. Alumni comments about the impact you had on them. ① ② ③ ④ ⑤

g. Your chair's or dean's comments on your service contributions to the institution. ① ② ③ ④ ⑤

10. For each statement below, fill in the circle that best expresses your level of agreement.

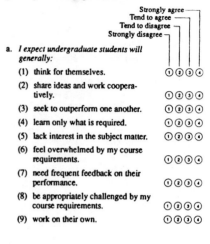

Strongly agree  
Tend to agree  
Tend to disagree  
Strongly disagree

a. *I expect undergraduate students will generally:*

(1) think for themselves. ① ② ③ ④

(2) share ideas and work cooperatively. ① ② ③ ④

(3) seek to outperform one another. ① ② ③ ④

(4) learn only what is required. ① ② ③ ④

(5) lack interest in the subject matter. ① ② ③ ④

(6) feel overwhelmed by my course requirements. ① ② ③ ④

(7) need frequent feedback on their performance. ① ② ③ ④

(8) be appropriately challenged by my course requirements. ① ② ③ ④

(9) work on their own. ① ② ③ ④

Strongly agree  
Tend to agree  
Tend to disagree  
Strongly disagree

b. *I assume undergraduates learn best when:*

(1) course content is determined by the teacher. ① ② ③ ④

(2) pace is set for the group by the teacher. ① ② ③ ④

(3) course content is perceived to have immediate relevance to the students' lives. ① ② ③ ④

(4) course content is determined cooperatively by students and the teacher. ① ② ③ ④

(5) conditions are established that let students discover new concepts or principles. ① ② ③ ④

(6) competition among students is fostered. ① ② ③ ④

(7) students progress at their own pace. ① ② ③ ④

6

11. Below are sets of words and phrases that faculty have used to describe the valued faculty member on their campuses. The first set has to do with skills and abilities of these faculty members. The second set consists of values and attitudes ascribed to these people. The third set contains personality characteristics respected faculty members are said to possess.

First, fill in the circle in column I that best represents the extent to which the word or phrase characterizes the faculty members you believe are valued on your campus. Then, in column II, indicate how characteristic the skills, the beliefs/attitudes/values, and the personality characteristics are of you. Last, in column III, **for the skills only,** fill in the circle corresponding to how difficult each is for you. (Go across the sheet for each item.)

| | I Characteristic of valued faculty | II Characteristic of you | III Difficulty for you |
|---|---|---|---|
| | Highly characteristic / Somewhat characteristic / Slightly characteristic / Not at all characteristic | Highly characteristic / Somewhat characteristic / Slightly characteristic / Not at all characteristic | Very difficult / Difficult / Of average difficulty / Not very difficult |

**a. Skills**

| | | I | II | III |
|---|---|---|---|---|
| (1) | Teaches effectively | ① ② ③ ④ | ① ② ③ ④ | ① ② ③ ④ |
| (2) | Keeps abreast of developments in the discipline | ① ② ③ ④ | ① ② ③ ④ | ① ② ③ ④ |
| (3) | Obtains grants | ① ② ③ ④ | ① ② ③ ④ | ① ② ③ ④ |
| (4) | Communicates well | ① ② ③ ④ | ① ② ③ ④ | ① ② ③ ④ |
| (5) | Publishes | ① ② ③ ④ | ① ② ③ ④ | ① ② ③ ④ |
| (6) | Is organized | ① ② ③ ④ | ① ② ③ ④ | ① ② ③ ④ |
| (7) | Works skillfully with students | ① ② ③ ④ | ① ② ③ ④ | ① ② ③ ④ |
| (8) | Responds to requests | ① ② ③ ④ | ① ② ③ ④ | ① ② ③ ④ |
| (9) | Is an excellent lecturer | ① ② ③ ④ | ① ② ③ ④ | ① ② ③ ④ |
| (10) | Knows how to work the system | ① ② ③ ④ | ① ② ③ ④ | ① ② ③ ④ |

**b. Beliefs/Attitudes/Values**

| | | I | II |
|---|---|---|---|
| (1) | Is highly committed to teaching | ① ② ③ ④ | ① ② ③ ④ |
| (2) | Is concerned about students | ① ② ③ ④ | ① ② ③ ④ |
| (3) | Believes in the virtue of hard work | ① ② ③ ④ | ① ② ③ ④ |
| (4) | Is highly committed to research | ① ② ③ ④ | ① ② ③ ④ |
| (5) | Holds high standards | ① ② ③ ④ | ① ② ③ ④ |
| (6) | Has integrity | ① ② ③ ④ | ① ② ③ ④ |
| (7) | Respects others | ① ② ③ ④ | ① ② ③ ④ |
| (8) | Is dedicated to the liberal arts | ① ② ③ ④ | ① ② ③ ④ |
| (9) | Is a team player | ① ② ③ ④ | ① ② ③ ④ |
| (10) | Is devoted to the institution | ① ② ③ ④ | ① ② ③ ④ |

**c. Personality Characteristics**

| | | I | II |
|---|---|---|---|
| (1) | Is supportive | ① ② ③ ④ | ① ② ③ ④ |
| (2) | Is understanding | ① ② ③ ④ | ① ② ③ ④ |
| (3) | Is open | ① ② ③ ④ | ① ② ③ ④ |
| (4) | Is candid | ① ② ③ ④ | ① ② ③ ④ |
| (5) | Has a sense of humor | ① ② ③ ④ | ① ② ③ ④ |
| (6) | Is personable | ① ② ③ ④ | ① ② ③ ④ |
| (7) | Is dedicated | ① ② ③ ④ | ① ② ③ ④ |
| (8) | Is ambitious | ① ② ③ ④ | ① ② ③ ④ |
| (9) | Is competitive | ① ② ③ ④ | ① ② ③ ④ |
| (10) | Is perseverant | ① ② ③ ④ | ① ② ③ ④ |

7

327

12. Most faculty members have an idea of what an effective administrator is like. Rate both your immediate administrator (e.g., chair/director, division head) and the next higher level individual (e.g., dean, academic vice president/provost) on each of the following attributes that can affect your work. Fill in the circle that most closely corresponds to your overall level of satisfaction.

|  | Immediate Administrator | Next Higher Level Administrator |
|---|---|---|
| | Very satisfactory<br>Somewhat satisfactory<br>Somewhat dissatisfactory<br>Very dissatisfactory | Very satisfactory<br>Somewhat satisfactory<br>Somewhat dissatisfactory<br>Very dissatisfactory |
| a. **Administrative skills** (those things the administrator does to make the organization function; e.g., communicate with faculty, students, alumni; reach and carry through on decisions) | ① ② ③ ④ | ① ② ③ ④ |
| b. **Values** (the core values he or she holds about what is important in academia, and how to best achieve these goals for students and faculty members) | ① ② ③ ④ | ① ② ③ ④ |
| c. **Professionalism** (the integrity with which he or she conducts business; her or his knowledge of and commitment to the institution; dedication to the role of being an effective administrator) | ① ② ③ ④ | ① ② ③ ④ |
| d. **Experience/Background** (knowledge of faculty life; preparation, formal and informal, as an administrator; educational credentials; ability to fulfill special requirements such as fundraising) | ① ② ③ ④ | ① ② ③ ④ |
| e. **Personality** (those aspects of her or his demeanor that make it more or less easy to work with her or him) | ① ② ③ ④ | ① ② ③ ④ |

13. During the *current term,* how much time are you giving to teaching, scholarship/professional growth, research, and service in a typical week? (*Teaching* is the time spent preparing for teaching, scheduled classroom and laboratory instruction, grading, working with students. *Scholarship/Professional Growth* is the time spent enhancing your knowledge or skill in ways which may not necessarily result in a concrete product—library work, reading, exploratory inquiries, computer use. *Research* is the time spent in activities that lead to a concrete product—article, report, monograph, book, grant proposal, software development. *Service* is the time spent in college/university meetings, community activities, professional association involvements.)

a. Divide your work-time over the four principle activities. First, complete column I by entering the percent of time you give to each. Then go to column II and partition the major activity types into the sub-categories that are shown. For example, if you had reported teaching as 60% in column I, your three parts in column II might be 20%, 30%, and 10%.

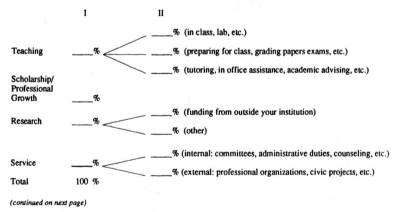

*(continued on next page)*

8

328

*(continued from previous page)*

13. b. Now complete the distribution two more times. First, indicate how you believe your institution wants you to allocate your effort. Then indicate how you would prefer to distribute your time to these four kinds of activities. (In all cases, be sure the percentage's total is 100.)

| | My perception of institutional preference | My personal preference |
|---|---|---|
| Teaching | ____ | ____ |
| Scholarship/ Professional Growth | ____ | ____ |
| Research | ____ | ____ |
| Service | ____ | ____ |
| Total | 100% | 100% |

c. In a typical calendar week, how many *hours* are you giving to the above activities? ____ (hours).

Compared to five years ago, is this:

① More?
② About the same?
③ Less?

d. For your classes this term, what is the largest enrollment? ____

Smallest? ____

Compared to five years ago, is your average class size:

① Larger?
② About the same?
③ Smaller?

e. How many hours of student assistance do you get per week? (If none, enter 0.) ____

Compared to five years ago, is this:

① More?
② About the same?
③ Less?

f. How many hours of clerical assistance do you have per week? (If none, enter 0.) ____

Compared to five years ago, is this:

① More?
② About the same?
③ Less?

g. How many thesis or dissertation committees are you currently chairing? ____

Serving on? (If none, enter 0.) ____

h. How many comprehensive exam/ orals committees did you chair last year? ____

Serve on? (If none, enter 0.) ____

14. While it is impossible to capture the essence of a faculty career in a few words, sometimes a metaphor can come reasonably close. Some faculty have found that what makes being a faculty member personally meaningful can be expressed in a brief phrase or metaphor.

Read the following phrases. First, fill in the circle which most closely corresponds with what makes being a faculty member *personally* meaningful for you. Next, fill in the circle for the expression which is second closest for you. Last, fill in the circle for that which is *furthest removed* from you. **Mark only one per column.**

The most removed from me ┐
The next closest to me ┐ │
The closest to me ┐ │ │

a. An unending love affair with ideas. ⓪⓪⓪

b. The daily challenge of keeping student motivation high. ①①①

c. Having students become enthused with my subject. ②②②

d. Being simultaneously a playwright, a director, and a leading actor. ③③③

e. The excitement of the unknown, the yet to be discovered. ④④④

f. Facilitating the reaction between an idea and a student. ⑤⑤⑤

g. The challenge of retaining current students and attracting new ones. ⑥⑥⑥

h. The cultivation of an apprentice into a master. ⑦⑦⑦

i. The cyclical rhythm of academic life. ⑧⑧⑧

j. An opportunity to help students make significant changes in their lives. ⑨⑨⑨

*Thank you for taking the time to complete this survey.*

9

329

# Appendix I

# ADMINISTRATOR SURVEY

Administrators' Views of Faculty at Work:
A Survey of Motivations, Expectations, and Satisfactions

### General Directions

1. This survey is concerned with your views of full-time arts and science faculty who are teaching *undergraduates*. Please *keep this in mind* when you are responding to questions about classes and instruction.

2. The academic disciplines of the faculty with whom we are concerned include: biology, chemistry, mathematics, English, history, political science, psychology, and sociology. In several questions these eight disciplines are grouped under three main areas: Natural Sciences (biology, chemistry, mathematics), Humanities (English, history), and Social Sciences (political science, psychology, sociology).

3. The terms teaching, scholarship, research, and service have a range of definitions. For the purpose of this survey, please use these:

    *Teaching*:     Class preparation, scheduled classroom and laboratory instruction, grading, working with students.

    *Research*:     Activity that leads to a concrete product (an article, report, monograph, book, grant proposal, software development).

    *Scholarship*: Professional growth—enhancing knowledge or skills in ways which may not necessarily result in a concrete product (library work, reading, exploratory inquiries, computer use).

    *Service*:      Work in college/university meetings, community activities, professional association involvements.

4. We have tried to design the questionnaire so the greatest number of individuals can respond. Some questions, however, may be inappropriate for your own situation. Answer all the questions as well as you can from the perspective of your institution.

5. You'll enjoy the questions more if you take each at its most obvious intention and avoid making subtle (even when valid) distinctions.

Robert T. Blackburn, Project Director
Janet H. Lawrence, Associate Director
Jeffery P. Bieber, Research Assistant
Judith A. Pitney, Research Assistant
Kwang Suk Yoon, Research Assistant

The Center is funded by the University of Michigan and
the U. S. Department of Education's Office of Educational Research and Improvement
under OERI grant number G008690010.

330

Response Instructions

Most of the questions below can be answered by simply filling in the circle ● which identifies what you consider the most appropriate response.

It does not matter what type of pen or pencil you use.

If you change your mind or mark the wrong space, cross it out ✖ and fill in the space you wish.

1. Faculty implicitly or explicitly make some assumptions about teaching-learning processes. How concerned do you think faculty are with the following:

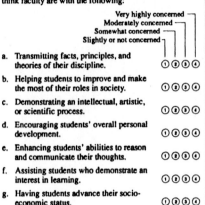

Very highly concerned
Moderately concerned
Somewhat concerned
Slightly or not concerned

a. Transmitting facts, principles, and theories of their discipline. ① ② ③ ④

b. Helping students to improve and make the most of their roles in society. ① ② ③ ④

c. Demonstrating an intellectual, artistic, or scientific process. ① ② ③ ④

d. Encouraging students' overall personal development. ① ② ③ ④

e. Enhancing students' abilities to reason and communicate their thoughts. ① ② ③ ④

f. Assisting students who demonstrate an interest in learning. ① ② ③ ④

g. Having students advance their socio-economic status. ① ② ③ ④

2. Below are several statements about the environment in which faculty work. For each statement, indicate the degree of truthfulness it has *for you* by filling in the appropriate circle.

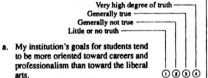

Very high degree of truth
Generally true
Generally not true
Little or no truth

a. My institution's goals for students tend to be more oriented toward careers and professionalism than toward the liberal arts. ① ② ③ ④

b. The most highly rewarded faculty members at my institution are those oriented primarily toward their own professional accomplishment. ① ② ③ ④

*(continued in next column)*

*(continued from previous column)*

Very high degree of truth
Generally true
Generally not true
Little or no truth

c. The support services for teaching (lab facilities, computers, libraries, clerical assistance, audio-visual aids, student assistance, etc.) help faculty teach what and how they would like. ① ② ③ ④

d. The support services available at my institution for scholarship help faculty conduct the kind of inquiries they desire. ① ② ③ ④

e. The collegial resources (faculty to contribute to each other's class, persons with whom to discuss appropriate topics) available at my institution help enrich teaching. ① ② ③ ④

f. Faculty are encouraged by my institution to work for the collective good of their units. ① ② ③ ④

g. Faculty can trust the administration to act in good faith for the betterment of the institution. ① ② ③ ④

h. Faculty can trust established faculty groups (e.g., governance committees) to act in good faith for the betterment of the institution. ① ② ③ ④

i. The faculty in this institution are more committed to teaching than they are to doing research in their disciplinary domain. ① ② ③ ④

j. Some units on this campus receive more than a fair share when it comes to the central administration's allocation of resources. ① ② ③ ④

k. An ineffective/unproductive faculty member at my institution can be changed into a contributing member of this organization. ① ② ③ ④

3

331

3. In responding to these statements about the environment in which faculty work, please indicate the degree of truthfulness you believe they have for faculty in the three major disciplinary areas indicated.

| | **Humanities** (English, history) | **Natural Sciences** (biology, chemistry, mathematics) | **Social Sciences** (political science, psychology, sociology) |
|---|---|---|---|

Very high degree of truth — Generally true — Generally not true — Little or no truth

a. There is a high degree of agreement among colleagues in this area about the content of their curricula.
   ① ② ③ ④     ① ② ③ ④     ① ② ③ ④

b. As a result of changes in this disciplinary area in the past decade, faculty have had to make significant changes in the content of their courses.
   ① ② ③ ④     ① ② ③ ④     ① ② ③ ④

c. As a result of changes in this disciplinary area in the past decade, faculty have had to make significant changes in their teaching methods.
   ① ② ③ ④     ① ② ③ ④     ① ② ③ ④

d. Faculty feel pressure from their colleagues to teach in a particular way.
   ① ② ③ ④     ① ② ③ ④     ① ② ③ ④

e. Faculty feel pressure from their institution to grade in a particular way.
   ① ② ③ ④     ① ② ③ ④     ① ② ③ ④

f. The faculty in this area are more committed to the teaching of their discipline than they are to adding to their discipline's knowledge base.
   ① ② ③ ④     ① ② ③ ④     ① ② ③ ④

---

4. The faculty's preference for how they allocate their time can differ from the administrator's preferred time allocations. Expectations can also vary considerably by disciplinary area. First, indicate how you believe the majority of faculty in the three areas want to allocate their effort. Then indicate how you, as an administrator, would prefer the faculty, on the average, to distribute their time.

(*Teaching* is the time spent preparing for teaching, scheduled classroom and laboratory instruction, grading, working with students. *Scholarship/Professional Growth* is the time spent enhancing your knowledge or skill in ways which may not necessarily result in a concrete product—library work, reading, exploratory inquiries, computer use. *Research* is the time spent in activities that lead to a concrete product—article, report, monograph, book, grant proposal, software development. *Service* is the time spent in college/university meetings, community activities, professional association involvements.)

The percentages are to total 100.

### Your Perception of Faculty Preference for Time Allocation

| | Humanitites | Natural Sciences | Social Sciences |
|---|---|---|---|
| Teaching | _____ | _____ | _____ |
| Scholarship/Professional Growth | _____ | _____ | _____ |
| Research | _____ | _____ | _____ |
| Service | _____ | _____ | _____ |
| Total | 100% | 100% | 100% |

*(continued on next page)*

4

332

*(continued from previous page)*

### Your Preference for Faculty Time Allocation

| | Humanitites | Natural Sciences | Social Sciences |
|---|---|---|---|
| Teaching | —— | —— | —— |
| Scholarship/Professional Growth | —— | —— | —— |
| Research | —— | —— | —— |
| Service | —— | —— | —— |
| Total | 100% | 100% | 100% |

5. Below are some outcomes that depend to varying degrees on faculty efforts. Fill in the circle that best corresponds to how much influence you think faculty have on each of the following:

Substantial influence ———
Some influence ———
Minor influence ———
Really no influence at all ———

a. Student learning. ① ② ③ ④

b. Departmental curriculum committee decisions. ① ② ③ ④

c. Having something they have written accepted for publication. ① ② ③ ④

d. Student career achievements. ① ② ③ ④

e. The salary increase they will receive next year. ① ② ③ ④

f. Selecting the next chair of their unit. ① ② ③ ④

g. Establishing student admissions requirements. ① ② ③ ④

h. Obtaining money for travel to professional association meetings (beyond standard institutional allocations). ① ② ③ ④

i. The personal interests they wish to pursue. ① ② ③ ④

j. Setting requirements for graduation. ① ② ③ ④

k. Selecting the next faculty member hired in their unit. ① ② ③ ④

l. Securing resources to maintain ongoing programs they consider important. ① ② ③ ④

m. Establishing criteria for annual review of faculty members. ① ② ③ ④

6. Faculty receive feedback on their work in a variety of ways and from different people. Fill in the circle that best corresponds with the degree of credence you give to each of the following :

A great deal of credence ———
Moderate credence ———
Some credence ———
Little or no credence ———
Never received ———

a. The unit chair's evaluation of a faculty member's teaching. ① ② ③ ④ ⑤

b. Colleagues' (faculty members at your institution) evaluations of one another's teaching. ① ② ③ ④ ⑤

c. Student responses on teaching evaluation forms. ① ② ③ ④ ⑤

d. The chair's or dean's comments on an individual's scholarly activities. ① ② ③ ④ ⑤

e. Colleagues' (faculty members at your institution) comments on one another's scholarly work. ① ② ③ ④ ⑤

f. Alumni comments about the impact faculty had on them. ① ② ③ ④ ⑤

g. The chair's or dean's comments on an individual's service contributions to the institution. ① ② ③ ④ ⑤

h. Peer (external) evaluations of faculty scholarship. ① ② ③ ④ ⑤

5

333

7. For each statement below, fill in the circle that best expresses your level of agreement.

Strongly agree ——
Tend to agree ——
Tend to disagree ——
Strongly disagree ——

a. *I expect undergraduate students will generally:*

(1) think for themselves. ① ② ③ ④

(2) share ideas and work cooperatively. ① ② ③ ④

(3) seek to outperform one another. ① ② ③ ④

(4) learn only what is required. ① ② ③ ④

(5) lack interest in the subject matter. ① ② ③ ④

(6) feel overwhelmed by course requirements. ① ② ③ ④

(7) need frequent feedback on their performance. ① ② ③ ④

(8) be appropriately challenged by course requirements. ① ② ③ ④

(9) work on their own. ① ② ③ ④

Strongly agree ——
Tend to agree ——
Tend to disagree ——
Strongly disagree ——

b. *I assume undergraduates learn best when:*

(1) course content is determined by the teacher. ① ② ③ ④

(2) the pace is set for the group by the teacher. ① ② ③ ④

(3) course content is perceived to have immediate relevance to the students' lives. ① ② ③ ④

(4) course content is determined cooperatively by students and the teacher. ① ② ③ ④

(5) conditions are established that let students discover new concepts or principles. ① ② ③ ④

(6) competition among students is fostered. ① ② ③ ④

(7) students progress at their own pace. ① ② ③ ④

8. Below are sets of words and phrases that faculty have used to describe the valued faculty members on their campuses. The first set has to do with skills and abilities of these faculty members. The second set consists of values and attitudes ascribed to these people. The third set contains personality characteristics respected faculty members are said to possess.

Fill in the circles that best represent the extent to which the word or phrase characterizes the faculty members you value on your campus.

Highly characteristic ——
Somewhat characteristic ——
Slightly characteristic ——
Not at all characteristic ——

a. **Skills/Abilities**

(1) Teaches effectively ① ② ③ ④
(2) Keeps abreast of developments in the discipline ① ② ③ ④
(3) Obtains grants ① ② ③ ④
(4) Communicates well ① ② ③ ④
(5) Publishes ① ② ③ ④
(6) Is organized ① ② ③ ④
(7) Works skillfully with students ① ② ③ ④
(8) Responds to requests ① ② ③ ④
(9) Is an excellent lecturer ① ② ③ ④
(10) Knows how to work the system ① ② ③ ④

b. **Beliefs/Attitudes/Values**

(1) Is highly committed to teaching ① ② ③ ④
(2) Is concerned about students ① ② ③ ④
(3) Believes in the virtue of hard work ① ② ③ ④
(4) Is highly committed to research ① ② ③ ④
(5) Holds high standards ① ② ③ ④
(6) Has integrity ① ② ③ ④
(7) Respects others ① ② ③ ④
(8) Is dedicated to the liberal arts ① ② ③ ④
(9) Is a team player ① ② ③ ④
(10) Is devoted to the institution ① ② ③ ④

c. **Personality Characteristics**

(1) Is supportive ① ② ③ ④
(2) Is understanding ① ② ③ ④
(3) Is open ① ② ③ ④
(4) Is candid ① ② ③ ④
(5) Has a sense of humor ① ② ③ ④
(6) Is personable ① ② ③ ④
(7) Is dedicated ① ② ③ ④
(8) Is ambitious ① ② ③ ④
(9) Is competitive ① ② ③ ④
(10) Is perseverant ① ② ③ ④

6

9. Fill in the circle that most closely indicates how often you have done the following during the *last year*.

More than 20 times
11-20 times
5-10 times
1-4 times
Never

a. Attended a visiting lecturer's presentation on campus. ① ② ③ ④ ⑤

b. Attended a campus seminar where a faculty member was presenting her or his work. ① ② ③ ④ ⑤

c. Conversed with faculty members about their research. ① ② ③ ④ ⑤

d. Attended a campus workshop on teaching. ① ② ③ ④ ⑤

e. Counseled a faculty member on her or his teaching. ① ② ③ ④ ⑤

f. Counseled a faculty member on her or his scholarship. ① ② ③ ④ ⑤

g. Counseled a faculty member on personal issues (e.g., stress, health, family, finances). ① ② ③ ④ ⑤

10. The following questions are about your background. Fill in the appropriate circle or write the response in the appropriate blanks.

a. List the highest academic degree you have earned, the institution granting it, the year in which it was obtained, and your major field of study.

Degree _____ Year _____

Institution _____

Major _____

b. Current position _____

c. How many years have you been at this institution (not including this year)? _____ (total years)

As an administrator _____ (years)

As a faculty member _____ (years)

d. How many years have you been at other colleges and universities? _____ (total years)

As an administrator _____ (years)

As a faculty member _____ (years)

e. What is your gender?

① Female  ② Male

f. In what year were you born? 19_____

*(continued in next column)*

g. Do you currently have an academic appointment?

① Yes  ② No

**If yes, answer questions h-l.**
**If no, skip to question m.**

h. What is your present rank? (Fill in one only.)

① Instructor
② Assistant Professor
③ Associate Professor
④ Professor
⑤ Lecturer
⑥ There are no ranks at my institution.
⑦ Other

i. How many years have you held your current academic rank (not including this year)? _____ (years)

j. What kind of appointment do you now hold? (Fill in one only.)

① Regular with tenure
② Regular without tenure
③ Yearly term appointment
④ Visiting
⑤ Other

k. If not tenured, are you in a tenure track position? (Leave blank if tenured.)

① Yes  ② No

l. As a faculty member, do your interests lie primarily in teaching or in research?

① Very heavily in research
② In both, but leaning toward research
③ In both, but leaning toward teaching
④ Very heavily in teaching

m. During this academic year, did you teach an undergraduate course?

① Yes  ② No

n. During this academic year, were you actively involved in disciplinary research?

① Yes  ② No

o. How fair is your salary in comparison with that of other administrators at your institution?

① More than I deserve
② About as much as I deserve
③ Somewhat less than I deserve
④ Much less than I deserve
⑤ I don't know.
⑥ I don't care.

p. How does your salary compare with those of your colleagues at peer institutions?

① Appreciably higher
② Somewhat higher
③ About the same
④ Somewhat lower
⑤ Appreciably lower
⑥ I don't know.
⑦ I don't care.

*(continued on next page)*

*(continued from previous page)*

q. Your race or ethnic group is:

  ① White/Caucasian
  ② Black/Negro/Afro-American
  ③ Native American/American Indian
  ④ Mexican American/Chicano
  ⑤ Puerto Rican
  ⑥ Hispanic
  ⑦ Oriental
  ⑧ Other Asian
  ⑨ Other

r. Comparing yourself with other college or university administrators of your age and qualifications, how successful do you consider yourself in your career?

  ① Very successful
  ② Fairly successful
  ③ Fairly unsuccessful
  ④ Very unsuccessful

s. In general, how do you feel about this institution?

  ① It is a very good place for me.
  ② It is a fairly good place for me.
  ③ It is not the place for me.

t. If you were to begin your career again, would you still want to be a college or university administrator?

  ① Definitely yes
  ② Probably yes
  ③ Probably no
  ④ Definitely no

11. Academic administrators can have varying levels of influence on the quality of *undergraduate* education at their institutions. For each item listed below, fill in the circle that identifies to what extent you feel you can affect decisions in that area.

Great deal of influence ———
Moderate influence ———
Some influence ———
Little or no influence ———

| | | | | |
|---|---|---|---|---|
| a. Curricula | ① | ② | ③ | ④ |
| b. Faculty salaries | ① | ② | ③ | ④ |
| c. Supplemental funds for instructional improvements | ① | ② | ③ | ④ |
| d. Student admissions standards | ① | ② | ③ | ④ |
| e. Academic support services (e.g., library, computing, audio-visual) | ① | ② | ③ | ④ |
| f. Student support services (e.g., tutoring, counseling) | ① | ② | ③ | ④ |
| g. Hiring of new faculty | ① | ② | ③ | ④ |
| h. Faculty development | ① | ② | ③ | ④ |
| i. Teaching and classroom facilities | ① | ② | ③ | ④ |
| j. Institutional resource allocation priorities as reflected in the annual operating budget | ① | ② | ③ | ④ |

12. Environmental factors can affect you and your institution. For each item listed below, fill in the appropriate circle.

a. Compared to five years ago, is your FTE undergraduate enrollment:

  ① More?
  ② About the same?
  ③ Less?

b. Compared to five years ago, is your FTE undergraduate enrollment:

  ① More part-time?
  ② Less part-time?
  ③ About the same?

c. Compared to five years ago, is your undergraduate student body:

  ① Older?
  ② Younger?
  ③ About the same?

d. Compared to five years ago, are your undergraduate students:

  ① More well-prepared?
  ② Less well-prepared?
  ③ About the same?

e. How would you describe the constraints on your institution's resources?

  ① Few
  ② Moderate
  ③ Serious
  ④ Severe

f. How would you describe the morale of the Humanities faculty at your institution?

  ① Generally high
  ② Uneven
  ③ Generally low

g. How would you describe the morale of the Natural Science faculty at your institution?

  ① Generally high
  ② Uneven
  ③ Generally low

h. How would you describe the morale of the Social Science faculty at your institution?

  ① Generally high
  ② Uneven
  ③ Generally low

i. Is your faculty unionized?

  ① Yes   ② No

  **If no, skip to question k.**

j. If yes, how has having a unionized faculty affected your job?

  ① My job is easier now.
  ② My job is more difficult now.
  ③ It has not changed the difficulty level of my job.

*(continued on next page)*

8

*(continued from previous page)*

k. How do you feel faculty salaries at your institution
   compare with those at your peer institutions?

   ① Faculty salaries here are less.
   ② Faculty salaries here are about the same.
   ③ Faculty salaries here are higher.

---

13. Most academic administrators have an idea of what an effective administrator is like. In column I rank order the characteristics in terms of how much you believe they contribute to an administrator's effectiveness. Assign "5" to the most important characteristic.

In column II rank order the characteristics according to what you consider to be your personal strengths as an administrator. Assign "5" to your greatest strength.

|  | **I**<br>**Effective Administrator** | **II**<br>**Personal Strengths** |
|---|---|---|
|  | Most important<br>Very important<br>Somewhat important<br>Slightly important<br>Not important | Great strength<br>Moderate strength<br>Little strength<br>Some weakness<br>Major weakness |
| a. **Administrative skills** (those things the administrator does to make the organization function; e.g., communicate with faculty, students, alumni; reach and carry through on decisions) | ① ② ③ ④ ⑤ | ① ② ③ ④ ⑤ |
| b. **Values** (the core values he or she holds about what is important in academia, and how to best achieve these goals for students and faculty members) | ① ② ③ ④ ⑤ | ① ② ③ ④ ⑤ |
| c. **Professionalism** (the integrity with which he or she conducts business; her or his knowledge of and commitment to the institution; dedication to the role of being an effective administrator) | ① ② ③ ④ ⑤ | ① ② ③ ④ ⑤ |
| d. **Experience/Background** (knowledge of faculty life; preparation, formal and informal, as an administrator; educational credentials; ability to fulfill special requirements such as fund-raising) | ① ② ③ ④ ⑤ | ① ② ③ ④ ⑤ |
| e. **Personality** (those aspects of her or his demeanor that make it more or less easy to work with her or him) | ① ② ③ ④ ⑤ | ① ② ③ ④ ⑤ |

---

*Thank you for taking the time to complete this survey.*

9

337

# NOTES

## Introduction

1. After Adelman's (1992) most appropriate title for curriculum problems.

2. Gender and ethnicity are also unevenly distributed across academic disciplines and institutional types. We develop these relationships in chapter 2.

3. These faculty constitute but a small percentage of the total population. The large constituency that we have also omitted is part-time faculty.

4. This decision means that professional school faculty receive less attention.

5. In the main, public college and university students outnumber their private counterparts. For example, the average public Res-I has 27,956 students, whereas the private average is 12,840, less than half that number.

6. In our 1988 data set, in almost every one of our studies—the exception is the study of administrators and faculty in two-year colleges (chapter 7)—we use data only on the public two-year institutions. They enroll over 95 percent of the students in two-year colleges. The private sector has a wide assortment of institutions—usually small, with an average enrollment of 700 in contrast to 4,404 for the public colleges—ranging from pure baccalaureate preparation to training for specialized vocations.

7. Some church-controlled colleges require that faculty members pledge to conform to a set of behavior standards before being hired. Only a few private colleges and universities have unionized faculty, in contrast to appreciable numbers in the public sector. Not infrequently, especially in the first few years, a unionized condition strains administrator and faculty relations. Faculty governance changes, and merit pay (reward incentive) often disappears.

8. The ratio varies appreciably within Res-I institutions, from more than 20 to 1 in their law schools to approximately 1 to 1 in their medical schools.

9. One can set aside the part-time numbers, for these faculty are all but impossible to census. NCES (1990a, p. 231) reports there were 180,000 regular part-timers, 131,000 temporary part-timers, and 23,000 temporary full-timers.

10. The survey reported in NCES (1990a) counted anyone who taught a course as a faculty member. Some institutions register only those who had half or more of their assignment in the professorial role. Others count administrators who hold a professorial title even though they neither teach nor engage in research.

11. However, because the 564 LAC-I's and -II's differ appreciably in their student-to-faculty ratio, the task would be a long one.

12. This statement is not true for historically black colleges and universities (HBCUs).

13. We frequently cite "national surveys" of faculty as the data source for figures and tables. There are 17 surveys, conducted between 1955 and 1989, that appear in the literature with some regularity (plus an unknown number of others of a private nature, most often conducted as a part of a dissertation). The ones we make use of are the larger and more comprehensive ones. (The others, while most often well carried out, sample either selected faculty populations or an institutional type.)

The first is the 1969 survey by the Carnegie Commission on the Future of Higher Education and the American Council on Education (Bayer, 1970; Trow, 1975). The second and third—virtual repeats of the first—are the 1972 survey by the American Council on Education and the 1975 one by the Carnegie Commission (Roizen, Fulton, & Trow, 1978). The next is the 1980 survey from UCLA conducted by the Higher Education Research Institute (1983). The fifth is the 1984 survey by the Carnegie Foundation for the Advancement of Teaching (1984). There were three surveys in 1988: an essential repeat by the Carnegie Foundation for the Advancement of Teaching (1989b); one at the University of Michigan conducted by NCRIPTAL, the National Center for Research to Improve Postsecondary Teaching and Learning (Blackburn & Lawrence, 1989); and one by the National Center for Educational Statistics of the U.S. Department of Education's Office of Educational Research and Improvement (NCES, 1990a), most often referred to as NSOPF-88 (*Faculty in Higher Education Institutions, 1988*). With the exception of the UCLA survey, the data for these surveys are publicly available through a number of sources. (There is a 1989–1990 UCLA survey that is also not available for use.) NCES has released its NSOPF-93 national survey, but not in time for data from it to be incorporated into this book.

The reader can tell by the dates used in the figures which survey the data came from.

14. In other words, ours is not an exhaustive literature review of all studies on faculty.

## Chapter 2. The Variables: Sociodemographics and Career

1. Opinions, perceptions, and beliefs contribute important data. As our research demonstrates, each influences behavior. However, they are not themselves behaviors.

2. As explained in the note to the figure, these data differ from those on the national surveys' uncorrected data tapes. They are the most accurate that exist. See the research note by Bentley, Blackburn, and Bieber (1990). Blackburn and Mackie (1992) report on the response rates and reliabilities of the various national surveys of faculty.

3. The 1989–1990 Higher Education Research Institute (n.d.) survey's age distribution report differs at most by 1 percent for each category.

4. Faculty live longer than the average U.S. citizen. With continuing health benefits to staff retirees and health costs rising at an exponential rate, institutions already face serious financial problems. For example, the University of Michigan

is currently paying $8 million per year for 4,000 retirees. This expense rises annually, with 200 to 300 people retiring each year and another 130 or so passing away but being survived by their spouses, whose health coverage continues until death.

5. During this era millions of dollars went into producing television courses and setting up language laboratories to make up for the expected shortage of teachers. Most of the "innovations," however, were never used except by the faculty members who designed the programs. (The language labs went out with the student revolution. Dropping language requirements for the B.A., M.A., and Ph.D. devastated foreign language departments nearly everywhere.)

6. See Western Interstate Commission on Higher Education (1991) for the best review of this literature.

7. The total number of U.S.-graduated Ph.D.'s is not declining. Decreasing numbers of U.S. citizens earning the degree have been offset by the number of foreign nationals studying in this country. It remains unknown, however, how many of them will return to their native country and how many will remain in the United States and take faculty positions. (Academics do not produce all new science, of course, but they publish the most and advance the theoretical basis on which many applied results depend.)

8. Wisconsin and, recently, Michigan set aside the national law with their own state provisions that no longer exempt public college and university tenured faculty from this discriminatory legislation. The Wisconsin experience has shown no difference in faculty retirement practices. Age 65 remains the norm. The exemption will most likely expire in 1994 rather than be renewed.

9. Scholars engaged in other than the traditional modes of investigation also attack this measure. Academics using new modes of analysis question the possibility of dispassionate investigation of a world divorced from the inquirer's claim. They also assert a lack of access to the "respected" (i.e., traditional) outlets. The debates over acceptable canons of research have spread from literature and history deep into some of the social sciences.

10. A few studies fall outside these categories. Some provide data for more than one. This section follows Blackburn and Lawrence's (1986) review of the literature on aging and faculty performance.

11. Stern (1978) examined the publication data on mathematicians and concluded that there is not an early peak followed by a decline, as has often been asserted. He found no relationship between age and creative discovery.

12. The data are cross-sectional, not longitudinal records of the same faculty. We discuss these database limitations for dealing with age-related data in greater detail below.

13. Bayer and Dutton (1977) have a variety of curves for different disciplines. They use a best-fit quadratic equation for each data set. They hypothesize different explanations for the different curves. By way of illustration, they interpret a productivity upturn by individuals in their mid-60s as a response to the motivation to clean up one's work before retirement.

14. Blackburn, Behymer, and Hall (1978) also used the 1969 Carnegie survey.

Pelz and Andrews (1976) relied on data collected in the 1960s. Bayer and Dutton (1977) used the 1972 Carnegie data, a sample drawn from the same population as the 1969 survey.

15. In 1969, $r = -.01$; in 1975, $r = -.05$; in 1980, $r = -.09$, a significant value.

16. See Lawrence and Blackburn (1985) and Horner, Rushton, and Vernon (1986) on using survey data for conducting cross-sequential studies for cohorts.

17. We follow Epstein's (1988, pp. 5–6) usage. *Sex* refers to attributes created by biological differences, and *gender* refers to socially and culturally created differences between men and women. However, when differences between the sexes are debatable, or when the term could have multiple meanings, we tend to use *gender*. We usually use *female* and *male* as adjectives and *men* and *women* as nouns, their order of presentation being alphabetical (*female* before *male, men* before *women*).

18. The parallel with faculty of color is strong along this dimension. "Black studies" started at about the same time.

19. The exception is the 1980 survey, one with a very low response rate and hence the most likely to be in error. Data on liberal arts and community colleges for 1988 are 23.0 percent, 30.4 percent, 35.4 percent, and 30.5 percent, respectively, for Comp-II's, LAC-I's, LAC-II's, and CCs, higher for each of these institutional types. In addition, including faculty from these four categories produces a higher percentage of women in every single discipline shown in the table. These are where the women are.

20. The exception being the same institutions and point in time mentioned in the previous note.

21. When initial Ns at time 1 are close to zero, even a meager increment translates into high percentage gains.

22. Strictly speaking, from an approximately 50 percent response rate, the best bet is one woman chemist per five institutions. That number remains a monstrous embarrassment to equity.

23. This section is taken from Trautvetter and Blackburn (1990). We have also borrowed extensively from the excellent review on status changes for female faculty from 1980 to 1990 conducted by Dwyer, Flynn, and Inman (1991).

24. Bentley and Blackburn (1992) used only the eight disciplines mentioned above. The findings reported here follow that study.

25. See chapter 4. Keep in mind that so far the productivity studies have predominantly been conducted with men.

26. The figures, however, do show gains over time.

27. For example, contrary to accepted beliefs, Lutjens (1988) found no relationship between the proportion of women in a department and their publication rate; that is, tokenism does not explain female productivity.

28. Widom and Burke (1978), J. R. Cole (1979), and Rothblum (1988), among others, call attention to the existence of discrimination quite irrespective of various rules and regulations.

29. We take *race* to be a social construction, one that has no biological basis.

We prefer *ethnicity*, also a social construction but one that identifies a group of people on some common grounds (e.g., religion, nationality, culture) other than skin color. However, *race* is the term frequently used in government and national survey reports. "Race" identifiers having different terms for the same ethnic group—*American Indians* and *Native Americans, blacks* and *African Americans*—exacerbate the problem of proper terminology. We stay with NCES terminology when reporting NCES data. Otherwise we most often use *African Americans* (not *blacks*), *Asian Americans,* and the like, and *Caucasian* rather than *white. Hispanic* we retain even though it improperly collects Cubans, Chicanos, and others under this general title, as does *Latino.* (The absurdity of this business reached its peak when the U.S. government classified natives of India as whites; not until 1993 did it begin placing them in the Asian category.)

30. While NCES includes Asian Americans as minorities, some colleges and universities do not when employing affirmative action practices. This ethnic group's representation in the professoriate exceeds its proportion of the U.S. population.

31. Hispanic faculty are smaller in number—although increasing more rapidly both in percentage of the professoriate and in real numbers—and more recent in entrance to faculty positions.

The NCES (1990a, pp. 164–171) survey also displays comparative data on a number of variables—highest degree held, rank, tenure status, age, hours worked, publications, salary, satisfaction, and others. However, the minority data are aggregated. That is, NCES presents Native Americans, African Americans, Asian Americans, and Hispanics as a single group. However, African American faculty in education in HBCUs are likely to have appreciably lower salaries than Asian faculty in engineering in doctoral universities. That their combined average income is approximately the same as that of Caucasian faculty misleads more than it informs.

32. In many ways there are but two faculty ethnic groups, African Americans and non–African Americans.

33. Thomas (1987), Pruitt (1989), Blackwell (1987), and Pearson and Bechtel (1989) are important sources on black graduate students and the professions.

34. All these studies are on African Americans.

35. These two surveys have been the largest to date. The 1969 has over 60,000 respondents and the 1990 over 50,000.

36. Logan (1990) had a very high response rate in her dissertation study. However, the data she collected did not include information on research and publication.

37. The low response rate from HBCUs is understandable. With the never-ending threats of closure from state houses and foreclosure from banks, HBCUs cannot trust the white establishment collecting information that could be used to show their "inferiority" and jeopardize their continuance.

38. Freeman used the data from the 1969 Carnegie Commission and American Council on Education surveys and the 1972 ACE survey.

39. This study is not a direct black-white comparison.

40. But African American faculty frequently earned their bachelor's degree at an HBCU.

41. While this assertion is literally true, in reality the socioeconomic status into which one is born makes an appreciable difference in academic careers just as it does in other occupations. Being born in Winnetka rather than on the South Side of Chicago means a home rich with books, parents who promote education and who can afford an expensive college—the entire gambit. Today's faculty come principally from professional and business families with above-average means, the exception being faculty in community colleges. Religious upbringing also matters. For example, Jews place a very high value on education. Children raised in Jewish homes who become faculty far exceed their percentage in society as a whole. In addition, they publish at an above-average rate.

42. Our assertions are never without exceptions. A statement claiming an "unquestionable" relation such as this one really means "most often," "almost always," or "with a few exceptions."

43. While research universities pay according to market prices and will have physicists earning twice what historians of art earn, institutions emphasizing teaching have nearly equal salaries across the disciplines. Highest degree, rank, and career age will be the principal determiners of pay. If faculty are unionized, salaries are much more likely to be comparable across disciplines, even in institutions emphasizing research. Pay discrepancies lead to grievances being filed, and unions do not like grievances. They are expensive and breed worker discontent with the union. Few research university faculty have unionized.

44. A discipline can also be described by the work faculty do. See Watkins (1989) for a Marxist analysis of English departments.

45. One can make comparisons by introducing standard scores within each discipline. That is, the researcher finds high and low producers in two or more disciplines and looks at the correlates to assess comparability of factors that predict publications.

46. Or as Billie Holiday sings in "God Bless the Child," "Them that has, gets."

47. How well they will perform in the pedagogical role receives less attention. Liberal arts colleges care more about teaching ability. We will see later that the individual relationship between teaching and research is not strong, but it is positive. That is, contrary to the belief of many students, and some faculty, the two roles are not mutually exclusive, nor are they conflicting to the degree that one role blunts success in the other.

48. No-degree cases are rare. Universities hire an Eric Hoffman and established musicians and artists as faculty, but their numbers are small.

49. A number of faculty earn their doctorate before taking a community college position, posts they most often took because they were the only openings available during the lean hiring times of 1975–1985, especially in the humanities. More often, however, the faculty member acquires the doctorate after joining the community college faculty.

50. Almost all historically "non-Ph.D." fields have steadily elevated their re-

quirements to the doctorate. Nursing and social work research university departments now hire only faculty who have the Ph.D.—or promote only those who attain it, if they were hired with a master's degree.

51. Many liberal arts colleges—four-year institutions with no graduate programs and without adequate resources for conducting research—do not require faculty research publications for a successful career. Still, these institutions typically seek persons with a Ph.D. (although the percentage of their faculty who possess the degree is less than it is in most comprehensive, doctoral, and research universities). They also believe that their public image as a high-quality institution depends upon having a highly pedigreed staff—faculty with Ph.D.'s from leading graduate universities.

52. See below for degrees earned in other fields and observe what happens when Ph.D.'s earned by non-U.S. students are removed from the totals.

53. Recent preliminary reports indicate the beginnings of another rise.

54. Fewer faculty move up than down the institutional ladder. Those who move up have made significant and visible scholarly contributions. In addition, the relationship between place of work and place of graduation has other career implications that extend beyond our concerns. It is precisely these career variables that produce the existing stratified system of colleges and universities. See Breneman and Youn (1988) and Deitsch (1989) for an account of mobility patterns.

55. While a few assistant professors are tenured and a smaller number of associate professors are not, in the main the percentages of associate plus full professors gives the percentage of faculty who were tenured at each time of data collection.

56. The 1969, 1975, and 1988 surveys are the same ones reported earlier. These data have not been corrected for sampling errors. The differences between female and male academics, however, are not affected.

57. In addition, most often these people do not have the normal accouterments of health care, institutional retirement payments, and the like.

58. Status and promotion in rank depend upon training (education) and performance. Possessing the doctorate is almost a mandatory requirement in arts and science disciplines in universities. Performance almost always relies most heavily on scholarly publications.

59. As seen, nearly all faculty in universities have the doctorate. Most often that is the prerequisite for an assistant professorship and marks the beginning of the person's "real" career. Individuals may have done some part-time teaching at a neighboring institution while completing the dissertation, but the first full and regular appointment—that is, the beginning of their career—coincides with receiving the Ph.D. Consequently, our procedure ascertains career age reasonably accurately.

60. Assertions of this kind—namely, predictions of future conditions—rest on the validity of assumptions whose certainty is never known. In this case student enrollment and adequate institutional finances to hire new staff will affect the prognosis. Right now that prognosis appears dismal.

## Chapter 3. The Variables: Self-Knowledge, Social Knowledge, Behaviors, and Environmental Constructs

1. I had some control over where I went to graduate school and where I now work (career variables). Even though the institution I am now at may not have been my first choice, I could have refused to take employment here. I think my job performance has had something to do with my rank and tenure status. However, once I became a full professor (circa age 40), no further promotions were available. Still, over the last 25 to 30 years of my career my interest in, say, teaching has fluctuated (as it does even on a daily basis—from euphoria to considering options for retirement). So has my assessment of how influential I think I am in, say, determining who the next person hired for my department will be. I occasionally change my view of how supportive my colleagues and administrators are. Others' perceptions of themselves and the environment will not be identical to mine.

2. Whenever possible, we continue to present data on the variables at successive points in time. Unfortunately, more often than not, earlier faculty surveys did not include many of the self-knowledge variables.

3. The faculty's principal complaint is that they do not have enough time to do what they want to do. Their grumbling is well founded. Faculty have more work interests than can possibly be satisfied.

4. Of course, I am accountable to my students. I am also accountable to my immediate (departmental) colleagues. Peer pressure can be strong and can be exercised at tenure and promotion time.

5. Note that in table 3.1 we grouped institutions and that the categories are not a single institutional type. Those placed together are similar in faculty publication output. (See the table's note.) We exclude LAC-II's and two-year colleges because their modal faculty publication output is zero.

6. A 0.5 average means that half the faculty had a higher interest in teaching, half a higher interest in research.

7. See appendix H for the survey instrument. Question 13 of the survey has three parts—percentage of time actually allocated to the role, preferred allocation, and believed institutional expectation, the latter being a variable we explain in the section on social knowledge.

8. These data exist only for 1988, so we have no knowledge as to how preferred allocation of effort to the different roles has changed over time.

9. One obvious explanation, of course, is that Caucasian men made the rules by which success is judged.

10. One needs to keep in mind that noted differences (and similarities) are always "on average." There are always individuals within each group who are higher or lower than individuals in the other.

11. There is a debate as to whether women have a moral voice different from men's. Gilligan says yes; Colby and Damon say no. See their chapters in Walsh (1987).

12. As for students, Acker (1978) finds that women in graduate school change

their goals more often than men do, and they do not expect to be as scholarly as men. Cole and Fiorentine (1991, pp. 217–220) report that women are as likely as men to aspire to become doctors, but only about half as many end up applying to medical school.

13. For example, women are succeeding in psychology, but not in economics; in literature, but not in philosophy.

14. Caesar (1992, pp. 145–165) also writes about the invisible college, but his story is about what it is like to be teaching at an institution no one has heard of.

15. A perceived gap between personal and institutional preference for a role can create dysfunctional stress—guilt, colleague criticism that one is not carrying one's share of the load, peer pressure to uphold the reputation of the unit.

16. We discussed the end product at the outset of chapter 2. We mention it here again simply to have the reader imagine the variety of possible outcomes other than quantity of publications. There is, for example, a qualitative distinction, such as acceptance by a leading journal or a highly selective university press. There are also any number of products other than publications. A prizewinning video program and graduating a Ph.D. are but two examples; Blackburn and Trowbridge (1973) researched the latter.

17. Hildebrand (1972) found that those faculty rated highest and lowest by students spent equal amounts of time preparing for class.

18. Carol Hughes's ongoing dissertation research has added this dimension to our theoretical framework, and so have we in a study of University of Michigan faculty about to be launched.

## Chapter 4. Faculty Research

1. This is not the first time the discovery of scholarship has affected faculty and the country's higher-education institutions. In the last half of the 19th century, some Americans traveled to Germany for advanced study and a Ph.D. They came home infected with scholarship. Some became the prime movers who produced the American university (Veysey, 1965). While they created a new type of institution, research did not become central until the period on which we concentrate.

2. To tell the complete story would require another book, not our aim.

3. These are mind-boggling numbers. How is one to keep abreast of current scholarship even in one's own specialty? In a neighbor's? In the larger context? The Renaissance scholar, the person who knows everything about everything, is not a foregone dream. It is a biological impossibility.

4. Bieber, Blackburn, and De Vries (1991) had somewhat better success for physical chemists, but the data were too sparse to allow definitive conclusions. The differences are understandable. In Kuhn's (1970) terminology, chemists enjoy comparatively high paradigm agreement and a high consensus on experimental procedures. Literary criticism continues to foment a state of turmoil in the humanities.

5. That these journals reject about 85 percent of the manuscripts they receive,

most of which are from leading scholars in the field, provides another indicator of raised standards and hence higher quality. Many rejects find their way into print in the next tier of periodicals and possibly raise the quality level of those less respected journals.

6. A revision of this paper has been published in *Research in Higher Education*. See Blackburn, Bieber, Lawrence, and Trautvetter, 1991.

7. This same source serves for most subsequent inquiries reported in this and the following chapters.

8. A full technical report (Blackburn & Lawrence, 1989) is available from the Inter-University Consortium for Political and Social Science Research (ICPSR), University of Michigan.

9. A plateau effect creates problems with categorical publication data because many faculty in research universities are in the top category, one that is typically stated sometimes as "11 publications or more" and sometimes as "20 or more." The variable loses its power to discriminate because the actual number remains unknown. For example, a woman publishing 25 times in two years receives no higher a score than a colleague publishing 11 times.

10. The theoretical framework assumes that environmental responses are the result of behavior and productivity at one time ($T_1$) and influence subsequent behavior and productivity at a later time ($T_2$) to the extent that organizational feedback modifies social knowledge and self-knowledge. Therefore, we only use environmental responses to predict social knowledge.

11. The data set permits approximation of one aspect of environmental conditions, namely, shared beliefs about the institution. However, we decided that the views of faculty in eight disciplines were inadequate to operationalize this construct. Furthermore, we lacked factual data on the institution. However, each institution is a separate variable. Since there were no survey items about family or involvement in non-work-related activities, we could not estimate the effects of social contingencies.

12. After this critical demonstration of our theoretical framework, we will present the statistical testing data in a much simplified form. We will also lead the reader through the first of these forthcoming regression analyses. In this note we will deal with betas and what their magnitudes and plus or minus signs mean.

When a regression analysis is run, one set of numbers that comes out are called betas. There is a beta for each variable, a number ranging from $-1.0$ to $+1.0$. The number is an indicator of the strength of that variable in predicting the outcome variable when all of the other variables are held constant. That is, the beta tells the direct effect of the predicting variable on the dependent variable—most often, in this chapter, publications. The program also gives the significance level for the beta, and we can see if it is, say, less that .05, the level we have been using. The limitation of this "pure" beta is that its magnitude depends upon the scale used to measure the variable. When these are not the same for all variables, you cannot compare the beta for one variable with that for another and know if the larger beta really is a stronger predictor. For example, a score of 4 on a seven-point scale is not relatively as high as is a 3 on a four-point scale, yet the beta for the former will be larger. What programs do, then, is convert the scores for every variable to the same scale. The order of the scores stays exactly the same during the conversion so that the highest is still the highest, the next remains next highest, and so on. The converted scores are called standardized betas; that is, they are all on the same yardstick. Standardized betas are what we have in the table. Now the betas can be compared with one another regardless of the differences in variable scales. Larger numbers are stronger predictors.

SATs are an example of standardized scores. No matter how many items are on the test, the scores are converted to a scale from 200 to 800, math and verbal. A 685 on the math is higher than a 550 on the verbal quite irrespective of the actual number of questions answered correctly on either examination. GREs, IQs, and other human measures are put into standardized form so that effects can be estimated.

No plus or minus sign before a beta means that the beta is greater than zero. It also means that that variable is a contributor to the explained variance. For example, we coded female = 1 and male = 0. When the beta alongside sex is positive (no plus or minus sign), it means that being female predicts the outcome. If the beta has a minus sign in front of it, then being male is the predictor.

13. This finding may be due in part to the fact that the items with the strongest loading on the administrator and faculty factors had to do with teaching evaluation.

14. As already noted, the behavior variables had the largest betas.

15. We expected a positive beta for psychology, for there has been grant money in that discipline. However, the Reagan years were hard on the social sciences, and that is when the survey was conducted.

16. Note that the standard deviations are larger than the means in all three cases. This indicates that the distributions are skewed, and in this case that there are more faculty producing no or few publications that are counterbalanced by a small number of faculty producing a large number. The distortion from a normal curve is greatest for the Comp-I faculty.

17. There are enough new variables not used in the first test paper (described in the previous section of this chapter) that the reader should consult this appendix.

18. This analysis closely parallels the preceding one. However, (1) environmental responses are different, and (2) we report only the variables that entered the regression analysis. Consequently, the findings differ slightly (e.g., percentage of explained variance here is 58 percent vs. 50 percent in the test of the theoretical framework). We include the Res-I institutions again in this form so that comparisons can be made with other institutional types.

19. We make distinctions between the concepts of research and scholarship. On our survey instrument that yielded the data analyzed here, we defined *research* as an activity that results in a product—an article, for example. We defined *scholarship,* on the other hand, as professional growth, time spent enhancing knowledge or skill in ways that may not necessarily result in a concrete product—

activities such as library work, reading, exploratory inquiries, or computer use. We explore this behavior in detail in chapter 6.

20. Faculty may credit their administrators with securing the resources needed for success, but we do not have that information.

21. *Dummy* is the technical statistical term for dealing with categorical variables, ones that do not have a scale (like, say, interest in research, where one can score the degree of interest over varying degrees, say from 5 being very high to 1 being very low). One is either female or male, and any number assigned to the sex variable has no meaning of higher or lower. Yet the statistical technique requires numbers, not words. We arbitrarily, but consistently, have coded female as 1 and male as 0. This makes sex a dummy variable, and the numbers produced by the program come out either positive (i.e., with no sign) for female or negative for male.

22. This investigation uses the term *natural sciences* for the three disciplines unless a difference occurs among the disciplines that needs to be noted. Furthermore, since part-time faculty and those at two-year institutions differ substantially as a group from their full-time four-year-institution counterparts in background, training, and work activities (Finkelstein, 1984a), this inquiry limits itself to full-time academics at four-year colleges and universities.

23. Since over 80 percent of faculty in two-year institutions and liberal arts colleges II do not publish at all (Ladd, 1979), we excluded the faculty in these institutions.

24. When appropriate, Cronbach reliability tests were run on the variables and are reported.

25. We cannot conclude causality. Women who publish may in turn increase their research self-competence and publish even more.

26. It at first seems contradictory that more experienced and lower-ranked male professors publish more. However, the lower-ranked professors can also be the more experienced female faculty members who have been trapped in lower ranks but are high publishers.

27. For example, some past publications may be invited chapters in books, writing that most often does not involve new research.

28. These are the first studies using faculty in professional schools.

29. The fact that the individuals selected in this study are all male was not controlled for by the researchers; it is an artifact of the original sample frame. The sample was chosen exclusively on the basis of year of appointment as assistant professor.

30. See the original paper (Lawrence, Bieber, Blackburn, Saulsberry, Trautvetter, Hart, & Frank, 1989) for the tables and statistical data. With such small numbers, traditional data analyses are weak. Our aim here is to witness the theoretical framework's power in dealing with primarily qualitative data. (When we do report differences, they are statistically significant unless we note otherwise.)

31. The perception of today's faculty differs significantly. Now faculty believe that promotion to associate and to full professor are equally rigorous and depend upon scholarly publications being both plentiful and of high quality.

32. Julius and Krauss's (1993) collection of papers on an aging workforce will be helpful to administrators dealing with an older faculty constituency.

33. If an institution has an Andrew J. Wiles on its faculty, then there is no problem. His devotion of seven years to one mathematical proof (Fermat's last theorem) bespeaks personal traits beyond genius. See McDonald (1993).

## Chapter 5. Faculty Teaching

1. Some colleges and universities have "teacher of the year" awards, but in a random sample the number of faculty who would have received such awards would be too small to analyze.

2. There is a low positive correlation between student ratings and student learning, most often measured by grade received or final examination score (Cohen, 1981). Neither outcome measure will be the right measure of learning unless, among numerous other conditions, initial level of knowledge and aptitude for the subject are controlled. See below.

3. A slight modification of the third paper has been published in *Research in Higher Education;* see Blackburn, Lawrence, Bieber, and Trautvetter, 1991. We have differentially modified the other three papers.

4. Before addressing the analyses and results, note that the comparatively small Ns within institutional cells eliminate the possibility of advanced statistical analysis.

5. The change index consisted of responses to questions asking the extent to which the faculty member changed or adjusted her or his teaching, scholarly, and service activities as a result of last year's evaluation.

6. The extent to which this instrument can discriminate among levels of faculty quality of effort is considered elsewhere (Blackburn, Knuesel, Yoon, & Brown, 1988).

7. Discipline effects were estimated using seven dummy variables to represent the eight areas in which the respondents taught.

8. Although the survey includes several retrospective measures, the data are not longitudinal.

9. Administrators probably do take such matters into account but end up throwing up their hands because they are unable to change organizational priorities.

10. See Feldman (1976, 1977, 1986, 1989) for reviews of this literature.

11. The Ns are shown in table 5.7. We do not argue that all disciplines within a field are alike with respect to what will predict effort given to teaching; there will be some differences among, say, psychology, political science, sociology, and other disciplines within the social science field. What we believe is that the differences within a field will be smaller than those across fields (e.g., the differences between psychology and political science will be smaller than those between psychology and English or chemistry).

12. Preliminary analyses showed there to be but negligible differences between private and public institutions, so the data used here are from both sectors for the

Res-I's and Comp-I's. As noted above, we used only the public two-year institutions.

13. Only research universities on the next to last variable in table 5.8 extend beyond the plus-or-minus-1 range, a fact we return to later.

14. With one exception, it turns out that neither the self-competence nor the self-efficacy variable remains significant in the final regressions. See below. (The exception is self-competence for chemistry faculty in CCs.)

15. The two are co-related. Hence, if one is not a good predictor, the other is not likely to be either.

16. We retain research, scholarship, and service variables in order to show their relationships to teaching.

17. Many of these other doctoral degrees would meet the requirements for a faculty position in a four-year college. The D.A. degree was created for those who wanted to be teachers more than to be researchers. The J.D. would qualify one for several of the social sciences, as would the M.D. for biology.

18. The factor called dissemination did not load with any other teaching or research variables. We decided it was more likely to be a measure of dissemination of teaching activities and practices than disciplinary research activities and treated it accordingly.

19. However, the studies described in the preceding sections of this chapter did not find these variables to be effective predictors.

20. Blackburn and Pitney (1988) reviewed the theoretical and applied literature of performance appraisal and feedback with respect to faculty.

21. Wylie and Fuller (1985) have reported the GLCA project.

## Chapter 6. Faculty Service and Scholarship

1. Public service was subsequently dropped from the analyses because we had but a single, unacceptable behavioral item in that category.

2. See chapter 4, at the discussion of table 4.6, on how to read this and the following tables in this chapter.

3. From Blackburn, Bieber, Lawrence, and Trautvetter, 1991.

4. The *r*s are retest reliability coefficients—correlations calculated between individuals' responses on the original questionnaire and the responses they gave about six weeks later on this item. See Blackburn and Mackie (1992).

## Chapter 7. Administrative and Faculty Views of the Workplace

1. Financial officers, student personnel people, and a host of other administrative positions are another story. They require no faculty experience even when they require the Ph.D.

2. We have Native American, Mexican American, Puerto Rican, Hispanic, Oriental, other Asian, and "other" categories. However, the numbers are so small that these groups have been collapsed into "other"—an unhappy resolution that

unfairly represents the ethnic groups as all alike, not as distinctive from one another.

3. These are "full-time faculty" (50 percent or greater appointment as a teacher), not "administrators."

4. "Support" is twice that, namely, from 2 (low) to 8 (high).

5. There is some intersection with the results of the first study reported above. However, here we deal only with teaching institutions. We also treat each college as a separate environment rather than collecting them and treating the aggregation as if it were but one institution. In addition, we add morale/satisfaction as an outcome, a condition important for effective organizations.

6. Comparisons of means for preferred distribution of effort by professors in the humanities, natural sciences, and social sciences indicated little disciplinary variation. In our analyses we used the average of these three means as an indicator of the administrator's preference.

7. For the administrators, the natural science disciplines were biology, chemistry, and mathematics; the humanities disciplines were English and history; the social science disciplines were political science, sociology, and psychology; a category designated "other" included professional degrees. High-level administrators were chief executive officers such as presidents or chancellors; middle-level administrators were deans; and low-level administrators were directors of admissions, library, support services, and the like.

## Chapter 8. Findings, Theories, and Next Steps

1. Correlations with calendar age had been low, not significant, but positive through the early national surveys. However, they turned negative—still low, and not significant—in the most recent national surveys. The youngest are producing at the highest rate, a consequence of the very selective hiring practices that universities exercised in response to the oversupply of new Ph.D.'s in the late 1970s and early 1980s. (See Bentley & Blackburn, 1990.)

2. Past publications—used only in the first test of the model—is, we suspect, an even stronger predictor than other career variables. As we employ it in current investigations, it continues to account for a significant portion of the variance. Past behavior is always a good predictor of current behavior, no matter what the activity.

3. While we accounted for significant percentages of the variance, especially in comparison with earlier studies, most often more than half the variance remained unexplained.

4. We have over 3,000 research studies on faculty in our reference file.

5. One needs to consult other authors on this topic. A good start would be Fausto-Sterling (1992). Current claims on sexual orientation (homosexual vs. heterosexual men) advance a brain difference. The empirical data are based on but a few cases, and the conclusions continue to be controversial. Now a female-transmitted gene has been temporarily identified with male homosexuality.

6. Now cultural factors enter. That is why we qualified Hudson and Jacot's hypotheses by limiting them to the geographical societies we mentioned.

7. See Clark and Corcoran (1985), who incorporated this phenomenon into their interviews with University of Minnesota faculty.

8. In order not to lengthen the final questionnaire, we recommend that the inquiry focus almost exclusively on one role, either research or pedagogy, not both as we did. This will be a necessity if our recommendations for additions to the self-knowledge and social knowledge categories are accepted.

9. There is some evidence that "success" differs for men and women. A man's aspirations are often national and international; a woman's are more likely to be institutionally based.

## Epilogue

1. In the introduction we cited critics Anderson (1992), Cheney (1990), Douglas (1992), D'Souza (1991), Huber (1992), Kimball (1990), Smith (1991), and Sykes (1988, 1990). To this collection we can now add Roche (1994). In addition to financial mismanagement, Roche sees 1960s radicals lingering on the faculty, writing trash (when they write anything at all) and demanding protection for pedophiles.

2. Interestingly, Roche uses identical numbers. He says, "Colleges and universities have increasingly adopted a 'cattle-car' approach to education. . . . Classes crammed with 500 to 1,000 students are now commonplace."

3. Had we instead selected today's PC rather than a liberal education as our target, we believe we would soon have uncovered the blind, uncompromising demand for black and feminist studies, red faculty converting naive students to communism during the Joseph McCarthy era and to socialism during the Great Depression—selected events only occasionally supported by the historical record and grossly inflated with regard to their effects.

4. See Edmundson (1993, pp. 8–9) for his commentary on Kimball and D'Souza and for the chapters in his edited volume *Wild Orchids and Trotsky* for attempts by others to set the record straight. Byrne (1993) uses Lewis Carroll's *Hunting of the Snark* to characterize claims made as to why women are inferior to men when it comes to science.See also Rudolph's (1992) review of Smith's book and his violations of the historian's creed.

5. William Bennett is reported to have made $240,000 in 1990 for his speeches alone (Kinsley, 1993, p. 6).

6. We saw in chapter 6 that faculty members' service activities occupy the smallest portion of their work time. We therefore address only teaching and scholarship.

# REFERENCES

Abelson, R. P., & Levi, A. (1984). Decision making and decision theory. In G. Lindzey & E. Aronsen (Eds.), *Handbook of social psychology*. Reading, MA: Addison-Wesley.

Acker, S. S. (1978). Sex differences in graduate student ambition. (Doctoral dissertation, University of Chicago, 1978). *Dissertation Abstracts International, 39*(4-A), 2569.

Adams, C. W. (1946). The age at which scientists do their best work. *Isis, 36*, 166–169.

Adelman, C. (1992). *Tourists in their own land*. Washington, DC: United States Office of Education, Office of Educational Research and Improvement.

Ahern, N. C., & Scott, E. L. (1981). *Career outcomes in a matched sample of men and women Ph.D.s: An analytical report*. Washington, DC: National Academy Press.

Aisenberg, N., & Harrington, M. (1988). *Women of academe: Outsiders in the sacred grove*. Amherst: University of Massachusetts Press.

Allen, F. C. L. (1990). Indicators of academic excellence: Is there a link between merit and reward? *Australian Journal of Education, 34*(1), 87–98.

Allison, P. D., & Long, J. S. (1990). Departmental effects on scientific productivity. *American Sociological Review, 55*, 469–478.

Allison, P. D., & Stewart, J. A. (1974). Productivity differences among scientists: Evidence for accumulative advantage. *American Sociological Review, 39*(4), 596–606.

American Council on Education. (1987). *Fact book*. Washington, DC: American Council on Education.

Anderson, B. E., et al. (1978). *The state of black America*. New York: National Urban League.

Anderson, M. (1992). *Impostors in the temple*. New York: Simon & Schuster.

Anderson, R. E. (1983). *Higher education in the 1970's: Preliminary technical report for participating institutions*. New York: Columbia University, Teachers College Press.

Andrews, F. M. (1975). Social and psychological factors which influence the creative process. In I. R. Taylor & J. W. Getzels (Eds.), *Perspectives in creativity* (pp. 117–145). Chicago: Aldine.

Andrews, F. M. (Ed.). (1979). Scientific productivity: The effectiveness of research groups in six countries. Cambridge: Cambridge University Press.

Angelo, T. (1993, April). A teacher's dozen. *AAHE Bulletin, 45*(8), 3–7, 13.

Armour, R., Furhmann, B., & Wergin, J. (1990, April). *Racial and gender differences in faculty careers.* Paper presented at the annual meeting of the American Educational Research Association: Boston.

Astin, H. S. (1969). *The woman doctorate in America: Origins, career, and family.* New York: Russell Sage Foundation.

Astin, H. S. (1978). Factors affecting women's scholarly productivity. In H. S. Astin & W. Z. Hirsch (Eds.), *The higher education of women* (pp. 133–157). New York: Praeger.

Astin, H. S. (1984). Academic scholarship and its rewards. In M. W. Steinkamp & M. L. Maehr (Eds.), *Women in science* (pp. 259–279). Greenwich, CT: JAI.

Astin, H. S. (1991). Citation classics: Women's and men's perceptions of their contributions to science. In H. Zuckerman, J. Cole, & J. Bruer (Eds.), *The outer circle: Women's position in the scientific community* (pp. 57–70). New York: Norton.

Astin, H. S., & Bayer, A. E. (1979). Pervasive sex differences in the academic reward system: Scholarship, marriage, and what else? In D. R. Lewis & W. E. Becker (Eds.), *Academic rewards in higher education* (pp. 211–230). Cambridge, MA: Ballinger.

Atkinson, J. W. (1957). Motivational determinants of risk-taking behavior. *Psychological Review, 64,* 359–372.

Atkinson, J. W. (1977). Motivation for achievement. In T. Blass (Ed.), *Personality variables* (pp. 25–108). Hillsdale, NJ: Erlbaum.

Atkinson, J. W., & Feather, N. T. (Eds.). (1966). *A theory of achievement motivation.* New Work: Wiley.

Atkinson, J. W., & Raynor, J. O. (Eds.). (1974). *Motivation and achievement.* Washington, DC: Hemisphere.

Austin, A. E., & Gamson, Z. F. (1983). *Academic workplace: New demands, heightened tensions* (ASHE-ERIC Higher Education Report No. 10). Washington, DC: Association for the Study of Higher Education.

Babchuk, N., & Bates, A. P. (1962). Professor or producer: The two faces of academic man. *Social Forces, 40*(4), 341–348.

Baird, L. L. (1991). Publication productivity in doctoral research departments: Interdisciplinary and intradisciplinary factors. *Research in Higher Education, 32*(3), 303–318.

Baldwin, R. G., & Blackburn, R. T. (1981). The academic career as a developmental process: Implications for higher education. *Journal of Higher Education, 52*(6), 598–614.

Baltes, P. B., & Brim, O. G. (1983). *Life span and development and behavior.* New York: Academic Press.

Bandura, A. (1977a). Self-efficacy: Toward a unifying theory of behavioral change. *Psychological Review, 84*(2), 191–215.

Bandura, A. (1977b). *Social learning theory.* Englewood Cliffs, NJ: Prentice-Hall.

Bandura, A. (1982). Self-efficacy mechanisms in human agency. *American Psychologist, 37*(2), 122–147.

Bandura, A., & Wood, R. E. (1989). Effect of perceived controllability and performance standards on self-regulating complex decision making. *Journal of Personality and Social Psychology, 56,* 805–814.

Banks, W. M. (1984). Afro-American scholars in the university: Roles and conflicts. *American Behavioral Scientist, 27*(3), 325–338.

Barbezat, D. A. (1989). The effect of collective bargaining on salaries in higher education. *Industrial and Labor Relations Review, 42*(3), 443–455.

Bargh, J. A., & Pietrononaco, P. (1976). Automatic information processing and social perception: The influence of trait information present outside of conscious awareness on impression formation. *Journal of Personality and Social Psychology, 43,* 437–449.

Bar-Haim, G., & Wilkes, J. M. (1989). A cognitive interpretation of the marginality and underrepresentation of women in science. *Journal of Higher Education, 60*(4), 371–387.

Bayer, A. E. (1970). *College and university faculty: A statistical description* (Vol. 5, No. 5). Washington, DC: American Council on Education.

Bayer, A. E. (1973). *Teaching faculty in academe, 1972–73* (American Council on Education Research Reports Vol. 8). Washington, DC: American Council on Education.

Bayer, A. E., & Astin, H. S. (1975). Sex differentials in the academic reward system. *Science, 188*(4190), 796–802.

Bayer, A. E., & Dutton, J. E. (1977). Career age and research-professional activities of academic scientists: Tests of alternative nonlinear models and some implications for higher education faculty policies. *Journal of Higher Education, 48*(3), 259–279.

Bayer, A. E., & Folger, J. (1966). Some correlates of a citation measure of productivity in science. *Sociology of Education, 39*(4), 381–390.

Becher, T. (1981). Towards a definition of disciplinary cultures. *Studies in Higher Education, 6*(2), 4–6.

Becher, T. (1989). *Academic tribes and territories: Intellectual enquiry and the culture of disciplines.* Bury St. Edmunds, England: Society for Research into Higher Education and Open University Press.

Belenky, M. F., Clinchy, B. M., Goldberger, N. R., & Tarule, J. M. (1986). *Women's ways of knowing: The development of self, voice, and mind.* New York: Basic Books.

Bensimon, E. M. (1992). Lesbian existence and the challenge to normative construction of the academy. *Journal of Education, 174*(3), 98–112.

Bentley, R. J. (1990). *Faculty research performance over time and its relationship to sources of grant support.* Unpublished doctoral dissertation, University of Michigan, Ann Arbor.

Bentley, R. J., & Blackburn, R. T. (1990, November). *Relationship of faculty publication performance with age, career age, and rank.* Paper presented at the annual meeting of the Association for the Study of Higher Education: Portland, OR.

Bentley, R. J., & Blackburn, R. T. (1991). Changes in academic research performance over time: A study of institutional accumulative advantage. *Research in Higher Education, 31*(4), 327–353.

Bentley, R. J., & Blackburn, R. T. (1992). Two decades of gains for female faculty? *Teachers College Record, 93*(4), 697–709.

Bentley, R. J., Blackburn, R. T., & Bieber, J. P. (1990). Research note: Some corrections and suggestions for working with the national faculty survey databases. *Research in Higher Education, 31*(6), 587–603.

Berger, B. (1991). The idea of the university. *Partisan Review/2, 58*(2), 315–349.

Bernard, J. (1964). *Academic women.* University Park: Pennsylvania State University Press.

Berube, M. (1991, June). Public image limited: Political correctness and the media's big lie. *The Village Voice.*

Beyer, J. M., & Stevens, J. M. (1974, October). *Differences between scientific fields in patterns of research activity and productivity* (Paper No. 195). Buffalo: State University of New York at Buffalo, School of Management.

Bieber, J. P., & Blackburn, R. T. (1993). Faculty research productivity, 1972–1988: Development and application of constant units of measure. *Research in Higher Education, 34*(5), 551–567.

Bieber, J. P., Blackburn, R. T., & De Vries, D. (1991, April). *Faculty knowledge production: Changes in quality, 1972–1988.* Paper presented at the annual meeting of the American Educational Research Association: Chicago.

Bieber, J. P., Blackburn, R. T., Lawrence, J. H., Okoloko, V. P., Ross, S., & Knuesel, R. (1988, April). *Effects of personal attributes and environmental forces on faculty teaching behaviors.* Paper presented at the annual meeting of the American Educational Research Association: New Orleans.

Bieber, J. P., Lawrence, J. H., & Blackburn, R. T. (1992, July). Through the years: Faculty and their changing institutions. *Change, 24*(4), 28–35.

Birnbaum, R. (1975, September). Using the calendar for faculty development. *Educational Record, 56,* 226–230.

Blackburn, R. T. (1970). Legends of academe U.S.A., 1970: Filters, philtres, and potions. *Australian Journal of Higher Education, 4*(1), 4–12.

Blackburn, R. T. (1985). Faculty career development: Theory and practice. In S. M. Clark & D. R. Lewis (Eds.), *Faculty vitality and institutional productivity* (pp. 55–85). New York: Columbia University, Teachers College Press.

Blackburn, R. T., Behymer, C. E., & Hall, D. E. (1978). Research note: Correlates of faculty publications. *Sociology of Education, 51*(2), 132–141.

Blackburn, R. T., Bieber, J. P., Lawrence, J. H., & Trautvetter, L. C. (1989, November). *Faculty at work: Focus on research, scholarship, and service.* Paper presented at the annual meeting of the Association for the Study of Higher Education: Atlanta, GA.

Blackburn, R. T., Bieber, J. P., Lawrence, J. H., & Trautvetter, L. C. (1991). Faculty at work: Focus on research, scholarship, and service. *Research in Higher Education, 32*(4), 385–413.

Blackburn, R., Boberg, A., O'Connell, C., & Pellino, G. R. (1980). *Project for faculty development program evaluation.* Ann Arbor: University of Michigan, Center for the Study of Higher Education.

Blackburn, R. T., Chapman, D. W., & Cameron, S. M. (1980). *Cloning in academe: Mentorship and academic careers.* Paper presented at the annual meeting of the American Educational Research Association: Boston.

Blackburn, R. T., & Clark, M. J. (1975). An assessment of faculty performance: Some correlates between administrator, colleague, student, and self-ratings. *Sociology of Education, 48*(2), 242–256.

Blackburn, R. T., & Havighurst, R. J. (1979). Career patterns of distinguished male social scientists. *Higher Education, 8,* 553–572.

Blackburn, R. T., & Holbert, B. (1986). The status of women academics, 1964–1984. In J. Figueira-McDonough & R. C. Sari (Eds.), *Gender, deviance, and social control: Catch-22 strategies in the maintenance of minority status* (pp. 296–317). New York: Sage.

Blackburn, R. T., Horowitz, S. M., Edington, D. W., & Klos, D. (1987). University faculty and administrator responses to job strains. *Research in Higher Education, 25*(1), 31–41.

Blackburn, R. T., & Knuesel, R. E. (1987, February). *Validating a quality of faculty effort instrument.* Paper presented at the annual meeting of the Association for the Study of Higher Education: San Diego, CA.

Blackburn, R. T., Knuesel, R. E., Yoon, K., & Brown, R. (1988, April). *Attributes of valued faculty members.* Paper presented at the annual meeting of the American Educational Research Association: New Orleans.

Blackburn, R. T., & Lawrence, J. H. (1986). Aging and the quality of faculty performance. *Review of Education Research, 23*(3), 265–290.

Blackburn, R. T., & Lawrence, J. H. (1989). *Faculty at work: Final report of the national survey.* Ann Arbor: University of Michigan, NCRIPTAL.

Blackburn, R. T., Lawrence, J. H., Bieber, J. P., & Trautvetter, L. C. (1988, November). *Faculty at work: Focus on teaching.* Paper presented at the annual meeting of the Association for the Study of Higher Education: St. Louis, MO.

Blackburn, R. T., Lawrence, J. H., Bieber, J. P., & Trautvetter, L. C. (1991). Faculty at work: Focus on teaching. *Research in Higher Education, 32*(4), 363–383.

Blackburn, R. T., Lawrence, J. H., Hart, K. A., & Dickman, E. M. (1990). *Same institution, different perceptions: Faculty and administrators report on the work environment.* Ann Arbor: University of Michigan, NCRIPTAL.

Blackburn, R. T., Lawrence, J. H., Okoloko, V. P., Bieber, J. P., Meiland, R., Ross, S., & Street, T. (1986). *Faculty as a key resource.* Ann Arbor: University of Michigan, NCRIPTAL.

Blackburn, R. T., Lawrence, J. H., Okoloko, V. P., Bieber, J. P., Ross, S., Street, T., & Knuesel, R. E. (1987). *Faculty in their teaching roles: Case studies.* Ann Arbor: University of Michigan, NCRIPTAL.

Blackburn, R. T., & Mackie, C. J. (1992). Test-retest coefficients and the national faculty surveys. *Review of Higher Education, 16*(1), 19–39.

Blackburn, R. T., & Pitney, J. (1988). *Performance appraisal for faculty: Implications for higher education.* Ann Arbor: University of Michigan, NCRIPTAL.

Blackburn, R. T., Pitney, J., Lawrence, J. H., & Trautvetter, L. C. (1989, March). *Administrators' career background and their congruence with faculty beliefs and behaviors.* Paper presented at the annual meeting of the American Educational Research Association: San Francisco.

Blackburn, R. T., & Trowbridge, K. W. (1973). Faculty accountability and faculty workload: A preliminary cost analysis of their relationship as revealed by Ph.D. productivity. *Research in Higher Education, 1*(1), 1–12.

Blackburn, R. T., Wenzel, S., & Bieber, J. (1994). Minority vs. majority faculty publication performance: A research note. *Review of Higher Education, 17*(3), 271–282.

Blackburn, R. T., & Young, D. (1985). Faculty quality in black and white public colleges and universities in selected southern states. *Teachers College Record, 86*(4), 593–613.

Blackman, S. (1986). The masculinity-femininity of women who study college mathematics. *Sex Roles, 15*(1–2), 33–42.

Blackwell, J. E. (1987). *Mainstreaming outsiders: The production of black professionals.* Dix Hills, NY: General Hall.

Blau, J. R. (1974). Patterns of communication among theoretical high energy physicists. *Sociometry, 37*(3), 391–406.

Blau, P. M. (1973). *The organization of academic work.* New York: Wiley.

Boice, R. (1989). Procrastination, busyness, and bingeing. *Behavior Research and Therapy, 27*(6), 605–611.

Boice, R. (1992). *The new faculty member: Supporting and fostering faculty development.* San Francisco: Jossey-Bass.

Boice, R., & Jones, F. (1984). Why academicians don't write. *Journal of Higher Education, 55*(5), 567–581.

Bonzi, S. (1992). Trends in research productivity among senior faculty. *Information Processing and Management, 28*(1), 111–120.

Bonzi, S., & Day, D. I. (1991). Faculty productivity as a function of cohort group, discipline, and academic age. *Proceedings of the American Society for Information Science, 28,* 267–275.

Booth, W. C. (1988). *The vocation of a teacher: Rhetorical occasions, 1967–1988.* Chicago: University of Chicago Press.

Bouillon, J. (1987). *Research productivity and rewards in academe: Gender and field differences.* Unpublished doctoral dissertation, University of California, Los Angeles.

Bowen, H. R., & Schuster, J. H. (1986). *American professors: A national resource imperiled.* New York: Oxford University Press.

Bowen, W. G., & Sosa, J. A. (1989). *Prospects for faculty in the arts and sciences: A study of factors affecting demand and supply, 1987–2012.* Princeton, NJ: Princeton University Press.

Bowman, C. C. (1938). *The college professor in America.* Philadelphia: University of Pennsylvania Press.

Boyer, C. M., & Lewis, D. R. (1985). *And on the seventh day: Faculty consulting and supplemental income* (ASHE-ERIC Higher Education Report No. 3). Washington, DC: Association for the Study of Higher Education.

Boyer, E. L. (1987). *College: The undergraduate experience in America.* New York: Harper & Row.

Boyer, E. L. (1990). *Scholarship revisited: Priorities of the professoriate.* Princeton, NJ: Carnegie Foundation for the Advancement of Teaching.

Braskamp, L. A., & Ory, J. C. (1994). *Assessing faculty work: Enhancing individual and institutional performance.* San Francisco: Jossey-Bass.

Braxton, J. M. (1983). Department colleagues and individual faculty publication productivity. *Review of Higher Education, 6*(2), 115–128.

Breneman, D. W., & Youn, T. I. K. (1988). *Academic labor markets and careers.* New York: Falmer.

Bridgwater, C. A., Walsh, J. A., & Walkenbach, J. (1982). Pretenure and posttenure productivity trends of academic psychologists. *American Psychologist, 37*(2), 236–238.

Brophy, J. E., & Good, T. L. (1974). *Teacher-student relationships: Causes and consequences.* New York: Holt, Rinehart, & Winston.

Brown, S. V. (1988). *Increasing minority faculty: An elusive goal.* Princeton, NJ: Educational Testing Service.

Budd, J. M., & Seavey, C. A. (1990). Characteristics of journal authorship by academic librarians. *College and Research Libraries, 51*(5), 463–470.

Buss, D. M., & Craik, K. H. (1983). The act frequency approach to personality. *Psychological Review, 90,* 105–126.

Byrne, E. M. (1993). *Women and science: The snark syndrome.* London: Falmer.

Caesar, T. (1992). *Conspiring with forms: Life in academic texts.* Athens: University of Georgia Press.

Cantor, N., Mischel, W., & Schwartz, J. (1982). A prototype analysis of psychological situations. *Cognitive Psychology, 14,* 45–77.

Carnegie Foundation for the Advancement of Teaching. (1984). *Technical report: 1984 Carnegie Foundation national surveys of higher education.* Princeton, NJ: Opinion Research Corporation.

Carnegie Foundation for the Advancement of Teaching. (1987). *A classification of institutions of higher education* (rev. ed.). Princeton, NJ: Carnegie Foundation for the Advancement of Teaching.

Carnegie Foundation for the Advancement of Teaching. (1989a). *The conditions of the professoriate: Attitudes and trends, 1989.* Princeton, NJ: Carnegie Foundation for the Advancement of Teaching.

Carnegie Foundation for the Advancement of Teaching. (1989b). *Survey among college and university faculty.* Princeton, NJ: Carnegie Foundation for the Advancement of Teaching.

Carter, D., & Wilson, R. (1987). Minorities in higher education: Fifth annual status report. *AAHE Bulletin, 39,* 11–14.

Cartter, A. M. (1966). *An assessment of quality in graduate education.* Washington, DC: American Council on Education.

Carver, R. B., & Scheier, M. F. (1983). A control-theory approach to human behavior and implications for problems in self-management. *Advanced Cognitive Behavioral Research and Theory, 2,* 127–193.

Cattell, R. B., & Devdahl, J. E. (1955). A comparison of the personality profile of eminent researchers with that of eminent teachers and administrators. *British Journal of Psychology, 46,* 248–261.

Centra, J. A. (1973, December). Effectiveness of student feedback in modifying college instruction. *Journal of Educational Psychology, 65*(3), 395–401.

Centra, J. A. (1975). Colleagues as raters of classroom instruction. *Journal of Higher Education, 46*(1), 327–337.

Centra, J. A. (1977). Student ratings of instruction and their relationship to student learning. *American Educational Research Journal, 14*(1), 17–24.

Chamberlain, M. (1988). *Women in academe: Progress and prospects.* New York: Russell Sage Foundation.

Chambers, J. (1964). Creative scientists of today. *Science, 145,* 1203–1205.

Change Magazine. (1993). Opening the classroom door. *Change, 25*(6), 4–58.

Cheney, L. V. (1990). *Tyrannical machine: A report on educational practices gone wrong and our best hopes for setting them right.* Washington, DC: National Endowment for the Humanities.

Choy, C. (1969). *The relationship of college teacher effectiveness to conceptual systems orientation and perceptual orientation.* Unpublished doctoral dissertation, University of Northern Colorado, Greeley.

Christensen, K. W., & Jansen, D. G. (1992). Correlates of research productivity for industrial education faculty. *Journal of Industrial Teacher Education, 29*(4), 23–40.

Chubin, D., Porter, A. L., & Boeckman, M. (1981). Career patterns of scientists. *American Sociological Review, 46,* 488–496.

Clark, B. (1986). *The intellectual enterprise: Academic life in America.* Princeton, NJ: Carnegie Foundation.

Clark, B. (1987). *The academic life: Small worlds, different worlds.* Princeton, NJ: Carnegie Endowment for the Advancement of Teaching.

Clark, M. J., & Centra, J. A. (1985). Influences on the career accomplishments of Ph.D.s. *Research in Higher Education, 23*(3), 256–269.

Clark, S. M., & Corcoran, M. (1985). Individual and organizational contributions to faculty vitality: An institutional case study. In S. M. Clark & D. Lewis (Eds.), *Faculty vitality and institutional productivity* (pp. 112–138). New York: Columbia University, Teachers College Press.

Clark, S. M., & Corcoran, M. (1986). Perspectives on the professional socialization of women faculty: A case of accumulative disadvantage. *Journal of Higher Education, 57*(1), 20–43.

Clark, S. M., Corcoran, M., & Lewis, D. R. (1986). The case for an institutional perspective on faculty development. *Journal of Higher Education, 57*(2), 176–195.

Clemente, F. (1973). Early career determinants of research productivity. *American Journal of Sociology, 79*(2), 409–419.

Clemente, F., & Hendricks, J. (1973). A further look at the relationship between age and productivity. *Gerontologist, 13*(1), 106–110.

Clemente, F., & Sturgis, R. B. (1974). Quality of department of doctoral training and research productivity. *Sociology of Education, 47*(2), 287–299.

Cohen, C. E. (1981). Goals and schemata in person perception: Making sense from the stream of behavior. In G. Gintor & J. F. Kihlstrom (Eds.), *Personality, cognition, and social interaction* (pp. 45–68). Hillsdale, NJ: Erlbaum.

Cohen, P. A. (1980). Effectiveness of student rating feedback for improving college instruction: A meta-analysis of findings. *Research in Higher Education, 13*(4), 321–341.

Cohen, P. A. (1981). Student ratings of instruction and student achievement: A meta-analysis of multisection validity studies. *Review of Educational Research, 51*(3), 281–309.

Cole, J. R. (1979). *Fair science: Women in the scientific community.* New York: Macmillan.

Cole, J. R., & Cole, S. (1973). *Social stratification in science.* Chicago: University of Chicago Press.

Cole, J. R., & Zuckerman, H. (1984). The productivity puzzle: Persistence and change in patterns of publication of men and women scientists. In M. Steinkamp and M. Maehr (Eds.), *Advances in motivation and achievement: Women in science* (pp. 217–258). Greenwich, CT: JAI.

Cole, J. R., & Zuckerman, H. (1987). Marriage, motherhood, and research performance in science. *Scientific American, 256*(2), 119–125.

Cole, S. (1979). Age and scientific performance. *American Journal of Sociology, 84,* 958–977.

Cole, S., & Fiorentine, R. (1991). Discrimination against women in science: The confusion of outcome with process. In H. Zuckerman, J. Cole, & J. Bruer (Eds.), *The outer circle: Women's position in the scientific community* (pp. 205–226). New York: Norton.

Coltrin, S. A., & Glueck, W. F. (1977). The effect of leadership roles on the satisfaction and productivity of university research professors. *Academy Management Journal, 20,* 101–116.

Connor, P. E. (1974). Scientific research competence is a function of creative ability. *IEEE Transactions on Engineering Management, EM-21,* 2–9.

Cornette, M. L. (1987). *Perceptions of university faculty members' involvement in research and other creative activities.* Unpublished doctoral dissertation, Colorado State University, Fort Collins.

Crane, D. (1965). Scientists at major and minor universities: A study of productivity and recognition. *American Sociological Review, 30*(5), 699–713.

Crane, D. (1972). *Diffusion of knowledge in scientific communities.* Chicago: University of Chicago Press.

Crawley, S., Wenzel, S., & Blackburn, R. T. (1993, October). *Grants as a faculty product: Does a publication model apply?* Paper presented at the annual meeting of the Association for the Study of Higher Education: Pittsburgh, PA.

Creswell, J. W. (1985). *Faculty research performance: Lessons from the sciences and the social sciences* (ASHE-ERIC Higher Education Report No. 4). Washington, DC: Association for the Study of Higher Education.

Creswell, J. W., Seagren, A., Wheeler, D., Vavrus, L., Grady, M., Egly, N., & Wilhite,

M. (1987). *The faculty development role of department chairs: A naturalistic analysis.* Paper presented at the annual meeting of the Association for the Study of Higher Education: Baltimore, MD.

Crittenden, K. S., & Wiley, M. G. (1985). When egotism is normative: Self-presentational norms guiding attribution. *Social Psychology Quarterly, 48*(4), 360–365.

Cropley, A. J., & Field, T. W. (1969). Achievement in science and intellectual style. *Journal of Applied Psychology, 53,* 132–135.

Cross, K. P., & Angelo, T. (1988). *Classroom assessment techniques: A handbook for faculty.* Ann Arbor: University of Michigan, NCRIPTAL.

Dannefer, D. (1984). Adult development and social theory: A paradigmatic reappraisal. *American Sociological Review, 49*(1), 100–116.

Davis, W. E. (1990). *Changes in the lives of male college and university faculty.* Unpublished doctoral dissertation, University of California–Davis.

de Meuse, K. P. (1987). The relationship between research productivity and perceptions of doctoral program quality. *Professional Psychology: Research and Practice, 18*(1), 81–83.

Deci, E. L. (1975). Effects of externally mediated rewards on intrinsic motivation. *Journal of Personality and Social Psychology, 18*(1), 105–115.

Deci, E. L., Nezlek, J., & Sheinman, L. (1981). Characteristics of the rewarded and intrinsic motivation of the rewardee. *Journal of Personality and Social Psychology, 40,* 1–10.

Deitsch, M. S. K. (1989). *Prestige mobility in academic careers.* Unpublished doctoral dissertation, New York University.

Dennis, W. (1956). Age and productivity among scientists. *Science, 123,* 724–726.

Dennis, W. (1966). Creative productivity between the ages of 20 and 80 years. *Journal of Gerontology, 21*(1), 1–8.

Deskins, D. R. (1990). *Prospects for minority doctorates in the year 2000: Employment opportunities in a changing American society.* Ann Arbor: University of Michigan, Rackham Graduate School.

Deutsch, K. W., Platt, J., & Senghaas, D. (1971). Conditions favoring major advances in social science. *Science, 171,* 450–459.

Dickson, V. A. (1983). The determinants of publication rates of faculty members at a Canadian university. *Canadian Journal of Higher Education, 13*(2), 41–49.

Dossey, J. A., Mulles, I. V. S., Lindquist, M. M., & Chambers, D. L. (1988). *The mathematics report card: Are we measuring up?* (1986 National Assessment Report No. 17-M-01). Princeton, NJ: Educational Testing Service.

Douglas, G. H. (1992). *Education without impact: How our universities fail the young.* Secaucus, NJ: Carol Publishing Group.

D'Souza, D. (1991). *Illiberal education: The politics of race and sex on campus.* New York: Free Press.

Dunkin, M. J. (1986). Research on teaching in higher education. In *Handbook on research on teaching* (3rd ed.) (pp. 754–777). New York: Macmillan.

Dunkin, M. J., & Biddle, B. J. (1974). *The study of teaching.* New York: Holt, Rinehart, & Winston.

364

Dwyer, M. M., Flynn, A. A., & Inman, P. A. (1991). Differential progress of women faculty: Status 1980–1990. In J. C. Smart (Ed.), *Higher education: Handbook of theory and practice* (Vol. 7, pp. 173–222). New York: Agathon.

Eccles, J. P. (1984). Sex differences in mathematics participation. In M. W. Steinkamp & M. L. Maehr (Eds.), *Advances in motivations and achievement* (pp. 93–137). Greenwich, CT: JAI.

Edgerton, R. (1993, July/August). The reexamination of faculty priorities. *Change, 25*(4), 10–26.

Edgerton, R., Hutchings, P., & Quinlan, K. (1991). *The teaching portfolio.* Washington, DC: American Association for Higher Education.

Edmundson, M. (Ed.). (1993). *Wild Orchids and Trotsky: Messages from American Universities.* New York: Penguin.

Eiduson, B. T. (1962). *Scientists: Their psychological world.* New York: Basic Books.

Elmore, C. J., & Blackburn, R. T. (1983). Black and white faculty in white research universities. *Journal of Higher Education, 54*(1), 1–15.

Endler, N. S. (1977). Research productivity and scholarly impact of Canadian psychology departments. *Canadian Psychological Review, 18*(2), 152–168.

Entrekin, L. V., & Everett, J. E. (1981). Age and midcareer crises: An empirical study of academics. *Journal of Vocational Behavior, 19*(1), 84–87.

Epstein, C. (1988). *Deceptive distinctions: Sex, gender, and the social structure.* New Haven, CT: Yale University Press.

Erickson, G. R., & Erickson, B. L. (1979). Improving college teaching: An evaluation of a teaching consultation procedure. *Journal of Higher Education, 50*(5), 670–683.

Erikson, E. H. (1963). *Childhood and society* (2nd ed.). New York: Norton.

Etaugh, C., & Kasley, H. C. (1981). Evaluating competence: Effects of sex, marital status, and parental status. *Psychology of Women Quarterly, 6,* 196–203.

Evans, R. I. (1968). *Resistance to innovation in higher education.* San Francisco: Jossey-Bass.

Exum, W. (1983). Climbing the crystal stair: Values, affirmative action, and minority faculty. *Social Problems, 30,* 383–399.

Exum, W. H., Menges, R. J., Watkins, B., & Berglund, P. (1984). Making it at the top: Women and minority faculty in the academic labor market. *American Behavioral Scientist, 27*(3), 310–324.

Fairweather, J. S. (1993). Faculty reward structures: Toward institutional professional homogenization. *Research in Higher Education, 34*(5), 603–623.

Fausto-Sterling, A. (1992). *Myths of gender: Biological theories about women and men* (2nd ed.). New York: Basic Books.

Featherman, D. L. (1983). Life-span research in social science research. In P. B. Baltes & J. O. G. Brim (Eds.), *Life-span development and behavior* (pp. 1–57). New York: Academic Press.

Feldman, K. A. (1976). The superior college teacher from the student's view. *Research in Higher Education, 5,* 243–288.

Feldman, K. A. (1977). Consistency and variability among college students in rating their teachers and courses: A review and analysis. *Research in Higher Education, 6*(3), 223–274.

Feldman, K. A. (1986). Perceived instructional effectiveness of college teachers as related to their personality and attitudinal characteristics: A review and synthesis. *Research in Higher Education, 24*(2), 139–213.

Feldman, K. A. (1989). Instructional effectiveness of college teachers as judged by teachers themselves, current and former students, colleagues, administrators, and external (neutral) observers. *Research in Higher Education, 30*(2), 137–194.

Feldman, S. D. (1973). *Escape from the doll's house.* New York: McGraw-Hill.

Ferber, M. A., & Loeb, J. W. (1973). Performance, rewards, and perceptions of sex discrimination among male and female faculty. *American Journal of Sociology, 78*(4), 995–1002.

Finkelstein, M. J. (1984a). *The American academic profession: A synthesis of social scientific inquiry since World War II.* Columbus: Ohio State University Press.

Finkelstein, M. J. (1984b). The status of academic women: An assessment of five competing explanations. *Review of Higher Education, 7*(3), 223–246.

Fishbein, M., & Ajzen, I. (1975). *Beliefs, attitudes, intention, and behavior: An introduction to theory and research.* Reading, MA: Addison-Wesley.

Fisher, C., & Gitelson, R. (1983). A meta-analysis of the correlates of role conflict and ambiguity. *Journal of Applied Psychology, 68,* 320–333.

Fox, M. F. (1983). Publication productivity among scientists: A critical review. *Social Studies of Science, 13,* 285–305.

Fox, M. F. (1985a). Location, sex-typing, and salary among academics. *Work and Occupations, 12*(2), 186–205.

Fox, M. F. (1985b). Publication, performance, and reward in science and scholarship. In J. C. Smart (Ed.), *Higher education: Handbook of theory and research* (Vol. 1, pp. 255–282). New York: Agathon.

Fox, M. F. (1991). Gender, environmental milieu, and productivity. In H. Zuckerman, J. Cole, & J. Bruer (Eds.), *The outer circle: Women's position in the scientific community* (pp. 188–204). New York: Norton.

Fox, M. F., & Faver, C. A. (1981). Achievement and aspiration: Patterns among male and female academic-career aspirants. *Sociology of Work and Occupations, 8*(4), 439–463.

Fox, M. F., & Faver, C. A. (1982). The process of collaboration in scholarly research. *Scholarly Publishing,* pp. 327–339.

Fox, M. F., & Faver, C. A. (1984). Independence and cooperation in research: The motivations and costs of collaboration. *Journal of Higher Education, 55*(3), 347–359.

Freeman, R. B. (1978). Discrimination in the academic marketplace. In T. Sowell (Ed.), *American ethnic groups* (pp. 167–202). Washington, DC: Urban Institute.

Freidson, E. (1973). *Profession of medicine.* New York: Dodd, Mead.

French, J. R. P., Tupper, C. J., & Mueller, E. F. (1965). *Work load of university professors.* (Cooperative Research Project No. 2171, Office of Education,

U.S. Department of Health, Education, and Welfare). Ann Arbor: University of Michigan, Institute for Social Research.

Frieze, I. H., & Hanusa, B. H. (1984). Women scientists: Overcoming barriers. In M. Steinkamp & M. Maehr (Eds.), *Advances in motivation and achievement: Women in science* (pp. 139–163). Greenwich, CT: JAI.

Fulton, O., & Trow, M. (1974). Research activity in American higher education. *Sociology of Education, 47*(1), 29–73.

Gage, N. L. (Ed.). (1963). *Handbook of research in teaching.* Chicago: Rand McNally.

Gallant, J. A., & Prothero, J. W. (1972, January). Weight-watching at the university: The consequences of growth. *Science, 175,* 381–388.

Garkland, K. (1990). Gender differences in scholarly publication among faculty in ALA accredited library schools. *Library and Information Science Research, 12*(2), 155–166.

Gaston, J. (1978). *The reward system in British and American science.* New York: Wiley-Interscience.

Geertz, C. (1983). *Local knowledge: Further essays in interpretive anthropology.* New York: Basic Books.

Gersick, D. J. G., & Hackman, J. R. (1990). Habitual routines in task performing groups. *Organizational Behavior and Human Decision Processes, 47,* 65–97.

Gilligan, C. (1982). *In a different voice.* Cambridge, MA: Harvard University Press.

Gist, M., & Mitchell, T. (1992). Self efficacy: A theoretical analysis of its determinants and malleability. *Academy of Management Review, 17*(2), 183–211.

Gless, D., & Smith, B. (1992). *The politics of liberal education.* Durham, NC: Duke University Press.

Glueck, W. F., & Thorp, C. D. (1974). The role of the academic administrator in research professors' satisfaction and productivity. *Education Administration Quarterly, 10*(1), 72–90.

Gordon, G., & Morse, E. V. (1970). Creative potential and organizational structure. In M. J. Cetron & J. D. Goldha (Eds.), *The science of managing organized technology* (Vol. 2). New York: Gordan & Breach.

Gould, R. (1978). *Transformations.* New York: Simon & Schuster.

Gross, E., & Grambsch, P. V. (1968). *University goals and academic power.* Washington, DC: American Council on Education.

Hall, D. T., & Mansfield, R. (1975). Relationships of age and seniority with career variables of engineers and scientists. *Journal of Applied Psychology, 60,* 202–210.

Hammel, E. (1980, January). *Report on the task force on faculty renewal.* Berkeley: University of California, Program in Population Research.

Hamovitch, W., & Morgenstern, R. D. (1977). Children and the productivity of academic women. *Journal of Higher Education, 48*(6), 633–645.

Hansen, W. L., Weisbrod, B. A., & Strauss, R. P. (1978, October). Confirmations and contradictions: Modeling the earnings and research productivity of academic economists. *Journal of Political Economy, 86,* 729–741.

Hargens, L. L. (1978). Relations between work habits, research technologies, and eminence in science. *Sociology of Work and Occupations, 5,* 97–112.

Hargens, L. L., McCann, J. C., & Reskin, B. (1978). Productivity and reproductivity: Fertility and professional achievement among research scientists. *Social Forces, 57,* 154–163.

Heath, J. A., & Tuckman, H. P. (1989). The impact of labor markets on the relative growth of new female doctorates. *Journal of Higher Education, 60*(6), 704–715.

Helmrich, R., Spence, J., Beane, W., Lucker, G. W., & Matthews, K. (1980). Making it in academic psychology: Demographic and personality correlates of attainment. *Journal of Personality and Social Psychology, 39,* 896–908.

Heydinger, R. B., & Simsek, H. (1992). *An agenda for reshaping faculty productivity.* Denver, CO: State Higher Education Executive Officers and the Education Commission of the States.

Hickson, M. (1991). Prolific scholarship in mass communications, 1924–1985. *ACE Bulletin* (75), 75–80.

Higher Education Research Institute. (1983). *Technical report to 1980 national survey.* Los Angeles: University of California–Los Angeles, Higher Education Research Institute.

Hildebrand, M. (1972, January). How to recommend promotion for a mediocre teacher without actually lying. *Journal of Higher Education, 43*(1), 44–62.

Hill, W. W., & French, W. L. (1967). Perceptions of power of department chairmen by professors. *Administrative Science Quarterly, 11*(4), 548–574.

Hollenshead, C. (1992, February). *Women at the University of Michigan.* Ann Arbor: University of Michigan, Office of the President.

Holley, J. W. (1977). Tenure and research productivity. *Research in Higher Education, 6,* 181–192.

Hood, J. C. (1985). The lone scholar myth. In M. F. Fox (Ed.), *Scholarly writing and publishing: Issues, problems, and solutions* (pp. 111–125). Boulder, CO: Westview.

Horner, K. L., Rushton, J. P., & Vernon, P. A. (1986). Relation between aging and research productivity of academic psychologists. *Psychology and Aging, 1*(4), 319–324.

Horner, M. (1972). Towards an understanding of achievement-related conflicts in women. *Journal of Social Issues, 28,* 157–175.

Hornig, L. S. (1984, November). Women in science and engineering: Why so few? *Technology Review, 87*(8), 30–41.

House, J. S. (1981). *Work stress and social support.* Reading, MA: Addison-Wesley.

Huber, R. M. (1992). *How professors play the cat guarding the cream.* Lanham, MD: George Mason University Press.

Hudson, L., & Jacot, B. (1991). *The way men think: Intellect, intimacy, and erotic imagination.* New Haven, CT: Yale University Press.

Hughes, C. (in progress). *The influence of the campus information environment on faculty publishing output.* Unpublished doctoral dissertation, University of Michigan, Ann Arbor.

Humphreys, L. G. (1984). Women with doctorates in science and engineering. In M. W. Steinkamp & M. L. Maehr (Eds.), *Women in science* (pp. 197–216). Greenwich, CT: JAI.

Hutchings, P. (1993). Introducing portfolios. *AAHE Bulletin, 45*(9), 14–17.

Jackson, K. W. (1991). Factors associated with alienation among black faculty. *Research in Race and Ethnic Relations, 6,* 123–144.

Jacoby, R. (1987). *The last intellectuals: American culture in the age of academe.* New York: Farrar, Straus, & Giroux.

James, J., & Farmer, R. (Eds.). (1993). *Spirit, space, and survival: African American women in (white) academe.* New York: Routledge.

Jauch, L. R., Glueck, W. F., & Osborn, R. N. (1978). Organizational loyalty, professional commitment, and academic research productivity. *Academy of Management Journal, 21,* 84–92.

Jencks, C., & Riesman, D. (1968). *The academic revolution.* Garden City, NY: Doubleday.

Johnsrud, L. K., & Saddao, K. C. (1993, November). *Ethnic and racial minority faculty within a research university: Their common experiences.* Paper presented at the annual meeting of the Association for the Study of Higher Education: Pittsburgh, PA.

Julius, N. B., & Krauss, H. H. (Eds.). (1993). *The aging work force: A guide for higher education administrators.* Washington, DC: College and University Personnel Association.

Kanfer, R., & Ackerman, P. L. (1974). Motivation and cognitive abilities: An integrative/aptitude=treatment interaction approach to skill acquisition. *Journal of Applied Psychology, 59,* 657–689.

Kanter, R. M. (1977). Some effects of proportions on group life: Skewed sex ratios and responses to token women. *American Journal of Sociology, 82*(5), 965–990.

Kasten, K. (1984). Tenure and merit pay as rewards for research, teaching, and service at a research university. *Journal of Higher Education, 55*(4), 500–514.

Katz, J., & Henry, M. (1988). *Turning professors into teachers.* Phoenix, AZ: American Council on Education/Oryx.

Keller, E. F. (1985). *Dynamic autonomy: Reflections on gender and science.* New Haven, CT: Yale University Press.

Keller, E. F., & Moglen, H. (1987). Competition: A problem for academic women. In V. Miner & H. E. Longino (Eds.), *Competition: A feminist taboo?* (pp. 21–37). New York: Feminist Press.

Kerlin, S. P., & Dunlap, D. M. (1993, May). For richer, for poorer: Faculty morale in periods of austerity and retrenchment. *Journal of Higher Education, 64*(3), 348–377.

Kihlstrom, F. (1983). Conscious, subconscious, unconscious. In K. S. Bowers & D. Meichenbaum (Eds.), *Unconscious processes: Several perspectives.* New York: Wiley.

Kimball, R. (1990). *Tenured radicals: How politics has corrupted our higher education.* New York: Harper & Row.

Kinsley, M. (1993, May 17). Editorial. *New Republic,* p. 6.

Knapp, R. (1963). Demographic, cultural, and personality attributes of scientists. In C. Taylor & F. Barron (Eds.), *Scientific creativity: Its recognition and development* (pp. 205–216). New York: Wiley.

Kuhn, T. S. (1970). *The structure of scientific revolutions.* Chicago: University of Chicago Press.

Kyvik, S. (1990). Motherhood and scientific productivity. *Social Studies of Science, 20*(1), 149–160.

Ladd, E. C. (1979). The work experience of American college professors: Some data and an argument. *Current Issues in Higher Education, 2,* 3–13.

Ladd, E. C., & Lipset, S. M. (1973). *Professors, unions, and American higher education.* Berkeley, CA: Carnegie Commission.

Ladd, E. C., & Lipset, S. M. (1975). *The divided academy: Professors and politics.* New York: McGraw-Hill.

Landino, R. A., & Owen, S. V. (1988). Self-efficacy in university faculty. *Journal of Vocational Behavior, 33*(1), 1–14.

Langer, E. G. (1989). Minding matters: The mindlessness, mindfulness theory of cognitive activity. In L. Berkowitz (Ed.), *Advances in experimental social psychology* (Vol. 22, pp. 137–173). New York: Academic Press.

Langstom, C., & Cantor, N. (1989). Social anxiety and social constraint: When making friends is hard. *Journal of Personality and Social Psychology, 56*(4), 649–661.

Lawrence, J. H., Bieber, J. P., Blackburn, R. T., Saulsberry, K., Trautvetter, L. C., Hart, K. A., & Frank, K. (1989). *Predicting individual change in faculty research productivity.* Paper presented at the annual meeting of the American Educational Research Association: San Francisco.

Lawrence, J. H., & Blackburn, R. T. (1985). Faculty careers: Maturation, demographic, and historical effects. *Research in Higher Education, 22*(2), 135–154.

Lawrence, J. H., & Blackburn, R. T. (1986). *Age and faculty distribution of their work effort.* Paper presented at the annual meeting of the Association for the Study of Higher Education: San Antonio.

Lawrence, J. H., & Blackburn, R. T. (1988). Age as a predictor of faculty productivity: Three conceptual approaches. *Journal of Higher Education, 59*(1), 22–38.

Lawrence, J. H., Blackburn, R. T., & Hart, K. (1990, November). *Predicting faculty teaching behaviors: Testing of a theoretical model of motivation.* Paper presented at the annual meeting of the Association for the Study of Higher Education: Portland, OR.

Lawrence, J. H., Blackburn, R. T., Hart, K., Mackie, C. J., Dickman, E. M., & Frank, A. A. (1991). *Motivation for changing teaching: Institutional and personal barriers to change.* Paper presented at the annual meeting of the American Educational Research Association: Chicago.

Lawrence, J. H., Blackburn, R. T., Hart, K. A., & Saulsberry, K. (1989). *Faculty in community colleges: Differences between the doctorally and non-doctorally prepared.* Paper presented at the annual meeting of the Association for the Study of Higher Education: Atlanta, GA.

Lawrence, J. H., Blackburn, R. T., Pitney, J., & Trautvetter, L. (1988, November). *Faculty and administrator views: The organizational climate for teaching.* Paper presented at the annual meeting of the Association for the Study of Higher Education: St. Louis, MO.

Lawrence, J. H., Blackburn, R. T., & Trautvetter, L. C. (1989). *Predicting faculty publication output: Evaluation of a causal model across institutional types.* Paper presented at the annual meeting of the Association for the Study of Higher Education: Atlanta, GA.

Lawrence, J. H., Blackburn, R. T., Trautvetter, L. C., Hart, K. A., & Herzberg, G. (1990, April). *Women in selected "female" and "male" disciplines: A view of professional behavior at three points in time—1969, 1975, and 1988.* Paper presented at the annual meeting of the American Educational Research Association: Boston.

Lawrence, J. H., Blackburn, R. T., & Yoon, K. (1987). *Changing faculty distribution of their work effort, 1968–1984.* Paper presented at the annual meeting of the Association for the Study of Higher Education: San Diego, CA.

Lawrence, J. H., Frank, K., Bieber, J. P., Bentley, R. J., Blackburn, R. T., & Trautvetter, L. C. (1989, March). *Faculty scholarly output: Development of a theoretical model.* Paper presented at the annual meeting of the American Educational Research Association: San Francisco.

Lawrence, J. H., Hart, K., Linder, V., Saulsberry, K., Dickman, E. M., & Blackburn, R. T. (1990, November). *Comparisons of the teaching goals, assumptions, and behaviors of community college and transfer institution faculty.* Paper presented at the annual meeting of the Association for the Study of Higher Education: Atlanta.

Lazarsfeld, P. F., & Thielens, J. W. (1958). *The academic mind: Social scientists in a time of crisis.* Glencoe, IL: Free Press.

Lehman, H. C. (1953). *Age and achievement.* Princeton, NJ: Princeton University Press.

Lehman, H. C. (1958). The chemist's most creative years. *Science, 127,* 1213–1222.

Lehman, H. C. (1966). The psychologist's most creative years. *American Psychologist, 21,* 363–369.

Lepper, M. R., Greene, D., & Nisbet, R. E. (1973). Undermining children's intrinsic motivation with extrinsic rewards: A test of the over justification hypothesis. *Journal of Personality and Social Psychology, 28,* 129–137.

Levinson, D. J., Darrow, C. N., Klein, E. B., Levinson, M. H., & McKee, B. (1978). *The seasons of a man's life.* New York: Knopf.

Lewis, L. S., Wanner, R. A., & Gregorio, D. I. (1979). Performance and salary attainment in academia. *American Sociologist, 14,* 157–169.

Liebert, R. (1976). Productivity, favor, and grants among scholars. *American Journal of Sociology, 82,* 664–673.

Liebert, R. (1977). Research-grant getting and productivity among scholars. *Journal of Higher Education, 48,* 164–192.

371

Lightfield, E. T. (1971). Output and recognition of sociologists. *American Sociologist, 6*(2), 128–133.

Lincoln, Y. S. (1992, November). *Virtual community and invisible colleges: Alterations in faculty scholarly networks and professional self-image.* Paper presented at the annual meeting of the Association for the Study of Higher Education: Minneapolis, MN.

Lindsey, D. (1989). Using citation counts as a measure of quality in science: Measuring what's measurable rather than what's valid. *Scientometrics, 15*(3–4), 189–203.

Linn, M. C., & Hyde, J. S. (1989). Gender, mathematics, and science. *Educational Researcher, 18*(8), 17–27.

Linville, P. W., & Clark, L. F. (1989). Production systems and social problem solving: Specificity, flexibility, and expertise. In R. S. Wyer & T. K. Srull (Eds.), *Advances in social cognition* (Vol. 2, pp. 131–152). Hillsdale, NJ: Erlbaum.

Lipset, S. M., & Ladd, E. C. (1971). *Jewish academics in the United States: Their achievements, culture, and politics.* New York: McGraw-Hill.

Logan, C. J. (1990). *Job satisfaction of African-American faculty at predominantly African-American and predominantly white four-year state-assisted institutions in the South.* Unpublished doctoral dissertation, Bowling Green State University, OH.

London, H. B. (1978). *The culture of the community college.* New York: Praeger.

Long, J. S. (1978, December). Productivity and academic position in the scientific career. *American Sociological Review, 43,* 889–908.

Long, J. S. (1987). Problems and prospects for research differences in the scientific career. In L. Dix (Ed.), *Women: Their underrepresentation and career differentials in science and engineering—Proceedings of a workshop* (pp. 157–169). Washington, DC: National Academy Press.

Long, J. S. (1990). The origins of sex differences in science. *Social Forces, 68*(4), 1297–1315.

Long, J. S. (1992). Measures of sex differences in scientific productivity. *Social Forces, 71*(1), 159–168.

Long, J. S., Allison, P. D., & McGinnis, R. (1979, October). Entrance into the academic career. *American Sociological Review, 44,* 816–831.

Long, J. S., Allison, P. D., & McGinnis, R. (1993). Rank advancement in academic careers: Sex differences and the effects of productivity. *American Sociological Review, 58,* 703–722.

Long, J. S., & McGinnis, R. (1981). Organizational context and scientific productivity. *American Sociological Review, 46,* 422–442.

Longino, H., & Doell, R. (1987). Body, bias, and behavior: A comparative analysis of reasoning in two areas of biological science. In S. Harding & J. F. O'Barr (Eds.), *Sex and scientific inquiry* (pp. 165–186). Chicago: University of Chicago Press.

Louis, K. S., Blumenthal, D., Gluck, M., & Stoto, M. A. (1988, October). *Entrepreneurs in academe: Exploration of behaviors among life scientists.* Paper presented at the annual meeting of the Association for the Study of Higher Education: Boston.

Lutjens, N. V. (1988). *The effects of gender ratios on research productivity of female faculty in research universities.* Unpublished doctoral dissertation, University of Denver, CO.

MacKie, M. (1985). Female sociologists' productivity, collegial relations, and research style examined through journal publications. *Sociology and Social Research, 69*(2), 189–209.

Maclean, N. (1983). *A river runs through it.* Chicago: University of Chicago Press.

Maehr, M. L., & Braskamp, L. A. (1986). *The motivation factor: A theory of personal investment.* Lexington, MA: Heath.

Marsh, H. W., & Roche, L. (1993). The use of students' evaluations and an individually structured intervention to enhance university teaching effectiveness. *American Educational Research Journal, 30*(1), 217–251.

Maslow, A. H., & Zimmerman, W. (1956). College teaching ability, activity, and personality. *Journal of Educational Psychology, 47,* 185–189.

McCain, B., O'Reilly, C., & Pfeffer, J. (1982). The effects of departmental demography on turnover: The case of a university. Unpublished manuscript, University of Iowa, Iowa City.

McClelland D. C. (1961). *The achieving society.* Princeton, NJ: Van Nostrand.

McClelland, D. C., Atkinson, J. W., Clark, R. A., & Lowell, E. L. (1953). *The achievement motive.* New York: Appleton-Century-Crofts.

McCormmach, R. (1982). *Night thoughts of a classical physicist.* Cambridge, MA: Harvard University Press.

McDonald, K. A. (1993, July 7). Princeton professor appears to have proved Fermat's last theorem. *Chronicle of Higher Education,* pp. A8–A10.

McKeachie, W. J. (1979a). Student ratings of faculty: A reprise. *Academe, 65*(6), 384–398.

McKeachie, W. J. (1979b). What motivates faculty behavior? In D. L. Lewis & W. E. Becker (Eds.), *Academic rewards in higher education* (pp. 1–20). Cambridge, MA: Ballinger.

McKeachie, W. J. (1986). *Teaching tips* (8th ed.). Lexington, MA: Heath.

McKeachie, W. J., Pintrich, P. R., Lin, Y., & Smith, D. A. (1986). *Teaching and learning in the college classroom: A review of the research literature* (Tech. Rep. No. 86-B-001). Ann Arbor: University of Michigan, NCRIPTAL.

McKeachie, W. J., Salthouse, T. A., & Lin, Y. G. (1978). An experimental investigation of factors affecting university promotion decisions: A brief report. *Journal of Higher Education, 49,* 177–183.

McNamee, S. J., Willis, C. L., & Rotchford, A. M. (1990). Gender differences in patterns of publications in leading sociology journals, 1960–1985. *American Sociologist, 21*(2), 99–115.

McNeece, C. A. (1981, September). Faculty publications, tenure, and job satisfaction in graduate social work programs. *Journal of Education for Social Work, 17*(3), 13–19.

Meador, M., et al. (1992). Academic research productivity: Reply, still further results. *Economics of Education Review, 11*(2), 161–167.

Menand, L. (1991, December). What are universities for? The real crisis on campus is one of identity. *Harper's Magazine,* pp. 47–56.

Merton, R. K. (1968). The Matthew effect in science. *Science, 159,* 56–63.

Merton, R. K. (1973). *The sociology of science.* Chicago: University of Chicago Press.

Milem, J. P., & Dey, E. L. (1993, November). *Are we approaching equal pay for equal work? Gender differences in academic salaries, 1972 to 1989.* Paper presented at the annual meeting of the Association for the Study of Higher Education: Pittsburgh, PA.

Miller, E. (1988). *Person/role conflict, stress, and their relationship to teaching effectiveness among college faculty.* Unpublished doctoral dissertation, New York University.

Mitchell, T. R., & Beach, L. R. (1990). Do I love thee? Let me count: Towards an understanding of intuitive and automatic decision making. *Organizational Behavior and Human Decision Processes, 47,* 1–20.

Mooney, C. J. (1991, May 22). In 2 years, a million refereed articles, 300,000 books, chapters, monographs. *Chronicle of Higher Education,* p. A17.

Moore, D. P., et al. (1992). Accreditation and academic professionalism in business administration. *Journal of Education for Business, 67*(4), 218–223.

Moore, K. M. (1983). *The top-line: A report of presidents', provosts', and deans' careers.* University Park: Pennsylvania State University, Center for the Study of Higher Education.

Moore, K. M., & Garden, P. D. (1992). *A study of faculty job satisfaction and mobility at Michigan State University.* East Lansing, MI: Michigan State University, Collegiate Employment Research Institute.

Moore, K. M., & Sagaria, M. A. (1982). Differential job change and stability among academic administrators. *Journal of Higher Education, 52*(5), 501–513.

Moos, R. (1976). *The human context: Environmental determinants of behavior.* New York: Wiley.

Moos, R. (1979). *Evaluating educational environments: Procedures, measures, findings, and policy implications.* San Francisco: Jossey-Bass.

Moos, R. H. (1987). Person-environment congruence in work, school, and health care settings. *Journal of Vocational Behavior, 31,* 231–247.

Namenwirth, M. (1986). Science seen through a feminist prism. In R. Beleier (Ed.), *Feminist approaches to science* (pp. 18–41). New York: Pergamon.

National Center for Educational Statistics (NCES 89-648). (1989). *Projections of education statistics to 2000.* Washington, DC: U.S. Department of Education, Office of Educational Research and Improvement.

National Center for Educational Statistics (NCES 90-365). (1990a). *Faculty in higher education institutions, 1988 (NSOPF-88).* Washington, DC: U.S. Department of Education, Office of Educational Research and Improvement.

National Center for Educational Statistics (NCES 90-333). (1990b). *Institutional policies and practices regarding faculty in higher education (NSOPF-88).*

Washington, DC: U.S. Department of Education, Office of Educational Research and Improvement.

National Research Council. (1990). *Summary report, 1989: Doctorate recipients from United States universities.* Washington, DC: National Academy Press.

National Science Board. (1981). *Science indicators, 1980.* Washington, DC: National Science Board, National Science Foundation.

National Science Board. (1989). *Support for U.S. academic R&D.* Washington, DC: National Science Foundation.

National Science Foundation. (1988). *Doctoral scientists and engineers: A decade of change.* Washington, DC: National Science Foundation.

National Science Foundation. (1989). *Science and engineering indicators—1989.* Washington, DC: National Science Foundation.

Neumann, Y. (1978). Predicting faculty job satisfaction in university departments. *Research in Higher Education, 9,* 261–275.

Neumann, Y., & Finaly-Neumann, E. (1990). The support-stress paradigm and faculty research publication. *Journal of Higher Education, 61*(5), 565–580.

Newcombe, N., Bandura, M. M., & Taylor, D. G. (1983). Sex differences in spatial ability and spatial activities. *Sex Roles, 9*(3), 377–385.

Nisbet, R. (1992). *Teachers and scholars: A memoir of Berkeley in depression and war.* New Brunswick, NJ: Transaction.

Nisbett, R. E., & Ross, L. (1980). *Human inference: Strategies and shortcoming of social judgment.* Englewood Cliffs, NJ: Prentice-Hall.

Noble, D. F. (1992). *A world without women: The Christian clerical culture of western science.* New York: Knopf.

Noordenbos, G. (1992). Explanations for differences in publication rates between male and female academics and between productive and less productive women. *Bulletin de Méthodologie Sociologique, 35,* 22–45.

Nuttin, J. R. (1984). *Motivation, planning, and action: A relational theory of behavioral dynamics.* Hillsdale, NJ: Erlbaum.

Oromaner, M. J. (1973a, April). Career contingencies and the fate of sociological research. *Social Science Information, 12,* 97–111.

Oromaner, M. J. (1973b). Productivity and recognition of sociology departments. *Sociological Focus, 6*(1), 83–89.

Oromaner, M. J. (1975). Collaboration and impact: The career of multi-authored publications. *Social Science Information, 14*(1), 147–155.

Oromaner, M. J. (1981). The quality of scientific scholarship and the "graying" of the academic profession: A skeptical view. *Research in Higher Education, 15,* 231–239.

Over, R. (1982). Does research productivity decline with age? *Higher Education, 11,* 511–520.

Pace, C. R. (1980). Measuring the quality of student effort. *Current Issues in Higher Education, 3,* 10–16.

Paisley, W. (1972). The role of invisible colleges in scientific information transfer. *Educational Researcher, 1*(4), 5–8, 19–20.

Paludi, M. (1987). Psychometric properties and underlying assumptions of four objective measures of fear of success. In M. R. Walsh (Ed.), *The psychology of women: Ongoing debates* (pp. 185–202). New Haven, CT: Yale University Press.

Parsons, T., & Platt, G. (1968, March). *The American academic profession: A pilot study* (National Science Foundation Grant GS 513). Unpublished manuscript, Harvard University.

Pascarella, E. T., Terenzeni, P. T., & Hibel, J. (1978). Student-faculty interactional settings and their relationship to predicted academic performance. *Journal of Higher Education, 49*(5), 450–463.

Patitu, C. L., & Tack, M. W. (1991, November). *Job satisfaction of African-American faculty in higher education in the South.* Paper presented at the annual meeting of the Association for the Study of Higher Education: Boston.

Pavel, M. M. (1991). *Gender and organizational culture: A study in career orientation and satisfaction among liberal arts faculty.* Unpublished doctoral dissertation, California School of Professional Psychology, Berkeley.

Pearson, W., & Bechtel, K. H. (Eds.). (1989). *Black science and American education.* New Brunswick, NJ: Rutgers University Press.

Pellino, G. R., Blackburn, R. T., & Boberg, A. L. (1984). The dimensions of academic scholarship: Faculty and administrator views. *Research in Higher Education, 20*(1), 103–115.

Pelz, D. C., & Andrews, F. M. (1976). *Scientists in organizations* (rev. ed.). New York: Wiley.

Perrucci, R., O'Flaherty, K., & Marshall, H. (1983). Market conditions, productivity, and promotion among university faculty. *Research in Higher Education, 19*(4), 431–449.

Perry, W. G. (1968). *Forms of intellectual and ethical development in the college years: A schema.* New York: Holt, Rinehart, & Winston.

Persell, C. H. (1983). Gender, rewards, and research in education. *Psychology of Women Quarterly, 8*(1), 33–47.

Peterson, M., Cameron, K., Mets, L., Jones, P., & Ettington, D. (1989). *The organizational context for teaching and learning.* Ann Arbor: University of Michigan, NCRIPTAL.

Petty, R. E., Cacioppo, J. T., & Goldman, R. (1981). Personal involvement as a determinant of argument based persuasion. *Journal of Personality and Social Psychology, 41*, 847–855.

Pfeffer, J. (1981). Some consequences of organizational demography: Potential impacts of an aging work force on formal organizations. In S. Kiester, J. Morgan, & V. Oppenheimer (Eds.), *Aging: Social change* (pp. 291–326). New York: Academic Press.

Pfeffer, J., & Konrad, A. M. (1991). The effects of individual power on earnings. *Work and Occupations, 18*(4), 385–414.

Pfeffer, J., Leong, A., & Strehl, K. (1976, July). Publication and prestige mobility of university departments in three scientific disciplines. *Sociology of Education, 49*, 212–218.

Pfeffer, J., Leong, A., & Strehl, K. (1977, June). Paradigm development and particularism: Journal publication in three scientific disciplines. *Social Forces, 55,* 938–951.

Pirsig, R. M. (1974). *Zen and the art of motorcycle maintenance.* New York: Bantam.

Plomp, R. (1990). The significance of the number of highly cited papers as an indicator of scientific prolificacy. *Scientometrics, 19*(3–4), 185–197.

Price, D. J. D., & Beaver, D. D. B. (1966). Collaboration in an invisible college. *American Psychologist, 21*(11), 1011–1018.

Pruitt, A. S. (1989). Access and retention of minority graduate students. In W. E. Ward & M. M. Cross (Eds.), *Key issues in minority education: Research directions and practical implications* (pp. 73–96). Norman: University of Oklahoma, Center for Research on Minority Education.

Rafky, D. M. (1972). The attitude of black scholars toward the black colleges. *Journal of Negro Education, 41*(4), 320–330.

Ramaley, J. (1978). *Covert discrimination and women in the sciences.* Boulder, CO: Westview.

Raymond, J. C. (1967). *Publications, production of knowledge, and career patterns of American economists.* Unpublished doctoral dissertation, University of Virginia, Charlottesville.

Regan, C. E., & Volkwein, J. F. (1993, November). *The influence of organizational variables on disparities between male and female faculty salaries.* Paper presented at the annual meeting of the Association for the Study of Higher Education: Pittsburgh, PA.

Reskin, B. F. (1976). Sex differences in status attainment in science: The case of the postdoctoral fellowship. *American Sociological Review, 41,* 597–612.

Reskin, B. F. (1977). Scientific productivity and the reward structure of science. *American Sociological Review, 42,* 491–504.

Reskin, B. F. (1978, March). Scientific productivity, sex, and location in the institution of science. *American Journal of Sociology, 83*(5), 1235–1243.

Reskin, B. F. (1979). Age and scientific productivity. In M. S. McPherson (Ed.), *The demand for new faculty in science and engineering.* Washington, DC: National Research Council, Communication on Human Resources.

Reskin, B. F. (1985). Aging and productivity: Careers and results. In S. M. Clark & D. R. Lewis (Eds.), *Faculty vitality and institutional productivity* (pp. 86–89). New York: Columbia University, Teachers College Press.

Rice, E. E., & Austin, A. (1988, March). High faculty morale: What exemplary colleges do right. *Change, 20*(2), 51–58.

Rieger, S. R. (1990). *Characteristics of knowledge producers in teacher education.* Unpublished doctoral dissertation, Ohio State University, Columbus.

Roche, G. (1994). *The fall of the ivory tower: Government funding, corruption, and the bankrupting of American higher education.* New York: Regnery.

Rodgers, R. C., & Maranto, C. L. (1989). Causal models of publishing productivity in psychology. *Journal of Applied Psychology, 74*(4), 636–649.

Roe, A. (1952, December). A psychologist examines 64 eminent scientists. *Scientific American, 187,* 21–25.

Roe, A. (1953). *The making of a scientist*. New York: Dodd, Mead.

Roe, A. (1964). The psychology of scientists. In K. Hill (Ed.), *The management of scientists* (pp. 49–71). Boston: Beacon.

Roizen, J., Fulton, O., & Trow, M. (1978). *Technical report: 1975 Carnegie Council national surveys of higher education*. Berkeley: University of California–Berkeley, Center for Studies in Higher Education.

Rong, X. L., Grant, L., & Ward, K. B. (1989). Productivity of women scholars and gender researchers: Is funding a factor? *American Sociologist, 20*(1), 95–100.

Rosenfeld, R. A. (1981, December). Academic men and women's career mobility. *Social Science Research, 10*, 337–363.

Rosenfeld, R. A. (1984). Academic career mobility for women and men psychologists. In V. B. Haas & C. C. Perrucci (Eds.), *Women in scientific and engineering professions*. Ann Arbor: University of Michigan Press.

Rossi, A. S. (1970). Status of women in graduate departments of sociology, 1968–69. *American Sociologist, 5*(1), 1–12.

Rossi, A. S. (1980). Life-span theories and women's lives. *Signs, 6*(1), 4–32.

Rothblum, E. D. (1988). Leaving the ivory tower: Factors contributing to women's voluntary resignation from academia. *Frontiers, 10*(2), 14–17.

Rowe, A. R. (1976). Retired academics and research activity. *Journal of Gerontology, 31*(4), 456–461.

Rubin, A., & Powell, D. M. (1987). Gender and publication rates: A reassessment with population data. *Social Work, 32*(4), 317–320.

Rudolph, F. (1962). *The American college and university*. New York: Knopf.

Rudolph, F. (1992). Book report—Killing the spirit: Higher education in America (by Page Smith, 1990). *Teachers College Record, 92*(2), 319–321.

Rushton, J. P., & Meltzer, S. (1981). Research productivity, university revenue, and scholarly impact (citations) of 169 British, Canadian, and United States universities. *Scientometrics, 3*(4), 275–303.

Ryan, J., & Sackrey, C. (1984). *Strangers in paradise: Academics from the working class*. Boston: South End.

Schaie, K. W. (1983). Age changes in adult intelligence. In D. S. Woodruff & J. E. Birren (Eds.), *Aging: Scientific perspectives and social issues* (pp. 137–148). Monterey, CA: Brooks/Cole.

Schiebinger, L. (1987). The history and philosophy of women in science: A review essay. In S. Harding & J. F. O'Barr (Eds.), *Sex and scientific inquiry* (pp. 7–34). Chicago: University of Chicago Press.

Schiele, J. H. (1991). Productivity of African American social work faculty. *Journal of Social Work Education, 27*(2), 125–134.

Schoen, L. G., & Winocur, S. (1988). An investigation of the self-efficacy of male and female academics. *Journal of Vocational Behavior, 32*(3), 307–320.

Schuttenberg, E. M., Patterson, L. E., & Sutton, R. E. (1986). Self-perceptions of productivity of education faculty: Past, present, and future. *Education, 107*(2), 161–172.

Schwab, J. J. (1969). *College curriculum and student protest*. Chicago: University of Chicago Press.

Schweitzer, J. C. (1989). Factors affecting scholarly research among mass communication faculty. *Journalism Quarterly, 66*(2), 410–417, 452.

*Scientist.* (1993, May 3). Citation study reveals Moscow as leader in research paper publishing. *The Scientist,* p. 15.

Scott, R. R. (1981). *A social facilitation model of black faculty.* Washington, DC: National Institute of Education.

Selye, H. (1964). *From dream to discovery: On being a scientist.* New York: McGraw-Hill.

Sherman, B. R., & Blackburn, R. T. (1975). Personal characteristics and teaching effectiveness of college faculty. *Journal of Educational Psychology, 67*(1), 124–131.

Showers, C., & Cantor, N. (1985). Social cognition: A look at motivated strategies. *American Review of Psychology, 36,* 275–305.

Shulman, L. (1986). Paradigms and research programs in the study of teaching. In *Handbook of research on teaching* (3rd ed.) (pp. 3–36). New York: Macmillan.

Simon, R. J. (1974, August). The work habits of eminent scientists. *Sociology of Work and Occupation, 1,* 327–335.

Smart, J. C. (1991, June). Gender equity in academic rank and salary. *Review of Higher Education, 14*(4), 511–525.

Smart, J. C., & Bayer, A. E. (1986). Author collaboration and impact: A note on citation rates of single and multiple authored articles. *Scientometrics, 10*(5–6), 297–305.

Smith, P. (1991). *Killing the spirit: Higher education in America.* New York: Viking.

Snyder, M. (1981). On the influence of individuals on situations. In N. Cantor & J. Kihlstrom (Eds.), *Personality, cognition, and social interaction* (pp. 309–329). Hillsdale, NJ: Erlbaum.

Stark, J., Lowther, M., Ryna, M., Bomotti, S., Genthon, M., Havens, L., & Martens, G. (1986). *Reflections on course planning: Faculty and students consider influences and goals.* Ann Arbor: University of Michigan, NCRIPTAL.

Staw, B. M. (1983, June). Motivation research versus the art of faculty management. *Review of Higher Education, 6*(4), 302–321.

Stein, M. I. (1962). Creativity in the scientist. In B. Barber & W. Hirsch (Eds.), *The sociology of science* (pp. 329–343). New York: Free Press.

Steinberg, S. (1974). *The academic melting pot.* New York: McGraw-Hill.

Stern, N. (1978). Age and achievement in mathematics: A case study in the sociology of science. *Social Studies of Science, 8,* 127–140.

Stinchcombe, A. L. (1966). On getting "hung up" and other assorted illnesses. *Johns Hopkins Magazine,* 25–30.

Storer, N. W. (1966). *The social system of science.* New York: Holt, Reinhart, & Winston.

Super, D. (1980). A life-span, life-space approach to career development. *Journal of Vocational Behavior, 16,* 282–298.

Super, D., Crites, J., Hummerl, R., Moser, H., Overstreet, P., & Warnath, C. (1957).

*Vocational development: A framework for research*. New York: Columbia University, Teachers College Press.

Sykes, C. J. (1988). *Profscam: Professors and the demise of higher education*. Washington, DC: Regency Gateway.

Sykes, C. J. (1990). *Hollow men: Politics and corruption in higher education*. Washington, DC: Regency Gateway.

Tack, M. W., & Patitu, C. L. (1992). *Faculty job satisfaction: Women and minorities in peril* (ASHE-ERIC Report No. 4). Washington, DC: George Washington University, School of Education and Human Development.

Tavris, C., & Wade, C. (1984). *The longest war: Sex differences in perspective*. San Diego: Harcourt Brace Jovanovich.

Taylor, C. W., & Banon, F. (Eds.). (1975). *Scientific creativity: Its recognition and development*. Huntington, NY: Krueger.

Taylor, C. W., & Ellison, R. L. (1967). Biographical predictors of scientific performance. *Science, 155*, 1075–1080.

Taylor, M. S., Locke, E. A., Lee, C., & Gist, M. E. (1984). Type A behavior and faculty research productivity: What are the mechanisms? *Organizational Behavior and Human Performance, 34*, 402–418.

Terpstra, D. E., Olson, P. D., & Lockerman, B. (1982). The effects of MBO on levels of performance and satisfaction among university faculty. *Group & Organization Studies, 7*(3), 353–366.

Thomas, F. N., & McKenzie, P. N. (1986). Prolific writers in marital and family therapy: A research note. *Journal of Marital and Family Therapy, 12*(2), 175–180.

Thomas, G. E. (1987). Black students in U.S. graduate and professional schools in the 1980's: A national and institutional assessment. *Harvard Educational Review, 57*(3), 261–282.

Tidball, M. E. (1976). Of men and research: The dominant themes in American higher education include neither teaching nor women. *Journal of Higher Education, 48*(4), 373–389.

Tien, F. (1994). *Promotion, motivation, and faculty research productivity: Theory testing and model construction for a Taiwanese setting*. Unpublished Ph.D. dissertation, University of Michigan, Ann Arbor.

Tien, F., & Blackburn, R. T. (1993). *Faculty rank systems, research motivation, and research productivity*. Paper presented at the annual meeting of the American Educational Research Association: Atlanta, GA.

Tokarczyk, M. M., & Fay, E. A. (Eds.). (1993). *Working-class women in the academy*. Amherst: University of Massachusetts Press.

Toren, N. (1991). The nexus between family and work roles of academic women in Israel: Reality and representation. *Sex Roles, 24*(11–12), 651–667.

Trautvetter, L. C., & Blackburn, R. T. (1990, April). *Gender differences in predicting faculty publication output in the natural sciences*. Paper presented at the annual meeting of the American Educational Research Association: Boston.

Trigg, L., & Perlman, D. (1976). Social influences on women's pursuit of a nontraditional career. *Psychology of Women Quarterly, 1*(2), 138–150.

Trow, M. A. (1975). Technical report on the 1969 Carnegie Commission survey of faculty and student opinion. In M. A. Trow (Ed.), *Teachers and students.* Berkeley, CA: Carnegie Foundation for the Advancement of Teaching.

Tuckman, H. P. (1976). *Publication, teaching, and the academic reward structure.* Lexington, MA: Heath.

Tuckman, H. P., Gapinski, J. H., & Hagemann, R. P. (1977). Faculty skills and the salary structure in academe: A market perspective. *American Economic Review, 67,* 692–702.

Tuckman, H. P., & Leahey, J. (1975). What is an article worth? *Journal of Political Economy, 83*(5), 951–967.

University Committee on Minority Issues. (1989). *Building a multiracial, multicultural university community.* Palo Alto, CA: Stanford University.

Van House, N. A. (1990, July 24). *Library resources and research productivity in science and engineering: Report of a pilot study.* Berkeley: University of California, School of Library and Information Studies.

Vasil, L. (1991). *Self-efficacy expectations and causal attribution for achievement among male and female university faculty.* Unpublished doctoral dissertation, University of Florida, Gainesville.

Veysey, L. (1965). *The emergence of the American university, 1865–1915.* Chicago: University of Chicago Press.

Vroom, P. I. (1991). *Role conflict, commitment, and coping, and scholarly productivity and satisfaction of social work academics.* Unpublished doctoral dissertation, University of Michigan, Ann Arbor.

Vroom, V. H. (1964). *Work and motivation.* New York: Wiley.

Wahba, M., & House, R. (1981). Expectancy theory in work and motivation: Some logical and methodological issues. *Human Relations, 27*(2), 121–147.

Wallmark, J. T., & Sedig, K. G. (1986). Quality of research measured by citation method and by peer review: A comparison. *IEEE Transactions on Engineering Management, EM-33*(4), 218–222.

Walsh, M. R. (Ed.). (1987). *The psychology of women: Ongoing debates.* New Haven, CT: Yale University Press.

Wanner, R. A., Lewis, L. S., & Gregorio, D. J. (1981). Research productivity in academia: Sciences and humanities. *Sociology of Education, 54,* 238–253.

Watkins, E. (1989). *Work time: English departments and the circulation of cultural value.* Stanford, CA: Stanford University Press.

Weiner, B. (1985). An attributional theory of achievement motivation and emotion. *Psychological Review, 92*(4), 548–573.

Welch, L. B. (Ed.). (1992). *Perspectives on minority women in higher education.* New York: Praeger.

Wenzel, S. A., & Blackburn, R. T. (1993, April). *Predicting science and engineering rates.* Paper presented at the annual meeting of the American Educational Research Association: Atlanta, GA.

Wenzel, S. A., Crawley, S., & Blackburn, R. T. (1993, October). *In partnership with industry: Business and engineering faculty.* Paper presented at the annual meeting of the Association for the Study of Higher Education: Pittsburgh, PA.

# References

Western Interstate Commission for Higher Education. (1991). *The literature on factors affecting faculty supply and demand.* Boulder, CO: Western Interstate Commission for Higher Education.

Whitley, R. (1978). Types of science, organizational strategies, and patterns of work in research laboratories in different scientific fields. *Social Science Information, 17,* 427–446.

Widom, C. S., & Burke, B. W. (1978, August). Performance, attitudes, and professional socialization of women in academia. *Sex Roles, 4*(4), 549–562.

Wiemer, M. (Ed.). (1993). *Taking stock of what we know.* University Park: Pennsylvania State University, Center for the Study of Higher Education.

Wigfield, A., & Braskamp, L. A. (1985). Age and personal investment in work. *Advances in Motivation and Achievement, 4,* 297–331.

Wildavsky, A. (1989). *Craftways: On the organization of scholarly work.* New Brunswick, NJ: Transaction.

Wilkes, J. M. (1980). *Styles of thought, styles of research, and the development of science.* Worcester, MA: Worcester Polytechnic Institute.

Williams, R., & Blackburn, R. T. (1988). Mentoring and junior faculty productivity. *Nursing Education, 5,* 204–209.

Wilson, L. (1942). *The academic man.* New York: Oxford University Press.

Wilson, R. C., Woods, L., & Gaff, J. G. (1974). Social-psychological accessibility and faculty-student interaction beyond the classroom. *Sociology of Education, 47*(1), 74–92.

Wispe, L. G. (1969). The bigger the better: Productivity, size, and turnover in a sample of psychology departments. *American Psychologist, 24*(7), 662–668.

Wyche, K. F., & Graves, S. B. (1992). Minority women in academia. *Psychology of Women Quarterly, 16,* 429–437.

Wylie, N. R., & Fuller, J. W. (1985). Enhancing faculty vitality through collaboration among colleagues. In R. G. Baldwin (Ed.), *Incentives for faculty vitality* (New Directions for Higher Education, No. 51). San Francisco: Jossey-Bass.

Youn, T. I. K. (1988). Studies of academic markets and careers: An historical review. In D. W. Breneman & T. I. K. Youn (Eds.), *Academic labor markets and careers* (pp. 8–27). New York: Falmer.

Yuker, H. E. (1984). *Faculty workload: Facts, myths, and commentary.* Washington, DC: ERIC Clearinghouse for Education.

Zacharias, M. K., & Mathis, B. C. (1982). *The academic professions: Theory and method for research in career development.* Paper presented at the annual meeting of the American Educational Research Association: New York.

Zuckerman, H. (1967). Nobel laureates in science: Patterns of productivity, collaboration, and authorship. *American Sociological Review, 32*(3), 391–403.

Zuckerman, H. (1970). Stratification in American science. *Sociological Inquiry, 40,* 235–257.

Zuckerman, H. (1991). The careers of men and women scientists: A review of current research. In H. Zuckerman, J. Cole, & J. Bruer (Eds.), *The outer circle: Women in the scientific community* (pp. 27–56). New York: Norton.

Zuckerman, H., & Cole, J. R. (1975). Women in American science. *Minerva, 13*, 83–102.

Zuckerman, H., Cole, J. R., & Bruer, J. T. (Eds.). (1991). *The outer circle: Women in the scientific community.* New York: Norton.

# INDEX

This index is structured around our theoretical framework and will be most helpful for those who have read chapter 1 and examined figures 1.1 and 4.1 carefully. It identifies the key relationships for each of the principal constructs; however, it does not identify every occurrence of a word but rather only those where the text is most relevant. Italicized terms refer to the principal constructs.

# Index

with longitudinal data, 165–73
in professional schools, 164
in research, doctoral, and,
   comprehensive universities, 136–43
in research universities, 120–36

for women in sciences, 157–64
usefulness for predicting
   teaching behavior, 14–23, 37–52
   teaching effort, 8–14, 24–37

Library of Congress Cataloging-in-Publication Data

Blackburn, Robert T.
    Faculty at work : motivation, expectation, satisfaction / Robert T. Blackburn
& Janet H. Lawrence.
        p.    cm.
    Includes bibliographical references (p.    ) and index.
    ISBN 0-8018-4942-X (alk. paper)
    1. College teachers—United States.    2. College teachers—United States—
Psychology.    3. Education, Higher—United States.    I. Lawrence, Janet H.
II. Title.
LB1778.2.B53   1995
378.1'2'0973—dc20                                                          94-43255

Printed in the United States
44888LVS00004B/75